June 11 8/08

Dear Sandy —
Happy Birthday! Have fun in the Sun! Love You.
Love Ya.
Mum + Dad.

thegolfbook

the golf book

THE **PLAYERS** THE **GEAR** THE **STROKES** THE **COURSES** THE **CHAMPIONSHIPS**

INTRODUCTION BY **NICK BRADLEY**

LONDON, NEW YORK, MELBOURNE,
MUNICH, and DELHI

Senior Art Editor Michael Duffy
Senior Editor David Summers
Project Editors Chris Stone, Pip Morgan,
Tarda Davison-Aitkins
US Editor Jenny Siklós
Project Art Editors Adam Walker,
Philip Fitzgerald, Brian Flynn,
Phil Gamble, Dave Ball

Jacket design Lee Ellwood

Artwork Mike Garland

Production Editor Jonathan Ward
Senior Production Editor Vania Cunha

Managing Editor Stephanie Farrow
Managing Art Editor Lee Griffiths

Publishing Director Jonathan Metcalf
Art Director Bryn Walls

First American Edition, 2008

Published in the United States by
DK Publishing, 375 Hudson Street
New York, New York 10014

08 09 10 11 10 9 8 7 6 5 4 3 2 1

PD201–April/2008

Published in Great Britain by Dorling Kindersley Limited.

A catalog record for this book is available from the
Library of Congress.

ISBN 978-0-7566-3390-5

DK books are available at special discounts when
purchased in bulk for sales promotions, premiums,
fund-raising, or educational use. For details, contact:
DK Publishing Special Markets, 375 Hudson Street,
New York, New York 10014 or SpecialSales@dk.com

Printed and bound in China by Hung Hing
Offset Printing Company Limited

Discover more at
www.dk.com

CONTENTS

4 GOLFING LANDMARKS

5 THE GREATEST COURSES

6 THE RECORDS

INTRODUCTION

GOLF BOOKS HAVE BEEN A FUNDAMENTAL PART of my development as a golf coach and mentor to a number of the top players in the world. Taking up the game at the relatively late age of 16, I knew very quickly that the game of golf—specifically the teaching of it—would be my life's work. I needed to make up ground quickly, learn as much as I could and digest the intricacies of the sport in order to bring me up to speed with my peers. I did this largely through golf books; with five books on the golf swing, three books on course design, and a number of autobiographies of the best players, I started to compile quite a library.

However, what I actually needed was a golf book such as the one you presently have in your hands. *The Golf Book* is just that, a celebration of everything that is commendable, exciting, and worthwhile knowing in the sport of golf. This book distills a collective global knowledge of golf and binds it into one comprehensive document; it cuts to the chase with its information and presents essential text and images. This book would have saved me a considerable amount of time and much shelf space in my bedroom.

Like any new activity that one may take up, there is always that fragile gap between learning the basics and developing enough competency to then enjoy the activity itself. This is where golf is unique—there are so many aspects to the sport that a "trial and error" process may be timely. *The Golf Book* cuts through that trial and error, giving the reader the essential, important and usable information associated with every department of this great game. With "state of the art" presentation, the information is easily absorbed and remembered, making the process of reading this book light but extremely informative.

PLAYING THE GAME

Steve Newell, with whom I have worked on numerous occasions, expertly delivers the section on the golf swing, short game, and strategy. The photography and the art direction during this chapter leave nothing to the imagination, as its content gives the reader a concise and common-sense assessment of golf technique. In addition to the fundamental motion of the golf swing, there is also detailed advice on the short game and sloping lies—something we all face whenever we play. There are subtle yet important adjustments to be made when changing from club to club through the bag and this subject, along with fairway woods and the art of.

putting, is an integral part of this chapter. This section sums up great golf instruction: it informs you with drills, bullet pointed tips, and notable positions and feelings. It is a perfect way to receive great advice.

One of the beautiful aspects of golf is that we can play the same golf courses that great championships have been played on and top golfers have graced. I couldn't play soccer at Wembley or pitch a baseball at Shea Stadium, for example. The section "The Greatest Courses" provides the reader with some amazing insights into some of the great links around the world.

> What I . . .needed was a golf book such as the one you presently have in your hands. It distills a collective global knowledge of golf and binds it into one comprehensive document.

Each course you read about has made its own unique mark on the game. Waterville Golf Club in Ireland (my favorite course in the world), for example played host to one of the first transatlantic communication points between Europe and the United States. It was during the construction of this station that the workers unwittingly carved out the great links of Waterville as a form of recreation during their rest days. Blind luck or the luck of the Irish? Either way, it's a great links! The book also details the organic growth of a course like Augusta National. How did the course that we see every April in such magnificent condition evolve and become a benchmark in course design? Why do the players on the PGA Tour liken the 17th hole at Pete Dye's Sawgrass stadium course to enduring root canal tooth surgery? All of these courses are written about and complemented with some fantastic photographs and insights into their rich history.

In the 18 years that I have been a golf performance consultant, the biggest change I have seen in the game is in respect of the equipment we all use nowadays. Suffice to say that to a large extent it has actually been the equipment revolution that has been responsible for the evolution of the golf swing over the years. In the early days, the club makers could only forge and mold new designs with the materials that they had at their disposal—wood and steel.

So while clubheads and indeed the shafts often took on different guises, the actual difference in performance from club to club was marginal. Then manufacturers started to apply different composites to the shafts and the heads; titanium, graphite, beryllium, copper, and rubber inserts are just some of those examples. Instantaneously we started to "feel" different strikes from the clubface and the behavior of the ball took on another dimension. Dovetailing this composite evolution was the advancement in computer software and analysis; instant feedback on the ballistics of a strike can now be displayed on a screen in seconds—we don't even need to look up at the ball to see where it is going. We are at the point now where launch angles and spin rates are factors that we can genuinely "dial in" before the ball is even struck.

The ball has come full circle, too, no pun intended! We now have the ability to produce a hard-covered golf ball (for distance) that has a soft bounce (for control around the greens) and spin characteristics for a perfect combination. In what can be a minefield of technological jargon, this book strips this information down for you on a "need to know" basis.

I will enjoy studying and piecing together the information provided in *The Golf Book*.

Since its conception, golf has always delivered dynamic, colorful, and absorbing characters. Why is this? The answer can be found when you understand that golf at any level is fairly emotive and will always draw out the true character in most of us at some point. This book profiles the golfers that have played significant roles in the development of the game. It covers not only the champions but the larger than life personalities too.

To my mind Bobby Jones, Ben Hogan, Jack Nicklaus, Seve Ballesteros, Annika Sorenstam, and Tiger Woods have been the key instigators in the introduction and reintroduction of the sport to the masses. Their achievements, skills, records, and flamboyant play have captured the public imagination and driven people to their local driving ranges and golf courses all over the world.

Contained in this chapter are rare facts and insights into the careers of these golfers and many many more. This chapter in the book is a personal favorite of mine. It is essential when working with a top tour star to understand their character as much, if not more, than their golf swing technique. Introverts, extroverts, perfectionists, and showman alike make up a small portion of the tour's golfing fraternity. They seek one common goal, however—to get the best out of themselves and their games throughout their careers. So when you read about the extroverted Lee Trevino or the deeply introverted Ben Hogan understand that, although they walked the same path, they did so in completely different ways. That's the beauty of this game; a diversity of characters linked together by the common thread of hitting that little white sphere the least amount of times.

SOMETHING FOR EVERYONE

I see this book appealing to every genre of golfer. For the established player, the chapters that re-live the history of the great golfers, golf courses, and championships will serve to re-inspire and jog the memory pleasantly. The beginner will find that they have everything in the instruction section to save time and gain knowledge that will ultimately add to their enjoyment of this great game. The golfer or fan who currently plays on a regular basis has the chance to add further value to their experience as they read about the "where," "why," and "how" of the game that they pursue.

And for me, I will continue to look for the "x" factors that make up the DNA of a great golfer. You have never fully learned golf, you are continually learning it. So I will enjoy studying and piecing together the information *The Golf Book* gives me, ever expectant of a new clue that assists my own personal quest as a golf coach.

NICK BRADLEY, GOLF PERFORMANCE CONSULTANT

PLANET GOLF

Golf's origins

WINSTON CHURCHILL ONCE SAID "golf is a game in which you try to put a small ball in a small hole with implements singularly unsuited to the purpose." Golf always has been a difficult game, but that hasn't ever dented its appeal. The game taps into that strangely compulsive human desire to want to swing a stick in order to strike an object at rest on the ground.

Where it all started, nobody really knows. But it certainly began in the most primitive and basic form imaginable. Some visual and historical references bear little resemblance to the game of golf as we know it today, but are more closely related to hockey. By the 16th and 17th centuries, however, what might be described "real" golf was being played all along the east coast of Scotland. At that time it was genuinely a classless game, played with considerable enthusiasm by the poor, the good, and the great. The Royals weren't always eager to encourage such frivolity. King James II of Scotland did his best to stamp out the game, the suggestion being that it stopped youngsters from doing more constructive things with their time—such as archery practice. The Scots were, after all, at war.

GOLFING PIONEERS

However, it is comforting to know that golfers then were just like golfers today—once bitten by the golf bug, forever smitten. Not even the beheading of Mary Queen of Scots—among the charges laid against her was that she was playing golf the day after her husband was murdered—could deter these golfing pioneers.

By the mid-18th century, the first golf clubs were being established. Also key was the introduction of the first official Rules of Golf. There were only 13 rules, but they marked a vast improvement on the chaotic game that was typical of the era. Also at that time the Society of St. Andrews Golfers determined that a round of golf should consist of 18 holes. Golf was on the map.

▷ **THE ROYAL AND ANCIENT GOLF CLUB** of St. Andrews had, by the start of the 20th century, taken command of the rules of the game. This match was captured there in 1905.

△ **A GROUP OF GOLF ENTHUSIASTS** enjoy an evening's game at the seaside links at Musselburgh, near Edinburgh, in 1859. By this time golf clubs were being established around the coastal areas of Scotland.

Golf ball revolution

IT IS BELIEVED THAT by the mid-1800s, there were only 17 established golf clubs in the world; and of those, 14 were in Scotland. Incredibly, golf in Britain at this time was a game actually in decline. In some ways the foundations were in place for the game to blossom, but in other key respects, the general public were faced with insurmountable obstacles that deprived them of the opportunity.

Obviously, there was a shortage of places to play golf; but more crucially, golf equipment had become prohibitively expensive for the average man in the street. The manufacture of golf balls— a highly labor-intensive and skilled process that involved stuffing wet feathers into a leather pouch and then sewing it up— pushed unit prices way beyond the budget of ordinary people.

For a while, then, golf became very much a game for the wealthy and the privileged classes. It was a perception, and, indeed, in many respects a reality, that existed for decades and which prevented and put off many people from taking up the game.

THE GUTTA PERCHA ARRIVES

The arrival of the "gutta percha" golf ball changed everything. This rubbery substance was easy to fashion into golf balls, so they were cheap to produce. Whereas a skilled ballmaker could make four "featheries" a day, they could make 100 from gutta percha. The balls were also far more robust and lasted longer—if you did not lose them.

The ball was rolling, and with some considerable momentum. By the end of the 19th century, there were almost 2,000 golf clubs in Britain and the game had begun to spread into the far reaches of the British Empire. Golf exploded among the masses and the game never looked back.

Today, there is almost nowhere in the developed world where golf is not a multi-billion dollar industry. The technology used to make today's golf clubs and balls is unrecognizable from that used a century ago, but the essential appeal of the game of golf remains unaltered.

▽ **MASS PRODUCTION OF GOLF BALLS** was a key factor in making the sport more accessible. Today more than a billion golf balls are produced every year (see pp.44-45).

◁ **THE INVENTION OF THE GUTTA PERCHA BALL** was a turning point in the history of golf. Golf balls made of gutta percha were cheap and durable, helping to dispel golf's image as a rich man's past-time.

Golf's great triumvirates

THE ESTABLISHMENT OF GOLF'S early tournaments, in particular the Open Championship in the mid-to-late 19th century, brought with it the emergence of the game's earliest superstars and legends. And when superstars collide, rivalries are born. The history of golf is punctuated with great triumvirates—chapters in time where three outstanding players of a generation compete against and inspire each other throughout their playing careers.

Harry Vardon, J.H. Taylor, and James Braid were golf's first Great Triumvirate (see pp.106–07). All were from relatively poor backgrounds and born within 12 months of each other. For a 20-year period, they dominated the Open, winning 16 titles between them. Vardon won six times—a record that still stood at the turn of the 21st century.

They each left an indelible mark on the game, a legacy that went way beyond mere numbers and entries in the record books. Taylor was largely responsible for establishing the Professional Golfers Association; Vardon lent his name to the trophy awarded to the golfer with the lowest stroke average on the PGA Tour, and to the grip adopted by most of the game's top players; Braid became a successful golf course architect.

Next to take the baton were Walter Hagen (see pp.108), Gene Sarazen (see pp.109), and Bobby Jones (see pp.110–13). Between them they won 25 career Major titles and splashed the game of golf with a color, character, and sense of "joie de vivre" that has never since been surpassed.

Byron Nelson (see pp.116–17), Sam Snead (see pp.118–19), and Ben Hogan (see pp.120–21) followed in their footsteps. They were born within four months of each other, but here were three very different men with a distinct style and temperament. Nelson's career was spectacular but, through his own choosing, relatively brief. He retired at the age of 34. Hogan had a career of two halves—both brilliant, with a life-threatening car crash in between (see pp.220–21). No one played great golf for longer than Sam Snead. His talent was sublime, and his swing was blessed with the greatest rhythm of any golfer.

THE GREATEST RIVALRY

However, the greatest rivalry of them all was that between Arnold Palmer (see pp.128–31), Gary Player (see pp.132–35), and Jack Nicklaus (see pp.136–39). Between them they won an impressive 34 Major titles, and dominated the game in the 1960s and 1970s (see pp.224–25). Nicklaus and Player, in particular, managed a hugely impressive longevity at the absolute top of their games, with Big Jack's Major wins spanning 24 years.

In the 21st century, perhaps for the first time in the history of golf, the game has been defined by the domination of one golfer alone. Peerless in the modern game, Tiger Woods may well go down as the greatest golfer of them all (see pp.32–33).

△ **GENE SARAZEN INTERVIEWS** two-thirds of a celebrated triumvirate: Sam Snead (left) and Ben Hogan (right). Sarazen himself formed an illustrious threesome with Bobby Jones and Walter Hagen.

▷ **PICTURED HERE PLAYING TOGETHER** in the World Series of Golf, in 1962, Gary Player, Arnold Palmer, and Jack Nicklaus were great friends, as well as rivals. Their combined success led to them being known as "The Big Three" (see pp.224–25).

The Majors

GOLF'S MOST IMPORTANT championships are the four Majors—the Masters, US Open, the Open, and the USPGA. These are the tournaments that every golfer dreams of winning, the ones that matter the most.

It is no coincidence then, that the man considered by most people to be the greatest golfer who ever lived has the most victories in Major championships—Jack Nicklaus with 18. The number of Major victories is ultimately what determines a player's claim to greatness.

THE OPEN

It is not clear when the term "Major" was first used, but there is no doubt that the original Major was the Open Championship, first played in 1860 at Prestwick and won by Willie Park, from an entry of just eight players (see pp.210-11). The Open remained at Prestwick for the next 12 years, but soon it began to visit other courses. Today, the Open rota consists of nine of Britain's finest links courses—St. Andrews, Turnberry, Royal St. George's, Royal Troon, Hoylake, Carnoustie, Royal Birkdale, Muirfield, and Royal Lytham & St. Annes (see pp.248-79).

THE US OPEN

The first US Open was won by an English golfer, Horace Rawlins, who on October 4, 1895 shot 173 for four rounds at Newport, Rhode Island's nine-hole golf course. At that time the US Open was considered a sideshow to the more prestigious US Amateur Championship, and it was even tagged on to the end of that tournament,

◁◁ **THE FIRST OPEN CHAMPION** to receive the Golf Champion Trophy, commonly referred to as the Claret Jug, was the 1873 winner, Tom Kidd.

△△◁ **BEN HOGAN** holds the US Open trophy in 1948. Today, as then, the winner receives a replica of the Championship Cup for one year.

△◁ **GARY PLAYER** kisses the trophy, after winning the USPGA on July 22, 1962. Wealthy businessman Rodman Wanamaker first donated the trophy in 1916.

◁ **THE GREEN JACKET** was presented to winners of the Masters for the first time in 1949, and Sam Snead (left) was the first recipient.

allocated just one day's play as opposed to the three days it took to find an Amateur champion. The following year, the US Open moved to the 18-hole course at Shinnecock Hills, New York (see pp.278-79), and it didn't stay the second-class citizen for long.

THE USPGA

The USPGA Championship began its life as a matchplay tournament in 1916 and remained so until 1957. At least during its early years, the USPGA suffered in the same way as the US Open had, in the sense that professional golf tournaments were perceived as inferior to those of their amateur counterparts.

It wasn't long before Walter Hagen, the undisputed king of matchplay, began his reign. He dominated the event, reaching the final in six out of seven years and winning the title five times in the 1920s (see pp.218-19). He was an extraordinary man, a larger than life character.

THE MASTERS

The Masters was the last of the four Majors to arrive on the golfing calendar, although it wasn't immediately accorded Major status. It is the only one of the four tournaments to be played at the same venue every year—the sensational Augusta National in Georgia (see pp.296-99).

This tournament was originally merely an invitational event organized by Bobby Jones and was played for the first time in 1934. It was the following year's event that truly put the Masters on the map, however, thanks to Gene Sarazen's stroke of genius, holing a 4-wood from 220 yards for an albatross-two on the 15th in the final round.

The Masters gathered momentum as one of the game's premier tournaments, although it wasn't until 1949 when Sam Snead won the first of his three titles, that the organizers started handing out the now iconic green jacket to the winner.

The order of the Major championships runs: the Masters in April, the US Open in June, the Open in July, and then the USPGA in August.

Arnie's Army

IN THE EARLY 1950S, it is thought that less than 10 percent of households in the US owned a television set. Less than a decade later, that figure was approaching 80 percent. Despite this, golf didn't convert particularly well to the small screen. That is, until Arnold Palmer came along (see pp.128-31).

Golf can consider itself fortunate that when the television era dawned, its No 1 player—the undisputed star attraction—was Arnold Palmer. He had the kind of appeal that transcended his sport; Lee Trevino described him as "the greatest role model that any sport ever had."

Palmer was, by far, the most exciting personality in golf. He was good looking, with a physique more like that of a boxer than a golfer. He was photogenic, and possessed charisma that jumped out of the television screen and into people's living rooms. At the same time, he had that man-of-the-people appeal which made the public feel like he was one of them.

Not only was he a winner, but the manner of his winning was extraordinary to watch—an absolute rollercoaster of heroic shots, powerhouse drives, sublime chips and putts, and the occasional disaster.

Palmer always appeared to be walking the thin line between triumph and failure. The crowds adored him and soon "Arnie's Army" was on the march. Golf had seen nothing like it. Television and Arnold Palmer were made for one another and both parties benefited from this happy marriage. "It was a classic case of the right man being in the right place at the right time," said Palmer's great rival Jack Nicklaus.

Palmer's popularity grew beyond that of any other golfer in history and he was the first sportsman to establish the link between success on the field of play and lucrative product endorsements off it. He whipped up a frenzy of media and commercial interest, flooding the game with cash. He completely transformed the economics of professional sport, and television had a man who they could guarantee would bring in the ratings.

▷ **PALMER WAS GOLF'S FIRST SUPERSTAR.** His presence and his visionary manager Mark McCormack are partly responsible for the global popularity of golf (see pp.224-25).

△ **ARNIE'S ARMY FOLLOWED HIM** wherever he played and was most vocal in its support for him. They also bought the products he endorsed, and boosted the television ratings. When Palmer eventually retired, they turned out in the thousands to say farewell.

The golf business

IT IS A TRUISM OF MODERN SPORT that many leading protagonists make far more money off the field of play than on it. Certainly that is the case with the world's top golfers.

For this select band, golf is their passion, but it is also their business—a business as diverse as it is lucrative. Arnold Palmer was the first golfer to really connect with the public in such a way that companies were willing to pay him not-so-small fortunes to use and endorse their products (see pp. 24-25).

Product endorsement is easy money for today's top golfers, although there is such a spotlight on the game these days that you wouldn't catch a player endorsing a product he or she didn't either use or at least strongly believe in.

ENDLESS OPPORTUNITIES

By featuring a logo on a shirt or golf bag, and perhaps a few personal appearances, players now endorse anything from cars, technology, and watches, to global fashion brands, luxury resorts, and even health products. It is great exposure for the company, and nice business for the player.

Personal appearances and product endorsements are, however, just a small part of a player's commercial activity in a typical year. Golfers are lucky in that they have a longer shelf life than any other type of sportsperson. But they know all too well that a golfer's prime is relatively short-lived. Understandably, they want a life after golf, but one that keeps them in touch with the game.

Many are involved in golf course design. Ernie Els, one of the game's truly global players, designs golf courses all over the world, in established as well as emerging golf markets such as the Far East and India. And Els is not alone. Almost all of the top players are to some extent involved in golf course design. They start at the peak of their playing careers, so the business is established when their prime playing days are coming to an end.

For many golfers, the wine business has also proved attractive. Ernie Els, Nick Faldo, Greg Norman, David Frost, and Luke Donald have all launched their own wines. They're not just in it for fun, either. It is reasonable to expect the same traits in business that make them great players, so it is no surprise, then, that many of the golfers' wines have won awards.

Clothing is another area of outstanding opportunities for the business-savvy golfer. Tiger Woods has his own range within the Nike brand; Ernie Els has his own "Tour Collection" of golf clothing, as do former US Open champion Michael Campbell and the flamboyant Englishman Ian Poulter. All will play an active role in the design of the clothes that they wear and which then find their way on to the shelves of Pro Shops all over the world.

But don't for a minute think they're neglecting their games, though. Behind every successful golfer is a team of staff, managers, and advisors helping keep the wheels of industry turning (see pp. 40-41).

△ **WINE PRODUCING** has become a favored business opportunity for many modern golfers who are eager to develop an interest, and a future outside of golf.

◁ **MANY TOP GOLFERS** now have some interest in a clothing range, whether it is their own brand as with Ian Poulter, or a range incorporated by a sports manufacturer, as in Tiger Woods's case. It has become a way for golfers to create an identity for themselves while increasing their earnings.

A fine line...

IN SPORTS, ONE ASSUMES that there is a precariously fine line between success and disappointment. In the case of professional golf tournaments, this is certainly true. Between winning a golf championship and merely finishing in the top-five, we are talking about wafer-thin margins. However, comparing those at the top and bottom of the Tour money lists highlights a chasm that all aspiring young players would do well to contemplate.

For the purposes of this comparison, we introduce to you former US Open champion Jim Furyk and former Open champion Todd Hamilton. Both, as is evident from their Major-winning credentials, are great golfers, although Furyk is the more prolific. In the 2006 season, their fortunes were mixed, to say the least.

BEST ON TOUR

Jim Furyk was, for the purposes of statistical validation (determined by a player competing in a minimum number of tournaments), the best player on the PGA Tour in that season. Never mind that Tiger Woods won more money, Furyk won the Stroke Average. For the 24 tournaments in which he competed, his average score was 68.86. That was good enough to win him well over $7 million in prize money.

CONTRASTING FORTUNES

Todd Hamilton competed in a total of 27 tournaments in 2006. His stroke average was 72.84—hardly shabby, but, on average, four shots a round higher than Furyk. That's 16 shots over the duration of a four-round tournament (although Hamilton will have missed some cuts, and

therefore played only two rounds of golf). The vast gulf in prize money hits home more than any one of those 16 shots could. Hamilton won just $165,000 over the season—some way short of Furyk. And if anyone thinks that $165,000 for playing golf sounds like a pretty good living, think again. Hamilton's expenses traveling the tour will have eaten up as much as half of that amount, and then there's the tax man taking his chunk. It is lucky for him that he had some money behind him from winning the Open in 2004. He may well have sponsors picking up the tabs some weeks, too.

STATISTICS TELL THE STORY

The comprehensive performance statistics prepared by the PGA Tour (www.pgatour.com) tell the whole story. The only category where Hamilton beat Furyk was the category that matters least in the pro game—distance off the tee. Hamilton averaged 283 yards, Furyk 281. In every other department of the game, Furyk had the better of Hamilton, and by some margin. Furyk was 8th on tour for driving accuracy with 74 percent of fairways hit; Hamilton was 184th, averaging just 56 percent. Furyk was 4th for greens in regulation, hitting 70 percent; Hamilton was 196th with 57 percent. Furyk was 8th for putting average; Hamilton was 132nd.

And if you add up these differences, four shots a round is the end result. Not so much a fine line, then, more a gaping chasm. Like the Tour website says, at the higher echelons of the game, "these guys are good."

▷ **DURING HIS SUCCESSFUL 2006 SEASON,** Jim Furyk won three titles: (clockwise from top) the Nedbank Golf Challenge at the Gary Player Country Club, Sun City, South Africa; the Canadian Open at the Hamilton Golf and Country Club; and the Wachovia Championship at Quail Hollow Club, Charlotte, North Carolina.

▷▷ **HAVING WON THE OPEN IN 2004** Todd Hamilton had a less successful season in 2006. Out of the 27 tournaments he played in, he missed the cut in 19, and his best result was a tied for 10th place.

The women's game

FOR CENTURIES WOMEN GOLFERS have had to put up with restrictions of one form or another. Amazingly, until the end of the 19th century, it was even considered un-ladylike to swing the club above shoulder height. Although, looking at early images depicting the garments women golfers had to wear, you wonder if they had a choice.

Slowly the world changed and golf changed with it. First Joyce Wethered came along in the early part of the 20th century, winning championships with such style and panache that the great Bobby Jones proclaimed "she is the finest golfer I have ever seen" (see p.114).

The women's game went from strength to strength, especially in the US. The LPGA Tour, established in 1950, is a phenomenal success story. As far back as 1976 the leading money winner Judy Rankin won more than US$100,000 in a single season. At the start of the 21st century, the leading money winner on the LPGA Tour can expect to win US$2 million-plus in prize money. This figure compares favorably with the men's equivalent on the European Tour.

ROSY FUTURE

At club level the picture is equally rosy. For the most part, women golfers can boast a degree of equality, especially in the US. Indeed, there has been a world of difference between women's golf in the US and, for example, the UK.

Despite the fact that the UK has produced some of golf's best talent, at most golf clubs women have been restricted in the times that they can play, and even excluded from certain parts of the club-house. Happily, times are changing and many new golf clubs, and an increasing number of established clubs, are dispensing with such prehistoric values.

At the professional level the women's game has never been stronger. Golfers such as Annika Sorenstam (see pp.178-79),

Lorena Ochoa, Paula Creamer, Morgan Pressel, and Michelle Wie represent the biggest draw in the women's game (see pp.204-07). Each are inspirational role models and a marketing agent's dream, and it is reasonable to expect that young girls will aspire to be like them, and follow in their footsteps on the LPGA Tour.

This is the showcase for women's golf. Whether there is any additional benefit for women, such as Annika Sorenstam or Michelle Wie, playing in men's events is a subject that provokes debate. Would you rather watch them produce stunning performances to win the women's Majors, or see them struggle to make the cut against the men? The answer to this question settles the matter for most people.

△ **THERE HAS ALWAYS BEEN** scope to be daring with golf fashions, as demonstrated by Diana Fishwick, British Ladies Amateur Champion of 1930.

◁ **WOMEN'S GOLF HAS BECOME** a marketable sport in recent years, with young players such as Michelle Wie at the forefront. With vast amounts of money coming into the game in prize money and endorsements, this trend will only continue.

The greatest?

TIGER WOODS PLAYS THE GAME as it has never been played before. He hits career shots with every club in the bag. He has no weaknesses, only strengths, and none of those strengths is greater than his mind. It is what allows Tiger to do extraordinary things as a matter of routine. We've grown used to it, but we shouldn't ever forget how remarkable it is.

He has broken numerous records along the way. Playing in his first Masters as a professional, he won by 12 shots (see pp.232-33). At Pebble Beach in 2000, he won the US Open by 15 shots, breaking a Major record that had stood for well over a century (see pp.238-39). He won his first Open Championship by eight shots.

His appetite for setting new standards in the game is insatiable. By the time he turned 30 years of age, Tiger had played in 210 PGA Tour events, of which he had won 50—the youngest man by three years to reach that landmark. Just as remarkable, is that he had finished second in another 20, and third in 17. That's a top-three finish in 41 percent of the events he'd entered. Along the way he had banked more than

$60 million in prize money—nothing more than loose change, compared to the money he has received in endorsements.

Tiger Woods has enough money to sustain himself and his family, for the rest of their lives, and yet it is clear that his motivation shows no signs of waning. Woods is addicted to the thrill of winning and no record is safe. The leading PGA Tour winners are Arnold Palmer (62 wins), Ben Hogan (64 wins), Jack Nicklaus (73 wins), and Sam Snead (82 wins). Assuming he stays healthy, it is only a matter of time before Tiger overtakes them all.

Of more significance to Tiger is Jack Nicklaus's tally of 18 victories in Major championships. There was a time when most people found it hard to believe that any golfer would ever win more Majors than Nicklaus. Not now, though. Most experts believe that Tiger Woods will beat his record, and, in doing so, become the greatest golfer that has ever lived.

▷ **TIGER WOODS HAS REWRITTEN** the record books since bursting on to the scene. He has demonstrated a mental strength and steely determination that has set him apart.

△ **WOODS IS NOT THE LONGEST DRIVER** in professional golf, but a look at his official PGA Tour statistics reveals that he is on top, or ranked close to the top, in most areas of the game.

Behind the scenes

THE OPEN IS ONE OF THE GREATEST sporting shows on earth. It attracts the attention of the world's media, thousands of spectators, and millions of TV viewers, all of whom are focused on the very best golfers on the planet.

The Open is organized and administered by the R&A (Royal & Ancient), golf's world rules and development body. The R&A works in collaboration with the host club, of which there are nine on the Open rota. Each hosts the event once every 10 years, except St. Andrews which, typically, plays host once every five years.

Although the competition takes place over just four days, there are so many logistical considerations that it usually takes five or six years of planning to make sure that all the necessary arrangements are in place. What we see on TV gives only the briefest impression of what goes on behind the scenes.

THE MEDIA CENTER

At any Open the media center forever buzzes with activity—fingers tap-tapping on laptops, phones ringing, and voices from 101 different conversations filling the air. When a top player is ushered in through the door, a kind of black hole effect takes place—journalists are sucked into the interview room by the pull of a huge star.

Pre-tournament interviews with the leading players are prearranged, and once the tournament starts, the same leading players are expected to make an appearance after each round. For some there is no get-out clause; whether they shoot 65 or 75, they are obliged to sit and answer questions.

Running the media center is a huge task that falls to the R&A's press officer. "It's a 12-month planning process," says current incumbent Stewart McDougall. "As soon as one championship finishes, we start work on the next one. We meet with the golf writers and photographers to give them a chance to voice their opinions on what they feel were the pluses and minuses. We always listen. There's always something that can be improved on."

▽ **THE MEDIA CENTER** is the hub for all the journalists and the many marketing and public relations specialists. During the Open it is always open for business.

◁ **BUNKER KEEPERS ARE USUALLY VOLUNTEERS** who are employed to keep the bunkers manicured during the day. The bunkers are raked before and after the day's play, and also after any of the players have found themselves playing out of one of them.

▷ **THE SCOREBOARDS IN THE MEDIA CENTER** are constantly updated, from the first shot to the last putt of the day. Match officials walking with each playing group maintain radio contact with the scorers to provide real-time updates.

ARMIES OF VOLUNTEERS

The newly crowned Open champion will, almost without exception, pay tribute in his winner's speech to the armies of volunteers who help make sure that the event runs smoothly. It is a gracious touch and one that reflects the extraordinary efforts of those who are happy to be involved and take part not for money, but for the love of the game.

Steve Carr manned one of the scoreboards at the 1988 Open at Royal Lytham and loved every minute. "I remember in the final round when Seve [Ballesteros] and Nick Price were playing together," recalls Carr. "Seve was two shots ahead and we got the news that they'd both eagled the 7th. I updated Nick's score first, so it looked like he'd drawn level with Seve. Then I waited for a moment before I put up Seve's eagle. The crowd went bananas. It was brilliant. I was jumping up and down. I think the power went to my head! I realized I could control the crowd's reaction with a numbered magnetic strip."

Course marshals probably don't have quite so much fun, but they are very close to the action, which brings its own rewards. Tens of thousands of spectators sometimes need shepherding—although a line of rope is all it ever takes—and all the course marshals are given instructions at pre-round briefings about how to successfully carry out their jobs.

Greenkeepers from other clubs, taking time off from their day jobs, take care of the bunker-raking duties; one walks with every group on the course. It may be a busman's holiday, but walking inside the ropes alongside your heroes is about as good as it gets for any golf fan.

THE PRACTICE GROUND

There was a time when the practice ground at any tournament, even the Open, was populated almost solely by players and caddies. However, in recent years, this area had become so overcrowded that the authorities have put their collective feet down and restricted this area to only those working for the players (see pp.40-41).

That means caddies, obviously. And teaching gurus, too. You might only recognize the likes of David Leadbetter and

Butch Harmon, but on the practice ground at the Open, there are probably another dozen or so coaches, each working with their pupils, trying to fine-tune technique with the precision of a Swiss watchmaker.

Players' agents and managers can also be spotted, but they typically move in mysterious ways, recognizable to only the tour regulars. A nod here, a wink there; these are the deal makers. Most of the serious business is done behind the scenes, but the practice ground is a place for them to "press some flesh."

For the Tour reps of all of the major equipment manufacturers, the practice ground is their office. They set up camp in huge tour buses, resplendent in the company livery. A peek inside reveals every golfer's version of an Aladdin's Cave, filled wall-to-wall with clubs of every type. This is no place for the public, though. Each bus is effectively a mobile workshop where a team of skilled technicians is able to tweak any aspect of a club's set-up.

RULES EXPERTS

The appointed referees and rules experts have regular meetings in the months and weeks leading up to a tournament. These obviously become more frequent as the big week approaches.

During tournament week, official referees are responsible for the set-up of the golf course: the pin positions, the location of the teeing areas from one day to the next, the way the fairways and greens are cut, and the depth and texture of the sand. All of these crucial elements are overseen in conjunction with the greens staff. They must also adjudicate on any rules queries that arise during play.

These are not volunteers, however, but paid professionals with serious responsibilities. To referee at any Major, they must first pass a series of exams set by the PGA and the R&A. For many, this is the culmination of years of hard work, starting at small events and progressing up the golfing ladder. To referee at a Major is the ultimate accolade.

TELEVISION PLAYS A LARGE ROLE in the staging of the Open, and the broadcasting companies invest a huge amount of money in trying to improve their service.

Team orders

GOLF IS PERHAPS the ultimate individual sport—the golfer alone hits the shots. There is no one to blame when things go wrong; equally, there is no one else to soak up the warm glow of victory. But at the highest level, golf has also become something of a team game in the sense that every one of the leading golfers in the world has an entourage of various support staff. Each has a common purpose: to do everything in their specialist powers to bring out the best in their boss.

Some of these staff might be deemed surplus to requirements, but not the caddie. Players rely on their caddies to a large degree; they do much more than simply carry a heavy bag. The personal chemistry between a player and a caddie needs to be absolutely right; they need to know what to say, when to say it, and when not to say it. Basically, caddies require a deep knowledge of the game and of their player.

THE OPEN

Good caddies are worth their weight in gold—often, quite literally. During Tiger Wood's dominant phase at the start of the 21st century, his caddie Steve Williams was routinely the highest earning New Zealander in sport, based on the percentage he received of Tiger's on-course earnings. Typically, with most players, that will be 10 percent for a win and a reduced figure on a sliding scale based on the player's finishing position.

A coach will also tend to receive a percentage of a player's on-course earnings. As with the caddies, this is a job that comes with a huge degree of responsibility. A coach literally has a player's livelihood in his hands. Some players like their coach to be on hand most weeks and will even meet up in-between tournaments. Others might only get together with their coach five to ten times a year for their swing-health check-ups. It is very much a personal thing.

The mind coach is a relatively new feature in the modern game. Not all players are convinced of the need for such help,

▷ **ERNIE ELS HAD BOTH** his mind-coach and caddie to thank after his victory at the 2002 Open at Muirfield. Els triumphed in a four-man playoff that tested his mental strength.

▷▽ **CADDIE, COACH, AND MIND COACH** are each a key part of the Ernie Els team. Here they come together to support their player on the practice range at the 2003 US Open.

but there are others who could not do without one. The nature of conversations between both parties tends to be very private, but much of it is purely based around the need to get the player into a positive and stable frame of mind for tournament play—one they are then able to maintain in moments of pressure.

Almost all top golfers have a personal trainer. The level of fitness in the professional game is extraordinary; there really are some fine physical specimens out there on tour these days. In terms of physical fitness the game has changed beyond all recognition in the last 20 or 30 years. As former Ryder Cup star and BBC commentator Ken Brown says, "people just didn't go to the gym at tournaments in the 80s. I suppose I might have done a bit of jogging during the week, and some of the other players did too, but that was it really. To be honest, we felt like we needed to save our energy for playing golf!"

These days it is quite common for a Tour player to pay a visit to the gym and have a work-out before a round of golf, and possibly even afterward, too.

△ **STEVE WILLIAMS, TIGER WOODS'S CADDIE,** has been an essential part of the Tiger team since 1999. Woods has remarked on the importance of Williams to his success.

2

PLAYING THE GAME

Golf balls: the design

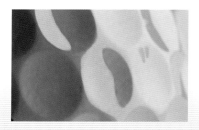

BUYING A SLEEVE OF GOLF BALLS used to be a simple task; almost the only ways to differentiate one ball from another were the manufacturer's stamp and the model number. With improvements in technology, however, has come a bewildering choice. Should you play cheap or premium brand, low compression or high compression, soft or hard, control or distance, XL or V1, XTour or Tour? Let's start with the basics.

VARIATIONS IN CONSTRUCTION

The dimensions and weight of the modern day golf ball are strictly monitored by the game's governing bodies, the United States Golf Association (USGA) and the Royal & Ancient (R&A). A golf ball must weigh not more than 1.62 oz (46 g) and it must have a diameter of at least 4.6 cm (1.68 in).

Companies use different materials for both the cover and the core. Many have a urethane cover, which is soft for improved feel, or surlyn, which is slightly harder. The core of a golf ball varies from one ball to another—a mixture of synthetic rubbers and special compounds. Golf balls are either one-piece, two-piece, three-piece, or even four-piece.

The USGA and R&A also put limits on the maximum initial velocity allowable under the current rules, a scientific measurement designed to prevent golf balls becoming too "hot" and therefore to preserve the integrity of today's golf courses and the inherent shot values.

There are also so-called "overall distance standards." The reasoning is the same; it is not in the interests of the game for the ruling bodies to allow manufacturers free rein in terms of how far a golf ball flies. It would soon get out of hand; the golf ball would, in essence, go too far—perhaps not in the hands of amateurs, but certainly in those of the leading pros.

The middle cover is unique to four-piece balls. It strikes a balance between the hard core and soft casing

The inner cover (a thin layer of enhanced rubber) is designed to transfer the energy from the strike to the core

The ball was not made as a perfect sphere and would therefore fly erratically

The inner core of two-, three-, and four-piece balls are made of solid rubber or liquid and are primarily intended to offer explosive distance

EARLY GOLF BALLS were simply hand-sewn cowhide bags stuffed with goose feathers. In wet weather the stitching tended to rot, rendering the ball useless.

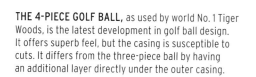

THE 4-PIECE GOLF BALL, as used by world No. 1 Tiger Woods, is the latest development in golf ball design. It offers superb feel, but the casing is susceptible to cuts. It differs from the three-piece ball by having an additional layer directly under the outer casing.

Outer casing is covered in aerodynamic dimples. For two-piece balls this is made from durable surlyn; for three- and four-piece balls it is made from softer urethane

DESIGNING THE DIMPLES

The important thing to understand is that the dimple patterns on golf balls vary, albeit subtly, from one ball to the next. It's all about aerodynamics (see box right). Those little dimples, in conjunction with the actual golf ball's construction, impact on the air flow around the ball and influence the trajectory of a ball's flight—how high or low it typically flies, how much it spins, how much it swerves in the air. A smooth golf ball would have reduced lift; basically dipping abruptly in flight.

The depth of the dimple indentation is usually standard, as is its spherical shape. However, in recent years Callaway have led the way in a new hexagonal dimple design.

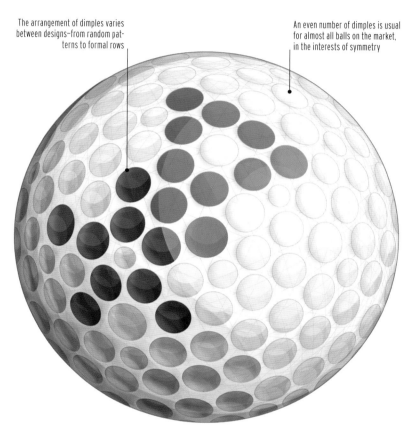

The arrangement of dimples varies between designs—from random patterns to formal rows

An even number of dimples is usual for almost all balls on the market, in the interests of symmetry

ALTHOUGH THERE ARE NO RULES governing the number of dimples on a ball, most manufacturers use between 300 and 450.

MAKING HISTORY

It is natural to assume that until the late 20th century, one golf ball was much like another. In fact, between 1931 and 1988 the R&A sanctioned a ball that was, at 1.62 in, a bit smaller than the now universal American/USGA ball of 1.68 1in. Although a subtle difference, it meant that the leading professionals from the PGA Tour and British circuit had to play with an unfamiliar golf ball when competing overseas.

■ A golf ball factory in the 1950s

PHYSICS OF THE GOLF BALL

The physics of golf ball design is concerned with the flow of air around the object when it is in flight. In scientific terms, there are two types of drag behind a sphere when it is airborne—laminar and turbulent. Laminar flow occurs over a smooth ball; the air separates very early in front of the ball, resulting in less carry. Turbulent flow occurs with a dimpled ball; it hugs the surface of the ball and separates later. The net result for the golfer is this: a player hitting a driver would carry the ball approximately 150 yards (137 meters) less with a smooth ball compared with a dimpled one.

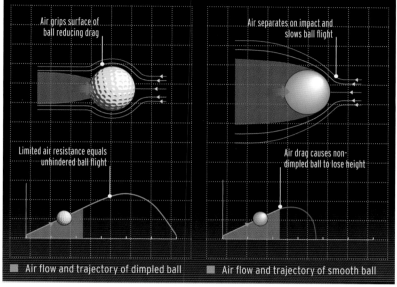

Air grips surface of ball reducing drag

Air separates on impact and slows ball flight

Limited air resistance equals unhindered ball flight

Air drag causes non-dimpled ball to lose height

■ Air flow and trajectory of dimpled ball   ■ Air flow and trajectory of smooth ball

IT'S ALL JUST SPIN

The many different types of golf ball exist for a reason; to offer golfers of all standards, whatever their preference or personal requirements, a ball that suits the way they play their game. Understanding what you want, and then matching the golf ball to your needs, is the single major factor in the buying process. Broadly speaking, golf ball types can be divided into three categories—distance, compromise, and control balls—although there is some blurring in these lines of definition.

Distance golf balls tend to be used by less-experienced golfers and high-to-mid handicappers; they have a relatively low spin rate, which offers good distance. The drawback is lack of control; they have a relatively hard feel off the clubface and the low spin rate can be a drawback for short shots around the green.

However, the drawbacks are less marked than, say, 20 years ago. Through clever construction techniques—essentially the materials and methods used in the inner core and outer layer of the golf ball—the manufacturers are able to offer golfers a compromise golf ball—one with more rounded qualities, so to speak. It means that many golf balls designed for distance now also offer soft feel and high performance control characteristics.

GOING FOR CONTROL

In the feel and control department, manufacturers cannot, however, compete with golf balls designed primarily for those purposes. This premium end of the market features golf balls designed for maximum feel and control, typically used by professional golfers and accomplished amateurs. The construction and dimple patterns are designed to generate a higher spin rate and, just as importantly, a soft feel off the clubface. This enables the player to hit a greater variety of "feel" shots from around the greens. The ball is more "workable" on long shots too.

Drivers: the design

THE EVOLUTION OF THE DRIVER has been an extraordinary success. Clubhead design, technology, and multi-material construction techniques are such that golfers today are more adept at hitting the driver than at any time in the history of the game. With so much choice, however, it is hard to know which club is best and, consequently, easier to make the wrong selection and buy a club that does not suit your game.

CLUBHEAD DESIGN

The use of light metals such as titanium and carbon composites has meant that driver clubheads have grown in size, although not in weight, and the effective sweet spot has consequently grown larger too. It is one of the reasons drivers have become comparatively easy to hit. That and the lower center of gravity, which makes it easier to get the ball airborne, and the clever weight distribution, which means that off-center strikes are not punished as severely as was the case a generation ago.

The actual shape of the clubhead is dictated by more than aesthetics. Form is dictated largely by function. Square-headed drivers are a 21st-century innovation. It seems bizarre, but the reasoning can be summed up with one phrase—moment of inertia, or MOI.

In layman's terms this means "resistance to twisting;" the significance for golf clubs being that the less a club twists when it strikes the ball, the straighter the shot flies. Square-headed drivers are found to possess high MOI.

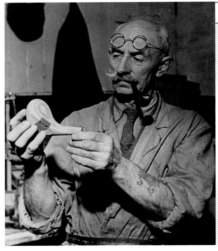

MAKING HISTORY

The principles of modern-day golf club manufacture, with its emphasis on moment of inertia and shaft bend profiles, are far removed from the origins of the game. As recently as the mid-1990s, driver heads were made of wood, especially persimmon, into which a metal face was screwed, representing the sweet spot. This is the origin of the phrase "hit it out of the screws"—a phrase used to denote a sweetly struck drive.

■ A clubmaker in 1950

THE PRINCIPLE OF MOVEABLE WEIGHTS, whereby players alter the characteristics of the club, is now commonplace. The rules state that these clubs can be set with a range of weight biases, provided this is not altered mid-round.

Heavy weights at the rear of the club promote a high launch angle

Weights positioned near the heel and toe of the clubhead can pre-set a right-to-left or left-to-right ball flight

Extra-large clubhead provides maximum forgiveness for off-center strikes

MOMENT OF INERTIA

The characteristics of MOI are designed to promote stability of the clubface and maximum efficiency of energy transfer from club to ball. The advantages this brings may be acutely evident with off-center hits.

Every club designer has at least one eye on MOI, but you don't have to go "square" to win at that game, which is why, if you lined up the ten current top-selling drivers at any given time, no two would be identical in shape. Form follows function in other ways too. Some drivers feature a clean, simple design and use moveable weights in the sole of the club to encourage a particular shape of shot—be that a fade, a draw, or a higher or lower ball flight.

Other manufacturers rely on the actual shape of the club to determine its playing characteristics, manipulating the club's center of gravity, balance, or clubface angle so the club has a draw or fade bias, for instance.

The combination of MOI geometry and weight-saving results in maximum distance, forgiveness, and accuracy

The club's face and body are made of titanium

Graphite shaft is standard in drivers. The lighter weight translates into higher clubhead speeds and greater distances

THE SQUARE-HEADED DRIVER uses light composite metals, except in the face and body, where strength and durability are key.

COMPARING THE SWEET SPOT

On modern golf clubs, the sweet spot is much larger than on traditional clubs (even those from 20 years ago), making solid hitting easier for all. On drivers, the sweet spot is positioned higher up the face. This is to encourage a higher launch angle, less spin, and extra distance.

Large sweet spot aids ball-striking

Smaller hitting area of the traditional "wood"

■ A metal-headed driver   ■ Traditional persimmon clubhead

THE LATEST DEVELOPMENT in club design, the square-headed driver, has particularly high moment of inertia.

The central crown with black finish is made of a composite material to reduce weight

Square shape delivers highest MOI in golf–29 oz in squared (5300 g cm squared)

With a greater mass, weight distribution away from the clubface is much easier

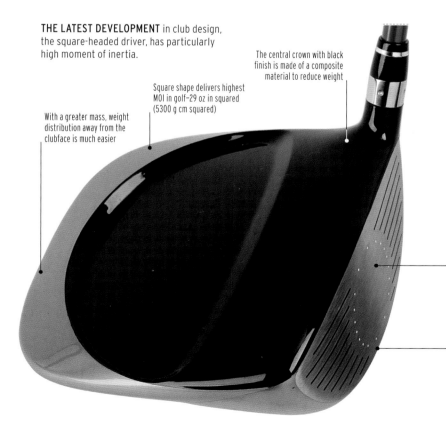

An enlarged sweet spot is a staple feature of all modern drivers–this assists ball-striking for high handicappers

There are no grooves at all on the sweet spot of this driver, which equals maximum forward momentum and no backspin

MULTI-MATERIAL CONSTRUCTION

Many 21st-century drivers are of multi-material construction; typically, the body of the clubhead and the face-insert itself will be made of different metals. Titanium is among the most popular metals used because it is durable and much lighter than steel.

This dual construction approach is more than just a sales gimmick. It allows the club manufacturers greater creative license to manipulate the weight distribution and performance of a club, typically in the body. However, the thickness of the face-insert can even be tapered to promote a particular type of launch angle, maximize ball speed, or offer greater forgiveness for the player when struck.

HOW BIG?

The R&A and USGA have placed limitations on the size of clubheads, with particular reference to the technological advancement of drivers. The volume of the clubhead must not exceed 28.06 cubic inches (406 cubic centimeters), and the distance from the heel to the toe (in the normal address position) cannot be more than 7 in (17.8 cm) and must not be greater than the distance from face to back.

ANGLE OF LOFT

Most modern-day drivers come in a range of different lofts, typically from around 7.5 degrees up to 11.5 degrees, although there is a slight variation from one manufacturer to another. A high loft produces a high launch angle; a low loft produces a low launch angle.

A DRIVER SHOULD BE CHOSEN depending on your ball flight. If your have a low ball flight, a 10 or 11 degree driver is better.

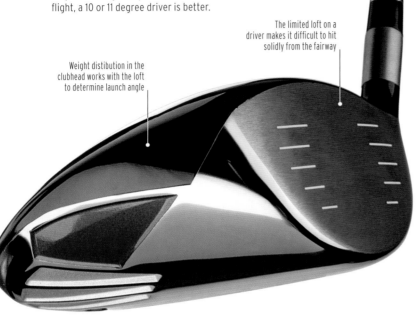

The limited loft on a driver makes it difficult to hit solidly from the fairway

Weight distibution in the clubhead works with the loft to determine launch angle

SHAFT MATERIALS

The shaft of a golf club is a complex piece of equipment and requires much consideration. There are three key factors that contribute to a shaft's overall performance characteristics—the material, shaft flex, and bend profile.

Materials come in two forms, steel or graphite. These days it is rare to see a driver fitted with a steel shaft. Graphite (essentially woven carbon fiber) is preferable, for expert and novice players alike. It is lighter and more flexible than steel and therefore helps a player generate more clubhead speed, which can be converted into distance.

STIFF SHAFTS are used by accomplished players who generate great speed and clubhead power with their swings. Professional players typically use extra-stiff shafts.

A stiff shaft will maximize speed and power through the drive

REGULAR SHAFTS have more flex than stiff shafts and are suited to the majority of amateur players who possess slower or medium swing speeds. Swinging too fast with this shaft may lead to a loss of accuracy.

This shaft weighs 2 oz (50 g). The letter "R" denotes regular

MANUFACTURERS PRODUCE specialist ladies' shafts, which are both lighter and more flexible than standard versions. These shafts are also suitable for junior golfers.

Made from graphite composite, this shaft is very light and flexible

OPTIMUM FLEXIBILITY

Shaft flex refers literally to the amount a shaft bends as a result of the forces generated in the golf swing. Powerful golfers and tour professionals require a stiffer-flex shaft. The less accomplished golfer requires a bit more "give," thus many amateurs will fare best with a regular-flex shaft. Matching the correct shaft flex to your swing and physique is essential in order that you optimize the performance of the club. Too "soft" a shaft may result in too much whip and a closed clubface at impact; too stiff a shaft often results in an open face.

The bend profile, which used to be known as kickpoint, essentially describes the point at which the shaft is most prone to flexing. It is possible to make two shafts of the same flex, but with different bend profiles. This in turn determines to some extent the trajectory of the golf ball.

Choosing the right shaft often requires more than just personal feel. It needs proper performance-related data, which only a launch monitor can accurately measure. This is why custom fitting is such an attractive option, whatever standard you play to.

The flex of the shaft may determine the angle of the clubface as it approaches impact

Power stored in the shaft and clubhead is unleashed from the top of the backswing

Shafts that bend at a higher point contribute to lower ball flights; low bend profiles lead to higher ball flights

USING A DRIVER FITTED with the correct shaft flex and bend profile will contribute to an improvement in your standard of play as surely as using an ill-suited shaft will hinder you.

A PERFECT FIT

There are a lot of different drivers and a dizzying number of options as regards loft, shaft, and head design. Hardly surprising, then, that a lot of golfers unwittingly use drivers that are not suited to either their swing or their physique, and that is sadly to the detriment of their golf game.

This is why custom fitting is so compelling. The process begins with a golfer hitting drives, while a computer known as a launch monitor captures all the data relating to the impact conditions of each shot—clubhead speed, ball speed, spin rate, launch angle, trajectory, ball flight, distance carried through the air, and the amount the ball runs on landing.

Through trial and error it is then possible to use this information to pinpoint the perfect club for a golfer's swing characteristics, one which optimizes the performance characteristics of the club to produce the best, most consistent drives off the tee with the tightest dispersion pattern. No golfer is skilled enough to be able to afford to ignore the potential benefits of custom fitting.

CUSTOM FITTING CENTERS measure data relating to your swing and translate it into a clubhead and shaft combination that best fits your game. Give custom fitting a try; it can only help your game.

DRIVING DISTANCES FROM PGA TOUR

The advancements in golf technology have resulted in players hitting ever-greater distances from the tee. Statistics from the PGA Tour demonstrate just how much impact this has had on the performance of the world's best players.

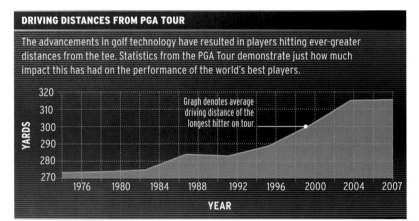

Graph denotes average driving distance of the longest hitter on tour

TIMES CHANGE

If anyone was ever in any doubt about the massive effect golf club technology, and in particular driver technology, has had on the pro game, they need look no further (literally) than the PGA Tour's performance statistics. Bubba Watson, the PGA Tour's biggest hitter, averaged a mighty 316 yards (289 meters) off the tee during the 2006 season. In 1983 Bill Glasson was the PGA Tour's biggest hitter and he averaged 276 yards (252 meters) that year. That's an increase in distance of nearly 15 percent.

THESE EXAMPLES of metal and persimmon-headed drivers were made less than 20 years apart, and are indicative of how far technology has come. The change is size, weight, and materials used is marked.

Aerodynamic design contributes to faster clubhead speed

Screws fix the metal sole plate to the clubhead

Persimmon is treated with oil to increase its resistance to impact

Woven strapping binds the clubhead to the shaft

Turnkey determines a single set of launch conditions

Despite having a much larger clubhead, the metal driver weighs less than the wooden alternative

Shaft is molded into the clubhead and set fast

Metal heads can be produced on a mass scale, unlike wooden drivers, so they dominate the market

◼ A persimmon driver from 1980s

◼ A modern titanium driver

On the tee

THE TEE SHOT SHOULD BE ONE OF THE EASIEST shots in golf; after all, you have the advantage of raising the ball off the ground using a tee peg. However, more often than not for the amateur golfer, this advantage is countered by the player adopting a poor set-up. All good golf swings start with a good set-up. There are three golden rules to follow: a neutral grip on the club; parallel alignment of the feet, knees, hips, and shoulders with the target line; and an athletic and comfortable posture. It is well worth making the effort to adopt these fundamentals.

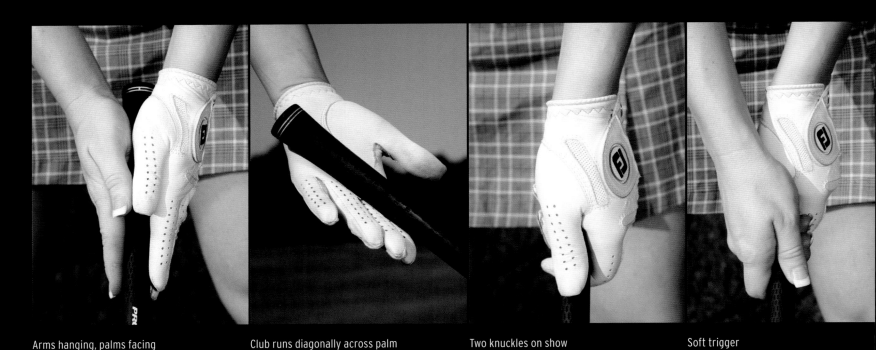

Arms hanging, palms facing | Club runs diagonally across palm | Two knuckles on show | Soft trigger

FORMING THE GRIP

To assume the perfect neutral hold requires some careful application.

▌ Start by letting your arms hang down free from tension, with your hands either side of the grip, palms facing one another.

▌ Now feed the club into your left hand, so the club runs diagonally from the first joint of your forefinger up into the fleshy pad at the top of your palm. Close your fingers around the grip.

▌ Your left thumb should rest on top of the grip, just right of center. In a mirror, only two knuckles on your left hand should be visible to you.

▌ To apply the right hand to the club, keep in mind the all-important palms-facing principle. Bring the right hand in toward the grip and wrap the fingers around it. The right hand should fit snugly on top of the left, the right thumb and forefinger forming a soft trigger around the grip.

> Start by letting your **arms hang down free** from tension, with your hands either side of the grip, palms facing one another

TYPES OF GRIP

The hands should now feel bonded together, as if one. How you join the hands together is a personal choice. Most top players adopt the Vardon grip, whereby the little finger of the right hand sits in the ridge created between the forefinger and middle finger of the left hand (left). Other players, including Tiger Woods, choose to entwine the little finger of the right hand with the left forefinger (right). Only you will know which feels most comfortable. Go with that.

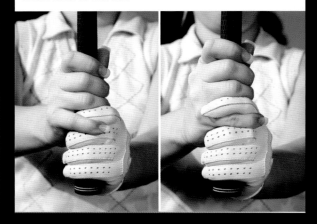

PERFECT ALIGNMENT

On the tee, good alignment is paramount. The principle c
perfect aim and alignment could not be simpler. Imagine
railroad track running down the fairway. The golf ball res
on the outer track, which points straight at the target. Th
where you aim the clubface. The inner track runs parallel
of that target line. This is where you align your feet, hips,
shoulders. Collectively, this is known as perfect parallel
alignment; it determines the path of your swing and is the
an essential requirement of powerful, straight driving.

PERFECT POSTURE

To hit perfect drives, your feet should be shoulder-width apart
with the toes splayed out slightly. The ideal ball position for the
driver is opposite the inside of your left heel, as that encourages
a sweeping angle of attack, striking the ball slightly on the upswing.
The weight should slightly favor your back foot–a ratio of about
60/40 is about right. This primes you for a good weight shift into
the right side in your backswing, essential for generating maximum
power in your swing.

FEET
The line formed by your feet should be
in parallel alignment to the target. Feet
should be shoulder-width apart and the
weight should be on the balls of the
feet in readiness for the swing

TARGET LINE
The clubface should be s
angles) to the target lin
outer track of a railroad

The drive

THE DRIVE IS A BIG SHOT IN MORE WAYS THAN ONE. The driver is, of course, the longest club in the bag and the club that we hit the furthest. It sets the tone for a hole, even for an entire round. A good drive puts you in the perfect position to attack a green and boosts your confidence. A good drive off the tee makes you believe you can shoot your best score...today! For all of these reasons, good driving is as much about position as it is about power. Although, of course, it is far better to have both.

THE FOUNDATIONS OF A GOOD SWING

The driver swing generates the most power, so the need for good foundations is paramount. Balance and posture need to be perfect. Think "shoulders over toes, hands under the chin." That should help get your posture in great shape every time you set-up to hit a drive. Also, parallel alignment should be achieved; the feet, hips, and shoulders all parallel to the target line (see pp.50–51). Good alignment promotes an on-line swing path.

GIVE YOURSELF TIME

Don't be in a hurry to get to the top; just keep your rhythm and tempo nice and smooth. Give yourself time to make a good shoulder turn and, more importantly, time to complete your backswing. For the perfect combination of arm swing and body turn, think "turn your back on the target and point the club straight at the target."

> Don't be in a hurry to get to the top: Just keep your rhythm and tempo nice and smooth

Strong foundations | Keep your rhythm smooth | Shift your weight with the club | Swing through and finish

LET YOUR WEIGHT FLOW

Poor weight shift drains the power out of your swing like nothing else. The key thing to remember is that you should let the weight move in the direction of the swinging clubhead. So, as you swing the club back the weight moves on to your right foot; then as you swing the club down, the weight moves on to your left foot. Now you can punch your weight off the tee.

SWEEP THROUGH AND HOLD YOUR FINISH

Let the club swing through. Keep your head down until the right shoulder comes through and raises it naturally. The intention to complete the swing with a well-balanced finish has knock-on benefits for your entire swing. It instils in your mind the need to keep your balance, a key requirement of solid ball-striking. Also, in doing that, you are less inclined to lose control or hit at the ball too aggressively. The swing stays smooth, which helps promote a pure and solid hit.

STAY IN CONTROL

- Many golfers feel that they should try to hit their drive shots as hard as they can. However, position, not power, is the most important factor off the tee. A shot of 250 yards (230 meters) that finds the middle of the fairway is always preferable to a shot of 300 yards (275 meters) that ends up in heavy rough.
- Most professional players hit their drives at 70-80 percent capacity. Less is often more when it comes to the golf swing; smooth rhythm is preferable to brute force. By employing this technique, you will discover that not only does your rhythm improve, but your distances are likely to be greater, too.
- For even greater control off the tee try gripping the club down the shaft a little and then make your normal swing. By "choking down" on the grip your swing will automatically become abbreviated—and a shorter swing results in greater control.

FREE-WHEELING
You should feel that the club is almost free-wheeling as it approaches the "hitting zone." It has little to do with brute force

WRIST ANGLE
Retain the angle in your wrists into your downswing, as this helps store the power in the swing

LEFT SHOULDER
As you start the downswing feel that you pull the left shoulder away from the chin

WEIGHT FORWARD
Keep your weight moving to the left as you swing into and through impact; do not under any circumstances allow yourself to fall backward away from the shot

THE MAGIC MOVE

There is no single part in the golf swing that could be said to be the key to great driving—golf isn't that simple. But if there is such a thing as a "magic move" then it is the split second transition from the completion of the backswing to starting the downswing. The weight shifts on to the left side, the hips start to unwind, the right elbow drops down to the right side and the shoulders stay back. The player is primed for the impact position.

PRACTICE MAKES PERFECT

Rehearse the "magic move" in slow motion and practice it in front of a mirror. Try to ingrain it into your practice swings, until it starts to feel comfortable and you feel you can replicate it in your actual swing. Repetition is a wonderful thing. Practice this move to train good driving habits.

STABLE BASE
Both feet should feel planted as the downswing starts, proving the stable base that is essential for making a controlled and well-balanced swing

BALL POSITION
With the ball correctly positioned opposite the left heel it is easier to achieve the desired sweeping angle of attack, promoting dead-solid contact

SWING SECRETS

Fully rotate the left shoulder under the chin

Keep the head down through impact

Ensure a smooth, one-piece takeaway

Align the ball with the left heel at address

Tee it high to maximize the driver's sweet spot

Big hitters: a masterclass

NOTHING RECEIVES GREATER ADMIRATION than a well-struck monster drive. It's the shot the galleries want to see. It's the shot club golfers want to hit most. New golf-club technology means that, when we get it right, we can achieve great distances, if not accuracy but, given that we will probably never be able to hit the ball as far as the world's best drivers, every golfer can learn from what they do.

ANGEL CABRERA'S FREE SWING

The tendency to hit at the ball with the driver is one of the biggest obstacles to achieving golf's Holy Grail—good distance and respectable accuracy. The trouble is, an overly aggressive approach tends to rob the swing of coordination and timing, which leads to poor distance and a loss of accuracy.

So, if you struggle with the driver, take a leaf out of 2007 US Open champion Angel Cabrera's book. The big Argentinian hits the ball a country mile (in 2007 his average driving distance according to PGA

Tour statistics was 303.2 yards), but it looks relatively easy. The secret lies largely in the freedom of motion.

Cabrera sets the club beautifully in his backswing and makes a big turn, which stores the power in his swing. Then in the downswing, he just lets it go; he swings the club down and almost free-wheels straight through the ball. It's a free swing, with the ball merely getting in the way of the club. That's a far more useful swing than trying to hit the ball as hard as possible and then having to deal with the problems associated with such a philosophy.

Make sure that you generate enough clubhead speed so the ball will spend enough time in the air to achieve a decent length

Driver shafts are generally made from graphite, because it is a light and very strong material

Big hitting does not come from brute force alone, but strong forearms, for example, will help generate a large amount of power and distance

THE GREATEST DRIVE

At the 1960 US Open at Cherry Hills in Denver, Arnold Palmer trailed leader Mike Souchak by seven shots going into the last round. Cue one of the greatest last-round charges in the history of golf. Palmer smashed his drive on to the green at the 346-yard 1st hole and two-putted for birdie, the first of six birdies in the first seven holes. Palmer went on to shoot 65, the lowest score ever in the final round by a winner, to win by two shots. It all started with that sensational drive on the 1st hole; surely the greatest drive ever.

■ Palmer lays down a marker

▷ **CABRERA'S BIG SHOULDER** turn enables him to free-wheel into the ball. This freedom of motion gives him great distance.

VIJAY SINGH'S RHYTHM

Rhythm in your golf swing is the key to consistent shot-making. Poor rhythm is debilitating with any club, but with a driver—the most unforgiving club in the bag—the effects are catastrophic. You will miss fairways, and lose balls, all day long.

Vijay Singh is a great scholar of the golf swing; and a man with a great swing himself. He advocates an old Bobby Jones adage, that you "start your downswing at the same speed as you took the club back."

It helps make smooth that crucial split-second transition from completing the backswing to starting the downswing. It gives you the time to coordinate the various moving parts in your swing, so that everything arrives at impact working in harmony. That is the essence of good timing. It is the way to hit drives long and straight, just like Vijay does.

▷ **VIJAY HAS A GREAT SWING** and excellent tempo, which is the same with every club in the bag. He is a great student of the game and renowned for the time he spends working on his swing.

ADAM SCOTT'S SHOULDER TURN

Adam Scott is not the strongest man in golf; he doesn't have the raw physical power of some bigger men on Tour. But he is a great driver of the golf ball, who has the ability to generate a lot of speed and distance, with good trajectory and a high level of consistency. A look at his PGA Tour statistics reveals that he hits the fairway almost 60 percent of the time, and averages over 300 yards in driving distance. The position he achieves at the top of the backswing is picture perfect and it is one of the main reasons why he drives the ball so well.

Scott makes a full shoulder turn, winding his body up like a coiled spring. All the time, he is resisting with his lower body, the hips turning only half as much as the shoulders do. This action generates a lot of resistance—in essence, latent energy waiting to be unleashed.

From the top of the swing, he can then basically recoil his upper body—like a spring unwinding – which drives his downswing forward at pace. He converts all of that power into the back of the golf ball with a good hand and arm action.

Again, with Scott and the other big hitters, the secret is that the hands, arms, and body work together toward impact. One doesn't reach its target before the other, meaning that every part of the swing is well coordinated and complementing each other.

◁ **SCOTT'S TECHNIQUE AND ABILITY** enable him to play and be successful no matter where in the world he plays. He has won on both the European and US Tours, as well as in Asia.

Metals and hybrids: the design

FAIRWAY METALS ARE THE DISTANCE CLUBS that don't bite. Like the driver, they have a relatively long shaft that helps generate distance. Unlike a driver, however, which has a relatively straight face, a fairway metal has a greater degree of loft on the clubface. This helps generate more height and more backspin, which in turn counteracts sidespin. This means that a fairway metal is easier to hit straight than a driver. It is more forgiving, too.

LOFTED METALS

Lofted metals come in a range of different designs. Aside from aesthetic considerations, which are of course important to any golfer, the focus of the club designer is on similar playability issues to that of the driver—maximum ball speed off the clubface, forgiveness, and moment of inertia (resistance to twisting at impact).

Versatility is also a key factor for this type of club, because a fairway metal will be required to perform in a greater variety of on-course situations—off the tee, from the fairway, and from light rough. There is much to gain—at least from the club golfer's perspective—in carrying more than one fairway metal, as it increases the range of shots at one's disposal.

However, in recent years there has been a revolution in the role of the lofted metal. It has in many ways been superseded by a new innovation that offers even greater playability.

THE HYBRID REVOLUTION

The hybrid or rescue club differs in appearance and design from the traditional fairway metal. It has a smaller clubhead, like an over-size long-iron with a bulbous back edge, and it produces the ball-flight characteristics of a long-iron without any of the hardships. The hybrid is incredibly versatile.

FAIRWAY METALS WITH HIGH LOFTS were traditionally the preserve of women and senior golfers until the revolution in hybrid clubs. Nowadays they feature in the bags of many professional players too.

Steel and graphite composite clubhead offers the perfect blend of distance and ease of use

Smooth sole area reduces drag and offers improved playabilty from a variety of different lies

Deep face and enlarged sweet spot forgives off-center strikes

■ View from the address position

METALS AND HYBRIDS VERSUS IRONS

Fairway metals, hybrids, and long-irons are interchangeable on the golf course. Each has its own advantages and disadvantages, but they travel similar distances. The key when considering your options is to think about the gap in distance between your 3-wood and the longest iron that you intend to keep in your bag—a 5-iron, for example. There will be a hybrid to fill that gap. Use the conversion chart below to build a set that best fits your game.

Lofts on metals and hybrids are comparable to long-irons

CONVERSION CHART			
210–230 yds	3-metal	1 hybrid	1-iron
190–210 yds	4-metal	2 hybrid	2-iron
170–190 yds	5/7-metal	3 hybrid	3-iron
160–180 yds	9-metal	4 hybrid	4-iron
150–170 yds	N/A	5 hybrid	5-iron

The rounded, compact clubhead makes light work of clingy rough. And it's a superb club to use off the tee on tight par 4s—the generous loft and relatively short shaft optimizes accuracy without any significant drain on distance.

Its performance advantages can be attributed to clubhead design and weight distribution. With a long-iron, the capability to distribute weight around the clubhead is limited. The rounded and slightly chunkier hybrid design, however, offers greater potential for redistributing the mass of the clubhead; this boosts the size of the sweet spot on the face and lowers the center of gravity, the dual effects of which make it more forgiving. It also increases the launch angle, enabling golfers to get the ball airborne far more easily. High-flying long shots—not a realistic proposition with a long-iron in the hands of the majority of amateur golfers—are very much back on the agenda.

GAME IMPROVEMENT

These clubs sit very nicely behind the ball, and this in itself gives golfers a great deal more confidence than if they were looking down at a long-iron. These psychological benefits combined with the tangible advantages in playability add up to a huge difference.

What is surprising is not that the hybrid has found its way into the golf bags of millions of golfers around the world, but that the world's best players are using them, too. One would have assumed that they hit their long-irons so well that they didn't need help from a hybrid. But the hybrid simply makes too compelling a case for itself to be ignored. The world's top-50 players have embraced this new concept club wholeheartedly.

One particular fan of the hybrid is 2007 Open champion Padraig Harrington (see pp.190). He believes there is a case for some golfers—especially seniors and those who perhaps don't generate much power in the swing—to carry only the irons numbered 6 and above. The 2, 3, 4, and 5-irons can therefore be replaced by the equivalent hybrid, which is easier to hit and offers more height, distance, and accuracy—a potent combination.

The bulbous clubhead results in a relatively low center of gravity

Perimeter weighting increases the club's resistance to off-center strikes

COMPACT AND FORGIVING, the hybrid is suitable for a wide range of shots; it is even used for chipping around the greens.

THE TRADITIONAL lofted metal features a wide clubhead. Not as versatile as the hybrid, it is best deployed from the tee or fairway.

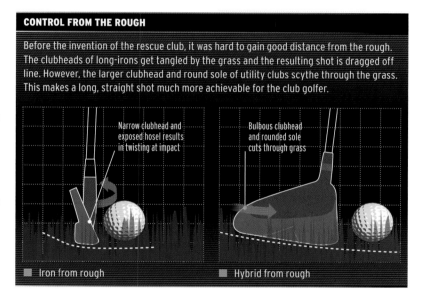

CONTROL FROM THE ROUGH

Before the invention of the rescue club, it was hard to gain good distance from the rough. The clubheads of long-irons get tangled by the grass and the resulting shot is dragged off line. However, the larger clubhead and round sole of utility clubs scythe through the grass. This makes a long, straight shot much more achievable for the club golfer.

Narrow clubhead and exposed hosel results in twisting at impact

Bulbous clubhead and rounded sole cuts through grass

■ Iron from rough   ■ Hybrid from rough

The smooth "speed plate sole design" reduces turf drag and promotes versatility from all lies

The center of gravity is positioned relatively far forward and close to the face to promote a low, penetrating ball flight

Tungsten-nickel weight lowers and deepens center of gravity for high launch and low spin

UTILITY METALS such as this example may feature an ultra-lightweight titanium head that has been designed to lower the club's center of gravity.

UTILITY METALS are available that come with a preset fade or draw bias. If a player has a persistent slice, a club with a draw bias will lead to straighter shots.

SOME HYBRIDS offer a degree of forgiveness via a combination of shock absorbtion technology, a high launch angle, and soft landing.

The fairway metal shot

MASTERING THE ART OF HITTING SOLID FAIRWAY METAL SHOTS gives you more strategic options on the golf course and ultimately makes you a more complete golfer. When you really need to hit a tight fairway, you can depend on a fairway metal to give you more accuracy than a driver, and with good distance. A fairway metal brings the green into play in two shots on those tough par-5s, and helps you generate good distance out of light rough. Fairway metals can be a golfer's best friends, if you know how to use them.

STATIC BUT ATHLETIC POSTURE

Your posture at address is integral to your chances of hitting a good shot because it determines the shape and quality of your body motion during the swing. It is easy to fall into bad habits, so when you practice, recreate perfect posture with this simple routine.
- Stand up straight with your feet shoulder width apart, your hands placed on the grip, and your arms extended comfortably around chest height.
- Bend over from the hips until the clubhead rests on the turf.
- Flex your knees, feeling some athletic tension in the thighs. Try to feel that your back is relatively straight, and hold your chin high.

The golf swing is a fluid motion and it is hard to make a good start from a totally static position. Waggle the club back and forth as you prime yourself to start the swing; this helps to banish tension from the hands, arms, and shoulders.

LEFT SHOULDER OVER RIGHT KNEE

Starting from the address position, begin the takeaway. Your body motion is the engine of the golf swing. Your body needs to move correctly and efficiently in order to drive your swing. Think of turning your left shoulder over your right knee, to promote a full turn. And make sure you keep that right knee flexed, just as it was at address, as that gives you a firm base from which to wind and unwind your body in the swing.

FULL ROTATION

As you swing your hands and arms through, the body needs to continue to unwind. The momentum of your swing will carry you through impact to a finish, but it helps if you think of completing your swing with your chest facing the target. This will get you "through the ball" better than ever.

Address routine

> Waggle the club back and forth as you prime yourself to start the swing; this helps to banish tension from the hands, arms, and shoulders

Address position | Smooth takeaway | Left shoulder over right knee | Rotate down and through the ball

PERFECT PLANE

There are several key checkpoints you can rehearse as you practice hitting balls; this is one of the best. As your left arm reaches parallel with the ground in the early stages of the backswing, make sure that the wrists are fully hinged, thus setting the club on the perfect plane.

Check it in a mirror; your hands should be right in front of your chest and the shaft of the club should be at an angle that hits the ground roughly equidistant between the golf ball and your toes. This is perfect plane. From there, you just keep turning your shoulders to complete the backswing.

SWING SECRETS

Hands stay in front of chest in backswing

Weight moves to the right as backswing progresses

Right foot stays planted in backswing

Left arm rotates to keep clubface neutral

KEEP IT TOGETHER
Feel that the arms swing at the same time as the body rotates

CHIN UP
Maintain your height, to make room for that shoulder turn, and keep your chin up

TURNING SHOULDERS
Turn your shoulders on a flat plane to complete your swing

FLEXED KNEE
Maintain the flex in your right knee

KNEES AND HIPS
Let your left knee work toward the ball as your hips turn

KEEP THE RHYTHM

You can expect good distance with fairway metal shots—they are the second longest clubs in the bag. But don't push it. Maintaining a smooth rhythm and focusing on dead-solid contact is the way to go, as that will promote sweet timing and the distance you seek, without sacrificing accuracy.

The hybrid shot

THE HYBRID IS A KEY STAGE IN THE EVOLUTION OF CLUB DESIGN. The neat clubhead and relatively short shaft makes a hybrid comparatively easy to hit and very forgiving, and it promotes a high launch angle. Because it also glides through rough better than the equivalent long-iron, it is incredibly versatile, too. To hit perfect hybrid shots from the rough, you need to keep in mind a few important factors that will determine the success of the shot.

▌ SET-UP RULES

You can never ignore the set-up; it has a huge bearing on the quality of your shot-making. A poor set-up almost invariably leads to a poor shot; a good set-up massively improves your chances of making a good swing and hitting a solid golf shot.

When hitting a hybrid from the rough, move the ball a little further back in your stance than you would for a shot from the fairway or off the tee. Somewhere around two balls'-widths inside the left heel is perfect. Also, make sure that your hands are slightly in front of the golf ball. Combined, these two measures will help promote the slightly descending angle of attack which is necessary to generate good contact and a strong ball-flight.

BE SMART

Smart shot selection is one of the keys to good scoring, which is one of the reasons a hybrid is such a useful tool to have in your bag. While attempting to hit a long-iron out of rough can lead to disaster, a hybrid is relatively easy to hit and therefore constitutes a smarter club selection. Don't be too ambitious, though. If you feel you'd struggle to hit a 7-iron from a particular lie, then you shouldn't be contemplating a hybrid, either.

Focus on set-up

Compact swing

Drive through

▌ THE PERFECT BLEND

A three-quarter backswing is more than enough for this type of shot—indeed, it has its advantages in the sense that a compact swing is easier to control and can help deliver a crisp blow to the back of the ball. But you must complete that full shoulder turn, allied to the appropriate arm swing. To arrive at the ideal top-of-the-backswing position, think in terms of making a "flat shoulder turn and an upright arm swing."

▌ PUNCH AND DRIVE

Hit down into the back of the ball, as though you're trying to hit a punch shot under the wind. This again reinforces the need, partly initiated in the nature of your set-up, to deliver a slightly descending strike. That helps make sure that the minimum amount of grass gets trapped between the clubface and the ball. It helps you make the best possible contact.

Descending strike

The hybrid chip and run

THE HYBRID IS MUCH MORE THAN THE DEFAULT OPTION from the fairway or rough from 150 to 200 yards (137 to 183 meters). It is also an excellent chipping club, frequently used by professionals. If you have a nice lie on the closely mown green fringe, and lots of green to work with, it is a smart play that produces neat chip-and-run shots. You can nudge the ball on to the putting surface with finesse and far more consistency than a lofted wedge shot.

▌CHOKE DOWN AND SET YOUR HANDS HIGH

You need to pre-set a few changes in your set-up in order to execute the hybrid chip-and-run well. First, place the ball in the middle of your stance, with your weight slightly favouring your front foot. Secondly, choke down on the grip, almost to the metal—you want to avoid any wrist hinge with this shot. Then stand as close to the ball as you comfortably can, with your hands a little higher than would be the case for a regular full shot.

> If the ball is **nestling in a tricky lie, the hybrid is best** choice as there is **no risk of the dreaded miss-hit**

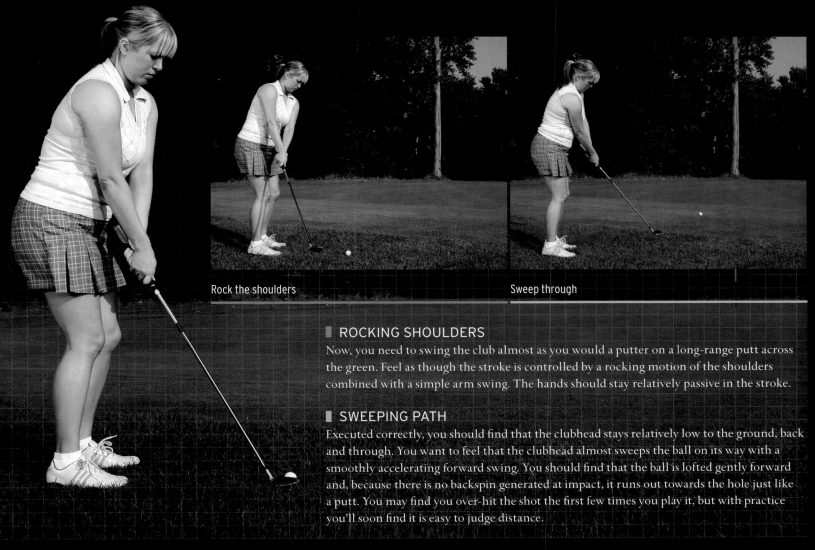

Rock the shoulders

Sweep through

▌ROCKING SHOULDERS

Now, you need to swing the club almost as you would a putter on a long-range putt across the green. Feel as though the stroke is controlled by a rocking motion of the shoulders combined with a simple arm swing. The hands should stay relatively passive in the stroke.

▌SWEEPING PATH

Executed correctly, you should find that the clubhead stays relatively low to the ground, back and through. You want to feel that the clubhead almost sweeps the ball on its way with a smoothly accelerating forward swing. You should find that the ball is lofted gently forward and, because there is no backspin generated at impact, it runs out towards the hole just like a putt. You may find you over-hit the shot the first few times you play it, but with practice you'll soon find it is easy to judge distance.

Choke down

Fairway metal: a masterclass

IF YOU WATCH A GOLF TOURNAMENT ON TELEVISION, especially a Major championship, where the golf courses tend to be set up with additional demands on accuracy as well as distance, you will see how frequently the top players rely on their fairway metals. Placement shots off the tee on tight par-4s, advancement shots on super-long par-5s, and shots into distant greens; these clubs are absolutely indispensable.

TIGER WOODS'S ANGLE OF ATTACK

The fairway metal is a different animal to the driver, but it needs very similar treatment to bring out its best qualities. The ball needs to be struck with a sweeping, shallow angle of attack. Many club golfers fail to achieve this all-important goal. They tend to think that, because the ball is sitting on the fairway and not on a tee-peg, it is necessary to hit down into impact—just like an iron shot. Wrong. It needs to be swept away.

Watch Tiger. He rehearses a very rounded swing motion when he is shaping up to hit a fairway metal. He knows the value of that sweeping angle of attack through impact; it's how you optimize ball-flight, distance, and accuracy.

Try to feel that the club works around your body in the backswing, allied to a good shoulder turn. This helps put you in the ideal position at the top of your backswing to approach the ball from the inside and on a shallow angle of attack. You'll sweep the ball away, with solid contact.

GREATEST SHOT

On the final day of the 1983 Ryder Cup at PGA National, Florida, Seve Ballesteros had driven into the fairway bunker on the 18th hole in his singles match against Fuzzy Zoeller. The situation looked lost. But Seve hit a 3-wood fully 240 yards on to the fringe of the green, an astonishing stroke of genius, to secure an unlikely half. The US Ryder Cup captain Jack Nicklaus described it as one of the greatest shots he had ever witnessed. Praise comes no higher.

■ Unbelievable Seve

▷ USING A METAL REQUIRES the golfer to round-out their swing and sweep it away, for position play; it's how Tiger Woods generates the perfect ball flight, coupled with accuracy.

Upper body rotation and a rounded swing are key when using a fairway metal

Neither hand should become dominant at any point of the swing—otherwise a loss of clubhead control will result

Don't get greedy with this club - it is about placement not distance

JIM FURYK'S POSITION PLAY

The fairway metal off the tee is a smart play; it gives you respectable distance and the extra loft on the face offers a greater level of accuracy than a driver. You can hit more fairways, which is a positive thing.

The key, once you've decided to hit a fairway metal off the tee, is making sure you don't try to make up the distance that in the back of your mind you know you're losing through not hitting a driver. That's an easy mistake to make, but not one made by Jim Furyk.

Furyk's swing may not be picture-perfect, but there is no one better at maintaining good rhythm and playing for position rather than for power. He believes in his swing, he knows exactly how far he hits the ball with that club, and he never pushes for more distance. That's why he hits more fairways than probably any other top player in the game.

So, when you're hitting a fairway metal off the tee, think position, not power. That's the whole point of the club.

◁ **JIM FURYK MIGHT NOT HAVE THE** most elegant swing on tour, but he is renowned for his consistency. Being able to keep the ball on the fairway is one of his greatest strengths.

PAUL CASEY'S WIDE ARC

It is astonishing the distances England's Paul Casey can generate with every club in the bag. The fairway metal is no exception. This swing trait, however, disguises the real source of Casey's power. He sweeps the club away on a wide arc in the backswing and makes a superb upper-body rotation. It is a potent combination, one that any golfer would do well to try to emulate.

Relaxed hands, arms, and shoulders at address is a crucial starting point. Tension is a total killer. Casey then sweeps the club away low to the ground for the first 30 in (76 cm) and at the same time the left shoulder starts to turn in behind the golf ball. That's the first power move. From here the swing just flows.

> He sweeps the club away on a **wide arc** in the backswing and makes a **superb upper body rotation**

▷ **CASEY HAS THE ABILITY** to create effective width in his backswing with a wide takeaway. This, coupled with a full shoulder turn, serves to store up power for the downswing.

Irons: the design

CHOOSING A SET OF IRONS used to be a choice between two very distinct options. Were you drawn to the purity and classic look of blades, or did you prefer the forgiveness of a peripherally weighted set with its trademark cavity-back? It was that simple. Times have changed, however, and immeasurably for the better as far as the golfer is concerned. The advancements in club technology mean that golfers of all levels have the potential to improve.

CAVITY-BACK IRONS

The main focus for golf club manufacturers is centered around game improvement. This is largely achieved by manipulating a club's center of gravity and weight distribution in order to optimize performance and forgiveness. In recent years the means by which they have strived to achieve this goal has become more varied.

Innovative and more sophisticated methods in the manufacturing and forging processes mean that cavity-back iron clubheads are stronger, easier to hit, better balanced, more consistent, and more forgiving than ever before. There are so many excellent cavity-back irons on sale, especially at the premium end of the market, that selection almost comes down largely to aesthetics.

THE DESIGN OF THE CAVITY-BACK IRON is concerned with redistributing the weight of the clubhead around the edge, leaving a cavity in the center. This weight transference means the clubhead is less likely to twist at impact with off-center strikes.

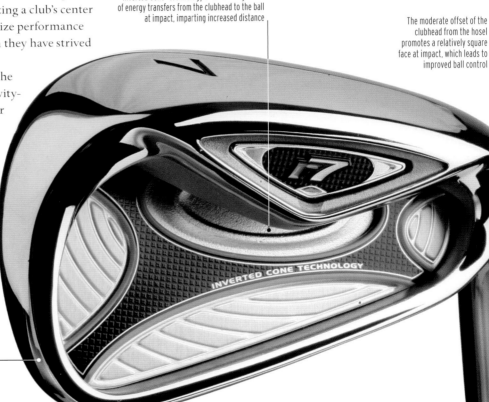

"Inverted Cone" technology ensures a high level of energy transfers from the clubhead to the ball at impact, imparting increased distance

The moderate offset of the clubhead from the hosel promotes a relatively square face at impact, which leads to improved ball control

Weight is transferred from the center cavity of the club and relocated around the perimeter –the essence of cavity-back technology

IN THE MAKING

As recently as the 1960s, many touring professionals spent their time between tournaments working in their club shop, making and refining their own golf clubs and servicing the needs of the club's members. Today the world's leading professionals receive round-the-clock service from golf equipment manufacturers and are given various sets of irons tailored specifically to their needs. Times have changed.

■ Sam Snead in his pro shop, 1949

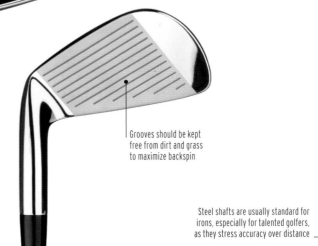

Grooves should be kept free from dirt and grass to maximize backspin

Steel shafts are usually standard for irons, especially for talented golfers, as they stress accuracy over distance

■ Iron face

MULTI-MATERIALS AND MOVEABLE WEIGHTS

Multi-material clubhead construction is a new technology. Some irons now feature lightweight titanium clubfaces, allowing more of the clubhead's weight to be located around the outer edges, specifically the sole of the club. Forgiveness is the major pay-off.

Other companies adopt a similar principle, involving specially constructed metal composite inserts, designed to help create a low center of gravity and high launch angle.

Moveable weights are another method used by designers of club heads. Progressive tungsten weights, which alter the playing characteristics of the club depending on loft, are the big selling point on some of the 21st century's newest irons. This innovation offers benefits in terms of the level of forgiveness and the optimization of the ball's launch angle.

Two shock absorption discs in the back of the clubhead produce a softer feel off the face at impact

Tungsten nickel weight lowers the center of gravity for a relatively high launch angle and reduced spin

CAVITY-BACK IRONS such as these are typical of the latest developments in club design. They feature a "WS system"– essentially a tungsten weight and shock absorption discs– as well as a cavity-back element.

TRADITIONAL BLADES

As well as the revolution in the design of game-improvement irons, there is also a wide choice of blades on the market. The leading manufacturers have in recent years successfully upgraded the forging process of the mild carbon steel typically used in the construction of blade clubheads. The purity of the forged steel results in supreme consistency and performance throughout the set, to help optimize distance control.

The muscle-back appearance of 21st century blades is an attractive design, but it also has a practical application, helping to concentrate the clubhead's center of gravity in the middle of the blade for solid hits and neutral shot bias throughout the set. It allows the more accomplished player a greater degree of shot-making control, to work the ball both ways through the air.

For many players there is nothing to beat a top-grade set of blades. These clubs are not very suitable for beginners, however—a player needs to be able to strike the ball well to get the best out of them.

Clubhead is finished in double nickel chrome plating for a durable and classic appearance

The muscle-back design (a partial cavity-back) helps concentrate the club's center of gravity in the middle of the clubhead

BLADED IRONS AND MUSCLE-BACKS are aesthetically pleasing but difficult for beginners to use due to a lack of peripheral weighting.

THE BEST OF BOTH WORLDS

For those who cannot decide between blades or cavity-backed irons, there is another option known as a "progressive" set, which provides the best elements of both. The long-irons, for years the bane of many an amateur golfer's life, feature a cavity-back design and slight offset to help you flight your shots properly; these also offer a good level of forgiveness.

However, rather than the whole set of irons featuring the same degree of cavity-back, the progressive set is different. Basically, as the loft increases, each club is progressively more bladelike in design and appearance, and features less offset.

It is the best of both worlds. The cavity-backed long-irons have a slightly bigger hitting area and the design is such that it goes through light rough a lot better than a traditional long-iron. Also, the offset head helps square the face at impact so there's less of a tendency to slice. And yet you don't have to compromise with the short-irons; you still get the enhanced feel and playability of a blade at that end of the set.

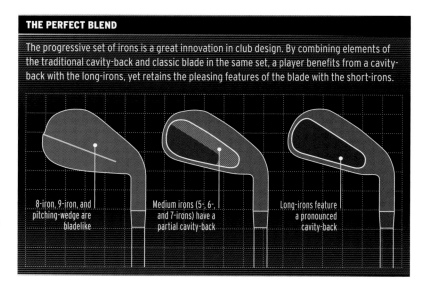

THE PERFECT BLEND

The progressive set of irons is a great innovation in club design. By combining elements of the traditional cavity-back and classic blade in the same set, a player benefits from a cavity-back with the long-irons, yet retains the pleasing features of the blade with the short-irons.

8-iron, 9-iron, and pitching-wedge are bladelike

Medium irons (5-, 6-, and 7-irons) have a partial cavity-back

Long-irons feature a pronounced cavity-back

IRON LOFT AND LENGTH

Loft is the essence of creative play on the golf course. If all clubs were the same loft, even the best players in the world would struggle to shoot low scores. There is a distinct variation between the loft of a 3-iron (approximately 22 degrees) and a pitching-wedge (approximately 48 degrees). Similarly, the length of the shaft in a standard set of nine irons differs; longer shafts are better for distance, shorter shafts more suited to precision play.

▷ **AS WELL AS THE OBVIOUS PROGRESSION** in loft in a set of nine irons, there is also a difference in the relationship between the sole and leading edge through the set.

▽ **THE SHAFT LENGTH** of a 3-iron is approximately 4 in (10 cm) longer than a pitching-wedge, with increments of half an inch for all clubs in between.

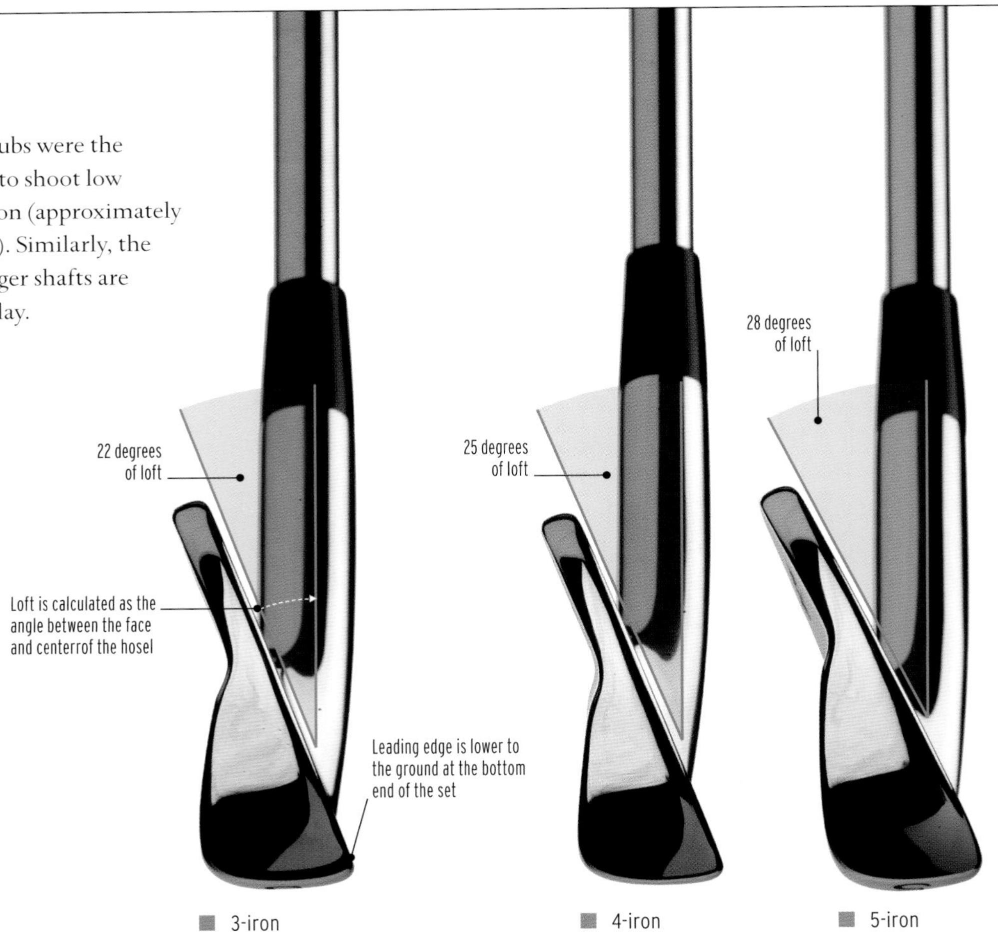

A 3-iron is 38.75 in (98.5 cm) long—a longer shaft promotes distance

A 6-iron has a shaft length of 37.25 in (94.5 cm)

A 9-iron is 35.75 in (91 cm) long—a shorter shaft is conducive to precision play

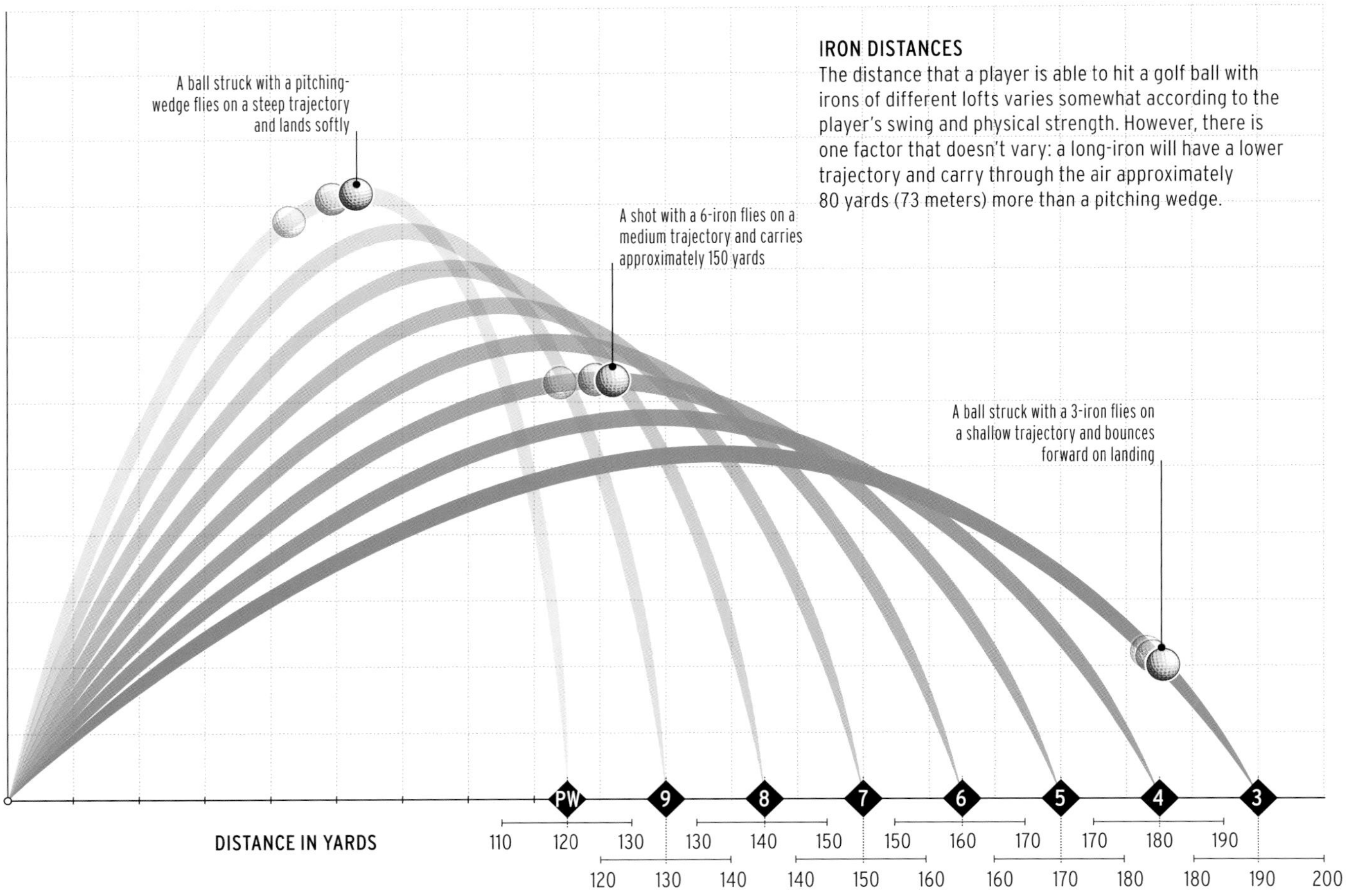

22 degrees of loft

25 degrees of loft

28 degrees of loft

Loft is calculated as the angle between the face and centerrof the hosel

Leading edge is lower to the ground at the bottom end of the set

■ 3-iron   ■ 4-iron   ■ 5-iron

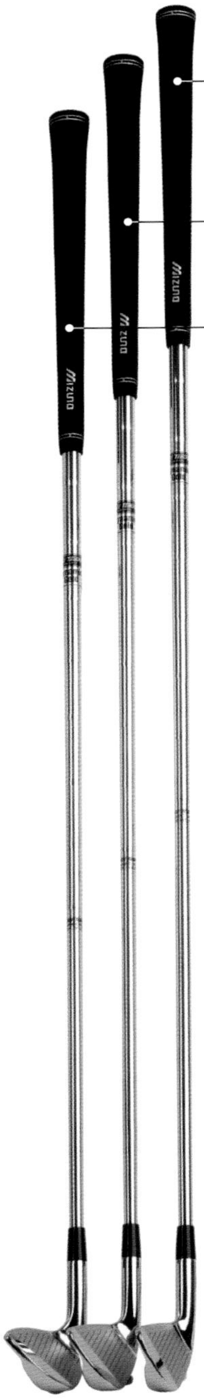

IRON DISTANCES

The distance that a player is able to hit a golf ball with irons of different lofts varies somewhat according to the player's swing and physical strength. However, there is one factor that doesn't vary: a long-iron will have a lower trajectory and carry through the air approximately 80 yards (73 meters) more than a pitching wedge.

A ball struck with a pitching-wedge flies on a steep trajectory and lands softly

A shot with a 6-iron flies on a medium trajectory and carries approximately 150 yards

A ball struck with a 3-iron flies on a shallow trajectory and bounces forward on landing

DISTANCE IN YARDS

PW	9	8	7	6	5	4	3
110 120	130	130 140	150	150 160	170	170 180	190
120	130 140	140	150 160	160	170 180	180	190 200

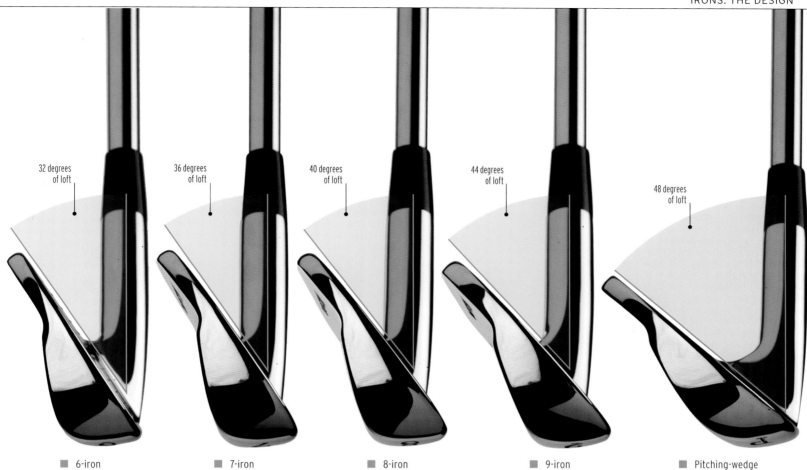

32 degrees of loft — 6-iron

36 degrees of loft — 7-iron

40 degrees of loft — 8-iron

44 degrees of loft — 9-iron

48 degrees of loft — Pitching-wedge

CUSTOM FITTING

Custom fitting provides the player with clubs tailored exactly to their specification. Fitting the perfect set is determined by various dynamic factors such as swing speed, angle of attack, launch angle, and so on. But it also takes account of various static measurements such as height, the size of a golfer's hands, and other considerations such as age and sex. The key measurements in the perfect set are as follows:

• Length: The ideal length of a club-shaft is determined by a player's height and, to a lesser degree, the distance from the tips of their fingers to the ground. Shafts can be shortened, or lengthened, accordingly.

AN ARRAY of different clubheads can be fitted to an equally diverse number of shafts to find the perfect combination for a player.

CLUB TECHNICIANS are constantly on hand at major tournaments to make any adjustments required to the equipment supplied by the manufacturers to the professional players they sponsor.

• Lie angle: This is the angle formed by the shaft and the bottom edge of the clubhead. Broadly speaking, short golfers require a flat lie angle on their irons; tall golfers require an upright lie angle.

• Shaft-type: There will typically be a range of shafts available from each manufacturer, with different weight, flex, and bend profile characteristics. As a rule, the stronger the hitter, the stiffer the shaft required.

• Grip size: Grips should be the correct size in order that the hands can work properly during the swing. If grips are too thin, the hands tend to be over-active, which causes problems. If grips are too thick, then it can lead to inactive hands where there is no zip to the swing in the hitting area.

The iron shot

THERE IS AN ART TO GREAT IRON PLAY. The clubs vary enormously in terms of loft, shaft-length, and of course the distance the ball flies, and yet they are all categorized in the same way. The great iron player must be able to cope with all of these elements – control their ball-flight, gauge distance, and control spin – using clubs as diverse as a 3-iron and a 9-iron. This is an art that can be learned, and every golfer can quickly improve their iron play. It's just a question of knowing where to look and how best to turn theory into practice.

UNDERSTANDING BALL POSITION

Ball position is a fundamental aspect of iron play. Any confusion or lack of awareness of this part of the set-up can, and probably will, have dire consequences on the state of your approach play.

▌ Here is a useful rule of thumb to work on. Play your wedge shots with the ball in the middle of your stance; then move the ball progressively further forward in your stance as the club gets longer. As a guide, the 5-iron is just over a ball's-width forward of centre; the 3-iron further forward still, inside your left heel.

The reason for doing this that it helps encourage the correct angle of attack as the clubhead approaches the ball – relatively steep with the wedge and progressively more shallow as the club gets longer. It is one of the keys to solid iron play.

▌ In terms of how far away from the ball you stand, again it depends on the club you are using. Quite simply, you stand progressively closer to the ball as the shaft of the club gets shorter. Use the posture drill at the start of the section of fairway metals (see p.58) to help you determine the distance you stand from the ball with every club in the bag.

 Ball position varies by club
 Club length is key

LEARN GOOD DISTANCE CONTROL

Good distance control is the foundation of successful iron play. What you need to do is try to establish your own personal yardages for each club. Use your time on the practice ground to establish how far you hit each club – on the fly, that is – by hitting 20 balls and discarding the longest five and the shortest five. That middle cluster of 10 balls represents your average distance with that club. Write down a number for each club. When you're on the golf course, get into the habit of using a yardage chart. That professional approach will pay off. Then learn to control your swing.

▌ Always make a smooth, well-balanced swing. You still need to commit to the shot through impact, but the overall motion of your swing must be within your own physical limits. Most top players swing at about 80-85 per cent of full power. It is the only way you can achieve the necessary consistency of strike and distance control.

WRAP THE SHAFT AROUND YOUR NECK

Anyone who tells you that the follow-through makes no difference to the quality of your iron shots is missing the point. Of course, the ball is gone and on its way, but if you have in your mind's eye a positive image of how you want to finish the swing, you can improve the execution of your iron shots.

▌ Here's a good image to have in mind. Wrap the shaft of the club around the back of your neck as part of a balanced finish to your swing. What this does is encourage a really positive release of the club into and through the ball. You'll hit consistently better iron shots as a result.

Poised follow-through

Practice with purpose and make a smooth swing

SWING SECRETS

Attention is focused on the back of the ball

Right arm stays close to side coming into impact

Right knee moves in towards the ball

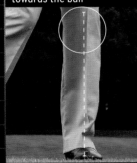

Left knee stays braced and does not collapse

ROCK STEADY
Head stays behind the ball, representing a fixed axis point for the swing

SHOULDER LINE
Right shoulder stays "under" to promote good swing path into impact

DESCENDING BLOW
Club approaches golf ball on a slightly descending angle of attack

HANDS LEAD THE CLUBHEAD

It's common for many amateurs to flick at the ball with their iron shots, in the belief that this will help the ball into the air and lead to better shots. It doesn't; it's one of the worst faults in the game.

Look at the top players. Their hands lead the clubhead into the ball, generating a downward angle of attack. The key aspect to have in mind is making sure that there is a degree of forward lean in the shaft at the moment of impact. This compresses the golf ball, and means that your shots will have a much more effective trajectory.

KEEP THE ARC
Left arm straightens to maintain arc of swing

CLEAR A PATH
Left hip clears out of the way, to make room for a free swing of the arms

Shaping shots

MOST AMATEURS ASSUME THAT INTENTIONALLY SHAPING shots different ways through the air is a game best left to the top players. But that needn't necessarily be the case. There are simple rules to help you shape shots – either with a draw or a fade, high or low – and anyone with ambition to improve their game can quickly develop these skills. It all comes down to practice and application. You'll find that there are many on-course situations in which your game will benefit hugely.

HOW TO HIT A DRAW

Shaping a draw involves moving the ball through the air from right to left for the right-hander and left to right for the left-hander.

▌ Aim the clubface straight at the target, as if you are hitting a straight shot. Then align your feet in the direction that you want your ball to start off, without adjusting the clubhead.

▌ Now make a normal backswing following the line of your feet.

▌ Through the hitting area pay extra attention to rolling your right hand over your left to encourage a good release of the clubhead.

▌ Then follow through to a well balanced finish. The opposing angles at address, and the resulting path of attack and clubface positioning at impact, impart the necessary sidespin and cause the ball to start off in one direction and curve away through the air.

Your weight shifts normally from the back foot to the front

Aim at the target   Swing normally   Roll the hands   Follow through

HOW TO HIT A FADE

Hitting a fade involves moving the ball through the air from left to right for the right-hander and right to left for the left-hander.

▌ Aim the clubface where you want the ball to finish – that is, straight at the target. The align your feet in the direction you want the ball to start, while maintaining the position of the clubhead.

▌ Then make a normal swing along your aim lines.

▌ As you approach impact, delay the release of your hands – the opposite of rolling your hands, shown above – to make sure that the face stays open through the hitting area.

▌ Proceed with your follow-through to a balanced finish. With this shot and the draw, the key is to practise it enough that you can control the amount of movement through the air. Your ultimate aim is to be able to shape the ball to suit different situations.

The clubface is open at the top of the backswing

Aim at the target   Swing normally   Delay the hands   Hold your finish

Backswing reaches to only three-quarters of its normal length

Ball back, weight forward | Abbreviated backswing | Stay back | Punchy follow through

HOW TO HIT IT LOW

For the low shot, where you need to keep the ball under an obstacle, such as a tree branch, a couple of adjustments at address are essential.

▮ To begin with, choke down on the grip an inch or two. Place the ball further back in your stance and hold your hands ahead of the ball; this de-lofts the clubface. You are effectively pre-setting a lower-than-normal ball flight. Place extra weight on your front foot.

▮ There is no need to make fancy moves in your swing. Make a three-quarter length backswing, with a full shoulder turn.

▮ In the downswing, try to feel as though your chest "covers" the ball through the hitting area. You should drive the club through low to the ground, with your hands very much ahead of the point of impact. Cultivate a sense that the clubhead stays low to the ground through the ball.

▮ The abbreviated follow-through is a sign of a controlled, well-balanced, and punchy swing.

Do not be tempted to hit the ball harder. Just hit it better. Dead-solid contact is the real key with this shot. Remember, a lower ball flight will result in extra run of the ball upon landing, so allow for this when choosing your club.

Hands are level with the ball at address

Through the swing, weight remains on the right side longer

Ball forward, hands back | Get the hands high | Hold your weight back | Balanced finish

HOW TO HIT IT HIGH

Hitting a high ball is probably not a shot you'll need to call on all that frequently. But if you have an obstruction in your way, such as a tree, or you need to attack a very tight pin position over a bunker, this is a useful shot to know.

Drastic changes to the set-up and swing are not advisable. It is far better in this case to keep things subtle.

▮ You need a higher-than-normal ball flight, so it is necessary to pre-set a little more loft on the clubface at address by positioning the ball further forward in the stance. And rather than the hands being ahead of the ball, as was the case with the low shot, this time place them level with the ball.

▮ Now make a slightly more upright backswing, getting the hands high at the top.

▮ The feeling through impact is of staying behind the ball, your weight just hanging on the right side a fraction longer than normal.

▮ With the ball on its way, proceed through to a well-balanced finish with the weight slightly more on the right side than usual.

Iron shots: a masterclass

THE SIMPLEST YARDSTICK OF GOOD IRON PLAY is the number of greens hit in regulation. The players at the top of the rankings hit as many as 80 percent of the greens they aim at. As with other areas of the game, there is much we can learn from the professionals, but there is more to great iron play than hitting greens. Strategy comes into play, as does the ability to move the ball through the air and to hit shots pin high.

Keep the clubhead online with the target through the shot

The right arm should be fully extended through impact

The legs provide a solid platform for the powerful unwinding of the body and a free swing of the arms

ERNIE ELS'S EXTENDED ARMS

Ernie Els is one of the greatest ball-strikers in the game, his seemingly effortless and beautifully rhythmic swing disguising serious power and great compression of the golf ball at impact. It's one of the many reasons why his iron shots fly so pure, straight, and far.

There is much in Ernie's swing that every golfer can learn from, such as the way his arms are fully extended as he swings the clubhead into and through the ball. This helps him carry good speed into the ball and deliver that all-important descending blow.

To emulate Ernie's positive move through impact, visualize your right arm extending fully toward the target and the clubhead traveling low to the ground after the ball. This will encourage you to swing freely through the ball; and extend your arms like Ernie does.

◁ THE ELS STYLE IS LEGENDARY and the envy of many players. His seemingly effortless swing and rhythmic tempo is complemented by the way he extends his arms through the ball.

THE GREATEST IRON SHOT

Sergio Garcia was playing in the final round of the 1999 USPGA when he hit an iron shot of pure genius. His drive on the 16th came to rest against the roots of a large oak tree, 189 yards from the pin. Initially he thought he would have to chip out, but then he saw an opening. He grabbed a 6-iron, opened the face, and hit it hard as he could with his eyes closed. When he opened them, he could see it going exactly where he wanted and slicing. It made the green, some 35 ft (10 m) from the hole and he almost holed the putt for birdie.

■ Garcia goes for broke on the 16th

COLIN MONTGOMERIE'S CONTROL

Scotland's Colin Montgomerie, a record-breaking eight-time winner of the European Tour's Order of Merit, may not have the most conventional-looking golf swing, but no one in the modern era could be said to have better controlled the distance of their iron shots into greens. Monty has hit the ball pin-high probably more times than any golfer in the last 20 years.

One of Monty's great strengths, which is something which every amateur or club golfer can easily carry into their own game, is the way his swing maintains its rhythm no matter which club he is using, from the 3-iron to the 9-iron. And, specifically, the way he maintains the same rhythm in that crucial transition from finishing his backswing to starting his downswing. He doesn't snatch the club down. He gives himself time. Therein lies a lesson for every golfer. Keep that first move down silky-smooth.

▷ **WHILE THERE MAY BE FLAWS** in his character, in terms of his temper and his concentration, the same cannot be said of Monty's iron play, which is smooth, free-flowing, and accurate.

▽ **SORENSTAM HAS A POLICY** of attacking the pin wherever possible, and rarely lays up to get out of trouble. Her approach play is considered and she makes very few mistakes.

ANNIKA SORENSTAM'S GOOD ROTATION

Annika Sorenstam is the greatest woman golfer of the last 20 years and certainly one of the greatest players in history. She has set new standards in the women's game—much like Tiger Woods has in the men's game. She is the very much the complete golfer, and has no real weaknesses to speak of.

She has one little quirk to her swing, however, which is unconventional. She turns her head markedly to the left as she delivers the clubhead to the ball. It is perhaps a dangerous move to mimic precisely, as every player will have a unique element to their swing that works just for them, but there are elements of this which would help improve many golfers' impact position. It's a case of taking a little, rather than a lot, of what Annika does and using it to the benefit of your own swing.

With a subtle turn of the head, Annika encourages good rotation of the upper body through the ball; it also helps her clear the left side out of the way, and in doing so, she gives herself enough room to enable her arms to swing freely.

She has one little quirk to her swing, however, which is unconventional. She turns her head markedly to the left as she delivers the clubhead to the ball

Sloping lies

NO GOLF COURSE IS COMPLETELY FLAT. In fact, the only time you can guarantee a totally level lie is on the tee and that accounts for a small percentage of the shots you'll play in a round of golf. Whether uphill, downhill, or sidehill you have to be able to cope with various sloping lies because the fact is you'll face them every time you set foot on the golf course.

BALL ABOVE YOUR FEET

The first thing to understand when the ball lies above the level of your feet is that you'll have a tendency to pull the ball down the slope. There are a few swing changes to adopt to compensate for this.

▌ Firstly, aim to the right of your target. Then, choke down on the grip. This shortens the club and thus compensates for the fact that the ball is effectively higher than it would be on a level lie. Also, stand a little more upright with slightly less knee flex.

▌ The combined effects of the slope and the nature of your stance will encourage a slightly more rounded swing plane – the feeling being that you are swinging the club more around your body. That's how it should feel; just try to maintain your original height and spine angle as best you can.

▌ Then rotate your body through to a finish, all the while maintaining your balance.

Maintain solid foundations through the swing

Aim right, choke down, stand tall | Maintain your height | Keep your balance

BALL BELOW YOUR FEET

Once again, the slope influences the ball flight and you must accept that the awkward nature of this lie and your stance tends to limit your body rotation.

▌ The ball will tend to fly right, so aim to the left of the target. At address, bend from the hips more than you would normally, to get yourself down to the level of the ball. Plenty of knee flex is also advisable, as is a wider stance, to give you more stability.

▌ Due to your inhibited turn, your backswing will be more arms-dominated, and therefore shorter and more upright. You'll generate less power, so club-up accordingly, and maintain a nice smooth rhythm.

▌ Swing through as freely as possible within the confines of the slope.

The key to this shot is maintaining your original height and spine angle until the ball is struck. Any tendency to gain height, an easy mistake given the nature of the situation, will result in a topped or thinned shot.

Grip the club towards the end of the shaft

Aim left, bend knees and hips | Shorter, upright swing | Make a free follow-through

BALL ON AN UPSLOPE

This is probably the easiest of all the shots from sloping lies, because there's a sense of being able to launch the ball into the air. However, there are a few ways to make sure you play it well.

▮ Your right shoulder should be markedly lower than your left and your weight favouring the back foot. Adopt a slightly wider stance and aim right of the target, because the ball tends to hook from an upslope.

▮ Try to swing in harmony with the slope and maintain your balance. Do not get thrown back onto your right foot, or lean into the slope.

▮ Keep your weight stable and your head down through impact. Let the natural momentum of your swing pull you into the finish position.

Steady backswing works in harmony with the slope

Align shoulders with slope   Maintain your balance   Keep your head down

UNDERSTANDING LAUNCH ANGLES

Club selection isn't as straightforward when you're playing from an upslope or a downslope. The main thing to keep in mind is the change in the initial launch angle. On a downslope, it will be significantly lower, so you can afford to take less club - say, a 6-iron instead of a 5-iron. On an upslope, the opposite is true. The launch angle is higher, which means you can take more club - for instance, a 7-iron instead of an 8-iron. Don't fight that slope effect - just go with it. Remember - less club on a downslope, more club on an upslope.

BALL ON A DOWNSLOPE

This is the toughest of all the sloping lies, because the downslope gives you the sense that it is very difficult to get the ball airborne. It is not imagined. The nature of a downslope means that you are deprivesd of loft, and it is all too easy to scuttle the ball straight along the ground.

▮ Make sure your shoulders and hips are as close to parallel with the slope as possible — your left shoulder feeling lower than the right. Place the ball back in your stance. This is a very important point. You will tend to want to put the ball forward in your stance, as it feels natural to generate some elevation from there, but this will prevent you from getting the ball airborne.

▮ Pick the club up a little steeper in your backswing with an early wrist hinge. This sets the club in a position from which you can more easily generate the necessary steep angle of attack into impact. Make sure you maintain your weight distribution all the way to the top of the backswing.

▮ As you swing down into impact, try to feel as though you are chasing after the ball down the slope, staying well down through impact so that the clubhead follows the contours of the ground. Never try to help the ball into the air.

Keep your head down through impact

Try your best to maintain your balance throughout the swing

Ball back in stance   Early wrist hinge   Stay down through impact

Problem shots

WHEN YOU PLAY A ROUND OF GOLF, you are taking on Mother Nature, a skilled golf course architect, and the capricious nature of the game itself. The accomplished player knows how to cope with the varied challenges that are thrown at them. Whether you are battling with a gusty wind, trying to excavate your ball from clinging rough, or have found a bunker with your drive, there are ways you can use the elements or improve your chances of recovery.

USE THE WIND, DON'T FIGHT IT

The wind is an ever-present challenge virtually every time you play golf. And whether it is merely a gentle breeze or a strong and gusting wind, you have to know how to play it.

Playing into the wind you should take a bigger club and swing it easier; the ball flight will penetrate the wind far more effectively. Don't make the common mistake of taking the same club and just trying to hit it harder, as that never works.

When playing downwind, take less club and again swing easier. Don't take the same club and try to ease up on the shot; you will probably miss-hit it. Also, consider taking a 3-wood off the tee, rather than a driver. The extra height will allow you to benefit more from the tailwind and thus gain distance.

▌ Playing with a crosswind, tour professionals will often work shots into the wind—for instance, hit a draw into a left-to-right wind—as they feel it gives them more control over distance and spin. This is the advanced option. Most times, however, it is easier to use the wind, rather than fight it. In a right-to-left wind, simply shift your aim focus to the right of target. Then hit a straight shot and let the wind do the rest for you.

Aim right and use the crosswind

PLAYING OUT OF THE ROUGH

In the rough the main problem is grass getting trapped between the clubface and ball. This drains the power out of the shot and loses you distance. The key is to train a steeper angle of attack into impact, as this gives you the best possible contact with the golf ball, which leads to a more "normal" iron shot.

▌ Put the ball back in the middle of your stance, with your hands ahead of the ball. Hinge the wrists a little sooner in the backswing.

▌ Hit down into the back of the ball, with your hands leading the clubhead through impact, and make sure you make a full follow-through.

> The key is to train a **steeper angle of attack** into impact, as this **gives you the best possible contact**

Hands ahead, break wrists early   Steep angle of attack, full follow-through

THE LONG BUNKER SHOT

Rule number one from any fairway bunker is to take a club with sufficient loft to clear the front lip. If it so happens that club has the distance to also reach the green, consider that a bonus. Clean contact is everything with this shot, because sand soaks up the energy in the swing and therefore even slightly heavy contact results in catastrophic loss of distance.

▌ Choke down on the grip about an inch. This will hold the clubhead up off the sand and help to promote a clean contact with the ball.

▌ Shuffle your feet into the sand to give yourself a secure footing. This will lower the base of your swing, so choking down on the club is key.

▌ Make a smooth, well-balanced swing and make sure you hit down into the back of the ball, rather than trying to help it into the air.

▌ You should strike the back of the ball, rather than the sand. If you catch the sand before the ball, it will feel "heavy."

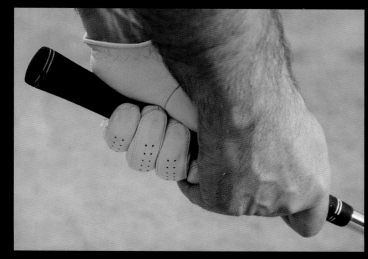

Shorten the club

Shuffle down

Strike the ball, not the sand

A secure footing will enable you to make a balanced swing

GREAT PRACTICE

Finding yourself in a fairway bunker during the course of a normal round of golf might rightly be considered a negative, but you can use this scenario very much to your advantage in a practice environment.

One of Vijay Singh's favorite practice drills is hitting full iron shots from a fairway bunker. It is a wonderful way to train clean, pure contact with the golf ball. Vijay, of course, is one of the best ball-strikers in the world, so if it works for him...

Make a smooth swing

Wedges: the design

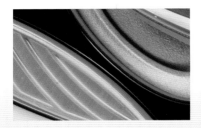

AS RECENTLY AS THE 1990S THE SCOPE OF THE WEDGE in any golfer's bag was very narrow. There was simply the pitching-wedge and the sand-wedge. If a player wanted to produce extra loft on a shot they had to open the clubface and improvise. Today, these two staple clubs have been largely replaced in the market by a series of wedges ranging from 52 to 64 degrees and offering players of all levels greater versatility.

PRECISION TOOL

Although it does not promise booming tee shots, like the driver, or holed putts and tumbling scores, like the putter, the wedge does have its own charms. It is a precision tool and it wins its place in a golfer's bag by offering an alluring combination of feel, high spin, and maximum control. From a playing perspective that is plenty for any golfer to get excited about.

Perhaps it is just that the wedge doesn't get the hard sell, like drivers, putters, and hybrids. This is partly because, for designers, there is a limited window of opportunity in terms of how they can maximize the performance of a wedge. A club's performance is therefore influenced by more basic considerations, such as the groove configuration and the type of metal used. None of this has quite the same "tech appeal" as "moment of inertia" and "center of gravity".

But these considerations matter a great deal: a large percentage of the shots you play in a round of golf are from inside 100 yards (91 metres). Aside from putts, then, it means the wedges in your bag get plenty of action.

THE DESIGN OF WEDGES tend to be more blade-like in appearance than long-irons, because they are easier to hit. The sole is more rounded and the leading edge higher off the ground. Peripheral weighting is of secondary importance to feel and the pursuit of precision striking.

Black nickel finish is softer than chrome and affords the player more feel around the greens

The rounded sole helps the player execute shots from sand or lush grass

Clubhead is made of grain flow forged carbon steel for distance control and a pure feel

The loft of a pitching wedge, measured from the center of the hosel, is approximately 46 degrees

Rounded sole with relatively low bounce angle

■ Toe-end view

IN THE GROOVE

The R&A and USGA, who together govern golf worldwide, set rules relating to grooves in golf clubs, including the width, depth, and distance between each groove. Spin is the name of the game with wedges so club manufacturers take groove sizes to the extremes of legality. Amateur golfers who struggle to spin the ball probably wish there were no restrictions.

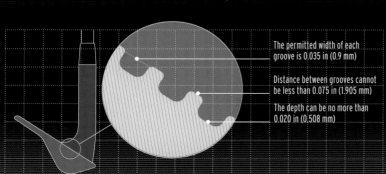

The permitted width of each groove is 0.035 in (0.9 mm)

Distance between grooves cannot be less than 0.075 in (1.905 mm)

The depth can be no more than 0.020 in (0.508 mm)

BELIEVING THE SPIN

High spin-rate is the key selling point of any wedge. The finish on the face of the club and the groove pattern are both designed to create friction when the clubface meets the ball, and to produce increased spin. Grooves on the faces of the modern wedge are so effective that professional golfers are able to generate amazing amounts of spin even from the rough, although of course the strike needs still to be precise.

HEAD CONSTRUCTION

The type of metal used in the construction of the wedge clubhead has not only a practical application—in the sense that some metals are softer than others and therefore offer greater potential for feel—but also an aesthetic quality. The classic chrome finish is still the most popular option, although a light satin finish is also available. As too is an "oil can" finish, which eliminates glare and also gives a slightly softer feel.

Other companies offer a "rusty" or "vintage" finish. The effect is the same; these clubheads rust over time, affording the player greater control. There are also jet black clubheads in many manufacturers' wedge range. The choices are wide; the decision is an entirely personal one.

WEDGES COME IN A RANGE of finishes– from chrome and black to copper, "oil can", and rusty.

Copper and bronze finishes are favored because they have a softer feel than other metals

A jet black finish is achieved via a complex oxydization process. The effect is to reduce glare at address

■ Groove detail

BY CARRYING A RANGE of wedges in a set, players give themselves different options on the course. Players should carry at least two- or ideally three–wedges.

The lob-wedge is typically the most lofted club in the bag

Every golfer should carry a sand-wedge (56 degrees)

The "gap" wedge fills the distance gap between pitching-wedge and sand-wedge

LOFTY MATTERS

No golfer should ever carry just one wedge in their set. Two is the absolute minimum; three is advisable. In terms of "building" a set of three wedges, the key is to make sure you have an evenly spaced loft progression, aiming for approximately four degrees between each club. Use your 9-iron as a starting point and work your way up to whatever maximum loft you feel is appropriate for your needs.

The most lofted club in many golfers' bags is a 60-degree lob-wedge, which is sensible. Phil Mickelson has been known to carry a 64-degree wedge, which is probably too extreme for the average player.

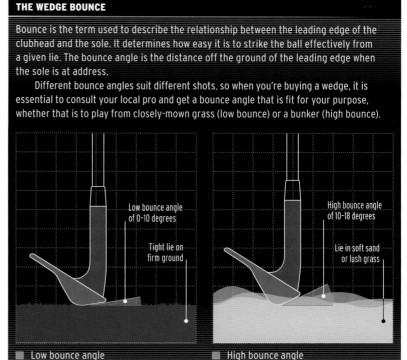

THE WEDGE BOUNCE

Bounce is the term used to describe the relationship between the leading edge of the clubhead and the sole. It determines how easy it is to strike the ball effectively from a given lie. The bounce angle is the distance off the ground of the leading edge when the sole is at address.

Different bounce angles suit different shots, so when you're buying a wedge, it is essential to consult your local pro and get a bounce angle that is fit for your purpose, whether that is to play from closely-mown grass (low bounce) or a bunker (high bounce).

Low bounce angle of 0-10 degrees

High bounce angle of 10-18 degrees

Tight lie on firm ground

Lie in soft sand or lush grass

■ Low bounce angle   ■ High bounce angle

The pitch shot

ONE OF THE GREATEST SKILLS YOU CAN HAVE as a golfer is the ability to pitch well. On par-4s it helps you save par if you've been in trouble off the tee. On par-5s it can help set up birdie chances when the green is out of reach in two. That ability to turn three shots into two will have a dramatic effect on your average scoring. It is a wonderful skill to have and one that is definitely worth working on.

Set up secrets

SMOOTHLY DOES IT

There is no place for ego in the world of pitch shots. It is not about how far you can hit your pitching wedge; it is about how close the ball finishes to the flag. That is the only meaningful measure of success. For that reason, leave aside any thoughts of trying to force your pitch shots. A smoothly-accelerating swing is far more effective. If you feel you need to hit a pitch shot hard to reach the target, then you are using the wrong club.

▌ FOUR SET-UP ESSENTIALS

Poor quality pitching often stems from a poor set-up. Here are four steps to a better set-up and more successful pitching action.
• Make sure that your feet are only slightly open, and that your shoulders are square.
• Choke down on the grip. This gives you maximum feel and clubhead control as you swing.
• Put the ball back in your stance and hold your hands forward.
• Keep your chin up. This simple move tends to lead to a better posture, with the spine angle more erect, and it gives you space under your chin to turn your left shoulder. Try to feel as though you are almost looking down your nose at the golf ball.

▌ MAINTAIN THE TRIANGLE

The wedge swing is often a difficult one to master, partly because a lot of amateurs view this shot as less-than-full and therefore assume they have to do something different. The most common tendency is to get a little too "handsy" in the swing, with the body almost going to sleep. That leads to poor strikes and distance control.

   This may not be a power shot, but you should still endeavour to make the perfect blend of arm swing and body turn as you start the club away from the ball. A useful swing thought is to visualize the triangle formed by the shoulders and the arms, then to maintain that for the first 30in (75cm) of the backswing. Let your body turn in harmony with the swinging arms, your left shoulder moving behind the ball as the backswing continues.

▌ CRISP CONTACT

The ideal pitch shot is one where the ball rises steeply to the top of its flight and then lands softly with little or no run. With this in mind, on the downswing you should encourage a slightly descending angle of attack. The goal is crisp, ball-turf contact and lots of backspin. However, you must not quit on the shot at impact; this will result in too large a divot and a loss of distance. Instead stay focused on making a positive swing through the ball to a neat finish.

Keep your hands, arms, and body in unison during the backswing   Make crisp ball-turf contact and hit through the shot

SHAFT ANGLE
Take the club back just
beyond the vertical position

LOW HANDS
The hands swing to shoulder
height in the backswing, then
through to shoulder-height in
the follow-through

HANDS AND CHEST
To help promote a synchronised golf
swing, think of the hands staying in
front of the chest throughout

BODY ROTATION
Body rotates in harmony
with the arm swing

NARROW STANCE
Legs are only slightly apart,
creating a narrow stance

SHOULDER-TO-SHOULDER SWING

One of the most common mistakes that amateurs make
when hitting pitch shots is to make a full swing and try to
hit the ball too hard. The ball tends to balloon into the air,
with no control of spin or trajectory.

Remember, pitch shots are all about control. It's not a
contest of how far you can hit it. So, think in terms of
making a "shoulder-to-shoulder swing". That is, the hands
travel to shoulder-height in the backswing and shoulder-
height in the follow-through.

Your only other focus should be on maintaining a
smooth rhythm in your downswing and a sense of "natural
acceleration" into and through impact. This encourages a
sweet and consistent strike, making it easier for you to
judge line, length, and spin.

SWING SECRETS

Position the ball in the
middle of your stance

Point the butt-end of the
club at the ground

Hands lead the clubhead
into impact

Head stays over the point
of impact, to stabilize swing

Keep your left arm
fairly straight

Pitching: a masterclass

THE GREAT PITCHERS IN GOLF are able to control the spin of their shots, the trajectory, the distance, and the accuracy. It is why, faced with 100 yards (91 meters) or less, they will more often than not get down in just two shots. Many amateurs, on the other hand, will tend to miss greens with pitch shots and often take three, even four shots, from 100 yards (91 meters) and in. By studying the best players you too, can learn to pitch like a pro.

Keep a firm left arm through impact

Hands lead the clubhead into the ball

Focus on the back of the ball for solid ball-turf contact

LUKE DONALD'S OPEN CLUBFACE

On most pitch shots, it is advisable to adopt a slightly open clubface at address. The reason being, it is easier to control your ball-flight and have some finesse in your game if there is some loft on the clubface. Also, it allows you to commit to striking down and through the shot, without the fear of over-shooting the green.

Look at a great pitcher of the ball, someone like England's Luke Donald. His swing is blessed with a wonderful sense of rhythm and timing right through the bag. And it doesn't matter if he is pitching from 80 yards (73 meters) or half that distance, he always commits to the shot fully through impact.

Keep in mind is that it is not a hard hit; rather, a positive and committed strike delivered with a sense of the arms and body working together. It is controlled.

◁ A GOOD PITCHING ACTION affords you the chance to hit the ball close and save strokes on your score. With an action that commits fully to the shot, Luke Donald has one of the best in the game.

THE GREATEST PITCH SHOT

The 1995 Ryder Cup at Oak Hill was a typically close contest. What became evident as the last day progressed was that the singles match between Nick Faldo and Curtis Strange would probably be pivotal. The pair came to the 18th hole all-square and, having driven into deep rough, Faldo had punched his ball out to within 100 yards (91 meters) of the green. Faldo hit a sublime pitch to five feet. He holed the putt for par, Curtis made bogey, and the Ryder Cup was soon in European hands again, after the 1993 defeat at the Belfry.

■ Faldo's pitch wins the Ryder Cup

RETIEF GOOSEN'S ANGLE OF ATTACK

Retief Goosen is very much his own man in the sense that he doesn't have a swing coach, but that hasn't stopped him from developing one of the soundest and most admired swings in the game. His pitching action is a joy to watch and, naturally, it is blessed with one of the key requirements of a successful technique; namely, a relatively steep angle of attack coming into the ball which pinches the ball cleanly, thus generating lots of spin and optimum control of distance.

Here's a useful swing thought to help you emulate "The Goose." As you play the shot imagine hitting the ball under a park bench right in front of you. This encourages a downward strike, with the hands leading the clubhead into the ball. Try it in your next practice session. It helps get you into a much better impact position, and consequently you'll strike the ball with far greater authority.

▷ **BY ADOPTING A STEEP ANGLE OF ATTACK** on the downswing, Goosen generates good backspin and distance control. It is one of the attributes that has made him a two-time US Open champion.

▽ **DECELERATION INTO IMPACT** is one of the worst faults among amateur golfers. In contrast, all the world's best players, including Thomas Bjorn, accelerate into the ball for better pitching.

THOMAS BJORN'S ACCELERATION

It has been proven by short-game guru Dave Pelz that an accelerating clubhead is far less prone to miss-hits. On pitch shots, a positive hit is required, with good acceleration through impact. And there is no better exponent than Dane Thomas Bjorn, a wonderful pitcher of the golf ball; his action through the ball is sublime.

Think along these lines. The length of your backswing should always be such that you can accelerate smoothly through impact to send the ball the required distance. Too short a backswing and you need to force the hit; too long a backswing means you have to decelerate in order to not hit the ball too far.

There is no **better exponent than Dane Thomas Bjorn**, a wonderful pitcher of the ball; **his action through the ball is sublime**

The chip shot

IT WOULD BE NICE TO THINK THAT WE COULD ALL one day play to a standard where we hardly ever missed a green, thus eliminating the need to play any chip shots at all. But the game of golf just isn't like that. Even the best players in the world miss greens—on average perhaps three or four a round. Part of the reason they are so successful in the game is that they can so often tidy-up with a neat chip and a single putt, or often, just a chip. It is a wonderful skill to have, one that every golfer should spend some time working on.

▌ SET-UP RULES

It is an oversimplification to say that bad chipping always stems from a bad set-up. But it is certainly true to say that a lot of golfers make life extremely difficult for themselves by neglecting this important aspect of the chip shot.

The correct set-up for 99 percent of all chip shots can be expressed in one simple sentence "ball back, hands and weight forward." This promotes a shape of swing that makes the clubhead approach the ball on a slightly descending angle of attack, leading to crisp ball-turf contact.

"SEE" THE SHOT

Good imagination is an absolute prerequisite of an all-round successful chipping game and something that all the top professionals empoy to great effect. You need to be able to visualize the flight of the ball, landing position and amount of run in different situations, in order to match the club to the job and then execute the shot with conviction.

Ball back, hands forward   Hands lead the clubhead through the hitting area   Maintain a smooth rhythm

▌ HOLD HANDS FORWARD

One of the golden rules of chipping is to make sure that the hands lead the clubhead through the hitting area, thus guaranteeing that all-important descending angle of attack. That is a crucial point of understanding for amateur golfers; if the hands stay ahead, a clean and consistent strike is far more likely. If, however, you allow the clubhead to overtake the hands coming into impact, the arc of the swing effectively bottoms-out before it reaches the golf ball. In that instance, a miss-hit is virtually assured.

▌ KEEP FOREARMS SOFT

As you may have learned from previous sections in this book, any tension in your hands, arms, or body destroys your chances of hitting solid, consistent golf shots. And so it is the case with chipping. To prevent this insidious fault creeping into your action, try to make sure your forearms stay soft as you swing the club back and through. That thought alone effectively "oils" the swing with a lovely smooth rhythm. It also helps to keep the acceleration smooth through the hitting area, so that the ball comes off the face not too "hot," but on a soft and easily controllable ball flight.

CLUB SELECTION

The set-up and the simple swing required to hit neat chip shots can be applied to different clubs. When you need to play a chip to carry some rough or a bunker between you and the flag—go with lots of loft, such as a wedge. If a low-running chip shot is required, go with less loft—a 7- or 8-iron. The swing stays the same. All you have to do is make sure that in your set-up the ball is back and your hands and weight are forward, and that your hands lead the clubhead into the ball. Trust your swing and just let the loft do the rest.

The left wrists stays firm as the club swings through

Legs stay flexed, supporting the swinging motion

Spine angle stays constant to promote good contact

Wrists stay "quiet" with no excessive hand action

Loft on the club does the work

HEAD POSITION
Head only comes up long after the ball is on its way

UPPER BODY MOVEMENT
Hands, arms, and torso should work as a unit, turning together

TURN YOUR BODY

The typical chip shot involves a relatively short swing, but that doesn't mean to say that the body can stop working. Indeed, poor contact with the ball is often the result of the body not turning as the arms swing down, which often causes the clubhead to overtake the hands. So always think of turning your chest back and through in harmony with your arm swing. This gives the swing some nice momentum and, providing you keep your hands in front of the ball, helps keep the club on the correct downward angle of attack.

SOFT GRIP
Grip pressure remains soft, for maximum feel

FLEXED
Adopt a narrow stance with flexed knees

LOW CLUB
Clubhead stays low to the ground through impact and rises only at the end of the swing

FOLLOW-THROUGH
Clubhead travels through further than it traveled in the backswing

Chipping: a masterclass

ONE OF THE REAL PLEASURES OF WATCHING THE BEST PLAYERS in action is admiring their skill around the green. They play chip shots of such great variety, and with wonderful touch and feel, that it is a joy to behold. And great chipping is within the compass of every golfer in the world because there are no physical limitations. You don't need to be incredibly strong–this is a short and relatively simple swing.

◁ **OLAZÁBAL IS NOT AFRAID** to hit the ball with pace because he knows that the spin imparted on the ball will make it stop.

The upper body must remain as still as possible as you swing from the shoulders and arms

At the point of impact, the hands should be in front of the ball

JOSÉ MARIA OLAZÁBAL'S ACCELERATION

Spain has through the years had a great reputation for producing golfers with exquisite short games; two-time Masters champion José Maria Olazábal is among the very best. He is sometimes let down by his driving, which means that his ability to scramble sometimes has to make up for it.

A golfer who can chip (and putt) will always be dangerous, and Olazábal is blessed with a chipping action that imparts wonderful acceleration through the ball, with the hands very much in front of the clubhead throughout the stroke. It is a very crisp, positive action, which produces low-flying shots that tend to skip forward and then spin and stop.

This is a good image to have in mind when you chip. Indeed, conjuring a mental picture of the Olazábal style of chipping has a number of benefits for the golfer who sometimes struggles with chipping. It prevents any deceleration into the ball. It also encourages the hands to stay ahead of the clubhead at the point of impact.

His chipping action **is blessed with a wonderful sense of acceleration** through the ball, **with the hands very much in front of the clubhead** throughout

K. J. CHOI'S CONSISTENT ACTION

South Korea's K. J. Choi, a regular winner on the PGA Tour, ranks highly in the Tour's so-called "scrambling" statistics; a figure based on the number of times during the year that a player has a chip and a single putt, or just a chip, to secure at least par.

One of Choi's great qualities as a player is the way he keeps his chipping action essentially the same for every chip shot, simply varying the club selection in order to conjure the trajectory, height, and spin required for any given situation. For any amateur this is a good example to follow, as you will quickly become more comfortable with your chipping technique and better able to repeat it on a consistent basis.

The alternative method, adopted by some top players, is to mostly use the same chipping club, but vary the technique in order to manipulate the loft on the clubface and thereby produce shots of varying heights. It has its merits, and will improve your range of shots, but bear in mind it requires considerably more skill and practice.

▷ **FOR A BIG MAN** (before becoming a professional golfer, he was a power-lifter), Choi has a soft hands and great touch around the greens.

THE GREATEST CHIP

In the 1987 Masters local boy and rank outsider Larry Mize made it into a playoff with Seve Ballesteros and Greg Norman. Seve bogeyed the first play-off hole, and was eliminated. On the par-4 11th, Mize missed the green to the right. Norman, meanwhile, hit the green in regulation and was two putts away from the Masters title. However, Mize played a deft pitch and run; the ball skipped on to the green, trickled down towards the hole ... and in! Norman, missed his birdie putt, meaning Mize had won.

■ Mize chips in to win the Masters

SEVE BALLESTEROS'S IMPROVISATION

Seve Ballesteros was the most creative golfer of his generation and he also had by far the best short game. These two qualities are inextricably linked. A good imagination is a prerequisite of a successful short game. You first have to be able to visualize different chip shots around the green and then develop the touch and feel to turn those shots into reality. Chipping is not a one-dimensional affair. It demands variety.

So, always practice your short game with a selection of clubs by your side and make sure you constantly vary your target from one shot to the next. Each time, visualize in your mind's-eye the flight of the golf ball: where you want it to land; how much run is required to get it close to the hole. Remember, every shot is different. Once you have a picture in your mind of the shot you want to play, select the club that best performs that function. The key is to change the club to vary the shots that you play—some high with very little run; others low with lots of run.

Never stand by the side of the practice green and simply hit the same shot to the same target for long periods—there is no real challenge in that—and thus your short game won't benefit in any meaningful fashion.

◁ **BALLESTEROS** was one of the most imaginative shot-makers of his generation. He was always able to think around a problem and invent an improbable solution.

The bunker shot

THE SAND-WEDGE IS A BESPOKE PIECE OF EQUIPMENT designed entirely on the principle that form should follow function. We have Grand Slam winner Gene Sarazen (see pp.109) to thank for this, for it was he that first identified the need for a broader sole on the wedge. Up until that point, the implements used to extricate a golf ball from sand were not entirely fit for the purpose. The straight leading edge and narrow flange, much like a classic blade in profile, tended to dig too deep into the sand, meaning that too much of the energy in the swing was dissipated.

HOW A SAND-WEDGE WORKS

Gene Sarazen's inspiration for creating the sand-wedge was part that of a golfer frustrated with his equipment and part that of a man with a lively imagination. He claimed he had been studying ducks landing on water, observing the way that their rounded underbellies skimmed across the surface. He designed a sand-wedge that had a similar rounded underbelly, what we now call the flange or sole of the club, and found that the clubhead would slide through the sand very efficiently.

When you play a bunker shot the flange of the club works in such a way that when the clubhead is delivered on a shallow and slightly descending angle of attack, it slides through the sand. This creates a splash of sand at impact, which propels the ball forwards and out of the bunker. This is why the perfect escape from a bunker is sometimes referred to as a "splash shot".

▌ ADOPT AN OPEN SET-UP

In order for you to utilize the bounce-effect of the sand wedge, you must adhere to a couple of simple set-up rules that will affect the shape of the swing.
• The stance must be open – that is, the feet aligned to the left of the target.
• The clubface must be open – that is, aimed to the right of the target.

▌ SWING ALONG YOUR AIM LINES

By addressing the ball correctly, the swing becomes immeasurably easier. The secret is to swing along the lines of your body – in other words, across the line on an "out-to-in" path.
• Focus on a spot in the sand roughly two inches behind the ball; this is the intended point of entry for the clubhead.
• Swing back and through, combining your arm swing with your body turn.
• Strike down into the sand on your intended spot and accelerate the club through the sand under the ball, with the feeling of swinging the club to the left of the target through impact.
• Always follow through on every bunker shot.

GRIP IT RIGHT

Once you've opened your stance you can form your grip. Remember, the sand-wedge does its best work when the clubface is open. This aspect of the set-up is paramount, which is why it is wise to adopt this simple routine to ensure that the clubface is indeed open as you address the ball and then start your swing.

Hold the club out in front of you, just in your right hand and swivel the grip anti-clockwise in your hands until the clubface is open (below left). Then, without altering that clubface position, form your grip (below right). That way, the clubface will more than likely stay open during the swing, which is perfect; just what you need to play great bunker shots.

Open stance and club face   Swing along your aim lines, strike the sand behind the ball, and remember to follow through

SHUFFLE, THEN PICK YOUR SPOT

When you are standing in a bunker you are not on solid ground, so it is important to create a secure footing. Shuffle your feet into the sand to give yourself a solid base. Then, pick a spot behind the ball and commit to striking the sand at that point.

Strange as it sounds, the short-range bunker shot is the only shot in golf where you should not actually hit the ball. The club glides under the ball and the ball flies onto the green on an explosion of sand. Remember: shuffle into the sand, then strike it.

Fear of bunker play is common among amateur golfers, but it is easily banished once you adhere to the fundamentals

FORMING THE GRIP
It is hugely important that you open the clubface and then form your grip. If you do it the other way round, the clubface will tend to return to square at impact, completely ruining the shot

FLEXED KNEES
Knees are flexed at address and should stay that way during the swing.

HANDS ALIGNMENT
The hands can be slightly ahead of, or even level with, the golf ball for a regular greenside bunker shot

LOFT AND BOUNCE

The choice of loft on a wedge is, to some extent, determined by the nature of the bunkers on a golf course. A course with shallow bunkers and big greens has no real call for a highly lofted wedge; whereas on a links course–where the bunkers are typically deep and require escape shots of maximum elevation–a lot of loft is desirable.

It is also imperative that the sand-wedge should have a fair degree of bounce-angle, certainly more than eight degrees and as much as 12 or even 14. This bounce angle helps ensure that the clubhead slides through the sand, rather than digging into it (see pp.78-79).

WEIGHT DISTRIBUTION
The weight should favour the front foot, but only slightly

CLUBFACE
You can afford to open the clubface on a sand-wedge more than you realize

(see pp.78-79)

SWING SECRETS

Ball should be positioned forward of center

Shoulders, feet, and hips open to the target line

Strike the sand behind the ball

Feel the heel of the club entering the sand first

Spine angle remains constant into impact

Bunker play: a masterclass

ALL OF THE GAME'S TOP PLAYERS DISPLAY sublime greenside bunker skills. Indeed, there are some critics of the modern professional game who say, rather churlishly, that bunkers are no longer proper hazards, such is the dizzying array of skills on show at a typical tournament. We should continue to observe in wonderment the way the world's best players splash the ball out to within inches of the flag.

Both the shoulder turn and the follow through must be as full as possible

Concentrate on a spot about 2 in (5 cm) behind the ball, and strike the clubhead through the sand

GARY PLAYER'S PRACTICE METHODS

South Africa's Gary Player, the self-styled Black Knight, is the greatest bunker player who ever lived. He once famously proclaimed that the more he practiced the luckier he became. The man did himself an injustice. Yes, he practiced his bunker play probably more than any other golfer in his day, but there was nothing lucky about the results. The man was a genius in the sand.

There is a lot we can learn from Player's approach to practicing his bunker play. Some lesser players would always practice shots from the perfect lie. Not Gary Player. He would randomly throw handfuls of golf balls into the sand and then simply play each ball wherever it came to rest. Some would be in a good lie, others would not. It meant Player developed an incredible imagination and skill for hitting great bunker shots from all manner of different situations. He was prepared for any eventuality.

He would even set goals, say, challenging himself to hole three bunker shots before he could go in and join his wife or guests for dinner.

◁ **AS ONE OF THE HARDEST** working men in golf, Gary Player spent a lot of time working on his technique. The result was brilliant bunker play and nine Major championships.

THE GREATEST BUNKER SHOT

The European side were on the brink of victory on the last day of the 2002 Ryder Cup. Three times Paul Azinger had trailed Niclas Fasth by a margin of two holes, but the American produced one of the shots of the year on the par-4 18th, holing from a greenside bunker to keep this Ryder Cup contest alive.

■ High-fives all round after Azinger holes from the sand

PHIL MICKELSON'S WRIST HINGE

Phil Mickelson has probably the most creative short game of any player at the top of the game and can produce a range of magical shots from around the green, including bunker shots. Mickelson often carries an exceptionally lofted sand-wedge, often as much as 64-degrees, and uses this to generate greenside bunker shots where the ball climbs almost vertically skyward and stops abruptly on landing. It isn't all down to the equipment he uses, though. The skill is in the hands, too.

He hinges the wrists early in the takeaway to set the club on a very steep angle of attack; this in effect pre-sets a swing arc which is distinctly U-shape in profile. So, the club goes back steeply and then comes down steeply, too. Mickelson then zips the clubhead through the sand under the ball with a fast and aggressive hand action; that's the key, fast hands through the ball. The ball pops straight up in the air and stops virtually dead in its tracks. This is a shot to practice before attempting it on the course.

▷ **MICKELSON HAS THE ABILITY** to exert terrific control over a golf ball, so he can afford to have an agressive short game. His recovery shots from greenside bunkers is unique because of his choice of lofted sand-wedge.

▽ **GARCIA IS AN INTUITIVE** and imaginative golfer, who has great technique around the greens. He is a touch player and his soft hands complement his great feel.

SERGIO GARCIA'S SOFT HANDS

Sergio Garcia is another in a long line of Spanish golfers blessed with a sensational short game. He has a technique very much his own invention, one which might best be described as "handsy." Overall, it is an extremely difficult method to teach because of its individual nature, however, every golfer can learn from the soft hold he applies to the grip.

A soft hold on the club effectively spreads into the arms and shoulders, as well. It helps endow your swing with an "oily" rhythm back and through. Only by swinging in this fashion can you develop the wonderful sense of touch and feel that is characteristic of all great bunker players.

Increasing your touch is a difficult concept to grasp, but by gripping the club softly the way Garcia does, you will start to become a much better bunker player.

Every golfer can learn from the soft hold he applies to the grip

Putters: the design

THE INTERESTING THING ABOUT PUTTERS is that there is a greater variation in aesthetics than for any other club in the bag. Designs vary from the original blade putter, to heel-and-toe, mallet heads, and futuristic deep-backed putters with a high moment of inertia. Literally almost anything goes, obviously within the limits of what the governing bodies will allow.

PRINCIPLES OF DESIGN

The principle of peripheral weighting is fundamental to the design of many of the putters on the market today. By placing weight in both the heel and the toe of the putter and towards the back of the putter-head, its dynamic stability is increased. This means that the face stays square at impact, so the ball goes where you want it to, even with off-center strikes.

The two-ball and three-ball putters, for instance, have white discs the size of golf balls perpendicular to the face, which are used as alignment aids at address. There are many different interpretations of this basic design principle, each with the intention of being not only forgiving to off-center strikes, but easy to aim also. A golfer needs to make a decision based on personal preference.

WEIGHT AND TWIST

The key factor with a lot of these radical, deep-faced designs is moment of inertia, or MOI. The center of gravity is moved way back from the face, deep behind the ball, which promotes a high MOI and therefore improves the putter-head's built-in resistance to twisting at impact. The fact that a lot of tour pros are using putters of this type adds a good deal of credence to the manufacturers' bold claims.

Black line marks the sweet spot on the face

THIS SIMPLE, CLASSIC design, the Bettinardi "C Series," is forged from a single piece of carbon steel.

Moveable weights enable the player to alter the club's balance

MALLET-HEADED putters work on the principle of moving weight back in the putter-head to reduce twisting at impact.

THIS PUTTER by Robert J. Bettinardi is a classic modern example of the heel-and-toe weighting first developed by Ping in the 1960s. The purpose of peripheral weighting is to counter the propensity of the face to twist at impact.

The offsetting of the putter-head at the hosel helps sighting at address

Weighting the putter at the heel and toe reduces twisting of the putter face at impact

Bettinardi's patented honeycomb face promotes consistent ball-striking and a smooth roll

Carbon steel material is soft enough to promote good feel but the metal makes a solid "click" sound at impact

Weight is set back away from the face

TWO- AND THREE-BALL PUTTERS help players line up putts by placing the ball directly in front of the "virtual" balls.

THE PUTTER FACE

Feel is a major factor with any shot—none more so than putting, where judgement of distance is everything. In reality, feel probably has as much to do with the sound of the putter-face contacting the ball as anything physically felt through the hands.

This is why face inserts have become so popular in modern-day putters. These synthetic inserts are softer than the metals used in the construction of the putter-head. They sound different and therefore offer greater "feel" at impact; in a sense, more feedback, which helps the golfer judge the speed of the ball off the face more easily.

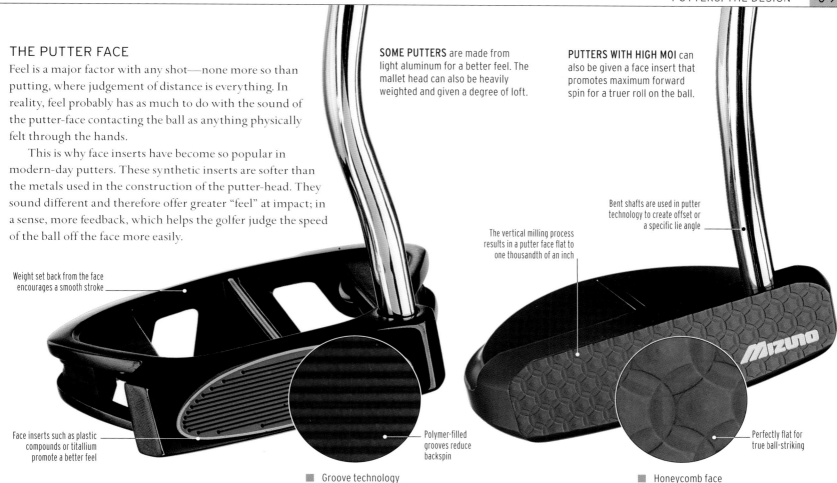

SOME PUTTERS are made from light aluminum for a better feel. The mallet head can also be heavily weighted and given a degree of loft.

PUTTERS WITH HIGH MOI can also be given a face insert that promotes maximum forward spin for a truer roll on the ball.

Bent shafts are used in putter technology to create offset or a specific lie angle

The vertical milling process results in a putter face flat to one thousandth of an inch

Weight set back from the face encourages a smooth stroke

Face inserts such as plastic compounds or titallium promote a better feel

Polymer-filled grooves reduce backspin

Perfectly flat for true ball-striking

■ Groove technology

■ Honeycomb face

SHAFT LENGTH

Which length putter-shaft you choose comes down to personal preference. The standard length is approximately 35–36 in (89–91 cm), but it's not uncommon for some of the world's best players to have a putter cut down to as little as 32–33 in (81–84 cm).

Some leading golfers take the matter of length to the other extreme, using one of the many different long-handled putters available. In addition to the broomhandle putter, for example, which is braced against the chin or breast-bone, there is also the belly-putter—or baby-broomhandle—that is secured in the midriff. These long-shafted models are available with a variety of putter-head designs, so a golfer can pick a model that best suits his or her game.

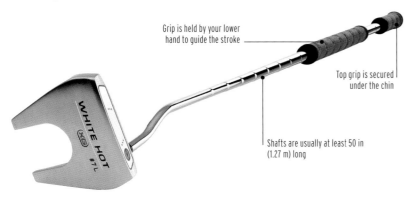

Grip is held by your lower hand to guide the stroke

Top grip is secured under the chin

Shafts are usually at least 50 in (1.27 m) long

THE BROOMHANDLE PUTTER became popular as a way to execute a smooth stroke. The putter is held under the chin and swung in a pendulum motion.

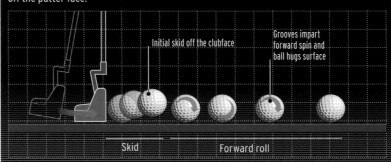

PUTTER TOPSPIN

As strange as it sounds, some putters impart a notable amount of backspin on the ball. This leads to a period of skidding shortly after impact, which affects the roll of the ball. Top-of-the-range putters are instead designed to promote topspin.

This feature, coupled with a putting stroke that strikes the ball on an ascending angle of attack, results in a pure roll. Provided that the putt is on line, a ball that hugs the surface of the green with topspin will find the target more surely than one that skids (with backspin) off the putter-face.

Initial skid off the clubface

Grooves impart forward spin and ball hugs surface

Skid   Forward roll

PAYING THE PRICE

Many golfers find it hard to swallow the high price tags of today's leading models, yet the putter is such an important club: if you don't hole out consistently your scores will never improve. There is a further justification for these prices. In a typical round of golf you will use your putter probably three times more often than your driver—a club which may have cost you twice the money of the putter. On a "cost per usage" basis, then, a putter is six times better value for money than a comparable driver.

The putting stroke

PUTTING IS THE MOST INDIVIDUAL ASPECT OF THE GAME. Just look at any tour event and you will see a multitude of different styles of putting stroke. So there is more than one way to get the ball into the hole on a consistent basis. There are, however, certain characteristics that are common to the majority of very fine putters. This is the conventional wisdom of great putting. You may have your own style, but if you want to make a lot of putts it pays to integrate these core elements into your technique.

EYES OVER THE BALL

Ball position is as important in the putting stroke as it is in the full swing. There are two factors to bear in mind. Firstly, the ball should be forward in your stance to encourage a slight ascending blow when the putter-face meets the ball. That imparts a good roll on your putts. Secondly, your eyes should ideally be directly over the ball, as this gives you the best perspective of the line from the ball to the hole.

One simple routine helps give you the perfect ball position. Adopt a comfortable posture and then drop a golf ball from the bridge of your nose. The spot on which it lands represents perfect ball position for you.

SHOULDERS AND EYES PARALLEL

Once you have the ideal ball position in your stance, the next key requirement is to have your shoulder-line and eye-line parallel to the path on which you want the ball to start. You can check very easily that these two crucial checkpoints are maintained.

Hold the shaft of the putter along the top of your chest. The line of the shaft should match the target line; if so, it will help promote an on-line stroke. Also hold the shaft along your eye-line and see if it corresponds with the target line. If so, it further improves your perspective to help you visualize the path the ball must take on its journey to the hole.

Drop a ball from your nose

Perfect ball position

Shoulders square

Check your eye line

TAKE DEAD AIM

The aim of the putter is obviously a crucial determining factor in how many putts you make. After all, if you don't aim correctly, how can you be expected to hit your target?

One method that should help you eliminate the likelihood of poor aim is to place the golf ball on the green in such a way that the manufacturer's name corresponds exactly with the line on which you want the ball to start its journey. You should then set the putter-face behind the ball so that it is exactly perpendicular to that line. Alternatively, draw a line on the ball. This is a very effective method, adopted by many of the leading players, because it provides you with a visual image of the perfect aim and path to the hole.

Taking aim

KEEP YOUR HEAD STILL

Any head movement before the ball is struck knocks the shoulders – and therefore the putter – out of its natural path; this leads to a crooked stroke and a missed putt. It is particularly common (and damaging) on short putts, where there is a tendency for golfers to take an anxious peek and see if the ball is heading towards the hole.

One of the key objectives for any good putter, therefore, must be to keep the head rock-still throughout the stroke. The simplest way to achieve this is to commit to keeping your head down until you hear the sound of the ball dropping in the hole.

SWING SECRETS

Maintain the angle in the back of the left wrist

Hands stay soft on the putter throughout the stroke

Think "left shoulder down" in the back-stroke

Think "left shoulder up" in the through-stroke

Keep the head down until your hear the ball drop

MAINTAIN THE PERFECT TRIANGLE

Throughout the putting stroke you should try to maintain the triangle formed at address by the shoulders and arms. The stroke should never be wooden, but neither should it have too many independent moving parts. It should be a soft yet coordinated motion that involves the hands, arms, and shoulders all working together.

To encourage this harmony of movement, think of the stroke being controlled predominantly by the rocking motion of the shoulders. The hands and arms then respond to the momentum created by this rocking motion, so that the putter tracks a neat path back and through.

It helps if you focus on maintaining throughout the stroke the triangle formed at address by the shoulders and the arms. Once again it is worth stressing that the hands should stay soft on the putter and that, while some softness in the wrists is desirable, there should not be too much independent wrist action as that can lead to an erratic stroke and lack of consistency.

KEEP STEADY
The head stays rock-steady until the ball is on its way

MAINTAIN THE UNIT
A slightly fatter-than-standard grip is popular with many top players, as it tends to help keep the hands and wrists "quieter" during the stroke

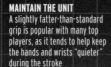

NO MOVEMENT
From the waist down, everything stays still during the stroke. Imagine your legs are set in concrete

KEEP ON TRACK
From short range, imagine the face of the putter looks at the hole through impact

SOLID BASE
Your weight should be evenly spread between both feet, with a sense that they are very much planted for a secure base to the stroke

The art of putting

PUTTING IS OFTEN DESCRIBED AS THE GAME WITHIN A GAME. It may be something of a cliché, but it captures the essence of putting better than any other single phrase. A bad ball-striking round can be saved by good putting as surely as a potentially good score can be ruined by poor putting. There are many different facets to the art of putting, and the fundamentals explained here will stand you in good stead as you strive to improve.

READING GREENS AND MAKING PUTTS

No green is totally flat. Thus, most putts have a degree of break on them – often subtle, sometimes severe. The best way to deal with breaking putts and sloping greens is to treat every putt as if it is straight. This is how it works.

▌ Identify how much break there is on a putt – for example, a 3ft (90cm) break from the left. The hole itself now ceases to be your target. Your new target is an imaginary hole positioned 3ft (90cm) to the left of the actual hole.

▌ As you go through your pre-shot routine, aiming the putter-face and aligning your stance, your focus should continue to be the imaginary target.

▌ Now hit a dead-straight putt at your imaginary target to the left of the hole, and the slope on the green takes care of the rest.

The advantage of this method is that you are far more likely to make a pure stroke when hitting a straight putt than you are when trying to guide the ball on a breaking putt.

> The best way to deal with **breaking putts** and **sloping greens** is to **hit it is straight** and let the green **take care of the rest**

Identify a target to the side of the hole

AIM TRUE
Take your time to identify the break, then pick your spot and hit a "straight" putt at the dummy target. Then simply let the slope do the work

Adopt your stance and aim at the imaginary target

Strike a normal putt and let the slope do the work

Make your preparations

Stroke through the pegs

THE PERFECT SHORT-PUTT DRILL

This is one of Tiger Woods' favourite putting drills.
Once during a tournament he practised it for 30
minutes every day and during the four rounds made
59 out of 60 putts from inside eight feet.

▌ It is best when practised on a relatively flat portion
of the green; the straighter the putt the better. Place
your putter on the ground and stick two tee-pegs either
side of the heel and toe of the putter-head, leaving about
a ½in (1.25cm) gap either side (you can reduce the gap as
your confidence grows).

▌ Now place a ball down and simply hit putts, trying
to swing the putter-head through the gate formed by
the two tee-pegs.

If your stroke is crooked, then either the heel or the toe
of the putter will collide with one of the tee-pegs
through impact. In this way the drill forces you to make
an on-line stroke. If you miss a lot of putts during this
practice drill, check the aim of the putter-face at
address. It could be that it is not square.

ROUND THE CLOCK

Another fun, and extremely useful, putting drill to try is as follows.
Line up 12 golf balls in a circle around the hole, one for each point
on the clock face. Then putt the golf balls one at a time into the
hole; each time you miss one you must start again until all 12 are
holed consecutively. Start at a distance of about 3ft (1m) from the
hole, then gradually increase the distance as you gain confidence
and your putting stroke improves.

▌ THE PERFECT LONG-PUTT DRILL

Good long putting is all about speed and rolling the ball
stone-dead. If the putt drops, so be it. That's a bonus.
But from 40ft (12m) or more every golfer, even the best,
is satisfied with a safe two-putt. One of the best ways to
improve your judgement of pace on long putts is to
rehearse this practice drill.

Place a handful of tee-pegs in the ground, starting
at about 20ft (6m) and working away from you at
intervals of about 3ft (1m). Use as many tee-pegs as
space on the green permits.

Now putt the first ball to the first tee-peg, the second
ball to the second tee-peg, and so on. The idea is that
you get one chance at each putt, just as is the case on
the golf course during a real round of golf. You can mix
things up a bit, too, by hitting putts randomly to the
various tee-pegs.

This drill is so effective because it trains you to see
a putt and then translate those visual messages into feel
for distance.

Refine your feel for distance

Putting: a masterclass

THE PROFESSIONAL GAME IS ALL ABOUT MAKING BIRDIES and that means making putts. The best players in the world average around 28 or 29 putts per round over the course of an entire season, which means they will typically single-putt probably seven or eight greens per round. That is impressive. As we already made clear, there is more than one way to putt well.

TIGER WOODS IS SOLID

Next time you watch Tiger Woods putt, ignore for a moment where the ball goes and focus instead on his hips and legs. You will notice that they stay absolutely rock-still throughout the stroke. This is hugely significant and one of the major points of difference between top players and many amateurs.

By keeping the hips and legs steady, Tiger establishes a solid foundation as he swings the putter back and through. It makes it easier to produce an on-line stroke on a more consistent basis, which leads to sweet strikes. This feature of Tiger's putting stroke is well worth copying.

THE GREATEST PUTT

The 1999 US Open at Pinehurst will go down as one of the most poignant tournaments in US Open history; Payne Stewart's last win before he lost his life in a plane crash, and the scene of arguably the greatest putt ever. Having holed a 25 ft (7.5 m) putt to save par on the 16th, Stewart then knocked a 6-iron to 3 ft (1 m) for birdie on the 17th, which meant he needed a par on the 18th to win his second US Open title. After driving into trouble, he played out into the fairway and hit a lob-wedge to 15 ft (4.5 m). "That putt to win the US Open". Stewart rolled the ball into the hole, right in the middle.

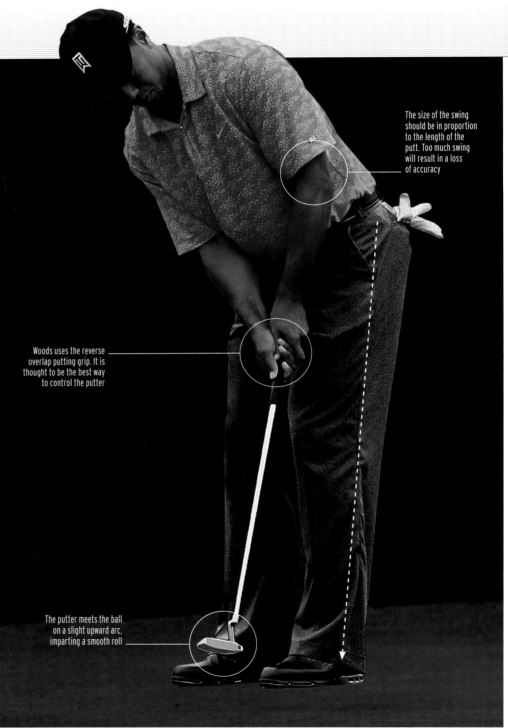

The size of the swing should be in proportion to the length of the putt. Too much swing will result in a loss of accuracy

Woods uses the reverse overlap putting grip. It is thought to be the best way to control the putter

The putter meets the ball on a slight upward arc, imparting a smooth roll

△ **WOODS HAS THE KNACK** of being able to sink the putts at the most crucial of times. He is a firm striker of the ball, secure in his ability to judge any putt to perfection. It is believed the ideal pace for holing a putt is such that, if the ball misses, it would travel 18 in (45 cm) past the hole.

■ Stewart's last Major win

PADRAIG HARRINGTON'S GRIP

The 2007 Open Champion Padraig Harrington, one of the finest all-round putters in the pro game, has used the same putting grip since he was a boy – a grip whereby the left hand sits below the right. He is not alone in that regard, either. Jim Furyk and Thomas Bjorn are just two of several other notable players who prefer this style of grip.

Positioning the left hand below the right has the effect of levelling the shoulders at address, which promotes a pendulum-type putting stroke. It helps maintain a firmer left-wrist position as the putter is delivered to the back of the ball, which eliminates any tendency to twitch putts to the left, a fault suffered by some. Other players find it also helps keep the putter closer to the ground on the way back and through, for a good roll.

If you feel frustrated with your performance on the greens, often it pays to try something different. The so-called "cack-handed" grip isn't for everyone, but the benefits are real and it should not be dismissed.

▷ **HARRINGTON** is one of the most reliable putters on the professional tour. He averages about 28 putts per round, which has helped push him up the world rankings.

▽ **THE FREE FLOWING** putting action of David Toms means that he is a great long putter. Leaving the ball very close to the hole from long range - "lag putting" - is a great attribute.

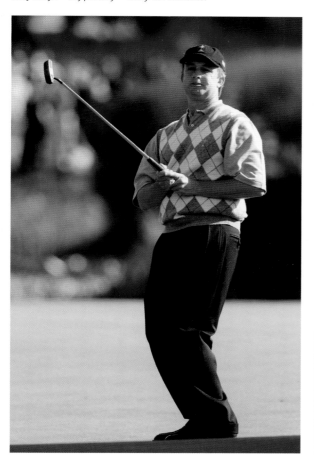

DAVID TOMS'S DEAD-WEIGHTED PUTTS

Rolling the ball stone dead – and very occasionally into the hole – from long distance is a wonderful skill that all top golfers possess. Former USPGA champion David Toms demonstrates this skill better than most of his contemporaries. He is a superb lag putter.

Of particular note to anyone wishing to learn from Toms' technique is the free and uninhibited swing of the putter. It stems from a very natural, upright address position where the arms hang comfortably. This allows him to swing the putter on a lovely flowing arc. It is almost as though there is no hit, just a sweeping motion with the ball simply getting in the way.

One other useful exercise, which Toms himself often replicates in his own putting strategy, is making practice putting strokes while looking at the hole. This helps give you a feel for the length and pace of stroke required and should improve your judgement of distance on long putts.

> Of particular note to **anyone wishing** **to learn from Toms' technique** is the free and **uninhibited swing** **of the putter**

Course management

IF THE SHOTS YOU HIT ARE THE TOOLS OF THE TRADE, then course management is perhaps best described as the manner by which you use those tools. It relates to the strategy you employ on the golf course and covers such areas as club selection, percentage play, staying out of trouble, getting out of trouble, and much more besides. The final section of this chapter provides a window into the mind of golf's great strategists. It should hopefully help you plot a less troubled path around the golf course.

> If you have a fade, teeing up on the right and playing down the left gives you a wider margin for error

▌ AVOID TROUBLE OFF THE TEE

Three-quarters of the world's amateur golfers flight their long shots on a left-to-right trajectory (right-to-left for the left hander) – a fade or slice. Therefore, trouble down the right-hand side of the fairway tends to be the biggest danger area for most golfers. If your typical ball-flight fits this description, a useful strategy to minimise the risk is to tee-up the ball on the very right-hand edge of the teeing area, then aim down the left-hand side of the fairway.

If the shot goes according to plan, the ball will assume its normal left-to-right flight and finish in the middle of the fairway. The great thing is, that you've also got a wide margin for error, for if the ball flies dead-straight it will finish only in the left rough and if the ball slices a little more than anticipated, probably the worse you can expect is to finish in the right rough.

THE DANGER AREA on this hole is the drop-off point past the rough to the right of the fairway. From here there may be no way back.

The shot starts on the line of the left rough and finishes in the middle of the fairway

SHAPE YOUR SHOTS

If you find yourself in a position whereby an obstruction blocks your way to the green, and you intend to play a shot with shape, it is important to bear in mind the simple rules of impact ballistics (see pp.70–71).

With a short shot which requires a lofted club, it is easier to hook or draw the ball than it is to fade or slice the ball.

With a longer shot which requires a less lofted club, it is much easier to fade or slice the ball than it is to hook or draw the ball.

Keep these factors in mind when considering which shape shot best gives you a route to the target. One option may be considerably easier than the other.

MAKE A GOOD START

However many warm up excercises and practice swings you make before a round, you will probably still be nervous on the first tee. Follow these rules to increase the likelihood of hitting a good shot, and to start the round as you mean to go on:

- Choose a club you are confident with; don't feel compelled to hit a driver
- Take a few deep breaths to lower your heartbeat
- Grip the club lightly
- Make a smooth swing

Draw with a short iron

Fade with a long iron

ALTHOUGH IT IS TEMPTING to aim for the green and take a chance on missing the trees, the sensible shot is to play out to the fairway

Playing it safe limits the risk of mistakes

▮ TAKE YOUR MEDICINE

Every golfer, even the best player in the world, makes mistakes. This is not the end of the world. But it is when you compound that initial mistake with another, and then another, that it becomes serious.

A lot of players are simply too ambitious; they'll hit the ball into trouble and then try to play a heroic recovery shot and land themselves in more trouble. They basically turn a five into a possible seven or eight.

If you find yourself in trouble – say, you've hit it into trees – make sure you get your next shot back in play. That's all. Don't try to punch the ball through tiny gaps in the trees or go for broke. Just play the simplest shot available to you. That way, your mistakes only ever cost you one shot.

ABOVE ALL, ENJOY IT

All golfers naturally want to play their best every time they set foot on the golf course. But don't let your ambition blinker you from the simple enjoyment to be gained from playing this game.

The great Walter Hagen, an 11-time Major champion, played the game with a joie de vivre that is unparalleled in the modern game, yet he was one of the greatest champions who ever lived. Hagen proved that you could have fun and win (see p.108).

Hagen sets a great example to us all. If you can maintain a state of equanimity, take the bad shots as they come, and above all keep your composure, you will in all probability not only enjoy the game more, but play better, too. It is one of the game's delicious ironies.

3 THE GREATEST GOLFERS

Old and Young Tom Morris

AMONG THE EARLY PIONEERS OF THE GAME, two families stand supreme. If your name was not Park or Morris, then winning the Open Championship in its formative years was almost impossible. Willie Park Senior and Old Tom Morris made the new Open into their personal duel—until Tommy, or Young Tom, arrived as the game's first star.

OLD TOM MORRIS STATS

BORN June 16, 1821; St. Andrews, Scotland
DIED May 25, 1908

MAJORS 4
THE OPEN: Won 1861, 1862, 1864, 1867

HONORS
Oldest winner of the Open Championship, aged 46

YOUNG TOM MORRIS STATS

BORN April 20,1851; St. Andrews, Scotland
DIED December 25 1875

MAJORS 4
THE OPEN: Won 1868, 1869, 1870, 1872

HONORS
Kept championship belt after hat-trick of victories

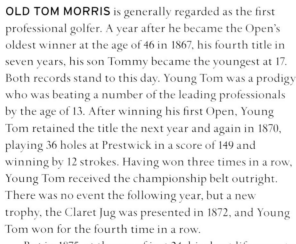

MORE THAN A CHAMPION golfer, Old Tom Morris designed the original courses at Muirfield, Prestwick, and Carnoustie.

OLD TOM MORRIS is generally regarded as the first professional golfer. A year after he became the Open's oldest winner at the age of 46 in 1867, his fourth title in seven years, his son Tommy became the youngest at 17. Both records stand to this day. Young Tom was a prodigy who was beating a number of the leading professionals by the age of 13. After winning his first Open, Young Tom retained the title the next year and again in 1870, playing 36 holes at Prestwick in a score of 149 and winning by 12 strokes. Having won three times in a row, Young Tom received the championship belt outright. There was no event the following year, but a new trophy, the Claret Jug was presented in 1872, and Young Tom won for the fourth time in a row.

But in 1875, at the age of just 24, his short life came to a heart-broken end when Young Tom's wife and child died in childbirth. Young Tom fell into a mighty depression, and died of a burst artery in his lung on Christmas morning.

Old Tom had been an apprentice ballmaker for Allan Robertson at St. Andrews before becoming Keeper of the Green at Prestwick, where he laid out the original 12-hole course; he also had a hand in designing the courses at Carnousite and Muirfield among many others. During

ST. ANDREWS GOLFERS, including resident club and ballmaker Allan Robertson (third from the right), in 1859. Old Tom Morris was Robertson's apprentice in the 1850s.

his time at Prestwick the first Open was played at the club and Old Tom was beaten by Willie Park. He had his revenge by winning the next two, finished second to Park again in 1863, then won again in 1864 and 1867. It is thought that Morris was responsible for modern greenkeeping development; was partly responsible for the standardization of the rules of golf and the number of holes to be played; and helped to design many of the hickory clubs that were used at the time. He returned to St. Andrews in 1865 to be the green keeper, and remained in that role until he finally retired to his workshop by the 18th hole in 1904. Golf's founding father died four years later.

YOUNG TOM MORRIS won four Opens and recorded the first hole-in-one, at Prestwick.

John Ball and Harold Hilton

ONLY THREE MEN HAVE WON THE OPEN CHAMPIONSHIP as an amateur and one of them was the legendary Bobby Jones. The other two were both Englishmen and both members of Royal Liverpool Golf Club at Hoylake. John Ball and Harold Hilton were not just contemporaries, but two of the finest players of their generation.

JOHN BALL playing the Amateur Championship at Royal St. George's, England in 1914. In 1927, at the age of 66, Ball played his last British Amateur game.

JOHN BALL WAS THE FIRST ENGLISHMAN to win the Open when he triumphed at Prestwick in 1890. A hugely determined man of few words, he was a joy to watch. Bernard Darwin wrote, "I have derived greater aesthetic and emotional pleasure from watching John Ball than from any other spectacle in the game." Ball was the most dominant force in British golf; much the same as Bobby Jones was in the US. He won a record eight Amateur titles between 1888 and 1912 (when he was 51), his most successful year being 1890, when he won both the Amateur and the Open titles. This victory in 1890 made him the only man other than Bobby Jones to hold the Open and Amateur titles in the same year.

Harold Hilton also matched Jones in being the only other golfer to hold the Amateur Championships of both Britain and the US at the same time. The year was 1911. After winning the third of his four British Amateur titles, Hilton was victorious in the US version at Apawamis at Rye, New York, winning the match play competition at the 37th hole against Fred Herreshoff of the US. He also won the Open twice, first in 1892 at Muirfield when the championship was extended to two days and 72 holes for the first time. He won again on his home links of Hoylake five years later.

DIFFERENT STYLES

Ball, a shy, modest man, was not the greatest putter to ever play the game, but he more than made up for this by being peerless with his long approach shots. Where others tried merely to find the green, he utilized his shotmaking ability to get as close to the hole as he possibly could. In contrast, Hilton went after the ball in a ferocious manner. "A little man jumping on his toes and throwing himself and his club after the ball with almost frantic abandon," wrote Darwin of Hilton's swing. A great enthusiast of the game, even after retiring from competitive golf, Hilton became the first editor of *Golf Monthly* magazine in 1911.

JOHN BALL STATS

BORN December 24, 1861; Hoylake, England
DIED December 2, 1940

VICTORIES 8
BRITISH AMATEUR: 1888, 1890, 1892, 1894, 1899, 1907, 1910, 1912

MAJORS 1
THE OPEN: Won 1890

HAROLD HILTON STATS

BORN January 14, 1869; West Kirby, England
DIED March 5, 1942

VICTORIES 5
BRITISH AMATEUR: 1901, 1911, 1913
US AMATEUR: 1911

MAJORS 2
THE OPEN: Won 1892, 1897

HAROLD HILTON was the was the first non-American born player to win to win the US Amateur championship.

Great Triumvirate

LONG BEFORE THE BIG THREE—Palmer, Nicklaus, and Player—there was the Great Triumvirate. At the turn of the century, the careers of Harry Vardon, JH Taylor, and James Braid had a profound effect on the development of the game not just in Britain, but around the world.

VARDON, TAYLOR, AND BRAID were all born within a year of each other, and from the age of 25, they dominated the nascent professional golf scene. They won the Open Championship 16 times in a 21-year period (1894–1914). It is a feat that will never be equaled.

Harry Vardon's six victories at the Open remains the largest haul in the history of the event. He was regarded as the best player of his time, and his fame spread far and wide. He made three long exhibition tours of the US and helped the game gain in popularity rapidly. In 1900 he won the US Open at the Chicago Golf Club, while on his other two appearances in the championship he was second on both occasions. Accuracy was the key to Vardon's game. He was a consistent driver and, playing from the fairway more

than anyone else, honed his iron play to perfection. It was said that if he played the same course twice in a day, he would be playing from the same divots in the afternoon. He wrote extensively about the swing, and the overlapping grip that he adopted, became known as the "Vardon grip;" where the so-called "St. Andrews" swing was flat, with the club swung around the body, Vardon favored a more upright action.

Born in Jersey, Vardon started caddying at a young age and quickly became besotted with the game. His first Open win came at Muirfield in 1896 after a playoff against Taylor. His last came in 1914. The second half of his career was afflicted by ill health; he suffered from tuberculosis. He also designed courses, including South Herts, the club to which he was affiliated for his last

JH TAYLOR STATS

BORN March 19, 1871; Devon, England
DIED February 10, 1963

MAJORS 5
THE OPEN: 1894, 1895, 1900, 1909, 1913

HONORS
Ryder Cup Captain: 1933

JAMES BRAID STATS

BORN February 6, 1870; Fife, Scotland
DIED: November 27, 1950

MAJORS 5
THE OPEN: 1901, 1905, 1906, 1908, 1910

HARRY VARDON STATS

BORN May 9, 1870; Jersey, England
DIED March 20, 1937

MAJORS 7
THE OPEN: 1896, 1898, 1899, 1903, 1911, 1914
US OPEN: 1900

■ JH Taylor wins the first Open outside Scotland

THE GREATEST GOLFER of his time, Harry Vardon won an unmatched six Open titles and the US Open in 1900.

Vardon played as if he was enjoying the game, Braid as if he were going through his day's work, and Taylor, in certain moods at any rate, as if he hated it.

BERNARD DARWIN

JH TAYLOR was made an honorary member of the Royal and Ancient Golf Club in 1947, and of Royal North Devon 10 years later.

THE 1902 OPEN CHAMPION, Sandy Herd, joins JH Taylor (back right), James Braid (front left), and Harry Vardon (front right).

three Open wins. Two trophies bear Vardon's name: for the winner of the European tour's Order of Merit, and for the stroke average title in the US.

JH Taylor learned the game at Westwood Ho! and, playing with the then traditional flat swing, was a master in the wind. He won two Opens before Vardon had won his first, and totaled five in all. His first, in 1894, came at the first Open held outside Scotland at Royal St. George's at Sandwich, Kent. He was a runner-up no less than six times in the Open, but his most satisfying achievement was winning at St. Andrews in 1900 when he produced the lowest score in every round to win by eight shots from Vardon. He became the professional at Royal Mid Surrey, one of the many courses he designed, and was instrumental in setting up the Professional Golfers' Association (PGA).

James Braid was a tall and powerful Scotsman who smashed the ball as far as he could, then looked for it. He was not the straightest hitting player, but he had a fine short game, making him a flamboyant and exciting player to watch. Like Taylor, Braid won five Opens, and although he was a later starter than his contemporaries—he gave Vardon a three Open start— he got to five titles first. Braid was the first professional at Walton Heath, Surrey, and became a distinguished course designer, with the Kings and Queens courses at Gleneagles being among his finest work.

Walter Hagen

GOLF'S FIRST GREAT SHOWMAN, Walter Hagen was colorful and flamboyant, brash and, to some, arrogant. But if he could talk the talk, then he could certainly walk the walk. Bringing golf to the attention of the Roaring Twenties, "Sir Walter," or "The Haig," as he was known, was also one of the game's greatest championship winners.

PLAYER STATS

BORN December 21, 1892; Rochester, NY
DIED October 6, 1969
HEIGHT 5 ft 11 in (1.80 m)

DEBUT WIN 1915 Massachusetts Open
TOUR WINS 51
PGA TOUR: 44
OTHER: 7

MAJORS 11
MASTERS: T11th 1936
US OPEN: Won 1914, 1919
THE OPEN: Won 1922, 1924, 1928, 1929
USPGA: Won 1921, 1924, 1925, 1926, 1927

HONORS
Ryder Cup Team: 1927, 1929, 1931, 1933, 1935

He was an irresponsible playboy;
and at the same time a keen and determined competitor

GRANTLAND RICE

WALTER HAGEN WON THE US OPEN TWICE, the UPGA Championship five times in six attempts, and crossed the Atlantic to win the Open Championship on four occasions. But his greatest and most lasting achievement was in inventing the role of the touring professional, and showing that it was possible to make a fortune playing exhibitions all over the world. Before Hagen there were only club professionals; he was the first to go "unattached."

The son of an immigrant family, Hagen began caddying at Rochester's first golf club at the age of seven. He left school to become an assistant professional, but his own game was entirely self-taught. He had the stance of a baseball player, and tended to lunge at the ball, but he played the game with the same gusto with which he lived his life. He enjoyed scrambling to recover a bad shot, he holed the putts that mattered, and was at his best at matchplay. He lost only once—in the final to Gene Sarazen in 1923 at the second extra hole—in six outings at the USPGA, then a matchplay championship. When the Ryder Cup started, he was a natural first US captain, and he won seven of his nine matches.

Hagen's raised the stature of the golf professional in the US at a time when the game was growing fast, but Britain lagged behind. At his first Open, at Royal Cinque Ports in Kent, in 1920, Hagen arrived in a chauffeur-driven Austro–Daimler

■ Cigarette card from 1920

limousine and dressed in a Saville Row overcoat. Told he could not enter the clubhouse, he changed his shoes in his car. Two years later he celebrated his first Open win by giving the check of £50 to his caddie. In 1923, at Troon, where he was the runner-up, the presentation ceremony was the only occasion that professionals were allowed in the clubhouse. Hagen declined the offer and bought drinks for the gallery at the local pub.

WALTER HAGEN WAS PART OF A US TEAM that traveled to Gleneagles, Scotland, in 1921 to play against Great Britain and Ireland. This event was the forerunner of the Ryder Cup.

Gene Sarazen

A SHORT MAN, ALWAYS DAPPERLY DRESSED in plus fours, Gene Sarazen was an engaging character whose enthusiasm for the game was infectious. He won seven Major championships, invented the sand-wedge, and later in life helped pioneer "Shell's Wonderful World of Golf" matches on television. He was one of the game's great ambassadors.

PLAYER STATS

BORN February 27, 1902; Harrison, NY
DIED May 13, 1999
HEIGHT 5 ft 5 in (1.68 m)

DEBUT WIN 1922 southern spring open
TOUR WINS 41
PGA TOUR: 39
OTHER: 2

MAJORS 7
MASTERS: Won 1935
US OPEN: Won 1922, 1932
THE OPEN: Won 1932
USPGA: Won 1922, 1923, 1933

HONORS
Bob Jones Award: 1992
Won a career Grand Slam
Ryder Cup Team: 1927, 1929, 1931, 1933, 1935, 1937

GENE'S SAND IRON

Sarazen invented the sand-wedge. With the trailing edge of the clubhead higher than the leading edge, he hit the sand behind the ball, "bouncing" the club upward, lifting the ball out of the trap.

■ Sarazen shows off his sand technique

BORN EUGENIO SARACENI, he changed his name at the age of 17 after it was reported in the newspaper that he had made a hole-in-one. "When I saw my name in print, I thought it looked like a violin player," he explained. "I wanted something that sounded more like a golfer."

It was a name that would soon become well known. In 1922, at the age of 20, he won the first of two US Open Championships and a month later won the first of three USPGA titles. He retained the USPGA Championship a year later, but in the era of Walter Hagen and Bobby Jones, he eventually found success hard to come by. What helped rekindle his career was his innovative mind. At the time, playing out of bunkers was regarded as a tricky business. Sarazen fiddled around with the loft and lie of his wedge clubs and eventually refined not only the implement now known as the sand-wedge, but the method of playing a bunker shot that allowed him to get up-and-down in two strokes.

Sarazen was not the best driver of a ball. He had a homemade swing and an unusual grip, with four knuckles showing on his left hand, but with his recovery play from bunkers hugely improved, confidence flowed through the rest of his game, and he won the US Open again in 1932. During that same summer, he returned to Britain, where he had first attempted to play in the Open in 1923 but failed to qualify, and won the only Open ever to be played at Princes in Kent. He won two more Major championships, the second of them the Masters in 1935, which meant he became the first player to win all four of the modern Grand Slam tournaments. Known as the "Squire," he remained an honorary starter at the Masters until shortly before his death at the age of 97.

SARAZEN IS CARRIED on the shoulders of enthusiastic fans after winning the US Open at Skokie Country Club, Illinois, in 1922. He beat Bobby Jones by one stroke.

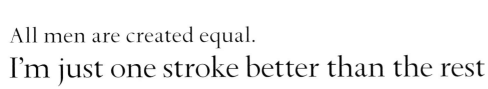

All men are created equal.
I'm just one stroke better than the rest

GENE SARAZEN

Bobby Jones was the **greatest championship golfer** in the history of the game, amateur or pro

CHARLES PRICE, AMERICAN GOLF WRITER

SPORT KINGS GUM

BOBBY JONES

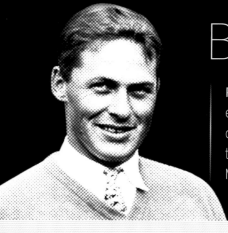

Bobby Jones

PERHAPS NO ONE CAN EVER BE DEFINITIVELY hailed as the greatest golfer ever to have played the game, but Bobby Jones might just have the strongest claim. His feat of winning the Grand Slam in 1930 is rivaled only by Ben Hogan's three titles in 1953 and Tiger Woods winning four consecutive Majors in 2000–01, but neither could be more beloved than Jones.

PLAYER STATS

BORN: March 17, 1902; Atlanta, Georgia, USA
HEIGHT: 5 ft 8 in (1.72 m)
DIED: 18 December 1971

TOUR WINS 9
PGA: 7
OTHER: 2

MAJORS 7
US OPEN: Won 1923, 1926, 1929, 1930
OPEN CHAMPIONSHIP: Won 1926, 1927, 1930
US AMATEUR: Won 1924, 1925, 1927, 1928, 1930
BRITISH AMATEUR: Won 1930

HONOURS
Grand Slam Winner: 1930
Walker Cup Team: 1922, 1924, 1926, 1928, 1930
Founded the Masters at Augusta National

FEW MEN, LET ALONE GOLFERS, have been as beloved as Bobby Jones–his admirers followed his every shot on the course.

BOBBY ON FILM

Jones made a number of coaching films. Here he is shown (third from the left) looking at the results of a recent shoot. In his series *Bobby Jones: How I Play Golf* (1931), Bobby is seen coaching some of the top celebrities of the time including W.C. Fields, and Loretta Young.

Watching how Bobby plays golf

ROBERT TYRE JONES was introduced to the game at an early age at the East Lake golf club in Atlanta. A sickly child, the fresh air was considered good for him but the youngster took to the game immediately; in fact he proved to be a prodigy. He won his club's junior title at the age of nine, beating a 16-year-old in the final, and by 12 he was the club champion. Two years later he was the Georgia State champion, and played in the US Amateur for the first time.

He was as enthralled with the mechanics of the game as actually playing it, learning his trade under the guidance of Stewart Maiden, a native of Carnoustie, at East Lake. But he was never just a golfer. He earned degrees in engineering from Georgia Tech and English literature from Harvard, then studied law and passed his bar exams after just a year. His professional career would be as a lawyer, but it was on the golf course that he was to become a hero.

By the time of his 21st birthday, Jones had been playing in national championships for seven years but had won nothing significant. He had all the physical attributes for playing the game to a level never seen before, but his temper often let him down. There was incidents of club throwing and verbal outbursts, and the president of the US Golf Association wrote a letter threatening to ban him from the main championships if his antics continued.

Jones suffered from nerves and anxiety and hardly played tournament golf outside the big events. "He was a fascinating personality," wrote American sports writer Al Laney. "Outwardly so gentle, so intelligent and pleasingly charming in a remarkably mature way; underneath lay concealed a furious often uncontrolled temper. In the young Bobby Jones, the emotions, the temperaments were a chaotic mixture with the fiercely choleric threatening to take control at times."

BOBBY JONES WITH THE TROPHIES of his 1930 season: (left to right) the Open, the US Amateur championship, the British Amateur Championship, and the US Open championship.

Yet Jones overcame himself to become a fearsome match player—no one ever beat him twice in championship play—and from 1923 to 1930, he produced an astonishing run of success. He won 13 of the 21 championships he entered—the Majors of the day to the amateur. He won the US Amateur five times, the US Open four times, the Open Championship three times, and the British Amateur once. From 1922 to his retirement, he played in the US Open and Open Championship 12 times, won on seven occasions and finished runner-up in four of the other five tournaments.

His breakthrough came at the US Open in 1923 when he looked a comfortable winner before finishing bogey, bogey, double bogey, to end up in a playoff. "I didn't finish like a champion," he said. "I finished like a yellow dog." But the playoff came down to the 18th hole and this time Jones did finish like a champion. From a sandy lie and over 200 yards away, Jones hit a 2-iron over the water and onto the green to six feet. It was one of the greatest shots he ever hit, and the legend was born.

BOBBY'S WAR

Robert T. Jones Jr. reports for duty as an officer of the Army Air Corp during World War II. He was initially assigned to the Aircraft Warning Service, an organization of civilian volunteers who manned observation posts along the Atlantic Coast, but later served overseas. During the war he allowed the US military to graze cattle on the grounds at Augusta National.

■ Bobby follows in his father's footsteps

THE MAKING OF A LEGEND

Part of the legend that grew up around Jones was his willingness to call penalty shots on himself, as during the 1925 US Open when, unseen by anyone else, his ball moved after being addressed. He ended up losing a playoff for the title but when asked about it he said, "There is only one way to play this game and that is by the rules. You might as well praise a man for not robbing a bank."

Jones won the Open for the first time in 1926 at Lytham, becoming the first man to win both the US and British titles in the same year. In preparation for the Open, he played a round of near perfection at Sunningdale. He shot 66 with 33 strokes to the turn, and 33 home. There were 33 strokes from tee-to-green, and 33 putts, only one of them a long one, and with a handful of missed chances.

PLANNING THE SLAM

In 1930 he planned an assault that became known as the Grand Slam—the Amateur and Open titles of both the US and Britain (see pp.212–13). The British Amateur came first at St. Andrews. It was the only time he won the title, involving head-to-head matches as it did, and was the key, he felt, to winning all four. Then came the Open at Hoylake, where he survived a double bogey seven at the final hole to win. The US Open was at Interlachen, where he holed from 40 ft (12 m) on the final green for the victory. The last leg of his mission was the US Amateur, which was, like the British equivalent, a matchplay event, but he again defeated all-comers. One report named the achievement the Impregnable Quadrilateral, but the phrase "Grand Slam" stuck.

Later that year at the age of 28 he announced his retirement to concentrate on his family and his business. Instead, along with some investors, he bought land in Augusta, Georgia and along with Alister Mackenzie created the Augusta National Golf Club and, from 1934, the Masters (see pp.214–15 and pp.296–99). In 1948 he played his last round of golf and was later diagnosed with the neuromuscular wasting disease, syringomyelia. He lived with the increasing incapacity for 23 years, deciding he would simply "do the best I could."

Pat Ward-Thomas wrote: "Jones was the champion of champions. No golfer has achieved or is ever likely to achieve a supremacy of all the players in the world for as long as he did. No golfer will command more lasting affection and respect for his qualities as a person."

JONES IS ESCORTED back to the clubhouse after winning the British Amateur at St. Andrews, the first leg of his Grand Slam.

1916
Wins the Georgia State Amateur title at the age of 14.

1923
Secures his first Major, the US Open, at Inwood Country Club, at the 18th hole in a playoff.

1927
Defends his Open title at St. Andrews with a record low score of 285.

1929
Wins his third US Open at Winged Foot after a playoff against Al Espinosa.

BOBBY JONES AT ST. ANDREWS

On first seeing the Old Course in 1921, Jones was less than impressed. In the third round of the Open he went to the turn in 43, double bogeyed the 10th, visited a bunker on the par-three 11th and was about to make another six when he picked up his ball. He did not tear up his card or storm off the course, but he had quit the tournament. Over the years his opinion of it changed significantly. "The more I studied the course, the more I loved it … the more I loved it the more I studied it," he said. In 1927 at St. Andrews, he won his second Open title, and in 1930 he won the first leg of the Grand Slam, the British Amateur, on the Old Course.

In 1936, on a short visit to Scotland en route to the Olympics in Berlin, Jones played a game at the Old Course and 5,000 people turned out to watch, even though there had been no official announcement of his visit. The rest of the town was deserted. "Our Bobby is back," the cry went up. In 1958, Jones added to his honorary memberships of the Royal and Ancient, St. Andrews, and New golf clubs by being awarded the Freedom of the Royal Burgh of St. Andrews in an emotion ceremony.

"If I could take out of my life everything but my experiences in St. Andrews I would still have had a rich, full life," Jones said. In 1972 there was a memorial service for Bobby in the town where Roger Wethered, the defeated finalist in the 1930 British Amateur, delivered the main address to "A golfer matchless in skill and chivalrous in spirit." The 10th hole on the Old Course is named "Bobby Jones."

△ **GENE SARAZEN** (left) and Jones (right) were great rivals. By winning the Masters in 1935, Sarazen helped Jones's new tournament become established.

◁△ **JONES REPRESENTED** the US in his fifth and final Walker Cup in 1930, at Royal St. George's. He was the playing captain in his last two matches.

■ A cigarette card from 1930

No one will ever replace Bobby Jones in the hearts of those to whom golf means more than a game

GRANTLAND RICE, SPORTS WRITER

1930	1930	1930	1930	1934	1958
Seals victory at the British Amateur Championship, beating Roger Wethered by seven shots.	Wins his third Open Championship–and the second part of the Grand Slam–at Hoylake.	Holes a 40 ft (12 m) putt on the final green to win the US Open at Interlachen.	Completes Grand Slam of Amateur and Open titles by winning the US Amateur at Merion.	Comes out of retirement to play in the inaugural Masters tournament in 1934 at his new course in Augusta, Georgia.	Is made a Freeman of St. Andrews, only the second American–after Benjamin Franklin–to be so honored.

Joyce Wethered

JOYCE WETHERED WAS TO THE WOMEN'S GAME what Bobby Jones was to the men's. She was the dominant player of the 1920s, virtually unbeatable in her short career. Jones was her hero. But the admiration was mutual, and it was Jones who described Wethered as the best golfer, man or woman, that he had ever seen. She was also a leading force in founding the Curtis Cup.

WETHERED TOOK UP THE GAME while on holiday in Scotland and was encouraged by her brother, Roger, one of the best amateur players of the era. She entered the English Ladies Championship at Sheringham in 1920, merely to keep a friend company, and ended up beating the then star, Cecil Leitch, in the final. Subsequently, she went on to win five consecutive English titles and the British Amateur four times. In the latter

championship she played 38 matches and won 36 of them. After winning her third British title in 1925, she retired from competitive golf, but made a comeback in 1929 at St. Andrews where she beat America's best player, Glenna Collett. After her famous win at the Old Course, she retired again from championship golf at the age of 28, as Bobby Jones would do at the same age a year later. She would be the first British captain in the Curtis Cup in 1932, having helped establish the competiton.

Jones often competed against Joyce's brother, Roger, and beat him in the final of the British Amateur at St. Andrews in 1930. A week later, Bobby and Joyce partnered each other in a fourball match off the back tees on the Old Course. Jones had a round of 75 to Joyce's 76, but Jones said he felt "utterly outclassed." "It was not so much the score as the way she made it," Jones said. "It was impossible to expect Miss Wethered would ever miss a shot—and she never did." As identified on film during her US tour of 1935, the pair shared a remarkably similar free-flowing swing. On that tour, Wethered played at Jones's home club of East Lake in Atlanta. Her partner, Charlie Yates, a future British Amateur champion, was outscored by Wethered for the first 14 holes. "I would have been pretty embarrassed, but I was hypnotized by watching her play," said Yates.

JOYCE WETHERED leads fellow players and spectators across a bridge at St. Andrews during the English Ladies' Championship in 1929.

WETHERED'S ELEGANT SWING was captured on film in 1932, three years after her last triumph in the Women's Amateur.

I never played golf with anyone, man or woman, amateur or professional, who made me feel so utterly outclassed

BOBBY JONES

Henry Cotton

ALTHOUGH HE DIED BEFORE BEING ABLE TO ATTEND Buckingham Palace for the investiture, Sir Henry Cotton was golf's first knight. Cotton became a patriarch of the European Golf Tour, authored a number of books, designed golf courses, and was the most respected British instructor of his time. He was Britain's finest golfer between the Great Triumvirate and Nick Faldo.

WHILE MOST PROFESSIONALS of his time had been caddies or the sons of golf professionals, Henry Cotton broke the mold. He was educated at private school in London and his middle class background would have suggested a career as an amateur. But Cotton wanted to make the most of his golfing abilities and to him that meant turning professional.

His first Open triumph ended an 11-year run without a British winner. It came at Royal St. George's in 1934, where he sprinted ahead of the field with opening rounds of 67 and 65. The latter score was a record that would stand for 43 years and was so amazing that a golf ball manufacturer wanted to commemorate the feat: the Dunlop 65 became the ball of choice for years to come. Cotton stuttered to a final round 79 but still won by five strokes. Three years later he won again at Carnoustie, against the full might of the American Ryder Cup team. The American writer Al Laney described Cotton as, "A strange, forbidding man in those days, but he could handle a golf club with his three-quarter swing more expertly than anyone I have seen since except Ben Hogan. When Cotton hit an iron to the green with chilling, humorless concentration, it seemed magic. Like Hogan... he gave the impression of coldness, but there was also the same feeling... that the ball had been given no option, that there was nothing he could not achieve."

Always one to winter in the sun, Cotton and his wife Toots lived in Penina, Portugal, to where professionals would make a pilgrimage for advice and guidance.

COTTON CHIPS onto the green during a match at the Royal Mid Surrey Course, England, in 1947, the year of his final Ryder Cup appearance.

PLAYER STATS

BORN January 26, 1907;
Holmes Chapel, England
DIED December 22, 1987

TOUR WINS 16

MAJORS 3
THE OPEN: Won 1934, 1937, 1948

HONORS
Ryder Cup Team: 1929, 1937, 1947
Ryder Cup Captain: 1947, 1953
Harry Vardon Trophy: 1938

■ Cotton speaks at the London Coliseum

Byron Nelson

BYRON NELSON BECAME FAMOUS FOR "THE STREAK" but will be remembered as the first gentleman of golf. His death, at the age of 94 in 2006, came as Tiger Woods was compiling a run of seven successive wins on the PGA Tour. In his historic season of 1945 Nelson won 11 in a row. However, 60 years after his retirement, the obituaries spoke of the man more than his remarkable deeds.

"LORD" BYRON'S 11 straight tournament victories in 1945 still stands as one of the sport's greatest records.

NELSON ONLY HAD A SHORT CAREER, but he

remained close to the game long after he finished playing; he was the first star player to become a television commentator, and mentored promising professionals, including Tom Watson and Ken Venturi. He served as a long-time honorary starter at the Masters, and since 1968 the Dallas Open has been known as the Byron Nelson Classic, the only US tour event named after a player. "Lord Byron," as he was affectionately nicknamed, was never less than a much-loved legend of the game, and the hand-written notes of congratulation or commiseration he sent to players became treasured keepsakes. Venturi, talking of their time playing exhibitions around the country, said Nelson would also check the course record and who held it. If it was the local club pro, they would leave it intact.

Nelson was born in the same year as Sam Snead and Ben Hogan, and in the same state of Texas as Hogan. They contested the final of the Glen Garden Country Club caddies' championship in 1927 with Nelson winning narrowly, a result which was repeated in their playoff at the 1942 Masters. Nelson won two Masters, two USPGA titles, and the US Open in 1939, after yet another playoff, but never the Open Championship.

As a player, he was the first big-name golfer to truly adapt to the new, larger ball and clubs with steel shafts, while his iron play was robotic; in the 1939 Open he hit the pin six times during the regulation 72-hole play. In testament to his consistency the USGA's equipment-testing machine was named "Iron Byron" and, at a time when only the leading 15 or 20 players received prize money each week, Nelson was "in the money" for 113 consecutive tournaments.

ABOUT THAT STREAK

A blood disorder prevented him from going to war and in 1944 he left his club job at Inverness in Toledo and just played on tour. He won eight times that year, but was not happy with his chipping and a number of careless shots—every round was noted in a diary and analyzed at length. The following year, he won 18 times on the tour, 19 times in total. His stroke average for the season was 68.34, only beaten by Tiger Woods in 2000. The 11 tournament winning streak began at a Fourball event in Miami, in March and ended when he lost at the Memphis Invitational in August, but he continued to win titles. It was said, unfairly and inaccurately, that the courses were easy, and the opposition limited, despite the fact that Sam Snead and Ben Hogan both won a number of tour events that year. "I don't care if he was playing against orangutans," said Jackie Burke. "Winning eleven straight is amazing."

He was victorious six times in 1946, but virtually retired at the end of the year, aged only 34. He bought a ranch near Fort Worth with his first wife Louise and freely admitted that his main motivation for every victory in the previous two years had been to earn money to buy another cow, or more land for his ranch. "I was tired and I'd accomplished everything I'd set out to do in golf," he explained. "It was time to move on. Once the ranch belonged to us, nothing else mattered."

■ Nelson features on a cereal box ad

> I don't know very much. I know a little
> bit about golf. I know how to make a stew.
> And I know how to be a decent man

BYRON NELSON

▷ **NELSON RETURNS TO THE CADDYSHACK,** where he started his career, beating rival Ben Hogan for the caddies championship at Glen Garden in 1927.

▷▷ **BING CROSBY** is excited to get the first gentleman of golf on camera at the Crosby tournament at Pebble Beach in 1951. Nelson won with a 54-hole total of 209.

▽ **NELSON MODERNIZED** the art of the golf swing, taking advantage of steel shafts and the larger ball. His iron play, in particular, was metronomic.

Sam Snead

"KNOWN AS "SLAMMIN' SAMMY," OR SIMPLY "SLAMMER," Sam Snead was blessed with one of the sweetest swings the game has ever seen. That sweet swing had such balance and rhythm, such touch and timing, that he was one of the longest hitters of his time. It was the hallmark of a career that spanned six decades and encompassed 162 tour victories; seven of them Majors.

PLAYER STATS

BORN May 27, 1912; Ashwood, Virginia
DIED May 23, 2002
HEIGHT 5 ft 11 in (1.80 m)
TURNED PRO 1934

DEBUT WIN 1937 Oakland Open
TOUR WINS 165
PGA TOUR: 82
SENIOR TOUR: 13
OTHER: 70

MAJORS 7
MASTERS: Won 1949, 1952, 1954
US OPEN: 2nd 1937, 1947, 1953/T2nd 1949
THE OPEN: Won 1946
USPGA: Won 1942, 1949, 1951

HONORS
PGA Tour Money Winner: 1938, 1949, 1950
PGA Player of the Year: 1949
Vardon Trophy Winner: 1938, 1949, 1950, 1955
Ryder Cup Team: 1937, 1947, 1949, 1951, 1953, 1955, 1959
Ryder Cup Captain: 1951, 1959, 1969

SNEAD'S ORIGINS were very humble indeed. He grew up and lived his whole life in Hot Springs, Virginia, in the foothills of the Blue Ridge mountains—huntin' and fishin' country. The youngest of five sons, Sam saw his elder brother, Homer, playing in the family pasture and copied his style, using homemade clubs fashioned from broken branches. He was a phenomenal athlete, his party tricks being one-armed press-ups and kicking cans off the top of doors. His golf may have been self-taught, but his big break came when he became the assistant professional at the Greenbrier in North Carolina, a club that he remained associated with until he died, four days short of his 90th birthday.

Snead's driving dramatically improved only after he was given a club by Henry Picard which had a stiffer shaft and suited his swing better than the old more flexible drivers. He became known as the longest, straightest driver of the ball on tour. Putting became his only weakness, as he tried many different styles, but to make up for it he was a demon pitcher and hit wonderful long-iron shots.

COUNTRY BOY

Snead became the greatest winner on the US tour, with 82 official victories—the last when he was 52—and more besides when traveling outside the US, something he generally disliked. Always a country boy at heart, his agent, Fred Corcoran, unashamedly promoted Snead's humble beginnings. Snead had a wicked sense of humor, but could be crude and definitely not politically correct, and the press reveled in his quaint and unpolished sayings. Asked once about the winning score in a US Open, Snead said: "Oh, I'll take 280, sit in a clubhouse, eat hot dogs, drink Cokes, and fart."

Snead won seven Major championships—three Masters, three USPGAs, and the Open, in 1946, but finished runner up no less than four times at the US Open. At times others did better, but on other

SNEAD HOLDS THE RECORD for most victories at one event, winning the Greater Greensboro Open eight times.

Any guy who would pass up the chance to see Sam Snead play golf would pull the shades driving past the Taj Mahal

JIM MURRAY, SPORTS WRITER

SNEAD BECAME THE GREATEST winner on the PGA Tour with 82 victories, the last of them coming at the age of 52.

occasions he simply fell apart. A triple bogey at the final hole lost it for him in 1937, as did a three-putt at the last hole of a playoff in 1947, while in 1949 and 1953 he had final rounds of 76 and even an 81. On one of those occasions he was asked if he had felt tight, and Snead replied, "Tight? I was so tight you couldn't a drove a flax seed up my ass with a knot maul."

Somewhat against his better judgment—the traveling expenses were greater than the first prize— Snead went to the Open Championship at St. Andrews in 1946, and from the train that was entering the town he said to a companion: "That looks like an abandoned golf course." Of course, it was the Old Course and news of the insult got around. "Snead, a rural American type, undoubtedly would think the leaning tower of Pisa is a structure about to totter and crash to his feet," wrote a correspondent from *The Times*. Nevertheless, Snead mastered the course, plotting his way around brilliantly in the gusty conditions and took the title by four strokes. It was said of Snead's swing: "He just walked up to the ball and poured honey all over it." Nothing was sweeter.

SAM'S BIG BREAK

Sam Snead's big break came when he played a foursome at the Greenbrier in West Virginia. He was offered the post of teaching professional, but almost lost it when he drove the green at the short par-4 5th and hit a hotel guest on the backside. The guest was a director of the railroad company that owned the hotel but, having seen Snead do it again the next day, he made him his personal teacher.

■ Snead in the Greenbrier pro shop

SNEAD WAS A PHENOMENAL athlete whose swing was as elegant at the end of his career as it was at the start.

Ben Hogan

"YOU HAVE TO DIG IT OUT OF THE DIRT," BEN HOGAN SAID. No one enjoyed practicing more or improved his swing as much as Hogan. From a slow start, compared to his contemporaries Byron Nelson and Sam Snead, Hogan dominated the game immediately after World War II despite suffering a near-fatal car crash. In 1953 he won three Major championships, including his one and only appearance in the Open.

PLAYER STATS

BORN August 13, 1912; Stephenville, Texas
DIED July 25, 1997
HEIGHT 5 ft 7 in (1.70 m)
TURNED PRO 1929

DEBUT WIN 1940 North and South Open
TOUR WINS 64
PGA TOUR: 64

MAJORS 9
MASTERS: Won 1951, 1953
US OPEN: Won 1948, 1950, 1951, 1953
THE OPEN: Won 1953
USPGA: Won 1946, 1948

HONORS
PGA Tour Money Winner: 1940, 1941, 1942, 1946, 1948
Vardon Trophy Winner: 1940, 1941, 1948
PGA Player of the Year: 1948, 1950, 1951, 1953
Ryder Cup Team: 1947, 1951
Ryder Cup Captain: 1947, 1949, 1967

BEN HOGAN WAS A COMPLEX MAN, who, at the age of only nine, had to deal with the death of his father who committed suicide by shooting himself. He came through the caddie ranks at Glen Garden in Fort Worth, Texas along with Byron Nelson, but struggled when he turned professional. He found himself broke at least a couple of times and did odd jobs in the winter, at one time working as a casino dealer. However, hours on the practice range eventually gave him a powerful but soft-landing fade, replacing his natural violent hook, which he once said was like having a "rattlesnake in your

pocket." Putting was not the best part of his game and would let him down later in his career, but few have perfected the game from tee-to-green as Hogan did. Like a machine "stamping out bottle top," said *Time* magazine.

He lost three years to military service, but in 1946, when he won 13 times, he discovered the key to his success was to concentrate on a few fundamentals. He won the first of nine Majors in 1946 at the USPGA, but it was when he won the US Open for the first time, that he started an incredible run of success: he won eight out of the 11 majors he entered between 1948 and 1953.

■ A Phoenix Open program

HOGAN WAS RENOWNED for his steely resolve and was reportedly unapproachable, but he was all smiles after the 1951 US Open.

HOGAN'S LUCKY ESCAPE

In 1949, driving along a road in Texas, Hogan's car ran into a Greyhound bus that was passing a truck. At the moment of impact, Hogan threw himself across the car to protect his wife. Both survived, but Hogan suffered a broken collar bone and fractures of his hip, ribs, and left ankle. He also suffered a blood clot and never had normal circulation in his legs again.

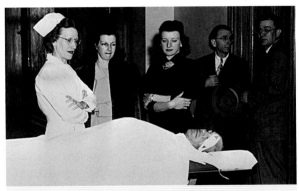

■ Hogan in a critical state after the car accident

After his car accident (see above and pp. 220–21) playing golf meant playing in pain, and in the most remarkable victory of his career at the US Open in 1950, he struggled through 36-holes on the final day, and then won an 18-hole playoff the following day. In 1951 he brought the monster Oakland Hills course to its knees to win the US Open once again, then two years later he won a second Masters and fourth US Open. In 1953, Hogan traveled for the first, and only time to Britain for the Open. He had stopped playing the USPGA due to its long matchplay format, and in any case the events overlapped. At Carnoustie he triumphed with a course record of 68 in the final round, and the "Wee Ice Mon" was immediately taken to the hearts of the Scots gallery.

He remains one of only five players to have won all four Major titles, and with Tiger Woods, the only other player to have won three Majors in the same season (see pp. 222–23).

HOGAN'S SWING was the envy of his fellow professionals and his methods live on–his technique is central to the teachings of many modern day coaches, including David Leadbetter.

> You hear stories about me beating my brains out practicing, but the truth is, I was enjoying myself. I couldn't wait to get up in the morning, so I could hit balls

BEN HOGAN

Babe Zaharias

BABE ZAHARIAS WAS THE FIRST WOMAN ATHLETE to become a national hero in the US. A brilliantly gifted all-around sportswoman, she was already a successful Olympic track and field athlete before she turned to golf, where she found lasting success. She also helped found the Ladies Professional Golf Association (LPGA) in 1950.

MILDRED DIDRIKSON changed her last name to Zaharias in 1938 after marrying professional wrestler George Zaharias. She had already become simply "Babe" after legendary baseball player Babe Ruth following a baseball game in which she hit five home runs. In fact, she was gifted at many sports, including basketball, tennis, diving, skating, bowling, billiards, not to mention athletics. At the US Olympic trials in 1932, she won six out of eight events, and at the Olympic Games in Los Angeles later that summer, she won gold medals in the javelin and the 80-meter hurdles. At the same Games she, albiet briefly, established a new high jump world record, but was later demoted to the silver-medal position because her technique was considered to be illegal.

AN OUTSTANDING AMATEUR
When she turned to golf on a full time basis, she could hit the ball vast distances, but took time to learn the game. After winning the Texas Amateur title in 1933, she was barred from playing in amateur events as she was considered to be a professional for earning money at other sports. She went on exhibition tours, but eventually regained her amateur status and went on a brilliant winning streak. She won the US Amateur in 1946, and the British Amateur at Gullane the following year.

Zaharias turned professional in 1947 and won the Women's US Open three times while heading the prize money list on the LPGA Tour in the first two years of its existence. In 1953 she was diagnosed with cancer but after surgery she returned to win the 1954 US Open by 12 strokes. It was her last great triumph, because in 1955 the cancer reappeared. On her hospital bed her final words to her husband were, "Honey, I ain't going to die".

ZAHARIAS WAS A LATECOMER to the game, and was introduced to it by the sports writer Grantland Rice during the 1932 Olympics in Los Angeles. In between events, Rice maintains she shot a round of 91.

FROM OLYMPIC STAR to golfing champion, Babe Zaharias was a sensational athlete blessed with a natural gift and rhythm.

She is the Ultimate Amazon and **the greatest athlete of all mankind for all time**

GRANTLAND RICE, SPORTS WRITER

Max Faulkner

AT A TIME WHEN THE OPEN CHAMPIONSHIP became dominated by visitors from Australia, South Africa, and, of course, the US, Max Faulkner was a beacon of hope, the last British champion for almost two decades until Tony Jacklin. Faulkner was a flamboyant character, a British version of Walter Hagen, who brightened up post-war golf. Portrush in 1951 was his lasting memorial.

FAULKNER ESCAPES from the rough at Royal Portrush on his way to winning the 1951 Open, his sole Major success.

IT WAS SAID IN A NEWSPAPER COLUMN, penned by the British sports journalist Ian Wooldridge, that Max Faulkner went around signing autographs that week with the addendum "Open Champion 1951." In fact, Faulkner had signed an autograph prior to the final round for a small boy whose father asked for the words to be added. Having obliged, Faulkner thought, "What have I done! I'd better win now."

He was six strokes ahead and duly took the crown and the £300 prize money with a final score of 285. A straight driver and iron player, Faulkner's putting that week was also superb. He had only 24 putts in the second round, but the especially light putter he used that week was just one of 300 he eventually collected, and used, most of which he'd made himself.

TEAM PLAYER

At the 1957 Ryder Cup at Lindrick in Yorkshire, England, Faulkner was left out of the singles but still had a vital role to play. Ken Bousfield, who claimed the winning point, recalled: "Those were the days before scoreboards out on the course and walkie-talkies. All of us playing out there have no idea what was happening in the other matches if it wasn't for Max. He was marvellous. And he seemed to bring good news every time I saw him. He'd nip up to me [and say], 'Rees is winning'; 'Brown's four-up'; 'We've got them on the run, Guv'nor'; 'Go on! You can beat this boy.' Then he'd dash off and come back ten minutes later with more good news. We might have won without him, but he was magnificent that day – I'll never forget what he did."

Bobby Locke

BOBBY LOCKE WAS THE FIRST GREAT PLAYER to emerge from South Africa, starting a dynasty that continued with Gary Player, and has progressed into the modern era with Ernie Els and Retief Goosen. Locke was also one of the finest putters the game has ever seen, his success on the greens bringing him four Open Championships between 1949 and 1957.

He was the greatest putter I have ever seen.

PETER ALLISS

LOCKE USED THE SAME HICKORY SHAFTED, rusty bladed putter for most of his career. Gripping the club very lightly, Locke had marvelous touch, and was a firm believer in easing the ball into the hole at "dead pace." His exceptional feel also showed in his distance control with his irons, and in his accurate chipping.

When Sam Snead traveled to South Africa, he came up against Locke, and was defeated 12–2 in a series of exhibition matches. But Snead was happy nonetheless to give him some career advice. The younger man once asked Snead if he could make a living in the US. "Make a living?" replied Snead, "you'll get rich, and very quickly." Locke did indeed win regularly in the US but, because many American players disliked a foreigner plundering their tour, he was resented and was briefly banned on the pretext of missing a couple of events he had entered. During his ban in the US, he played mainly in Britain, winning the Open for the first time in 1949, when he beat Harry Bradshaw in a playoff. It was when he started playing in Britain that he decided to change his natural fade to a draw, aiming away to the right and bringing the ball back. The change had a positive impact on his already impressive game.

The fourth and last of Locke's Open titles came at St. Andrews in 1957 when, on the final green, he moved his marker for another player but did not move it back to its original position. This was the first televised Open, and replays showed the error, but the committee ruled that the result should stand. Three years later Locke was injured in a car accident; he lost some of his sight in one eye and was never quite the same player again.

FOR MUCH OF HIS CAREER, Locke dressed almost exclusively in gray flannel trousers, white buckskin shoes, linen dress shirts with neckties, and white Hogan caps.

PLAYER STATS

BORN November 20, 1917; Germiston, South Africa
DIED March 9, 1987
TURNED PRO 1938

DEBUT WIN 1938 South African Open
TOUR WINS 72
PGA TOUR: 11
EUROPEAN TOUR: 23
SOUTHERN AFRICA TOUR: 38

MAJORS 4
MASTERS: 10th 1948
US OPEN: 3rd 1947, 1951
THE OPEN: Won 1949, 1950, 1952, 1957
USPGA: T33rd 1947

HONOURS
Named an honorary member of the Royal and Ancient Golf Club in 1976

LOCKE HOLDS THE CLARET JUG at Royal St. George's in 1949; it was the first of four Open victories.

Peter Thomson

WITH BOBBY LOCKE FLYING THE FLAG for South Africa, Peter Thomson arrived on the scene to do the same for Australia. The pair dominated the Open in the 1950s with Thomson winning the title four times, and five overall. He became a writer, commentator, and course architect and went on to become a tour winner all over again on the Seniors Tour.

PLAYER STATS

BORN August 23, 1929; Melbourne, Australia
TURNED PRO 1949

DEBUT WIN 1950 New Zealand Open
TOUR WINS 70
PGA TOUR: 6
AUSTRALASIA TOUR: 20
EUROPEAN TOUR: 26
SENIOR TOUR: 11
OTHER: 7

MAJORS 5
MASTERS: 5th 1957
US OPEN: T4th 1956
THE OPEN: Won 1954, 1955, 1956, 1958, 1965
USPGA: DNP

HONORS
Presidents Cup
Captain: 1998
President of Australian
PGA: 1962, 1963, 1994

THOMSON WAS A CEREBRAL PLAYER. He never believed in hours and hours of ball beating on the practice range. It was said that if he had a problem with his game, he would sit in a chair, analyze the possible causes and solutions, then only head for the range to confirm his theory with a dozen or so balls. He had a simplistic approach to the game; he would play for position and run the ball onto the green along the ground. In this way his game was ideally suited to the fast-running courses of Australia and the summer links of Britain. Having perfected his game, he considered the knack of competing to be the key ingredient of winning tournaments. Between 1952 and 1958 he finished either first or second at the Open.

THOMSON'S SON HOLDS the Australian Open trophy in 1967. Thomson was a prolific champion, winning the national championships of ten different countries.

CHAMPION OF THE OPEN

His first victory came at Royal Birkdale in 1954 and he would go on to become the first player since Young Tom Morris to win three consecutive Open Championships. A fourth title arrived in 1958, and the fifth in 1965 back at Royal Birkdale. By this time, the Open had been "rediscovered" by the best US players, and among his opponents were Arnold Palmer, Jack Nicklaus, Phil Rogers, and Tony Lema, the defending champion. It was his finest hour and finally cemented his reputation in the US. His ventures to the US had been brief and only brought him one victory, but when the Seniors Tour started up in the 1980s, he returned and plundered the circuit for a couple of years before finally retiring to television commentary and his course design business.

THOMSON BELIEVED that careful planning, calm and clear thinking, and common sense were the most important facets of golf.

Billy Casper

ANYONE WOULD LOOK A LITTLE LESS EXCITING when put alongside Arnold Palmer, but Billy Casper showed there was another way to forge a successful career. A conservative, patient, disciplined man compared to Palmer's aggressive and charismatic showman, Casper nonetheless showed that patience is a virtue. The 1966 US Open was his greatest triumph.

INEVITABLY, PERHAPS, it became known as the championship Arnold Palmer lost rather than for Casper's victory. Palmer led at the Olympic Club in San Francisco by seven strokes with nine holes to play. But his swashbuckling style suddenly suffered a massive collapse and Casper's steady consistency was rewarded. Palmer came home in 39, Casper in 32, to force a playoff. The following day, Palmer was again four ahead at the turn, but again capitulated. "I had seen other guys tense up, panic under pressure, but not Arnie," Casper said. "Once it looked like I was getting into his lead, his swing got shorter and faster."

Casper was an experienced winner. He won 51 times on the US tour between 1956 and 1975, including three Major championships. His 1966 win was his second US Open title, and he took the 1970 Masters in another playoff, this time against his fellow San Diegan, Gene Littler. Later he was successful on the Seniors Tour winning two Senior Majors (in 1983 and 1988) and seven other titles.

STEADY AS HE GOES

Casper's game was based on steadiness, straight driving, and wonderful putting. He said he was too lazy to go to the range so perfected his chipping and putting instead. But his peers knew of his great qualities. "To be a winner you have to have heart," said Jack Nicklaus. "You really have to control your emotions and your golf game. Billy Casper was wonderful at this and does not get the credit he deserves. He didn't have all the shots that others had, but he was able to will the ball into the hole."

On the course he based his demeanor on Ben Hogan's "ice man" image. Off it, it was reckoned that he was "so austere... that by contrast a Franciscan monk looks like a swinger," while Dave Hill wrote in his autobiography that he had, "as much personality as a glass of water." Members of the Mormon Church, Casper and his wife had 11 children, many of whom were adopted from poorer backgrounds overseas.

THE PUTTS usually dropped for Billy Casper, but on this occasion, at the Bob Hope Desert Classic in 1968, the birdie putt stayed out.

You must have the ability to **control your mind and your heart.** The golf swing is really a small part

BILLY CASPER

Julius Boros

A LATE STARTER AS A PROFESSIONAL GOLFER, Julius Boros still enjoyed a long and successful career. When he won the USPGA Championship in 1968 he became, at the age of 48, the oldest ever winner of a Major championship. Not bad for a former accountant who only turned to professional golf at the age of 30.

BOROS WAS OF HUNGARIAN DESCENT and lived in Connecticut. He played a lot of golf with Sam Snead and Tommy Armour, who was the professional at his local club, before he turned pro himself. When Boros decided to make a living from the game, Armour was not particularly encouraging, although he admitted he had a superb bunker game. However, Boros made an immediate impact. He placed ninth at his first US Open in 1950, finished fourth the following year, and then won at Northwood in 1952.

His game suited the US Open as he drove the ball straight, and always managed to maintain a relaxed demeanor. Lee Trevino once said of him, "I'm telling you, of all the guys up there on that leaderboard, he scares me more than anybody. When he putts you can't tell by looking at him whether he's just practicing or that it's for fifty grand if he sinks it." He did not practice much and, concerned that he might lock up

over a shot, he would walk casually up to his ball, shuffle into his stance in a distinctive manner, and then swing. Perhaps it all helped his longevity; 11 years after his first US Open victory, he triumphed at Brookline in 1963 after a playoff with Arnold Palmer and Jacky Cupit. Palmer was also involved five years later when Boros won the USPGA at Pecan Valley by one stroke from Arnie and Bob Charles.

Boros won the 1977 PGA Seniors' Championship, and two years later, in partnership with Roberto De Vincenzo, he won the Legends of Golf tournament after holing a birdie putt on the sixth hole of sudden death. It is widely acknowledged that this putt provided the impetus for the formation of the Senior PGA Tour in 1980.

▽ **BOROS TEES OFF** in the Los Angeles Open, the first tournament of the 1956 season, having ended the previous year as the tour's leading money winner.

△ **BOROS CONTEMPLATES** an iron shot during the 1968 Masters. He finished 16th that year, but won the USPGA four months later.

NICKLAUS AND PALMER line up a putt at the 1971 Ryder Cup. Their rivalry during the 1960s defined the sport.

ARNOLD PALMER BROUGHT a new audience to golf and wowed spectators around the world throughout his career.

Arnold Palmer

ARNOLD PALMER WAS GOLF'S WORKING CLASS HERO. If Bobby Jones received the sort of hero worship reserved for an untouchable god, Palmer was a man of the people. He was golfing royalty, but adored by all, men and women, rich and poor, golfer and non-golfer. He won seven Major championships, often thrillingly, within a span of six years, and his timing was perfect; television was just starting to broadcast the sport and Palmer was its first star.

PALMER GREW UP ON THE LATROBE COURSE on the outskirts of Pittsburgh, where his father, Deacon, was the greenkeeper and club professional. From the start, Palmer married natural ability with innate aggression. The aggression was channeled positively following an early club-throwing incident which earned him a reprimand. Arnold's father had placed a club in his hands at the age of three, shown him the right grip and Palmer never changed it. His father then said: "Just hit the ball as hard as you can and then go and find it." And that's how he played all his career.

Palmer went to college at Wake Forest and did military service in the Coast Guards. He won the US Amateur in 1954, then turned professional the following year, traveling in a RV with his young wife Winnie. He won a few tournaments and got to play in the Masters, but his style did not impress some of the veterans like Ben Hogan. In 1958 all that changed, as Palmer was tied with Sam Snead going into the last round at Augusta and won by four shots. At the 12th hole, his ball was over the green and plugged in the bank. There was confusion about how to proceed, but a rules official told him to play it as it lay, but to drop another ball and play that, too. He got a five the first time and then a par-three with the free drop. Mad as hell, Palmer made an eagle-three at the 13th hole and was only then told that the free drop at the 12th was allowable and his par-three would stand.

ARNIE'S GOLDEN YEARS

At 28, Palmer was only just starting to win Majors at the same age Bobby Jones had retired. Although Jack Nicklaus would eclipse his four titles, it was at Augusta

FASTEST AROUND THE WORLD

An eager private aviator, Arnold Palmer has held several flying records during his life. In 1976, he flew around the world in 58 hours in a Learjet 63. In 1996, he bought the first ever Cessna Citation X plane and promptly set a speed record with that over a closed 3,000 mile (5,000 km) course. His local airport was renamed The Arnold Palmer Regional Airport in his honor.

■ Palmer also enjoys more restrained modes of flight

that Palmer was at his best. It was here that Arnie's Army, a loyal band of supporters, was founded (see p.131). He won the title in alternate years between 1958 and 1964. In 1960 he birdied the last two holes to win by one shot. The following year, walking up the 18th fairway, he was distracted by a friend congratulating him. He took a double-bogey six and lost by one shot to Gary Player. In an 18-hole playoff in 1962, he beat Player and Dow Finsterwald by playing the inward nine in 31.

Perhaps his greatest triumph came at Cherry Hills in 1960, the only time he won the US Open. Palmer was seven shots behind Mike Souchak with a round to play. Having a hamburger in the locker room with a couple of players and journalist friends, Palmer suggested that a 65 might still win. "That would get me to 280, and 280 always wins the Open," Palmer said confidently. "Only when Hogan shoots it," someone replied. Taking this comment as a slight, Palmer promptly drove the short, par-four 1st hole and two-putted for a birdie. In fact, he birdied six of the first seven holes, scored 65 and won by two shots. Two years later he lost to Nicklaus in the US Open at Oakmont and the task of anyone else winning majors other than "the Bear"

> There has never been anyone like him before in the game ... and there probably won't be another like him again.

had suddenly become even harder. However, the pair would enjoy a friendly rivalry, both on and off the course, for the rest of their lives.

Having won the Masters and the US Open in 1960, Palmer headed to the Open at St. Andrews. On the plane he was thinking that there should be some professional equivalent of Jones's Grand Slam of the two Open and Amateur championships of the US and Britain. Palmer and Bob Drum, a journalist friend, came up with the idea for the modern Grand Slam— the Masters, the US Open, the Open, and the USPGA. Palmer came second to Kel Nagle at the 1960 Open, but won the title at Birkdale the following year, playing a shot from horrendous rough on what is now the 16th hole; there is now a plaque celebrating the wondrous thrash. He won again the following year at Troon, where the crowds overwhelmed the course, and it was Palmer who rekindled interest in the Open when it was flagging and encouraged his countrymen to travel across each summer.

FINAL FAREWELLS

As well as the triumphs, there were disappointing days for Palmer on the course, including the 1966 US Open at the Olympic Club in San Francisco where he was seven ahead with nine to play but ended up losing a playoff to Billy Casper the following day. Palmer was not a perfect golfer, but as with Seve Ballesteros, seeing him trying to get out of the trouble he had created was part of the wonder. "Trouble is bad to get into, but fun to get out of," he said. "I suppose there is a place to play it safe, but

> Success in golf depends a lot less on **strength of body** than upon strength of **mind and character**
>
> ARNOLD PALMER

as far as I'm concerned, it is not on a golf course." Without Palmer, modern day players would not be competing for the millions they do, and the senior circuit certainly would not exist to the same extent without Palmer so enthusiastically embracing the idea in the early 1980s. He simply loves to play golf.

Arnold Palmer, like other celebrities unwilling to leave the stage, was legendary for his farewells. There was the Open at St. Andrews, in 1990 and again in 1995. There were several at Augusta, where they did not bother to put up his scores on the last few appearances. Then there was the US Open at Oakmont, in his home state of Pennsylvania, in 1994. He was applauded every step of the way for 36 holes—ovations oblivious to the tournament going on. In the press room afterward, a towel around his shoulders, there were no questions. Palmer tried to

1954	1958	1961	1962	1962	1963
Having spent three years in the Coast Guard, Palmer returns to win the US Amateur title.	Palmer receives the Masters winner's medal from Bobby Jones–the first of four wins at Augusta.	Wins the first of his two Open Championships, at Royal Troon.	Claims the Open for a second time. His appearances in Britain breathed new life into the tournament.	Palmer wins seven other PGA Tour events during the season and his rivalry with newcomer Jack Nicklaus begins in earnest.	He is playing captain for the victorious US Ryder Cup team at East Lake, Atlanta. He featured in eight competitions as a player.

ARNIE'S ARMY

By the late 1960s, Palmer found himself being eclipsed by a new star, Jack Nicklaus. Although he increasingly began to lose out to his great rival, his huge fan base, known as "Arnie's Army", never waned. His popularity was instrumental in establishing the US Senior Tour, for which he became eligible in its inaugural season. He won ten tour events between 1980 and 1988, including five senior Majors.

■ Arnie with his adoring fans

△ **ARNIE AND JACK**. It was the rivalry to end all rivalries–golf's greatest hero, Arnold Palmer, against the game's greatest player, Jack Nicklaus.

△▷**PALMER ONLY KNEW ONE WAY TO PLAY** and his swashbuckling style continued on to the Seniors Tour which would not exist without him.

speak but dissolved into tears. Eventually he said: "It's been 40 years … When you walk up the 18th and get an ovation like that, I guess that says it all. I think you all know pretty much how I feel. It's been 40 years of work, fun, and enjoyment. I haven't won all that much. I won a few tournaments. I won some Majors. I suppose the most important thing is the game has been so good to me. I think that's all I have to say." He buried his head in the towel and then departed.

ONE FINAL WAVE to the gallery at the Masters as the four-time champion makes an emotional farewell from Augusta.

1973
Palmer competes in his last Ryder Cup as a player, as the US win 19-13 at Murifield.

1980
Brings his considerable presence to bear on the Seniors Tour, winning the PGA Championship in his first season.

1981
Palmer becomes the first person to win the US Open and US Senior Open.

1984
Won two of his five senior Major titles, the Senior PGA (pictured), and the Senior Players titles.

1994
Palmer makes his 32nd and final appearance in the US Open at Oakmont Country Club. He also bids farewell at the USPGA.

1995
On his 35th appearance bids farewell to the Open Championship, fittingly at St. Andrews.

△ **PLAYER WAS AS SUCCESSFUL** on the Champions Tour as he was on the PGA Tour, winning nine Majors on each.

◁ **KISSING THE OPEN TROPHY** in 1968 the "Black Knight," as he was nicknamed, was a distinctive character on the golf course.

Player, golf's Little Big Man, is of course a phenomenon. He rants about his religion, his dedication, and the searing nature of difficulties he has mastered. But there is no doubt about his place in the deity of the game

JAMES LAWTON, SPORTS WRITER

Gary Player

GARY PLAYER WAS PART OF THE "BIG THREE" with Arnold Palmer and Jack Nicklaus (see pp. 224-25). He won nine Major championships, more than any other golfer born outside the US, and he did it the hard way. He is said to have traveled approximately 15 million miles during his career, and while not as naturally talented as many others, but his dedication and belief took him to the very top of the game.

PLAYER STATS

BORN November 1, 1935; Johannesburg, South Africa
HEIGHT 5 ft 7 in (1.70 m)
TURNED PRO 1953

DEBUT WIN 1955 East Rand Open
TOUR WINS 163
PGA TOUR: 24
CHAMPIONS TOUR: 19
SOUTHERN AFRICAN TOUR: 73
OTHER: 47

MAJORS 9
MASTERS: Won 1961, 1974, 1978
US OPEN: Won 1965
THE OPEN: Won 1959, 1968, 1974
USPGA: Won 1962, 1972

HONORS
PGA Tour Money Winner: 1961
Presidents Cup Captain: 2003, 1995, 2007
9-time Senior Major Champion

GARY PLAYER WAS AS FIERCE a competitor as they come and his drive brought him nine majors.

PLAYER APPEARED IN THE MASTERS for the 50th time in 2007 and, into his seventies, still travels the globe. No one in golf has clocked up more air miles. In the early days of his career, international travel was more difficult than it is now, but Player would fly and tee up in virtually every continent. With his wife Vivienne, his staunchest ally, there was a time when Player traveled with all six of his children, more than 30 pieces of luggage, and would need a fleet of taxis once he had arrived at his destination.

When Player first left South Africa to play golf in Britain in 1955, his game was not ready. He broke even on the trip but was often dismissively told by his British peers that he might be better off heading back to Johannesburg and finding some other occupation. "It did me a great service to my drive and determination," he said. In 1956 he won the South African Open for the first time, and his game began to blossom. When he returned to England, he beat Arthur Lees, the local professional, in the 90-hole Dunlop tournament at Sunningdale, and a year later headed for the PGA Tour.

MAJOR BREAKTHROUGH

All the time he worked on improving his game, and his big breakthrough came at the Open at Muirfield in 1959. With one day, and 36 holes to go, he was behind by eight shots, but told his equipment representative, "You're going to see a small miracle tomorrow. In fact, you are going to see a big miracle. I'm going to win." And he did, with a final round 68.

Two years later, Player won the Masters, in somewhat fortunate circumstances. Arnold Palmer could have won the title, but he took a double bogey at the last to let Player sneak the victory. Player claimed the USPGA the following year, and then at the US Open at Bellerive in 1965 he beat Kel Nagle in a playoff. In doing so, he joined Gene Sarazen and Ben Hogan as the only golfers to have won all four of the modern Major championships. He achieved this Grand Slam before Jack Nicklaus, who completed it the following year, while Tiger Woods is the only other golfer to join the impressive list.

While Player's affairs were looked after by Mark McCormack, who also had Palmer and Player as clients, on the course he faced the sternest of tests. While Player was winning his nine Major titles, Palmer was winning six of his seven Majors, and Nicklaus 14 of his 18. There were also the likes of Lee Trevino, Johnny Miller, and Tom Watson to contend with in one of the most competitive eras the game has ever seen. He was a fine iron player, pitched well, and was aggressive with his

PLAYER LOVED THE FORMAT of matchplay golf. He won the World Match Play at Wentworth five times, making him the second most successful winner of the title.

chipping and putting. But if there was one part of his game that singled him out, it was his bunker play; he is one of the greatest bunker players the game has ever produced. While other players were happy simply to give themselves a chance at a putt to save par, Player would be looking to hole out from the sand.

Player won his second Open at Carnoustie in 1968, when he played a superb 3-wood shot at the par-5 14th to two feet for an eagle to hold off Nicklaus. It had been a superb duel between the two, but try as he might, the Bear could not catch the South African over the closing stretch. He won a third Claret Jug in 1974 at Royal Lytham, where he played a magical 9-iron from the rough at the 17th. He won by four strokes from Peter Oosterhuis and by five from Nicklaus.

There were three green jackets in total, with further wins coming in 1974, and famously in 1978, when he closed with a brilliant 64 on the last day, coming home in only 30 strokes. A second USPGA title was secured in 1972 at Oakland Hills, where again he hit a great 9-iron shot, from rough, over trees and water at the 16th hole to help him secure his victory.

BODY AND SOUL

His faith was always of great importance to Player, and he was always eager to acknowledge his God-given ability as a golfer. He was the first golfer to manage his diet, eat healthy foods, and would always take bananas and raisins on to the course to snack on during a round. He was also the first to employ a strict fitness regime at a time when golfers did not consider themselves to be athletes, and didn't believe that physical fitness was something that they needed to concern themselves with. Player was ahead of his time.

As well as being a pioneer, he courted controversy regarding his views on the South Africa's political stance. He found himself much criticized when he wrote that he was a proud South African and supported apartheid. In a later autobiography, he retracted what he had once believed, and worked to overcome the system by setting up a foundation educating underprivileged children.

In his book, *Grand Slam Golf*, Player described himself as, "Small, dark, deliberate, painstaking ... a man without talent who has done it all by sheer hard work and nothing else, a highly-strung faddist who bores

TOM WATSON helps Player into a Masters green jacket in 1978. It was his third victory at Augusta and his last Major win.

> You should look after your body. If you do, it could last you a lifetime

GARY PLAYER

1959	1961	1965	1965	1965	1969
At Muirfield, Player becomes the youngest golfer to win the Open Championship.	Player becomes the first non-American to win the Masters at Augusta.	Wins the World Series of Golf when it was an invitational event rather than a PGA Tour event.	Wins the US Open, to complete a career Grand Slam, at the age of 29.	Wins the first of five World Match Play titles, beating Peter Thomson 3&2 at Wentworth.	At the USPGA Championship black militants, perceiving him as a racist, throw a cup of ice in his face on the 10th tee.

THE MOSTLY BLACK, KNIGHT

There was a time when Player wore only white clothes, to reflect the sun, but for most of his career he wore all black—better to absorb the sun and keep his muscles warm. At the 1960 Open, he wore pants with one white leg and one black leg, but worried that it could be perceived as a political statement, never did so again, until one further occasion very late in his career.

Player tees off at the Old Course

PLAYER ESCAPES FROM THE SAND. Whenever possible he would play aggressively from a bunker rather than merely playing safely out of a sand trap.

the ears off you with weight-lifting and diets and nuts and raisins and talk of God, dark clothes, somber under big peaked cap, and, above all, a little fellow, a little man."

Player won over 150 titles around the world and was convinced that his determination and hard work could overcome any disadvantage or suffering, and that was his feeling from the very start. No one worked harder at all aspects of his game than Player, and the harder he worked, as he said, the more he was blessed with good fortune. "You know, I'll tell you something. The more I practice, the luckier I get." It was a winning mantra.

1974 Becomes the only golfer of the 20th Century to win the Open in three different decades.

1978 The last of Player's nine Majors comes at the Masters where he wins by just one shot.

1998 Becomes the oldest player to make the cut for the final rounds at the Masters.

2003 Captains the International team in the first Presidents Cup played in South Africa.

2007 Plays in his 50th Masters, tying Arnold Palmer's record for the most appearances at Augusta.

△△ **NICKLAUS STRIKES** a short iron to the green during a round at the 1969 Open at Royal Lytham.

△ **NICKLAUS TAKES POSSESSION** of the Open Claret Jug for the second time, at St. Andrews in 1978.

◁ **IT'S THERE!** Nicklaus holes for a birdie 3 on Augusta's 17th green on his way to victory in 1986.

Jack Nicklaus

JACK NICKLAUS WAS CONSIDERED THE BEST GOLFER OF THE 20TH CENTURY decades before anyone started planning for a Millennium party. Nicklaus's haul of 18 Major titles remains an Everest yet to be scaled, even if Tiger Woods is gaining ground. During a run of 154 consecutive Majors, Nicklaus finished in the top-10 in half of them, and second 19 times. The "Golden Bear" was a prolific winner, but also one of the most gracious players the game has seen.

PLAYER STATS

BORN January 21, 1940; Columbus, Ohio
HEIGHT 5 ft 10 in (1.78 m)
TURNED PRO 1961

DEBUT WIN US Open 1962
TOUR WINS 113
PGA TOUR: 73
CHAMPIONS TOUR: 10
OTHER: 30

MAJORS 18
MASTERS: Won 1963, 1965, 1966, 1972, 1975, 1986
US OPEN: Won 1962, 1967, 1972, 1980
THE OPEN: Won 1966, 1970, 1978
USPGA: Won 1963, 1971, 1973, 1975, 1980

HONORS
PGA Tour Money Winner: 1964, 1965, 1967, 1971, 1972, 1973, 1975, 1976
PGA Player of the Year: 1967, 1972, 1973, 1975, 1976
The only player to have won all four Majors at least three times
Finished 2nd in Major championships 19 times
8 Senior Major championships
Ryder Cup Team: 1969, 1971, 1973, 1975, 1977, 1981
Ryder Cup Captain: 1983, 1987
Presidents Cup Captain: 1998, 2003, 2005, 2007

NICKLAUS THROWS HIS BALL in celebration, having become the first player to retain the Masters, in 1966.

NICKLAUS GREW UP IN COLUMBUS, OHIO, and was encouraged in his golf by his father Charlie at the Scioto Country Club. An early club-throwing incident was the last of its kind, as his father instilled in the young Jack the values of the game—to act graciously, win or lose. Once, when Jack was about to break 70 for the first time, Charlie insisted that they went home, as they were expected for dinner. They later returned and Jack eagled the 18th for a 69.

At the age of 16, Nicklaus won the Ohio State Open. The event was over four rounds but only three days, with 36 holes on the final day. On the afternoon of the second day, after his round, Nicklaus flew across the state to play in an exhibition match with Sam Snead. Nicklaus lost, but was so inspired at having seen Snead play that he was determined to win the next day—which he did.

THE FUNDAMENTALS
Nicklaus's longtime teacher was Jack Grout, who had grown up in Texas playing with Ben Hogan and Byron Nelson. Grout preached the importance of getting the fundamentals correct, particularly keeping the head still. He would even take hold of Nicklaus's hair and make him swing, teaching him a painful lesson.

Nicklaus could thunder the ball off the tee, and brought the idea of powerful driving to a new level. He also hit magnificent iron shots, and he could putt. He once said that he did not hole many really long putts but, then, he rarely

missed any of the short ones. In fact, he holed more putts in the 10–15 ft (3–5 m) range than anyone else in the game. He was not the most naturally gifted—others did things better—but his head and his course management was better than anyone else's. He always played the right shot at the right time. He was a deliberate, almost slow player, but in the Majors, he figured out that the more he hung around without doing anything silly, the more everyone else would fall away. Some thought he only played really aggressive golf

ARNOLD PALMER PRESENTS NICKLAUS with the Masters green jacket on the occasion of his first win. He would claim the title a total of six times.

Jack knew he was going to beat you. You knew Jack was going to beat you. And Jack knew that you knew he was going to beat you

TOM WEISKOPF

THE CONCESSION

Jack Nicklaus had a profound effect on the Ryder Cup, and in 1969, his act of sportsmanship was rejoiced all over the world. Tony Jacklin had a short putt to win their match but Nicklaus conceded it, saying, "I don't think you would have missed that putt, but under the circumstances, I would never give you the opportunity." It meant that the overall match was tied but the US, as the holders, kept possession of the Cup.

■ Nicklaus and Jacklin share a moment

when he really needed to. Whether he would have won even more if he had pushed harder, we will not know. But, as he said, "I guess I could keep playing my game longer than they could keep playing theirs."

OUT OF HIS CAGE

Nicklaus won the US Amateur twice, in 1959 and 1961, and might have won the 1960 US Open, where he played the last 36 holes with the veteran Ben Hogan. "Today I played with a kid who could have won this Open by 10 shots if I'd be thinking for him," said Hogan. Two years later, Nicklaus's first professional title was no less than the US Open. If that was not already a mighty statement in itself, he defeated, after a playoff, the great Arnold Palmer in his home state of Pennsylvania. On the slick Oakmont greens, he had only one three-putt in 90 holes. "Now that the big guy is out of the cage, everybody better run for cover," said Palmer. Nicklaus, just out of college with a crew cut and on the tubby side, was the subject of abuse from the gallery, most of them Palmer fans. "Ohio Fats," and worse, was called out, but he never let it affect him, and after a few years Nicklaus also became a crowd favorite.

In 1966, Nicklaus became the first player to win successive Masters titles, and also won the Open at Muirfield—he liked the place so much he named his famed course in Ohio "Muirfield Village." The Open win gave him a complete set of the four Grand Slam titles, something he would achieve three times over. He won the Masters six times, the USPGA five times, the US Open four times, and the Open three. He considered winning the Open at St. Andrews a necessary part of

> I think when I play golf, yes, I have to make the world revolve around me. If you want to be the best at something, you have to make it revolve around what you are doing

JACK NICKLAUS

1961	1962	1966	1969	1972	1978
Claims his second US Amateur title with an 8&6 victory over Dudley Wysong. The tournament at that time was match play.	Wins the first of his 18 Major championships at the US Open. It is his first victory as a professional golfer.	Wins at the Masters, becoming the first golfer to successfully defend the title.	Makes his Ryder Cup debut at Birkdale. On the final day, he makes a famous concession to Tony Jacklin.	Becomes the first golfer to record a double career Grand Slam by winning the USPGA at Oakland Hills.	Named "Sportsman of the Year" by *Sports Illustrated* magazine.

△ **FOR A RECORD SIXTH TIME,** Nicklaus is presented with
a green jacket at Augusta, on this occasion by Bernhard
Langer, in 1986. At 46, Nicklaus remains the oldest winner.

◁ **NICKLAUS ACKNOWLEDGES** the crowd's applause
at Palm Beach Gardens, Florida, as he wins the USPGA
for the second time in 1971.

any complete golfing resumé and he did it twice, in 1970
and 1978. On the first occasion, Doug Sanders missed a
short putt on the 18th green to allow Nicklaus into an
18-hole playoff the next day. With the outcome still to be
decided at the short par-4 last, Nicklaus removed his
sweater and belted his drive through the green. He
chipped and putted for a three.

Nicklaus's last two Masters wins were special. In 1975
he held off Johnny Miller and Tom Weiskopf in a
remarkable three-way battle, which was settled when

Nicklaus holed from 45 ft (13 m) at the 16th.
In 1986, on the most exciting Sunday in
Masters history, Nicklaus swept to the
title at the age of 46 (see pp.230–31).

He kept winning when he went on to
the Seniors Tour, but didn't have the
appetite for "ceremonial" golf, as he put it.
Yet, the farewells were inevitable, and it all
ended on the Swilken Burn bridge on the
18th hole at St. Andrews in 2005.

1986
Wins the Masters for a record
sixth time—his last Major
victory—in his 25th year
as a golf professional.

1993
Comes back to win the
US Senior Open for the
second time after a
winless year in 1992.

1998
At 58, becomes the oldest player to
achieve a top-10 finish at a Major. A
plaque commemorating his career is
presented at the Masters.

2002
Teams up with Tiger Woods at the
made-for-TV "Battle of Bighorn."
The pair win and split the $1.2
million prize money.

2005
Nicklaus retires and is
also presented with the
Presidential Medal of
Freedom by President Bush.

Mickey Wright

MICKEY WRIGHT WAS NOT JUST THE ANNIKA SORENSTAM OF HER TIME, she possessed what is generally regarded as one of the best swings of any golfer, ever. Having left Stanford University at the end of her first year to pursue a golfing career, her early learning of the game and her sheer ruthlessness helped her to become the dominant player of her generation, winning a career Grand Slam by the time she was 27.

MICKEY WRIGHT WAS A SHY and modest character who simply let her clubs do the talking. Growing up in San Diego she broke 100 at age eleven, 90 a year later, and 70 at fourteen. When she arrived on tour she knew how to hit the ball exactly as she wanted.

Betsy Rawls, a friend and rival, suggested that "Mickey was able to move the club head so fast and hit the ball a very long way because her mechanics were so good. She was strong but she had no wasted movement in her swing, so that everything contributed to moving the club head."

Getting used to traveling and tour life didn't come easily to her. However, she threw herself into the golfing community, acting as secretary, treasurer, and president of the LPGA. Her first win came in 1956, but she had to learn one more important lesson before she could truly dominate, ironically from her rival Rawls. "Betsy taught me the most important thing of all: to take responsibility for everything that happens to you on the golf course; not to blame the greens for bad putting, the caddie for bad club selection, or the fates for a bad day."

Between 1956 and 1973 Wright won 82 times, including 13 Major championships. There were four US Open titles—her fourth in 1964 in San Diego in front of her parents being her personal favorite. In a four-year stretch between 1961 and 1964 she won 44 times, including 13 events in 1963 and eleven the following year. But the pressure was too great for her: if she didn't play the sponsors would threaten to withdraw their support, and she burned herself out playing too many tournaments. However, by the time she cut back her playing commitments she had won everything there was to win, and her success raised the profile of the women's game. Judy Rankin said, "Mickey's golf made the golf world sit up and take notice."

WRIGHT SHOWS OFF the Women's Titleholders Golf Tourney trophy in April 1961. She posted a score of 299, finishing one stroke ahead of the field.

PLAYER STATS

BORN February 14, 1935; San Diego, California, USA
HEIGHT 5 ft 9 in (1.75 m)
TURNED PRO 1955

DEBUT WIN 1956 Jacksonville Open
TOUR WINS 82 (all LPGA Tour)

MAJORS 13
LPGA CHAMPIONSHIP: Won 1958, 1960, 1961, 1963
US WOMEN'S OPEN: Won 1958, 1959, 1961, 1964
TITLEHOLDERS CHAMPIONSHIP: Won 1961, 1962
WESTERN OPEN: Won 1962, 1963, 1966

HONORS
LPGA Tour Money Winner: 1961, 1962, 1963, 1964

TALL AND STRONG, Mickey Wright had a classical swing and a sense of perfection that drove her to so many victories.

Perfection motivated me, doing it better than anyone who had ever done it, just as simple as that

MICKEY WRIGHT

Bob Charles

BOB CHARLES WAS A PIONEER and, in his time, was golf's greatest left-handed player. Until Mike Weir won in 1993, Charles was the first left-hander to have won a Major championship, and before Michael Campbell was victorious at the US Open in 2005, Charles was the only New Zealander to have won a Major. He is also the only golfer to become a Knight Companion of the New Zealand Order of Merit.

LIKE MICKELSON, BOB CHARLES is naturally right-handed, at least at everything except two-handed sports. His parents were both left-handed and so he learned the game that way, using some of their spare clubs. The availability of left-handed equipment has become much wider, which was not always the case, and as a result there are many more successful left-handed golfers than there once were. Charles's success, and endorsement of left-handed clubs, was a significant step in developing the market.

Charles won the New Zealand Open, for the first of four times, as an 18-year-old amateur, in 1954. But it was not until 1960 that he turned professional, having spent his time honing his game while working as a bank clerk.

His greatest triumph came after only three years as a professional when he won the Open at Royal Lytham & St. Annes in 1963. In the last ever 36-hole playoff in the Open championship, Charles defeated American Phil Rodgers by eight strokes. He had singled-putted 11 times in the morning round and it was his success on the greens that became the hallmark of his career. At the time, the UK *Sunday Telegraph* reporter wrote: "When he was on the green, the hole was never safe. Keeping his wrists unbroken and moving the club head more slowly under pressure than the game's case-hardened chroniclers had ever seen, Charles dropped putt after putt from any distance."

He soon started winning consistently and after a career of remarkable longevity and including his many years of winning on the Champions tour, he had collected over 66 titles on five continents. On the 30th anniversary of his Open win almost to the day, he claimed a second Senior British Open win, coming from one behind Tommy Horton on the last hole to win with a birdie. *Golf Weekly* reported: "If you had to put your life on someone sinking the winning putt in a Major, that someone would be Charles. When it comes to testing seven-footers there is no one better."

▷ **IN 1993 THE NEW ZEALANDER** returned to Royal Lytham, the scene of his Open triumph 30 years earlier, and won the British Seniors Open.

◁ **BOB CHARLES WAS THE FIRST** left-hander to win a Major championship. Here he lifts the Claret Jug, following his Open triumph.

PLAYER STATS

BORN March 14, 1936; Carterton, New Zealand
HEIGHT 6 ft 1 in (1.85 m)
TURNED PRO 1960

DEBUT WIN 1961 New Zealand PGA Championship
TOUR WINS 66
PGA TOUR: 6
AUSTRALASIAN TOUR: 8
CHAMPIONS TOUR: 36
OTHER: 16

MAJORS 1
MASTERS: T15th 1963
US OPEN: 3rd 1964/T3rd 1970
THE OPEN: Won 1963
USPGA: T2nd 1968

HONORS
Knight Companion of the New Zealand Order of Merit: 1999

> I'm an introvert. I take things seriously, particularly my golf. That's my business and the golf course is my office

BOB CHARLES

Lee Trevino

LEE TREVINO WAS ONE OF THE GREAT CHARACTERS OF GOLF. As both an entertainer and a golfer, he was of the highest order. He won six Major championships—the Open, the US Open, and the USPGA twice each—talking and wise-cracking all the way. And all after growing up in poverty in Dallas, and only making it to the tour at the age of 28.

PLAYER STATS

BORN December 1, 1939; Dallas, Texas
HEIGHT 5 ft 7 in (1.70 m)
TURNED PRO 1960

DEBUT WIN 1968 US Open
TOUR WINS 85
PGA TOUR: 29
CHAMPIONS TOUR: 29
OTHER: 27

MAJORS 6
MASTERS: T10th 1975, 1985
US OPEN: Won 1968, 1971
THE OPEN: Won 1971, 1972
USPGA: Won 1974, 1984

HONORS
Vardon Trophy Winner: 1970, 1971, 1972, 1974, 1980
Ryder Cup Team: 1969, 1971, 1973, 1975, 1979, 1981
Ryder Cup Captain: 1985
Champions Tour Rookie of the Year: 1990

Cover star, July 1971

TREVINO WON his first Major title (and first ever Tour title) in 1968 at Oak Hill, beating Jack Nicklaus by four strokes.

IN 1967, TREVINO CHALLENGED as an unknown at the US Open in his first season on tour. He did so well that he finished fifth (winning $6,000), and later that year, was named Rookie of the Year.

Before becoming a professional on the PGA tour, Trevino worked at golf courses and hustled in and around Dallas, Texas. In one of the numerous stories told about Trevino in his early days, he is said to have won many matches for money at the par-3 pitch-and-putt course where he worked, and instead of using a club, he would use a Dr. Pepper bottle. His golf may have been entirely self-taught, but his dedication to his sport was Hoganesque.

One of Trevino's first jobs was as the assistant golf professional at Horizon Hills in El Paso. He took part in money matches, and came into contact with professional golfers. When Ray Floyd visited the club, he was flabbergasted when he was told that he was playing the kid who took his clubs from the car to the locker room. But Floyd trailed after each of the first two rounds of the 54-hole match and needed an eagle at the last to win. When he got back on tour he told his peers, "Boys, there's a little Mexican kid out in El Paso. When he comes out here, you'll have to make way for him."

When he finally made it on to the tour, Trevino put down a marker by beating Jack Nicklaus by four strokes at the 1968 US Open. His big year however, when he was christened the "Super Mex," came in 1971, when in successive starts, he won the US Open, the Canadian Open, and the Open Championship at Birkdale. A year later at Muirfield, with Nicklaus trying to win a fourth major in a year and when Tony Jacklin was at his very best, Trevino won again. During the final round, he saw

WINNING A SECOND successive Open in 1972 at Muirfield was joy for Trevino, but misery for England's Tony Jacklin, when the American chipped in at the 17th hole in the final round.

Pressure? These guys don't know what pressure is. Pressure is when you're playing some hard-nosed gamblers for $25 and you've only got $10 in your pocket.

LEE TREVINO

THE HIGH-ROLLER

Lee Trevino was one of golf's great showmen. He loved spending the money he won, reportedly losing two fortunes, but luckily gaining three. He won two Major titles in 1971, indeed it was his most prolific year in terms of titles won, and by the early 1980s, he was second on the PGA Tour career money list, behind Jack Nicklaus.

Trevino liked to travel in style

off Nicklaus, but became involved in a furious duel with Jacklin. When he holed a chip for par at the par-5 17th, having made a mess of the hole, he had seemingly lost his chance as Jacklin seemed certain to birdie it. However, apparently unnerved by Trevino's recovery, Jacklin three-putted for a bogey, thus handing Trevino an unlikely victory.

Trevino won the USPGA in 1974 and 1984, but by then, he was suffering from severe back problems; in 1975 was hit by lightning at the Western Open and was never the same again. However, on turning 50 his career experienced a revival and Trevino had several good seasons competing on the Seniors Tour winning four of the tour's Major titles, two of them in 1992. He was indomitable of spirit throughout. "How can they beat me?" he said alluding to his life's misfortunes. "I've been struck by lightning, had two back operations, and been divorced twice."

Off the course, he was private; on it he was every bit the "Merry Mex." At the World Match Play in 1972, Jacklin made a simple request, "Lee, is it all right if we don't talk today?". "Sure, Tony," Trevino replied, "You don't have to talk, just listen."

"MERRY MEX" ONCE SAID, "I played the tour in 1967 and told jokes and nobody laughed. Then I won the Open... told the same jokes, and everybody laughed like hell."

Tony Jacklin

FROM THE VIBRANCY OF THE 1960s came a golfer to excite Britain like never before. Tony Jacklin was a product of his age and although his spell at the very top was brief, he was the brightest of stars. He won the Open and the US Open, but perhaps his greatest act for European golf was masterminding the Ryder Cup revival in the 1980s, turning it into a genuine contest.

◁ **JACKLIN EMERGED** as golf's brightest star of the Swinging Sixties and for a time eclipsed the achievements of even Jack Nicklaus.

▽ **AT ROYAL LYTHAM IN 1969** Jacklin became the first Englishman for 18 years to raise the Open Championship Claret Jug.

JACKLIN WAS FROM NORTHERN England but headed south, and developed his golf at the Potters Bar Golf Club in Hertfordshire under a hard taskmaster—the former Australian rugby league player turned golfer, Bill Shankland. He was a style-conscious character: for an interview early in his career he turned up wearing gold lame trousers, a gold cashmere sweater over a white polo neck, and gold shoes. Scotland's Eric Brown said of his first encounter with Jacklin, "I thought he was a big-headed so-and-so. But he has all the shots. Guts. Dedication. And he's cocky. He has a chance to win any tournament, including the Open."

Two years later, in 1969, Jacklin did just that, winning the Open at Royal Lytham. He was the first home champion since Max Faulkner in 1951, and it was the first crack in the dominance of US golfers. The next

CADY TO SCUNTHORPE

Tony Jacklin travels past assembled fans in a vintage white Cadillac in his home town of Scunthorpe, Lincolnshire. The motorcade was held to honor his victory in the 1970 US Open at Hazeltine. Jacklin led from the start, eventually securing a seven-shot victory over Dave Hill; it was the greatest winning margin for almost 50 years.

■ The US Open champion returns home

year he won the US Open at the new venue of Hazeltine in Minneapolis. He led after every round and won by seven shots to become the first British winner since Ted Ray in 1920. He was also the first Briton, since Harry Vardon in 1900, to hold both the British and US Opens at the same time.

Jacklin was a regular at the Open until 1972 at Muirfield, when Lee Trevino chipped in on the 71st hole for an unlikely par and Jacklin, shocked at the sudden turnaround, three-putted for a bogey. He was never quite the same player again. Off the course, his wife Vivienne died of a brain hemorrhage in 1988, and in business he was never a successful as he would have liked.

As a player he always battled greater opposition, but it was the Ryder Cup that cemented his place in history. In 1969 he was involved in the incident when Jack Nicklaus conceded his two-foot (60 cm) putt at the last to tie the match (see p. 264). When he held the captaincy in 1983, Jacklin did it his way. He demanded first-class treatment for the players, and they flourished under his inspirational leadership. With Seve Ballesteros leading the team on the course, Jacklin made light of a narrow defeat in 1983, then guided Europe to their first

Ryder Cup win for 28 years, in 1985, and a first ever win on US soil at Muirfield Village in 1987. He retired after the tied match at the Belfry in 1989, having played his part in re-establishing the cup as a viable contest, and one of the world's most exciting sporting events.

JACKLIN STRUGGLED in the late 1970s and early 1980s, but found a new role as an inspirational Ryder Cup captain.

This was my Everest, and no one can take away... that moment when I sat on its peak

TONY JACKLIN, ON WINNING THE 1969 OPEN

Raymond Floyd

RAYMOND FLOYD WON A FEW TIMES VERY EARLY in his career, but was much more successful later on. He went from being a playboy of the tour—the heir to Walter Hagen—to being a family man, and one of the game's revered elder statesmen. In 1993 he became the oldest man to play in the Ryder Cup, winning three points out of four at the Belfry.

> After you have won a tournament, you have a warm glow. When I was a bachelor, I used to celebrate some after I'd won
>
> RAYMOND FLOYD

FLOYD WAS THE SON OF A MILITARY MAN who opened a driving range when he left the army. He arrived on tour in 1963, aged 20, and four months later had his first victory. But winning came too easily. "Winning tournaments meant nothing to me," he said later. "I thought the tour was just one big ball, traveling from Miami to Los Angeles to New York, and all those other exciting places."

Floyd won the first of four Major titles at the USPGA in 1969. It was still party time, but in 1973 he met, fell in love with, and married Maria Primoli. She was to have the most profound affect on his life and his career. When Ray withdrew from a tournament in mid-round two days of soul-searching followed. "Maria jumped on me like a tiger," Floyd explained. "It helped put my life in proper focus. From that moment on, I was a more mature, patient, and responsible man."

Floyd's best golf was still to come. In 1976, he won the Masters by eight strokes, tying Jack Nicklaus's then tournament record of 271. A second USPGA title arrived in 1982, after an opening 63 at Southern Hills, the best round of his career, which included nine successive threes. In 1986 he won the US Open at Shinnecock Hills with a last round of 66, aged 43. Four years later he almost won the Masters again but lost in a playoff to Nick Faldo.

When Floyd learned how to focus on the scent of victory during a round, he would get a fixed look in his eyes, concentrating on nothing but the next shot. Fellow competitors called it "the stare." "When he gets that look in his eyes," said Lanny Wadkins, "he's hard to handle."

FAMILY MAN RAY FLOYD found lasting success late in his career, winning the US Open in 1986.

FLOYD COMBINED GREAT POWER with a soft touch, and is generally recognized as one of the best chippers the game has ever seen.

Hale Irwin

HE MISSED ONE OF THE SHORTEST putts in the history of Major championships—he actually missed the ball—but made one of the longest, at least one of the longer, important putts. Hale Irwin, three-time US Open winner, and the Tiger Woods of the Senior Tour was as intense a competitor as you could hope to find in any sporting arena.

IRWIN LEARNED THE GAME on a sand-greens course in Kansas. His first love was baseball, but in college he starred as a defensive player on the football field. "I was undersized, under speed, under everything," Irwin recalled. "But I had the determination to get it done. The intensity that I had to play at allowed me to compete with others with better skills."

His game was solid, but his strength, of consistently hitting fairways and greens, got its greatest reward at the US Open. The set up for the 1974 championship at Winged Foot was so difficult it became known as a "massacre." Battling a young Tom Watson and an old Arnold Palmer, Irwin won at seven over par. He won again at Inverness five years later, despite a poor final round in which he admitted "choking from the first tee."

That same year, in the 1979 Open at Royal Lytham, Irwin fought out the last two rounds with Seve Ballesteros and came off second best. Here was a clash of styles and personalities. Irwin was the anti-Seve and could not believe that driving the ball so waywardly could earn rewards. In 1983, at Royal Birkdale, Irwin finished runner-up to Tom Watson, but was left ruing a bogey at the 14th in the third round where he went to tap-in from two inches and hit an air shot—the putter hit the ground first and went over the ball.

But in 1990 at Medinah, a hat trick of US Open titles arrived, as he had dreamed it would two weeks earlier. He played the last eight holes in five under and holed from over 50 feet at the last hole, celebrating by circling the green high-fiving spectators. The putt got him into a playoff and he beat Mike Donald the following day.

Irwin qualified to play on the Champions Tour in 1995 when he reached the age of 50 and enjoyed great success, winning more than twice as many Champions Tour titles as PGA titles. Having won 45 times, including seven Major victories, he tops the all-time Champions Tour money list with earnings of over $23 million.

▽ **HALE IRWIN'S CONSISTENT PLAY** made him an ideal contender at the US Open, which he won on three occasions.

▷ **IRWIN CELEBRATES** the huge putt that got him into a playoff at the 1990 US Open at Medinah: he won the following day.

Nancy Lopez

AS A STAR WHOSE SUCCESS and personality helped massively to raise the profile of her sport, Nancy Lopez stands alongside Arnold Palmer and Seve Ballesteros. She arrived in the late 1970s like a ray of sunshine, and maintained a long career while also raising a family. She did it all … winning a host of awards and three Major Championships, but not the US Open.

PLAYER STATS

BORN January 6, 1957; Torrance, California
HEIGHT 5 ft 5 in (1.70 m)
TURNED PRO 1978

DEBUT WIN Bent Tree Classic 1978
TOUR WINS 52
LPGA TOUR: 48
OTHER: 4

MAJORS 3
LPGA CHAMPIONSHIP: Won 1978, 1985, 1989
KRAFT NABISCO: T3rd 1995
US WOMEN'S OPEN: 2nd 1975, 1977, 1989, 1997
DU MAURIER CLASSIC: 2nd 1979, 1996

HONORS
LPGA Player of the Year: 1978, 1979, 1985, 1988
Rookie of the Year: 1978
Curtis Cup Team: 1976
Solheim Cup Team: 1990
Solheim Cup Captain: 2005

LOPEZ WAS ONE OF THE BEST women golfers of all time. She showed promise an an early age by winning the New Mexico Amateur, aged 12. Lopez turned professional in 1977 and in her first full season on the tour, in 1978, she was a sensation. She won nine tournaments in all, including the LPGA Championship, but it was a run of five successive victories that captured the imagination of media and public alike.

It helped that she possessed a charming manner and a dazzling smile. She was a star but seemingly so down to earth. Her father, Domingo, was a three-handicap golfer who had encouraged her talent but never pushed. Her mother, Marina, died unexpectedly just as she was about to go on tour, a devastating blow that only strengthened her will to succeed. "I wanted to win for my parents because they sacrificed a lot for me to play golf," Lopez said. "They were always there when I needed them and I wanted them to be proud of me. I couldn't do anything except play golf to repay them."

AMERICAN IDOL
The great Mickey Wright said of the young Lopez: "Never in my life have I seen such control from someone so young." However, success could not last forever, and the wins became less frequent after she married baseball player Ray Knight and started a family.

She was runner up at the US Open on four occasions, the first in 1975 as an amateur. In 1997 she won for the 48th time on tour but yet again finished runner-up at the US Open, beaten by England's Alison Nicholas, who had grown up idolizing the American. "I probably won't sleep tonight because I'll be thinking about every shot... and what I could have done," Lopez sighed. But she was no loser. She was a great competitor and a great champion.

LOPEZ LEADS AMERICA to victory at the 2005 Solheim Cup, along with Christina Kim (left) and Natalie Gulbis (right).

> My image reflects on me, my husband, my family, my life.
> # Everyone should be good in public

NANCY LOPEZ

A SIGHT THAT was seen time and again in her early days as a sensational new star on tour–Lopez smiling in celebration of victory.

Johnny Miller

BACK IN THE MID-1970s, you might have been considered crazy to suggest that Johnny Miller would become better known as a golf broadcaster than a player. For a brief spell, the lanky, blond bombshell from California played the finest golf you could wish to see, and won two Major championships. These days he is one of the finest commentators on golf you could wish to hear.

PLAYER STATS

BORN April 29, 1947; San Francisco, California
HEIGHT 6 ft 2 in (1.88 m)
TURNED PRO 1969

DEBUT WIN 1971 Southern Open Invitational
TOUR WINS 30
PGA TOUR: 25
OTHER: 5

MAJORS 2
MASTERS: T2nd 1971, 1975, 1981
US OPEN: Won 1973
THE OPEN: Won 1976
USPGA: T11th 1977

HONORS
PGA Tour Money Leader: 1974
PGA Tour Player of the Year: 1974
Ryder Cup Team: 1975, 1981

△ **WINNING THE OPEN** at Birkdale in 1976, ahead of Jack Nicklaus and Seve Ballesteros, confirmed Miller as one of the game's best.

When I get going it's like I'm in a trance…
I can black everything out.

JOHNNY MILLER

WHAT A SHOW MILLER PUT ON between 1973 and 1976. He won the US Open at Oakmont in 1973 with a final round of 63, the first time anyone had scored so low during a Major championship, let alone en route to victory. Oakmont has the fastest and most devilish greens imaginable and is a beast of a course. There was a storm prior to the final round that softened the greens, but still Miller produced one of the finest rounds ever compiled. The 26-year-old Californian, who had learned his golf at Olympic Club in San Francisco, and Pebble Beach, opened with four straight birdies but still appeared to be a long way back. Having gone out in 32, Miller came home in 31 and set a target no one could beat.

In 1974 Miller won the first three tournaments he played in and eight in all. The following year he won four more titles, and was involved in a thrilling contest at the Masters in which Jack Nicklaus beat Miller and Tom Weiskopf. In 1976 Miller won the Open at Royal Birkdale with a final round of 66, leaving Nicklaus and a young Seve Ballesteros in his wake. Victories were sporadic after the Open, because he struggled on the greens. By the end of the 1980s, he had essentially retired from the tour and become a commentator for NBC television, where he is always known to speak his mind. One of the few events he still played in was the AT&T Pebble Beach Pro-am. In 1994, in a final-day tussle involving Tom Watson and Tom Kite, Miller pulled off a remarkable victory. "This isn't right, this is a fluke," he said. "I'm not a golfer, I'm a television announcer."

▷ **MILLER AT THE OPEN** at Royal Birkdale in 1971, the scene of his triumph five years later. He had top-five finishes at the Masters and US Open in 1971.

◁◁ **TOM WATSON HOLDS** aloft the Open Claret Jug for the fifth time at Birkdale in 1983. He beat Andy Bean and Hale Irwin by one stroke.

◁ **IN PARTNERSHIP WITH JACK NICKLAUS,** Watson was a member of the greatest ever American Ryder Cup team in 1981.

▽ **ON HIS WAY TO WINNING** his first green jacket at Augusta in 1977, Watson is watched by Ben Crenshaw as he tees off at the 4th.

Tom Watson

BY WINNING THE OPEN CHAMPIONSHIP FIVE TIMES, Tom Watson proved himself one of the greatest golfers of all time and endeared himself permanently to the British galleries. In the mid-1970s, he took over from Jack Nicklaus as the game's best player and, starting with the Open in 1975, won eight Major championships in as many years.

PLAYER STATS

BORN September 4, 1949; Kansas City, Missouri
HEIGHT 5 ft 9 in (1.75 m)
TURNED PRO 1971

DEBUT WIN 1974 Western Open
PROFESSIONAL WINS 62
PGA TOUR: 39
CHAMPIONS TOUR: 10
OTHER: 13

MAJORS 8
MASTERS: Won 1977, 1981
US OPEN: Won 1982
THE OPEN: Won 1975, 1977, 1980, 1982, 1983
USPGA: 2nd 1978

HONORS
PGA Tour Money Winner: 1977, 1978, 1979, 1980, 1984
Vardon Trophy Winner: 1977, 1978, 1979
PGA Tour Player of the Year: 1977, 1978, 1979, 1980, 1982, 1984
Ryder Cup Team: 1977, 1981, 1983, 1989
Ryder Cup Captain: 1993

THE VICTORIOUS RYDER CUP captain at the Belfry in 1993, when the US retained the trophy they won in dramatic circumstances at Kiawah Island in 1991.

Not as good as a few, but better than most.

Let's put it that way

TOM WATSON, SUMMING UP HIS CAREER

IT WAS WATSON'S GREAT PLAY that forced Jack Nicklaus to say, "I'm tired of giving it my best shot and coming up short." Some players briefly got the better of Nicklaus, but Watson managed it on a regular basis (see pp. 228–29) Between 1975 and 1983, he won eight Majors, and matched the achievement of James Braid, J.H. Taylor, and Peter Thomson by winning five Opens. He also led the money list in the US for four years in a row.

But when Watson, who grew up in Kansas City and has lived there ever since, graduated from Stanford University, he was unsure about what to do as a career. He had been introduced to the game by his father and turned professional in 1971 with the flimsiest of games. What held him together was his brilliant scrambling skills, his short game, and his bold putting. Initially, he could not win and was written off as a choker, but he worked with Byron Nelson and once he started winning, he could not stop.

Watson won the Open on his first appearance, at Carnoustie in 1975. Two years later he beat Nicklaus in the final round of the Masters and then again at Turnberry in the Open. They played together over the weekend, shooting 65s in the third round to distance themselves from the field before Watson edged out Nicklaus by one shot, shooting 65 on the final day. It was a round of electrifying golf as they pushed each other. One ahead playing the last, Watson hit his approach to two feet. But Nicklaus, who had been in trouble off the tee, holed from over 30 ft (9 m) for a birdie to keep the pressure on. They left the green arm-in-arm to wild scenes.

THE LOSS OF A FREIND

Watson was Player of the Year in 2003, but the year also was marked by sadness. His long time caddie, Bruce Edwards, was diagnosed with the progressive neurodegenerative disorder Lou Gehrig Disease. Watson helped found the organization Driving 4 Life to help fight the disease by donating $1 million.

Edwards was Watson's caddie for almost 30 years

HITTING THE WALL

Watson won again at Muirfield in 1980, Troon in 1982, and Birkdale in 1983. He had also taken the Masters again in 1981 and won the US Open at Pebble Beach in 1982, where he had played as a student. But in 1984 at St. Andrews, where he was trying to tie Harry Vardon's record of six Open titles, he went over the green at the 17th in the final round and finished against a stone wall. He lost to Seve Ballesteros and was never quite the same again. His putting went way off. On good days it was the Tom Watson of old, on bad, it was just old Tom Watson. But he kept at it, and in 1996 he won the Memorial after a nine-year gap, and two years after that, at the age of 48, became the oldest winner of the Colonial. He captained the US to victory in the Ryder Cup at the Belfry in 1993 and once he qualified for the Champions Tour, he won the Senior British Open three times.

◁ **SEVE IN FULL FLOW** was the most incredible sight European golf had ever seen. Fans were enraptured for three decades.

▽ **SEVE SHOWS OFF** his brilliant short-game skills at the Spanish Open in 1991. He won the title in 1981, 1985, and 1995.

▽▽ **HIS MOST FAMOUS** celebration—Seve winning the second of his three Open successes, at St. Andrews in 1984.

Severiano Ballesteros

IT WAS NOT JUST WHAT "SEVE" BALLESTEROS DID, but the way that he did it. He was thrilling, he was charismatic, he was swashbuckling, he never gave up; he might play an awful shot one minute but follow it with a brilliant recovery the next. He was the Arnold Palmer of Europe. Golf in Spain, across Continental Europe, and the whole European Tour owes him everything.

He's probably the most creative player who has ever played the game. He was a genius

TIGER WOODS

BALLESTEROS WAS THE LEADER. He was the first of the "Big Five"—Nick Faldo, Bernhard Langer, Sandy Lyle, and Ian Woosnam were the others—to be born, and he was the first at everything else. He was the first to win a Major, to win in the US, to win an American Major, to realize that the Americans could be defeated in the Ryder Cup.

His uncle, Ramón Sota, was Spain's most famous player before Seve. All four of his elder brothers caddied and played golf at the club in the small fishing village of Pedreña, near Santander in northern Spain. Seve followed suit but spent much of his early time playing only with a rusty 3-iron on the beach. There he learned the art, and not just the skill, of improvization.

Seve turned professional just before his 17th birthday, but it was at the Open Championship at Royal Birkdale in 1976 that the world discovered him. He led for the first three days, but was overtaken by Johnny Miller on the final day. But the youngster stole the show. He eagled the 17th, then played an audacious chip and run, between two bunkers, over the bumps and hollows, to tie Jack Nicklaus for second place. Between 1976 and 1995, he would win 87 times around the world. He won the World Match Play Championship five times, loving the head-to-head contests, and he thrived in Britain, where both the galleries and the press adored him.

OPEN GLORY
In 1979 he won the Open at Royal Lytham, playing alongside Hale Irwin over the weekend (see pp. 226–27). By then Irwin was a two-time US Open champion, adept at hitting the fairways and the greens, and playing steady golf. The contrast was absolute. Ballesteros blasted the ball with all his might and then set about the next shot, its brilliance usually in direct correlation to the trouble he found himself in. At the 16th hole in the final round, a temporary parking lot just off the fairway was in his way, but no matter. "Parking lot champion," they said in the US. It only made him win more.

At St. Andrews in 1984, Seve fought out a brilliant duel with Tom Watson, who was going for a sixth Open title. As Watson got into trouble on the Road Hole, Ballesteros rolled in a birdie putt on the 18th green that sparked the most joyous and triumphant fist-pumping celebration. It became his trademark and endeared him

▽ **IT WAS LOVE AT FIRST SIGHT** as the young Ballesteros became an instant hit with the British gallery at the 1976 Open at Birkdale.

even more to the public. Four years later, back at Royal Lytham once more, Seve scored a blistering 65 in the final round to beat both Nick Price and Nick Faldo. "I told him afterward it was the greatest round of golf I had ever seen," Faldo recalled.

The three Open titles were joined by two Masters green jackets. In 1980 he led by 10 strokes with nine holes to play, eventually winning by four. Three years later he shot a final-round 69 and won by four again from Ben Crenshaw and Tom Kite. His European contemporaries saw Ballesteros winning the biggest prizes and followed suit. At Augusta, six Europeans won a collective 11 green jackets between 1980 and 1999.

Seve had more chances to win the Masters without success, notably in 1986 when, in the last round, he hit an awful four-iron into the pond at the 15th hole and lost to Jack Nicklaus. From that day on, he was not quite the same golfer. More specifically, it was a long-term back complaint that ultimately meant his career would not be as long as some. His body could not stand up to the punishment of his violent swing and, always an instinctive player, he could not refine the technique. He won for the last time in Madrid, at the Spanish Open, at the age of 38, and following years of struggling with his game, he retired on the eve of the 2007 Open at Carnoustie.

RYDER CUP COLOSSUS

During Seve's last years on tour, his short game was still magnificent, but he could not get the ball on the fairway. In his last Ryder Cup singles match against Tom Lehman in 1995 he barely hit a fairway or a green in regulation but employed some mystical powers to extend the match to the 15th hole. However, the Ryder Cup brought out the best in Ballesteros.

Under Tony Jacklin's captaincy in 1983 in West Palm Beach, Europe lost, but only narrowly. Ballesteros played an awesome shot—the best Jack Nicklaus had ever seen—from a bunker over 200 yards from the green, with a 3-wood, from a lie that most would struggle to get a 6-iron to. It was his third shot, but it helped him escape with an unlikely half against Fuzzy Zoeller. Afterward, his European teammates were disconsolate but

Seve, recognizing a major shift in the balance of power, was upbeat. He encouraged the team to celebrate as if they had won. The next time, they did. In 1987, Europe was victorious for the first time in the US and Seve started a legendary partnership with José Maria Olazábal. They won 11 times together, halving two matches and losing only two. They had a "no sorrys" policy and never admitted that any precarious situation was irretrievable. "When Seve gets his Porsche going, not even San Pedro in heaven could stop him," Olazábal said. It was certainly the case when he charged around Valderrama on a buggy as captain in 1997. Victory on the only occasion the match has been played on Spanish soil was his "destino," like everything in his remarkable career.

◁ **DARK AND BROODING**, sometimes Ballesteros was at his best with the world– particularly Americans–against him.

▽ **SEVE CELEBRATES VICTORY** at St. Andrews in 1984. The joy is unconfined after an epic final-round duel with Tom Watson.

1976
Shoots to prominence by finishing runner-up to Johnny Miller in the 1976 Open at Royal Birkdale.

1979
Seve wins his first Open in 1979 at Royal Lytham, becoming the youngest winner of the century.

1980
He cruises to victory at the Masters. Aged 23, Seve becomes the second non-American and first European to wear the green jacket.

1983
At the Ryder Cup at West Palm Beach, Seve plays the shot of his career, but Europe loses narrowly.

1984
At St. Andrews a second Open Championship–and fourth Major–is won after a duel with Tom Watson.

Seve was golf's Cirque du Soleil.

The passion, artistry, skill, drama

NICK FALDO

THE SEVE TROPHY IN IRELAND

Great Britain and Ireland captain Nick Faldo receives the Seve Trophy from the captain of Continental Europe, Seve Ballesteros, after winning at the Heritage in Ireland in 2007. The event was started in 2000 to celebrate Seve's love of international team matchplay golf, with Seve himself lifting the trophy in the first year.

■ Faldo receives the Seve Trophy from Ballesteros

NOTHING IS IMPOSSIBLE

Throughout his career, Seve was renowned for going for high risk shots. At the European Masters in Switzerland in 1993, he put on a brilliant final-round charge, but all appeared lost when he sliced his drive at the last. He lay between two trees, with a 6 ft (2 m) wall just in front of him. He had to go over the wall, under the branches, then over a swimming pool, some tents, four more trees, and a bunker to reach the green. His caddie, Billy Foster, told him it was impossible, but Seve was indignant. He played the shot and the ball found the tiniest of gaps and landed just in front of the green. He then chipped in for his third successive birdie, but ultimately lost by one stroke. "It was difficult," he admitted later, "but I wanted to make a three, I wanted to win. I am always looking to go forward, not backward."

1985
Seve is an integral part of the first European Ryder Cup victory at the Belfry, winning 3.5 points.

1988
Wins a third Open Championship at Royal Lytham. His final-round 65 is too good for Nick Faldo and Nick Price.

1991
Seve claims his 5th World Match Play title, at Wentworth, equaling Gary Player's record.

1997
Captains the European Ryder Cup team to victory on home soil at Valderrama.

2000
Captains Europe to victory in the inaugural Seve Trophy.

Ben Crenshaw

BEN CRENSHAW WAS ONE OF THE BEST PUTTERS of his generation and twice he conquered the greens at Augusta National to win the Masters. He was nicknamed "Gentle Ben" but ironically he was an emotional character who was given to bouts of temper. This trait was highlighted when he captained the US team to victory at one of the most fiery Ryder Cup competitions of recent years.

PLAYER STATS

BORN January 11, 1952; Austin, Texas
HEIGHT 5 ft 9 in (1.75 m)
TURNED PRO 1973

DEBUT WIN 1973 San Antonio Texas Open
TOUR WINS 27
PGA TOUR: 19
OTHER: 8

MAJORS 2
MASTERS: Won 1984, 1995
US OPEN: T3rd 1975
THE OPEN: T2nd 1978, 1979
USPGA: 2nd 1979

HONORS
Ryder Cup Team: 1981, 1983, 1987, 1995
Ryder Cup Captain: 1999
Bob Jones Award: 1991

SEVE BALLESTEROS HELPS a delighted Crenshaw into a Masters green jacket at Augusta for the first time in 1984.

CRENSHAW BECAME A STAR of college golf and quickly made an impact when he won his first event on the PGA Tour at the Texas Open in 1973. He was from Austin, Texas, just as Tom Kite was, and the pair enjoyed a long-standing friendly rivalry. At least a rivalry was perceived. They were very different characters: Kite, organized, consistent, a more mechanical swing; Crenshaw, an emotional, more go-with-the-flow, feel player.

In 1984, Crenshaw won the Masters for the first time, coming from two behind Kite on the final day with a 68 to win by two from Tom Watson. Throughout his career, aside from brief periods of banishment from his bag, Crenshaw used "Little Ben"—a putter bought for him by his father when he was 16-years-old. "I leaned on that putter hard to bail me out," Crenshaw said. "It did some extraordinary things."

THE GREAT REVIVAL

Crenshaw's second Masters victory came at Augusta in 1995 in the most emotional circumstances. His life-long coach from Austin Country Club, Harvey Penick, had died the previous Sunday, so he and Tom Kite went back mid-week for the funeral. On the following Sunday, Crenshaw beat Davis Love III with a final round of 68 to take the title. "I had a 15th club in the bag and it was Harvey," an emotional Crenshaw said afterward. "It was like someone had their hand on my shoulder this week and guided me through."

In 1999, at Brookline, Crenshaw was the captain of the US Ryder Cup team. The US trailed by four points after the first two days, but at a press conference on the Saturday night, Crenshaw simply said, "I'm a big believer in fate. I have a

good feeling about this. That's all I'm going to say." The following day the American players won the singles by 8½ points to 3½, the biggest comeback ever in the event. Passions boiled over, however, and celebrations at the 17th green, when José Maria Olazábal was still to putt, made for a controversial finale (see p.236).

CRENSHAW WAS ONE of golf's finest putters, and his philosophy was simple: "The ball which arrives at the hole with the proper speed has an infinitely greater chance of falling in the hole from any entrance."

Bernhard Langer

BERNHARD LANGER IS A MAN OF PATIENCE AND PERSEVERANCE. Overcoming the yips on multiple occasions and yet still conquering the greens at Augusta illustrates this. Twice he was Masters champion and both times this devout Christian donned the green jacket on Easter Sunday. He also enjoyed a spectacular triumph as Ryder Cup captain on US soil.

THOUGH BEST KNOWN for using a broom-handled putter, Langer twice mastered the greens at Augusta with a conventional club.

LANGER'S CZECH-BORN FATHER escaped from a Siberia-bound prisoner-of-war train in 1945 and settled in Anhausen, Germany. From the age of eight Bernhard, with his brother Erwin, cycled the five miles to Augsburg Golf Club, where he started caddying. He fell in love with the game and went on to become his country's best and most famous player, winning the World Cup for Germany in 1990 and again 16 years later at the age of 49.

Langer's talent became evident when he won the Cacharel Under-25s title in 1979 by a remarkable 17 strokes. He suffered a number of near misses in the Open but twice won the Masters. In 1985 he was six behind before he eagled the 13th in the penultimate round. The next day, four birdies in six holes on the back nine sealed the win. In 1993 he eagled the 13th again to take the title.

WHATEVER IT TAKES

Although he would always go to whatever lengths necessary (see right), the hallmark of Langer's career has been an attention to detail and precision. Playing with him in the Ryder Cup, Colin Montgomerie revealed that when giving him a yardage Langer had responded: "Is that from the front of the sprinkler head or the back?." He suffered from bouts of nervous twitches, but each time he fought back: using the left-below-right putting method; then moving his left hand down the shaft and clamping his forearm to the shaft with his right hand; then going to the long putter. "I don't care what it looks like," he said, "We don't get paid for looking good." Which is just as well, as at the Masters in 1985 he wore a red top and admitted looking like a Christmas tree when he put on the green jacket, but he redeemed himself when winning the Masters again in 1993.

LANGER LEAVES NOTHING to chance, but at Fulford, England, in 1981 he decided his best option was to climb a tree before chipping to safety.

His Ryder Cup career was mixed. His worst moment came in 1991, when he missed a 6 ft (2 m) putt on the last green to lose his match, and the Cup. It was a devastating blow, but a week later he won the German Masters in a playoff. Under his captaincy in 2004, Europe recorded a record nine-point win at Oakland Hills.

> Good things can come out of everything. When you go through bad times, good can follow, because you learn more in bad times than in good times.

BERNHARD LANGER

Sandy Lyle

BLESSED WITH SO MUCH NATURAL TALENT and such an amiable character, Sandy Lyle is perhaps the most beloved of all modern British golfers. In 1985, at Royal St. George's, he became the first British player to win the Open since Tony Jacklin in 1969, and in 1988 he became the first Briton ever to win the Masters. That victory included one of the greatest shots in championship golf.

IN 1988 LYLE became the first Briton to win the Masters at Augusta, leading the way for Nick Faldo and Ian Woosnam to follow.

NO ONE WHO WAS AT AUGUSTA that Sunday afternoon, or watching late at night in Britain, will ever forget it. Needing a three to win at the sharply uphill 18th hole, Lyle was in a bunker off the tee. "I'm dead," Lyle thought as he walked off the tee, but the moment he saw the ball on the upslope of the face of the bunker, with a good lie, his mood improved. He hit a 7-iron, easily reaching the green and going over the pin. The ball almost stopped on the top tier, but then it ever so slowly began to roll back down the green, to the accompaniment of a huge roar from the gallery. Lyle was left with a 15-footer (5 m) to win and he holed the putt, before celebrating with a quirky jig. It proved the start of an amazing run of four successive British winners of the green jacket.

Lyle was literally born to golf. His Scottish father, Alex, had moved to become the professional at Hawkstone Park in Shropshire when Sandy was born, and he was hitting golf shots by the age of three. Always tall and strong for his age, he proved to be a prodigy. He was successful at boy, youth, and full amateur levels, playing for England as an amateur, but switching his allegiance to Scotland when he turned professional. Ian Woosnam was a local rival, but once on tour another appeared in the form of Nick Faldo. They could not have been more different; Faldo mightily driven, Lyle just naturally talented (see opposite).

It showed most in his ability to hit the hardest club in the bag: the 1-iron, a club few professionals now even carry. His ball-striking with the long-irons was so pure that he hit his 1-iron as far as most players hit their driver, and his short game was sublime. These qualities combined to overcome the odd disastrous shot and his perennial laid-back manner.

CHAMPION GOLFER OF THE YEAR

At Royal St. George's in 1985 Lyle found himself in contention for the Open on the final day. But he duffed a chip in Duncan's Hollow, beside the 18th green, and everyone felt the anguish with him. He got up and down for a bogey and, after a long wait for the remaining players to finish their rounds, no one had beaten him.

The next day he threw a party for his friends and most of the players on the tour turned up. He rushed out to get mountains of Chinese food and spent most of the party cleaning up. That was Sandy. His hospitable nature seemingly knew no bounds. "I'll tell you what my life's like with Sandy," his long-term caddie Dave Musgrove once remarked. "My wages must be the best on tour... and when I stay at his house at Wentworth, he brings me tea in the morning. That can't be bad, can it?."

His record as a golfer is truly brilliant
but what always made him stand out was his naturally spontaneous personality and humanity

SEVE BALLESTEROS

Three years after his triumph at Royal St. George's he won the Masters. It was far from a one-off victory on the US tour. The year before, Lyle had won the Players Championship at Sawgrass, the only British player to do so. Asked how the event compared with the Open Championship, the Scot replied: "About 100 years of history." After winning the Masters in 1998, Lyle won the World Match Play Championship at Wentworth, beating Faldo in the final after losing in previous years. He played in five successive Ryder Cups matches from 1979 and contributed to the victories in 1985 and 1987. But then his game deserted him. There were flashes of

form, but he was rarely able to put four good rounds together. Not one to get technical, he seemed unable to piece his swing back together. In 2006 he returned to the Ryder Cup as an assistant to the captain, Ian Woosnam, and tasted victory again at the K Club. Yet through the bad times, as in the good times, he remained the same old Sandy.

LYLE PLAYED SOME of his best golf in the worst conditions; his long-iron play was one of his greatest strengths.

At the Kenyan Open in 1980, Sandy Lyle put some tape on the top of his putter face to prevent glare from the sun. Nick Faldo, playing with Lyle, noticed after a few holes but didn't say anything until he saw a tournament official later on. Lyle was disqualified and a cool rivalry between the contrasting men, one a natural, the other dedicated and relentless, began.

On-course rivals, Faldo and Lyle

LYLE CELEBRATES WINNING the Open at Royal St. George's in 1985. The victory made him a hero of British golf.

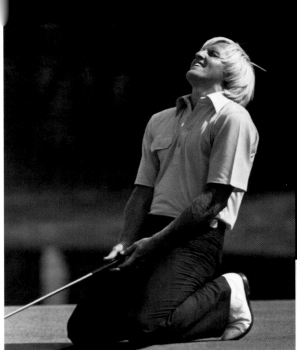

△ **IT WAS AT AUGUSTA** that Norman was christened the "Great White Shark" but it was also the scene of far too many near-misses for the Australian.

△ **NORMAN PARTNERS HIS SON** Gregory in the 2006 Father and Son event, in Orlando. More businessman than golfer, Norman plays in few tournaments these days.

◁ **NORMAN CELEBRATES MAKING** the putt that got him into a playoff at the 1984 US Open at Winged Foot ... but he lost the next day to Fuzzy Zoeller.

Greg Norman

WHEN THE MOST SEVERE criteria is used, Major championships won, the name of Greg Norman is not among those at the top end of the list. But, by sheer force of his personality, the "Great White Shark" dominated golf for a decade from the mid-1980s until the arrival of Tiger Woods. Norman twice won the Open, but he could—and with better fortune would—have won the Grand Slam.

BORN February 10, 1955; Queensland, Australia
HEIGHT 6 ft (1.83 m)
TURNED PRO 1974

DEBUT WIN 1976 West Lakes Classic
TOUR WINS 90
PGA TOUR: 20
EUROPEAN TOUR: 15
AUSTRALASIA TOUR: 39
OTHER: 16

MAJORS 2
MASTERS: T2nd 1986, 1987/2nd 1996
US OPEN: 2nd 1984, 1995
THE OPEN: Won 1986, 1993
USPGA: 2nd 1986, 1993

HONORS
Australia Tour Order of Merit Winner: 1978, 1980, 1983, 1984, 1986, 1988
PGA Tour Money Winner: 1986, 1990, 1995
PGA Player of the Year: 1995
Vardon Trophy Winner: 1989, 1990, 1994
Presidents Cup Team: 1996, 1998, 2000

THE GREAT JOURNEYMAN

Norman fulfils a dream of flying in a Navy jet and landing on an aircraft carrier in 1995. He loves to travel in style. He is no stranger to commuting by private boat, helicopter, or by jet, in order to manage his varied business interests across the world.

■ Norman has a keen interest in flying

I hate failure. The idea of failure is, I think, my driving force

GREG NORMAN

A NATIVE OF QUEENSLAND, Australia, Norman grew up on the beach and in the wild: surfing, fishing, and hunting. His mother, Toini, was an enthusiastic golfer for whom Norman caddied. He learned from her, too, but he didn't take up the game until he was 16. He was a scratch golfer two years later and, just before turning professional in 1976, he assured his club team mates that he would be a millionaire by the time he was 30. This he achieved easily.

First in Australia, then Europe, and finally in the US, the strong, blond Aussie charmer captivated the galleries with his smash-it-and-find-it attitude. It was a local paper in Augusta who gave Norman his distinct nickname on his Masters debut. He won 90 tournaments worldwide, and could have won the Grand Slam; instead he became the second man, after American Craig Wood, to lose playoffs at all four Majors.

THE SATURDAY SLAM

He should have won at Augusta, a course ideally suited to his attacking game, but it never happened for him. Against Jack Nicklaus in 1986 he fired his approach to the last hole into the crowd on the right. In 1987, on the second hole of a playoff, Larry Mize chipped in from 40 yards (35 m) at the 11th to deny him victory. In 1996, he led rival Nick Faldo by six shots but unraveled, eventually losing by six.

If the Mize shot was a blow, at the 1986 USPGA he lost in outrageous circumstances when Bob Tway holed a bunker shot at the last. That year he did the "Saturday Slam," leading after 54 holes at each Major, but he only won the Open trophy at Turnberry. After reining in his swing, under Butch Harmon, he became the longest, straightest driver in the game and the world No 1. In one of the greatest final days of them all, Norman beat Faldo

and Bernhard Langer to win the Open for a second time at Royal St. George's in 1993. Norman shot a final-round 64, and his four-round total of 267 remains the lowest ever in the Open.

With back surgery hampering any Seniors Tour ambitions that he may have been fostering, Norman turned to his business interests, which include course design, clothing, and restaurants.

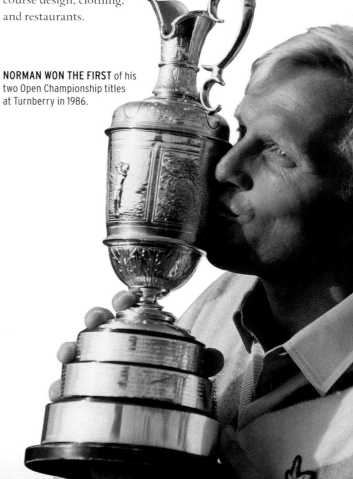

NORMAN WON THE FIRST of his two Open Championship titles at Turnberry in 1986.

△ **WITH SIX MAJOR CHAMPIONSHIPS**, Faldo became the greatest British player of his generation and probably of all time.

◁ **NICK FALDO CONSOLES** Greg Norman after coming from six shots behind to beat the Australian at the 1996 Masters.

There was something quietly beautiful about the relentless, slow-burning courage with which he played golf. Among British sportsmen, Nick Faldo ranks with the greatest of the great

HUGH MCILVANNEY, SPORTS WRITER

Nick Faldo

NICK FALDO IS NOT JUST THE GREATEST BRITISH GOLFER of the modern era, but one of the greats of all British sports. His achievement in winning six Major championships brought respect and admiration. To succeed at the highest level, he had to keep his emotions under close control. This meant he appeared cold and clinical at times, but golf is his passion and this became clearer as he got older, particularly when he moved into television.

PLAYER STATS

BORN July 18, 1957; Welwyn Garden City, England
HEIGHT 6 ft 3 in (1.91 m)
TURNED PRO 1976

DEBUT WIN 1977 Skol Lager Individual
TOUR WINS 43
EUROPEAN TOUR: 27
PGA TOUR: 9
OTHER: 7

MAJORS 6
MASTERS: Won 1989, 1990, 1996
US OPEN: 2nd 1988
THE OPEN: Won 1987, 1990, 1992
USPGA: T2nd 1992

HONORS
PGA Tour Player of the Year: 1990
European Tour Player of the Year: 1989, 1990, 1992
European Tour Order of Merit Winner: 1983, 1992
11 consecutive Ryder Cup team appearances: 1977–1997
Ryder Cup Captain: 2008

IT MIGHT HAVE TAKEN 18 pars in the final round to do it, but victory in the 1987 Open at Muirfield was just as sweet for Faldo.

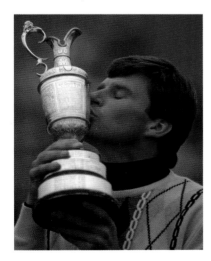

FALDO WAS ALWAYS an individualist in his sporting pursuits. He ran, he cycled, he swam. He did them all pretty well. But one night after watching Jack Nicklaus at the Masters, he switched his attention fully and irrevocably to golf. He was 13 and a slower starter compared to Sandy Lyle, who was hitting balls at the age of three. But Faldo more than made up for that with his determination to succeed. A school counselor suggested professional sports was to be avoided since only one in 10,000 make it. "Well, I'll be that one, then," Faldo replied. He won the English Amateur at the age of 18, in 1975, and turned professional a year later, having worn out the practice range at Welwyn Garden City where he first learned to play. A debut in the Ryder Cup followed in 1977, and his first big win, the PGA Championship, arrived at Royal Birkdale in 1978. The wins continued, and he had chances in the Majors, but a tall man with an aesthetically pleasing swing, he felt his willowy action was not consistent enough under pressure.

Faldo sought out David Leadbetter, an aspiring coach, and they worked on a tighter, more consistent swing. It took almost two years out of his career, but the reward was knowing he could hit the shots he needed to hit when the pressure was at its greatest. In 1987, at Muirfield, Faldo won the Open with a final round of 18 pars. It sounds monotonous, but in the conditions and the circumstances, the round was crafted from brilliance. He defeated Paul Azinger and never looked back. He won the Masters in 1989, after a playoff with Scott Hoch, and repeated the feat the following year, again winning in near darkness on the 11th green after a playoff against Ray Floyd.

Later that summer, Faldo arrived at St. Andrews as the world's best player and played like it to win a second Open crown at the home of golf. He fought off the challenge of Greg Norman in the third round and

FALDO AND DAVID LEADBETTER made one of the great pupil-teacher relationships, with Faldo completely remodeling his swing before finding Major success.

enjoyed a victory walk down the 18th on the final day. In 1992 he won again at Muirfield. Leading for much of the championship, he was suddenly two behind John Cook with four to play. "I've got to play the greatest four holes of my life," he said to himself—and he did. Afterward, in a less than gracious speech, he broke into a rendition of "My Way," and thanked the press "from the heart of my bottom." Faldo never had an easy relationship with the press. They thought he was boring, and he mistrusted them.

MAJOR FOCUS

A complex character, Faldo's whole approach was one of tunnel vision. His focus was on the golf and nothing else. He was never an easy teammate in the Ryder Cup but, aside from a couple of matches, in which his game was in trouble, he always gave his all, particularly in forming a partnership with Ian Woosnam that rivaled Ballesteros and Olazábal for reliability. By the end of his

COURSE FISHING

A passion for fishing began even before Faldo got into golf. His father introduced him to the sport and it became a life-long enjoyment—the perfect way to relax away from the golf scene. His fishing trips have taken him all over the world from Sweden to New Zealand and, in the company of musician Huey Lewis, to Montana.

■ A successful day's fishing

record 11th Ryder Cup appearance in, 1997, he had won more points than anyone else on either side. It was in 1995, at Oak Hill, that Faldo rallied over the last three holes to secure a vital point against Curtis Strange.

If that moment helped to turn admiration for Faldo into a warmer appreciation, so did his last great victory, at the Masters in 1996. Faldo started the final round six strokes behind his playing partner, Greg Norman. He knew he could not afford to make a single mistake if he was to claim a third green jacket, and he did not. The relentless excellence of his play finally told on the Australian, who started to fritter away strokes. Faldo's 67 enabled him to come from six behind to win by five. On the 18th green, Faldo took Norman in his arms and said "I don't know what to say. I just want to give you a hug."

A NEW CHAPTER

With six Majors, Faldo stood head and shoulders above his contemporaries, but Tiger Woods was the new force in the game and Faldo put the first green jacket on the young champion in 1997. Already interested in course design, with his Chart Hills course in Kent being well-received, Faldo started working in other areas of the game. One of his most fulfilling projects was setting up the Faldo Junior Series. The program has gone from strength to strength and in 2005 Nick Dougherty became the first former winner to become a champion on the European Tour. Rory McIlroy, the 18-year-old winner of the Silver Medal as the leading amateur at the 2007 Open, is also a graduate of the program, which includes mentoring and clinics from Faldo himself. Then along came television, which helped reveal his true love of the game.

Faldo turned 50 on the eve of the 2007 Open Championship at Carnoustie. He missed the cut, but the following week made his debut in the Senior Open Championship at Muirfield. He had a good first day but could not sustain the challenge. "Thank goodness I have a day job," he said. The "day job" is now television. After a few years working on tournaments for ABC television, Faldo was offered a huge contract to work almost weekly for CBS and

FALDO LEAPS FOR JOY after holing a putt for victory in the World Match Play Championship at Wentworth in 1989. He also lifted the crown in 1992.

1977	1978	1983	1987	1989	1990
Faldo becomes the youngest player to appear in the Ryder Cup at the age of 21.	Wins his first big tournament at the PGA Championship at Royal Birkdale.	Takes the European Order of Merit, winning five times during the season.	At the Open at Muirfield, Faldo manages to beat Paul Azinger by one shot with a historic final round of 18 pars.	Wins the first of three green jackets at Augusta after a playoff with Scott Hoch.	Becomes the first player since Jack Nicklaus to successfully defend the Masters title.

the Golf Channel. With his course design work and the Faldo Series, which has expanded from Britain to Asia, and in his four children, he says, actually playing golf is now his fifth priority. Years ago, his mother Joyce hoped he would become an actor. Now he says his aim is to match the ring tone on his cellphone, "The Entertainer."

In 2008, Faldo leads Europe as captain in the Ryder Cup at Valhalla. No one has bettered his 11 appearances in the transatlantic contest, from Royal Lytham in 1977 to Valderrama in 1997, nor put more points on the board. Inspiring others to success is his next challenge, but winning the Seve Trophy for Great Britain and Ireland in 2007 was a good start to his captaincy career.

"I'm just playing for the love of the game. And for the little cups," Faldo once said. He was never the machine some made him out to be. If he had been just a fairways and greens plodder he would probably have won either the US Open or the USPGA, instead of suffering near-misses in those events. Winning at Augusta and on the links of the Open rota requires flair. It was Faldo himself who hoped people would say of him: "I saw Nick Faldo play golf. He wasn't bad." He was the best of British.

FALDO VISITS MISSION HILLS in China on a site visit for another course design project. Faldo's design company has produced courses all over the world—from Cyprus, Turkey, and Egypt to Dubai, Mexico, and Ireland.

I went there with the intention of winning that Major, not just turning up and saying this feels good and I wonder what's going to happen

NICK FALDO

1990	1992	1996	1997	1998	2004	2007
Claims second Open title with an emphatic triumph at St. Andrews.	Victorious again at Muirfield claiming his third Open after playing "the greatest four holes of my life."	Seals a famous victory at the Masters, defeating Greg Norman, to collect his sixth and final Major championship.	Plays in a record 11th Ryder Cup and remains Europe's top point scorer.	Accepts his MBE at Buckingham Palace, in recognition of his golfing exploits.	Begins commentating regularly for US television after retiring from the tour.	Turns 50 and becomes eligible for the Seniors Tour. He shoots 68 in his first competitive round.

Curtis Strange

AT A TIME WHEN EUROPEAN GOLF WAS AT ITS STRONGEST, in the second half of the 1980s, Curtis Strange was the dominant American player. He won the US money list three times in the the space of four years, and in 1988 and 1989 became the first player since Ben Hogan in 1951 to win consecutive US Open titles. Then, suddenly, the success stopped.

WITH A REPUTATION for methodical play, Strange found a penchant for grinding out pars was crucial in his US Open wins.

THE SON OF A CLUB PROFESSIONAL from Virginia, Strange won 17 times on the American circuit between 1979 and 1989. For much of that period, he was known as a money machine, winning the money title in 1985, 1987, and 1988; in the last of those years he became the first player to win $1 million in a single season.

Strange was the quintessential grinder and once said of his making only one birdie in 35 consecutive holes during a US Open that it was, "as exciting as watching paint dry." He also disliked that he was described as a fiery competitor, but does admit to making the absolute most of his talent. That said, bringing such tenacity to the course every day did make him boil over. He was fined for using bad language and also declined to make several trips to Britain for the Open, partly because everyone told him he should go. He was to later admit that it was the "biggest mistake of my career. It didn't bother me then but it bothers me now. I should have gone. Sitting in your rocking chair, you don't want to have any regrets. That's one of mine."

Another regret may be how he started at the 1985 Masters. He recovered from an opening 80 with rounds of 65 and 68 and led by four with nine to play, but he went in Rae's Creek at the 13th and the pond at the 15th to lose to Bernhard Langer. Three years later, however, he made a superb up-and-down from a bunker to tie Nick Faldo at the US Open at Brookline and won the 18-hole playoff the next day. The next year at Oak Hill, he beat Ian Woosnam, Chip Beck, and Mark McCumber by one shot. Going for three in a row at Medinah in 1990, he finished six shots back and was then afflicted by a letdown in both his health, and his game. He suffered from headaches and lethargy and the intensity seeped from his game. The worse he felt he was playing, the more he tinkered with his swing. "Maybe I lost

enthusiasm because I knew my game was going south. I couldn't stop it for a while. The pressure to play well every day was part of it. We only have so much energy, mentally and physically, to be the best. The first thing that goes is the mental edge. Except for Jack Nicklaus, it's only for seven or eight years."

Strange never won again. He did make his fifth Ryder Cup appearance in 1995 at Oak Hill, but bogeyed the last three holes to lose an important singles to Nick Faldo. Later he spent many seasons as a television commentator.

STRANGE WON THE FIRST of his two successive US Open titles at Brookline Country Club in 1988 after beating Nick Faldo by four shots in an 18-hole playoff.

> I wasn't playing well... and I was getting worse and said, "To hell with it."
>
> STRANGE ON SWITCHING TO THE CHAMPIONS TOUR AGED 50

Ian Woosnam

IAN WOOSNAM WAS THE YOUNGEST of Europe's "Big Five," who were all born within a year of each other. Nick Faldo, Sandy Lyle, Seve Ballesteros, and Bernhard Langer all won Major championships, on both sides of the Atlantic. It would need something special for wee Woosie to be able to join the gang, but he possessed both a huge heart and one of the sweetest swings in the game.

PLAYER STATS

BORN March 2, 1958; Oswestry, Wales
HEIGHT 5 ft 5 in (1.65 m)
TURNED PRO 1976

DEBUT WIN 1982 Ebel Swiss Open
TOUR WINS 44
EUROPEAN TOUR: 28
USPGA TOUR: 2
OTHER: 14

MAJORS 1
MASTERS: Won 1991
US OPEN: T2nd 1989
THE OPEN: 3rd 1986/T3rd 2001
USPGA: 6th 1989

HONORS
Ryder Cup Team: 1983, 1985, 1987, 1989, 1991, 1993, 1995, 1997
Ryder Cup Captain: 2006
PGA Player of the Year: 1988
European Tour Order of Merit Winner: 1987, 1990

CADDIE TROUBLE

At the tournament immediately after the 2001 Open, the Scandinavian Open in Sweden, matters got worse for Woosnam's caddie, Miles Byrne (head bowed). He reported late for duty—forcing Woosnam to break into a locker to retrieve his clubs—and was fired.

■ Strained relationship

HIS SWING WAS A THING OF BEAUTY, it was a swing that drew admirers even among his peers, who would stop and watch him on the driving range, and it also allowed this small man of 5 ft 4 in (1.65 m) to smash the ball to kingdom come. It also matched his personality— a straightforward man who likes a beer and a smoke.

Woosnam got his strength from working on the family farm, but played golf at Llanmynech, which has 15 holes in Wales and three in England. Having learned his game in such humble origins, he attended the Qualifying School three times; later, as a struggling pro, he traveled the circuit in a camper van and ate cans of baked beans. Sandy Lyle, the same age, was an early rival. "One day I'll beat you," Woosnam said to Lyle after losing the 1969 Hereford Boys' Championship. "You'll have to grow a bit first, Woosie," replied the winner. In 1987 the pair met in a brilliant final at the World Match Play and Woosnam took his revenge. After the final, reminded of the earlier exchange, Lyle added, "If he ever grows up, he'll hit the ball 2,000 yards."

IAN WOOSNAM WON his only Major championship at the Masters in 1991. He celebrated the winning putt with passion, before being lifted off the ground by his caddie.

Winning the Order of Merit and the World Cup for Wales in 1987 capped Woosie's first great season. He won the money list again in 1990 and then claimed his biggest triumph at Augusta in 1991, winning by a shot from José Maria Olazábal. His one weakness was his putting, which may have prevented him winning more Majors. At Royal Lytham in 2001, he birdied the par-3 1st in the final round to take the lead, but then discovered that he had an extra driver in his bag and was penalized two shots for having 15 clubs (one too many). He lost to David Duval, but later in the summer became the first player to win the World Match Play in three different decades. His courage and determination made Woosnam a vital Ryder Cup player for Europe, and his passion as captain drove Europe to a third successive victory at the K Club in Ireland in 2006.

Payne Stewart

PAYNE STEWART'S DEATH IN A PLANE CRASH IN 1999 at the age of 42 came at the end of his most rewarding season. He had just won the US Open for the second time—his third Major—and off the course, the man known for his brashness and his outrageous clothing was more content than at any time in his life.

STEWART HAILED FROM THE HEART of America, and was on the US Tour for his individualism. He wore plus-twos, and for many years had a clothing contract with the NFL to wear the colors of the local teams. Unashamedly patriotic, Stewart was easily labeled "cocky" in the conservative world of American golf. He had won in Asia and Australia before making it in the US. His first Major title came at the 1989 USPGA, and two years later he won the US Open at Hazeltine, after an 18-hole playoff against Scott Simpson.

However, by 1999, he had not won in four years. He was runner-up twice in the Open Championship and was pipped on two occasions in the US Open by Lee Janzen, losing at Olympic Club in San Francisco in 1998. When asked what it was like playing with Stewart at the US Open, Janzen said, "He's more outgoing than most people on tour but his style of play is exactly the opposite. Nothing fancy, hit the fairways, hit the greens, and try and make a few putts."

Stewart said he never minded making a bogey at the US Open. This was probably because he had a an excellent short game, and was blessed with great imagination. At Pinehurst in 1999, he defeated Phil Mickelson, Tiger Woods, David Duval, and Vijay Singh, holing from 15 ft (4 m) at the last for the victory. To Mickelson, the runner-up whose wife was expecting their first child, Stewart said, "You'll win the Open, but now you have more important things to do. You'll be a great daddy." Age mellowed Stewart, and he traded his cocksure image for that of a fine family man, active at a Baptist church in Orlando. "This walk I am having in Christianity is being led by my children," he said.

Shortly after the Ryder Cup, where he had a spectator that was heckling Colin Montgomerie removed, he set out to visit a course he was designing. His private jet depressurized after take-off and all on board suffocated. The plane, on automatic pilot, finally ran out of fuel and crashed in South Dakota.

STEWART HOLDS ON tightly to the US Open trophy at Pinehurst in 1999. His third Major championship would, tragically, prove to be his last.

IN A TYPICALLY COLORFUL OUTFIT, the young Stewart won his first US Open at Hazeltine in 1991 after a playoff against Scott Simpson. His clenched-fist celebration became a common sight on the tour.

SMILING IRISH EYES

Payne Stewart enjoyed visiting Ireland, particularly Waterville, on golf trips and the Irish loved him. "If I ran for mayor... it would be a landside," he said. After his death the residents of Waterville erected a statue in his honor.

■ Stewart's statue at Waterville

John Daly

GOLF'S "WILD THING" HAS ENJOYED A TURBULENT LIFE, both on and off the golf course. His massive hitting, combined with a delicate touch around the greens, brought him two Major championships. The first, at the 1991 USPGA at Crooked Stick, Indiana, was one of the most surprising in the game's history; his second at the Open in 1995 at St. Andrews, was no surprise at all.

WILD SING

A talented singer and guitarist, Daly produced an album entitled *My Life*, which includes a track called "All my Exes wear Rolexes." "Music is my therapy," Daly says. "I think for all of us it is therapy, whatever style of music you are into. If I am driving my bus, I can't do it with no sound. The world can't exist without music."

Daly relaxes by playing the guitar

DALY'S "GRIP IT AND RIP IT" style of golf astonished the world when he came from nowhere to win the USPGA at Crooked Stick in 1991. Daly, a rookie on the US Tour who had been playing on mini-tours and in South Africa before that season, was the ninth reserve for the event. He drove for seven hours, arriving at his hotel at midnight before the first round, and didn't even have a practice round. But he played brilliantly, hitting long drives and putting superbly to win by three strokes. Suddenly his life became very public.

He grew up in Dardanelle, Arkansas, started playing golf at the age of four, and drinking at the age of eight. In his teens he was heavily into Jack Daniel's. He was already divorced once when he won at Crooked Stick. After the win he discovered his fiancée was 10 years older than she said, had a 13-year-old son, and was not yet divorced. They split up, and then got married when she became pregnant. Later, he was served divorce papers during the Masters. Throughout four marriages he has fought addictions to alcohol, gambling, chocolate, and Diet Coke—sometimes getting through 18 cans during a round. He has attended clinics, and wrecked hotel rooms, but has always strenuously denied accusations of wife-beating. "I play golf aggressively," explains Daly. "I like to go for it on the course, but now I'm better at not going for it off the course."

No matter what problems befall him—whether he has just walked off the course or been disqualified—he has always retained the loyalty of his many fans. In 2004 he won for only the fifth time on the US Tour, and the highlight of his career came when he won at St. Andrews in 1995, overpowering the Old Course with his length off the tee and making low scores with a superb touch on the huge double greens. In windy conditions he tied with Italian Costantino Rocca, and then won a four-hole playoff comfortably. Despite his Majors, he has never played in the Ryder Cup; he has not qualified by right, nor been picked by a captain as the ultimate wild card.

GRIP IT AND RIP IT, the Daly philosophy, produced big hitting but also gained the "Wild Thing" two Major championships and a fan base to rival any of the game's top players.

Fred Couples

FRED COUPLES DIDN'T SET OUT with the ambition of being the best player in the world, but for a short spell in 1992, that is exactly what he was. Winning the Masters and topping the money list was the pinnacle of his golfing career, but his laidback approach to the game and his humility made him hugely popular, especially in the US.

FRED COUPLES BECAME one of the most popular American golfers in the 1990s with his wonderfuly fluid swing and his laid-back approach to the game and to life.

> Fred would rather do his own thing than get involved in the business of being a celebrity. He is a very modest person.

DAVIS LOVE

FRED COUPLES LEARNED TO PLAY at a municipal course in Seattle. "I was playing with guys 60, 65-years-old, and having a blast," he recalled. "It was a good atmosphere; if I screwed around, some of the older guys let me know about it." Obviously talented, he was soon known as "Boom Boom" on tour for his great length, but although he won regularly, some critics wondered if he really had the ruthless streak to be a great champion. It did not help when Couples revealed he liked nothing better than being a television couch potato.

The turning point in his career was playing with Raymond Floyd in the 1991 Ryder Cup. "You can be friendly with them another time," Floyd told his partner when he started complimenting their opponents' shots. "For one week we are trying to beat these guys." They won two of their three matches together and some of Floyd's competitiveness must have rubbed off. He won twice early in 1992, arriving as a hot favorite at Augusta where he beat none other than Floyd by two strokes. His play more than justified the victory, but he profited from a moment of fortune at the short 12th; his tee short started to roll back toward the water but implausibly stayed on the bank. In the prime of his career, Couples joined up with Davis Love to win the World Cup four times in a row from 1992. But in 1994 he suffered a back injury that never really went away.

Off the course, there was the sadness of his parents dying within three years of each other, and a very public divorce, with his ex-wife later committing suicide. In 2003, five years after his previous win, came a popular victory at the Houston Open. But his attitude was simple. "Is it really important how many trophies you wind up with? I love golf, don't get me wrong, but there are other things I want out of life."

PLAYER STATS

BORN October 3, 1959; Seattle, Washington
HEIGHT 5 ft 11 in (1.80 m)
TURNED PRO 1980

DEBUT WIN 1983 Kemper Open
TOUR WINS 46
PGA TOUR: 15
EUROPEAN TOUR: 2
OTHER: 29

MAJORS 1
MASTERS: Won 1992
US OPEN: T3rd 1991
THE OPEN: T3rd 1991, 2005
USPGA: 2nd 1991

HONORS
PGA Tour Player of the Year: 1991, 1992
USPGA Tour Money Winner: 1992
Vardon Trophy: 1991, 1992
Ryder Cup Team: 1989, 1991, 1993, 1995, 1997
Presidents Cup Team: 1994, 1996, 1998, 2005

COUPLES WON REGULARLY on the US Tour before claiming his only Major at the 1992 Masters. He is also king of the Skins, winning five times between 1995 and 2004.

Laura Davies

LAURA DAVIES BECAME FAR MORE than the finest British woman player of the modern era. In 1994 she was the first European golfer to be ranked No 1 in the world, helping to make the women's game truly international. She hit the ball further than any other woman, she won around the globe, including four Major championships, and earned friends everywhere she traveled.

PLAYER STATS

BORN October 5, 1963; Coventry, England
HEIGHT 5 ft 10 in (1.78 m)
TURNED PRO 1985

DEBUT WIN 1985 Belgian Open
TOUR WINS 67
EUROPEAN TOUR: 39
LPGA TOUR: 20
OTHER: 8

MAJORS 4
KRAFT NABISCO: 2nd 1994
LPGA CHAMPIONSHIP: Won 1994, 1996
US WOMEN'S OPEN: Won 1987
DU MAURIER CLASSIC: Won 1996
WOMEN'S BRITISH OPEN: T8th 2004

HONORS
European Tour Order of Merit Winner: 1985, 1986, 1992, 1996, 1999, 2004, 2006
LPGA Tour Money Winner: 1994
LPGA Tour Player of the Year: 1996
Curtis Cup Team: 1984
Solheim Cup Team: 1990, 1992, 1994, 1996, 1998, 2000, 2002, 2003, 2005, 2007

IN 2007, MORE INTERNATIONAL PLAYERS than Americans teed off in the US Women's Open. Two decades earlier that would have been unthinkable, and it certainly would not have been possible without Laura Davies winning the 1987 US Open as a non-member of the LPGA Tour. For six days, Davies held both Open titles and only just failed to defend her Women's British Open —not then classed as a Major—the following weekend.

Davies was an instant success on the fledgling European circuit, winning the money list in her first two seasons in 1985 and 1986. Sensitive about her size, she used it to her advantage by hitting the ball huge distances, and as a natural gambler, on and off the course, she would attempt the most audacious shots in the manner of Ballesteros or Palmer. But she also had the delicate touch around the greens to recover when

DAVIES IS UNQUESTIONABLY Britain's most successful, golfer. She has won many golfing honors and holds the record for the most eagles in a season: 19 during 2004.

necessary. The putts did not always fall, and more than one putter finished up in a trash can, but the victories rolled in. Between 1994 and 1996, she won 24 times around the world, in 1994 becoming the first player, male or female, to win on five different tours; she won three more Majors in that time to add to her US Open.

Davies has also been instrumental in making the Solheim Cup a competitive match. When the women's version of the Ryder Cup was introduced, the US dominated the inaugural match. But at Dalmahoy in 1992, Davies inspired a young European team to victory and the transatlantic rivalry started in earnest.

DAVIES HAS BEEN ONE of Europe's most inspirational players in the Solheim Cup, and is Europe's second highest points scorer in the event.

José Maria Olazábal

JOSÉ MARIA OLAZÁBAL NOT ONLY FOLLOWED HIS COUNTRYMAN Seve Ballesteros in winning Major championships, but also formed with him perhaps the greatest partnership in the history of the Ryder Cup. Blessed with fierce determination, majestic iron play, and a brilliant set of recovery shots, he also overcame serious injury to continue his illustrious career.

OLAZÁBAL GREW UP WITH GOLF on his doorstep. He was born the day after the Real Golf Club de San Sebastian opened and practically lived on the course. First his grandfather, and then his father worked as green keepers and "Ollie" was introduced to the game with a cut-down club. He enjoyed success as an amateur, winning the triple crown of the British Boys, Youths, and Amateur titles. He won the tour qualifying school in 1985 and went on to win his first title the following year. In 1987 he played in the Ryder Cup for the first time, at the age of 21, and began his inspirational partnership with Ballesteros. They won 11 of their matches together, halving two and losing only two. Their sheer presence intimidated the opposition. They were never out of a hole, one of them conjuring up an unlikely escape. They had "no sorrys," they just got on with the next shot. At first Ballesteros was the senior man, but soon Olazábal proved the rock of the partnership. Though his driver could be erratic, his quick swing produced wonderful long-iron shots and his putting was deadly, which complemented his magic around the greens.

He won the Masters in 1994 and again, more emotionally, in 1999. In between he feared he would not play again, or might even end up in a wheelchair. For 18 months, from late in 1995, he was absent from the game and for six months in 1996 could barely walk, crawling from his bed to the bathroom. He was diagnosed with rheumatoid polyarthritis, but remarkably, returned to play his part in the Ryder Cup win at Valderrama in 1997. Having not played since 1999, Olazábal returned to the Ryder Cup in 2006 at the K Club, winning three matches out of three, and while hoping to play in 2008 he was named as a vice-captain designate by Nick Faldo, who marveled at the Spaniard's "great passion and incredible determination."

OLAZÁBAL HAS AMASSED a collection of trophies over his career. The highlights of his collection remain his two Masters green jackets.

OLAZABAL WAS ALWAYS at his inspired best in the Ryder Cup, forming an almost unbeatable partnership with Seve Ballesteros.

There are no sorrys between us if either of us hits a bad shot. We just make sure we get the next one right

SEVE BALLESTEROS ON PLAYING WITH OLAZÁBAL IN THE RYDER CUP

Nick Price

NICK PRICE IS SO NICE that he does not even mind being called nice. He is also downright talented and a great iron player. A long-term student of David Leadbetter, his crisp and efficient golf swing propelled him to three Major championship victories in as many years in the early 1990s. He proved the phrase "nice guys finish last" was nonsense.

PRICE WAS BORN TO AN ENGLISH FATHER, and a Welsh mother in South Africa. His mother told him, "I don't care how successful you are, what you've done in life, how much money you make—it doesn't matter. All I want to see every time I see you is a smile on your face." He grew up in what was then Rhodesia and went into the air force for his military service, which coincided the civil war of the late 1970s. The experience gave him a new perspective on the life of a professional golfer.

Price played in South Africa and Europe before heading to the US, where his first big win was beating Jack Nicklaus at the 1983 World Series of Golf. The year before he had started a career-long association with David Leadbetter. Though he had a quick rhythm, he became a great striker of the ball. If anything let him down it was his putting, which was a reason why he only started to win the biggest titles in the early 1990s. In 1992 he won the USPGA, and two years later he won both the Open, and the USPGA, and became the world's best player.

Twice he had come close to winning the Open; in 1982 he shot a final-round 73 to lose by one to Tom Watson, but in 1998 at Lytham he saw Seve Ballesteros rip the title away with a brilliant 65 to Price's 69. However, At Turnberry in 1994 his time had come. Jesper Parnevik led by one on the 18th tee but bogeyed the last; Price then eagled the 17th to win a fascinating duel. His caddie for all three of his Major wins was Jeff "Squeeky" Medlen, who died from leukemia at the age of 43 not long afterward. "He was diligent and conscientious and humble and simple and honest and all the good things any man should be," Price wrote in tribute.

In 2002 the Golf Writers Association of America inaugurated an award in the memory of the late *Los Angeles Times* writer Jim Murray to honor a player who, in being approachable and accessible, "reflects the most positive aspects of the working relationship between athlete and journalist." The first winner was Nick Price; the second was Arnold Palmer.

PLAYER STATS

BORN January 28, 1957; Durban, South Africa
HEIGHT 6 ft (1.83 m)
TURNED PRO 1977

DEBUT WIN 1979 Asseng TV Challenge Series
TOUR WINS 44
PGA TOUR: 18
EUROPEAN TOUR: 5
OTHER: 21

MAJORS 3
MASTERS: 5th 1986
US OPEN: 4th 1992/T4th 1998
THE OPEN: Won 1994
USPGA: Won 1992, 1994

HONORS
Sunshine Tour Order of Merit Winner: 1984
PGA Tour Money Winner: 1993, 1994
Vardon Trophy: 1993, 1997
Bob Jones Award: 2005
Presidents Cup Team: 1994, 1996, 1998, 2000, 2003

NICK PRICE HOLES a long eagle putt at the 17th hole at Turnberry on the way to winning the 1994 Open Championship.

I was impressed immediately.
It was his power, the sheer effortlessness of his swing

MARK ROE, EUROPEAN TOUR PLAYER

△ **IN A DRAMATIC** conclusion at Muirfield, including extra holes, Els finally triumphed to win the 2002 Open Championship.

◁ **ELS HAS ALWAYS** played around the world but is most successful at Wentworth where he has won seven World Match Play titles.

Ernie Els

A BIG MAN BLESSED WITH SUCH WONDERFUL NATURAL RHYTHM, Ernie Els became South Africa's next golfing superstar after Gary Player. At his best, the nickname of the "Big Easy" was perfectly apportioned. But any implication that there is not the will to win, the loathing of losing, the hard work and dedication applied, must be refuted. The rewards have been well earned.

PLAYER STATS

BORN October 17, 1969; Johannesburg, South Africa
HEIGHT 6 ft 3 in (1.90 m)
TURNED PRO 1989

DEBUT WIN 1991 Amatola Sun Classic
TOUR WINS 61
PGA TOUR 15
EUROPEAN TOUR 23
SOUTHERN AFRICAN TOUR: 19
OTHER 4

MAJORS 3
MASTERS: 2nd 2000, 2004
US OPEN: Won 1994, 1997
THE OPEN: Won 2002
USPGA: 3rd 1995, 2007

HONORS
PGA Tour Rookie of the Year: 1994
European Tour Order of Merit Winner: 2003, 2004
Sunshine Tour Order of Merit Winner: 1992, 1995
Presidents Cup Team: 1996, 1998, 2000, 2003, 2007

ELS WAS A NATURALLY TALENTED sportsman throughout his schooldays. He played rugby and cricket, as well as tennis, becoming the Eastern Transvaal junior champion at the age of 13. But, by the time he had reached the age of 14, he was a scratch golfer, and at the World Junior Championships in San Diego in 1984, he beat Phil Mickelson to the title in the 13-14 age group—Tiger Woods won the 9-10 age group.

After becoming South African Amateur Stroke Play Champion in 1989, Els completed his military service and—having had extensive surgery on a hand after being involved in a car accident—made his big breakthrough in 1992. He won six times in South Africa that year, including the triple crown of the South African Open, the PGA, and Masters titles. This was the year he also moved to Europe and he has played around the world ever since. Now based at Wentworth in England, he still competes in the US, Europe, Asia, and back home in South Africa every year.

Five years after turning pro, he won the 1994 US Open at Oakmont. He had announced himself to the world, beating Loren Roberts and Colin Montgomerie in a playoff. Monty always had trouble with Els. He was again on the losing end of an Els victory, this time at Congressional in the US Open of 1997, when the South African's wonderful approach at the 17th hole ended a terrific duel.

A PEERLESS MATCH PLAYER

Els had to wait until 2002 to win his third Major, the Open Championship at Muirfield. The old motto—"swing easy in the wind"—helped him survive the blustery conditions in the third round, but he still needed to recover over the closing holes before

ELS ANNOUNCES HIMSELF as a world player by winning at Oakmont in 1994 after a playoff against Loren Roberts and Colin Montgomerie.

GIVING TO THE COMMUNITY

As can be seen here, the "Big Easy" can swing a golf club and cricket bat with equal fluency. When he is not enjoying himself on the beach, however, he gives his time to promoting the Ernie Els & Fancourt Foundation. Started in 1999, it seeks to provide children who show promise in the game, with practical assistance and educational support.

■ Everything is easy for Els

winning a playoff against Thomas Levet, Stuart Appleby, and Steve Elkington. No one can win at Muirfield without being a master bunker player and Els is every bit as good as his compatriot Gary Player in that department.

One record Els took from Player, and Seve Ballesteros, was in winning the World Match Play Championship at Wentworth seven times. He has proved a dominant force in the 36-hole format, winning his first 11 matches, before losing to Vijay Singh in the 1997 final; but he was victorious in 26 of 31 matches by the time of his seventh title in 2007.

In the Majors, Els has not had it his own way, even as one of Tiger Woods' main rivals. He was the distant runner-up to Tiger in the US Open and the Open of 2000, and in 2004 had chances to win all four Majors but won none, losing in a playoff in the Open at Royal Troon. A knee injury while sailing in the Mediterranean in 2005 had a lasting effect on his swing, but he remains one of the most popular professionals in the game.

△ MONTY WINS THE Benson and Hedges International in 1999 on the way to a seventh consecutive Order of Merit crown.

△ LOYAL FANS FOLLOW the Scot wherever he plays and have supported him through the good times and the bad. His fanbase at the Open is second-to-none.

◁ MONTY HAS ALWAYS BEEN HAPPY to leave the heroics to others. He prefers to concentrate on hitting fairways and greens, and making putts.

Colin Montgomerie

IF MAJOR CHAMPIONSHIPS ARE THE MEASURE OF GREATNESS, and they have to be, Colin Montgomerie does not register. But the Scot's achievements in the game defy such a bleak characterization. His Ryder Cup successes and Order of Merit titles make him one of Europe's best ever golfers and an always enthralling, if unpredictable, individual.

The Ryder Cup brings out the best in me, and I'm grateful it does.

COLIN MONTGOMERIE

AFTER THE BOUNTIFUL MAJORS SUCCESS of Europe's big guns—the likes of Nick Faldo, Sandy Lyle, and Seve Ballesteros—a vacuum was left that was filled by Monty. His record of winning the Order of Merit seven times from 1993 to 1999 will surely never be bettered. It displayed his utter determination not to relinquish his crown as Europe's No 1 and it was achieved—he will be the last person that needs reminding—without adding the biggest prizes of all.

At his best, he rarely practiced; he just showed up and hit precise and consistent fades down the middle of the fairway—and into the green—every time. He was a magnificent putter, at least in the first half of his career, after years of giving himself so many birdie opportunities in the first place.

A MAJOR TALENT

The son of a former military man, who worked for Fox's Biscuits in northern England and then became secretary at Royal Troon, Montgomerie was a good amateur player, but not the best. José Maria Olazábal beat him in the final of the 1984 Amateur Championship.

Nevertheless, he improved by sticking to a simple method—by being more competitive than anyone else. He could be irascible and easily distracted by noise from the gallery, or a photographer in the wrong place.

At the Majors, he always came up just short, losing playoffs at the 1994 US Open and 1995 USPGA, and then finishing behind Ernie Els for the second time at the 1997 US Open. Later in his career, more chances presented themselves, although Tiger Woods was never

going to be beaten at the 2005 Open, the year Monty added an eighth Order of Merit. But at the 2006 US Open, a double bogey on the final hole ruined his best chance.

Yet, throughout his career, he has proved an inspirational figure at the Ryder Cup. He first played in 1991 and in 1997 at Valderrama he was Europe's main man: securing the winning point. At Brookline in 1999, the heckling in the US—which so obviously got under his skin—was at its worst, but he rose above it. In 2002 and 2006 he led off the singles matches, and secured yet another winning point at Oakland Hills in 2004.

MONTY CELEBRATES YET another Ryder Cup triumph, at Oak Hill in 1995. He beat Ben Crenshaw 3&1 in the singles to help Europe secure a one-point victory.

Annika Sorenstam

AT A TIME WHEN THE WOMEN'S GAME WAS BECOMING GENUINELY GLOBAL, Annika Sorenstam proved herself the best in the world and the outstanding candidate as the greatest player of all time. A friend and "rival" of Tiger Woods, during the 2001 and 2002 seasons, she was even more dominant on the women's circuit than Tiger. After each Major win, the pair exchanged text messages of congratulations.

SORENSTAM, WHOSE SISTER CHARLOTTA also became a professional, played tennis and skied to a high standard but found her single-minded approach best suited golf. She became a pupil of Pia Nilsson, who encouraged players not to limit themselves to two putts a hole, but to think about birdieing every hole. Sorenstam's initial run of success would have made for a satisfying career in itself (see p.240). She was the Rookie of the Year in Europe in 1993 and in the US the following year. In 1995 she topped the money lists on both sides of the Atlantic and won the US Open, which she would retain at Pine Needles the following year.

WINNING STREAK
More wins followed and she led the LPGA money list again in 1997 and 1998, but then she was overtaken by the likes of Karrie Webb and Se Ri Pak. Her determination to regain her top billing and start winning Majors again came to fruition in 2001. She won the Kraft Nabisco Championship, plus seven other events, and broke or tied 30 LPGA records, including shooting a round of 59. After working tirelessly on her fitness, she became one of the longer hitters on the women's circuit, while at the same time retaining her remarkable accuracy. In 2002 she won 13 times around the world, including the Kraft Nabisco Championship again. In 2003 she won the two Majors she had not previously won, the LPGA Championship and the Women's British Open at Royal Lytham. The following year she won 10 times, and in 2005 she won 11 times in 21 starts, including a third successive LPGA Championship (the first person in LPGA history to achieve this) and a record eighth LPGA Player of the Year award. In 2006, after a wait of ten years, she won a third US Open—her 10th Major. Her other achievements included being the first player in LPGA or PGA history to win the same event five consecutive years at the Mizuno Classic.

Sorenstam's game was based on a clinical precision from tee-to-green, while she also played occasional practice rounds with Tiger Woods in order to learn some of his short game secrets. In the Solheim Cup, the women's equivalent of the Ryder Cup, she has been supreme. She has played in eight cups and posted a record number of points. Although she was just one of a number of Swedish players to reach the top of the game, her influence led to the Solheim Cup being played twice in her home country, in 2003 at Barseback, where Sorenstam helped Europe to a famous victory, and at Halmstad in 2007, where the US retained the trophy.

SILENT ASSASSIN
Initially shy early in her career, as an amateur Sorenstam might three-putt at the last hole to avoid giving a winner's speech. When a coach decided that both the winner and the runner-up were required to

SORENSTAM CAUSED A SENSATION when she played in a men's event, the 2003 Colonial. It was a one-time occurance and a personal challenge.

SORENSTAM HOLDS the Kraft Nabisco trophy in 2002 after taking the traditional leap into the lake by the 18th green.

speak, she started to win. Something of a silent assassin on turning professional, she gradually developed a more expressive personality, as comfortable in front of a microphone as out on the fairways. Her locker-room speech at the 2000 Solheim Cup at Loch Lomond, sharing her passion and determination to succeed, helped Europe to victory that week.

COMPETING WITH THE MEN

In 2003, Sorenstam became the first woman for 58 years to play in a men's PGA Tour event, at the Colonial. She drew much attention and she prepared as if it was a Major championship. Not one of the longer courses on the men's tour, her accuracy worked in her favor, but it was not her best putting week. Some critics suggested that this was a fundamental flaw in her game but the number of times she has holed important putts in her many victories suggests this is incorrect. She just missed the cut at the Colonial but she believed the one-off experience—unlike others, she never saw it as a regular happening—helped her when she was trying to win women's Majors. Two of her next three victories were Majors. One of those victories came at the Weetabix Women's British Open at Royal Lytham where she beat Se Ri Pak in a thrilling duel. "I believe I have become a better player since playing at the Colonial," she said that night. "There were times today when I felt the pressure and then I thought it was not as bad as the Colonial."

TOP PLAYER, HEAD CHEF

One of Sorenstam's favorite hobbies is cooking. With more of a winter break in the women's schedule than on the men's tour, Sorenstam was able to develop her culinary skills. She spent her time off before the 2003 season working eight-hour shifts in the kitchens at the Lake Nona restaurant in Florida, near her home. She has talked of enrolling at a cookery school and she often participates in cooking demonstrations at tournaments, including with Robert Wegman, sponsor of the LPGA event in Rochester, New York.

■ Sorenstam at ease in the kitchen

I love to crunch numbers. I look at how many fairways I hit, how many greens I hit. I plan my way around the golf course

ANNIKA SORENSTAM ON HER APPROACH TO THE GAME

ANOTHER PUTT FINDS THE BOTTOM of the cup for Sorenstam. Initially not the most emotive on the course, Annika developed into a more charasmatic figure as her career progressed and the wins flowed.

I'm from the old school … Practicing is how I learned the game.

To practice and build a swing is a victory in itself

VIJAY SINGH

Vijay Singh

VIJAY SINGH'S JOURNEY TO BECOMING one of the best players of his generation is one of the longest and most unlikely ever seen. He grew up in Fiji, was outcast to Borneo, briefly acted as a nightclub bouncer in Edinburgh, won on every continent except Antarctica, and then won three Major championships. And he did it by practicing more than anyone else.

△◁ **AS BRYON NELSON NOTED**, Vijay never seems to rush, he swings fast through the ball but his rhythm doesn't seem to change.

◁ **DEDICATION ON THE** driving range and in the gym paid off for Singh when he became the world No 1 in 2004.

◁◁ **SINGH THANKS** the gallery in his new green jacket after winning the Masters at Augusta in 2000.

VIJAY WAS THE SON of an airport technician in Fiji and had to sprint across the runaway to get to his local course. He studied the golf magazines that were flown into the airport and focused particularly on American Tom Weiskopf, a similarly tall man. There were only approximately 200 golfers in Fiji at the time but, by the age of 15, Singh was the best of them. Though his father had helped to teach Vijay the game, Vijay angered his father by neglecting his school work in order to practice.

Eventually he turned professional and, with no backing, went to Australia. He won the Malaysian Open in 1994, but a year later was accused of doctoring his scorecard at the Indonesian Open. He claimed the marker had made the mistake, which he had not noticed, but as a result, he was suspended by the Asian Tour. He felt harshly treated, as such an offense—even if he had committed it—should have resulted in disqualification from the event, rather than a ban from the Tour.

EUROPEAN SUCCESS

Needing to make his living, Singh took a job as the club professional at a course in Malaysian Borneo and continued to hone his skills. His breakthrough was winning the Nigerian Open in 1988 and the Safari Tour Order of Merit. He got his card on the European Tour in 1988, having failed to gain access to the tour the previous year, and immediately became a regular winner. In 1993 he finished second at Bay Hill, and then won the Buick Classic to get his card in the US. In 2007 he won the Arnold Palmer Invitational at Bay Hill to claim his 31st victory on the PGA Tour.

Along the way he was notorious for being the first man on the practice range in the morning and the last to leave. When he was not hitting balls, he was working on his fitness. His work ethic was extraordinary, although he always said golfers get far more vacations than normal people do. "I have a family but golf was always me. I go to sleep thinking about it and wake up thinking about it. My mind is consumed with my career."

He experimented with different putting styles but won his biggest tournaments putting cross-handed with a conventional putter. He won the USPGA at

SINGH HOLDS ALOFT the huge Wanamaker Trophy after winning the USPGA Championship for the first time at Sahalee in 1998.

Sahalee in 1998 at the age of 35, and then claimed the Masters at Augusta in 2000 by three strokes from Ernie Els. Into his third decade as a pro, Vijay's rate of success actually increased, and he has won more titles than anyone else in their forties, beating the previous record set by Sam Snead. His second USPGA title came at Whistling Straits in 2004, when he won a playoff against Justin Leonard and Chris DiMarco. It was one of nine victories that season, which briefly put him above Tiger Woods as the world No 1, and earned him an astonishing $10 million in prize money. Vijay means "victory" in Hindu, and he has certainly lived up to the name: he has won more titles on the PGA Tour than any other non-American golfer.

Paul Lawrie

PAUL LAWRIE WAS A SLOW STARTER to the game of golf. Then in 1999 he shocked himself and the whole golfing world by winning the Open at Carnoustie. When Jean van de Velde stumbled, Lawrie seized his chance and took home the Claret Jug. He was the first Scot to win the title in Scotland for 68 years, and the last European to win a Major before Padraig Harrington won in 2007.

IT WAS NOT THAT LAWRIE WAS UNKNOWN. He had won twice on the European Tour in the three years prior to winning the Open, and won twice more in the following three years. But his route to becoming the "champion golfer of the year" was improbable. He turned professional at the age of 17, with a handicap of five, and worked as an assistant professional in the pro shop at Banchory Golf Club in Aberdeenshire, Scotland. He did not get on to the European Tour for another six years. In 1996 Lawrie secured his first victory—the Catalan Open. Then, several months before his Major triumph, he won in the wind in Qatar. Nevertheless, he still had to qualify for the Open at Carnoustie.

He was outside the world's top 150 and started the final round 10 strokes behind the leader but produced a brilliant 67. Jean van de Velde, on the other hand, teed off at the last hole with a three-shot lead but took a triple-bogey seven and limped into a playoff with Lawrie and Justin Leonard. In the playoff, Lawrie birdied the last two holes in the cold rain to claim the crown.

Lawrie had taken his opportunity. He was the leading points-scorer for Europe in the Ryder Cup later that year and he won the Dunhill Links Championship in 2001. But, with the media stuck on the Van de Velde story, Lawrie never got the credit he deserved. Not that he was seeking attention. "I didn't want to be a celeb in the papers every day saying 'look at me.' I am very much a person who does his work and then goes home," he said. Yet, at the age of 30, he had suddenly achieved his life's dream. As a result of winning the Open, Lawrie set up a junior program which has introduced hundreds of children in his hometown to the game.

△ **ALL SMILES AFTER** winning the Open Championship at Carnoustie—a brilliant but shock victory after a four-hole playoff.

▷ **LAWRIE STARTED** as an assistant in the pro shop at Banchory but years of hard work took the Scot to the very heights of the game.

Jesper Parnevik

THREE TIMES IN FIVE YEARS, Jesper Parnevik came close to winning the Open, and becoming the first Swedish player to win a Major championship. Although it never quite happened for him at the very highest level, Parnevik did become an inspirational Ryder Cup player, and with his unconventional style was one of the most popular players of his generation.

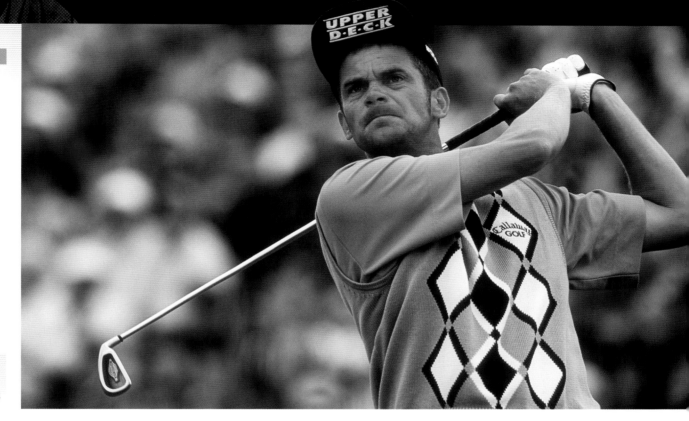

PLAYER STATS

BORN March 7, 1965; Stockholm, Sweden
HEIGHT 6 ft (1.83 m)
TURNED PRO 1986

DEBUT WIN 1993 Bell's Scottish Open
TOUR WINS 13
EUROPEAN TOUR: 4
PGA TOUR: 5
OTHER: 4

MAJORS 0
MASTERS: T20th 2001
US OPEN: T14th 1998
THE OPEN: 2nd 1994, 1997
USPGA: T5th 1996

HONORS
Ryder Cup Team: 1997, 1999, 2002

CRAZY GOLF

Whether on or off the course, Jesper Parnevik stands out as unique. Known for his outrageous fashion sense, he has been known to change outfits during the course of a round, and when he appeared in the Ryder Cup, he received a customized up-turned team cap. His style and individualism have made him hugely popular with the galleries.

■ Parnevik impersonators

PARNEVIK IS A FAMOUS NAME in Sweden because his father, Bo, was one of the country's foremost comedians. Parnevik learned to play by hitting floating golf balls into a lake behind the family house, and he developed into a great striker of the ball.

An early trademark developed after leaving the Swedish winter to practice in Florida for the start of the season. To improve his suntan, he flipped up the peak of his cap. He found his putting improved; he got into a playoff with Seve Ballesteros in his next event; the gallery loved it; and sponsors competed for the underside of the peak.

Parnevik, dubbed "the spaceman," is seen as quite the eccentric both on and off the course: he has tried a diet of volcanic sand and fruit; has used stroboscopic glasses; had his metal tooth fillings replaced with ceramic fillings; and named his children Peg (he had a tee peg in his pocket), Penny (his favorite marker was a penny), Phillipa (she was almost Pebble Peach), and Phoenix

THREE TIMES PARNEVIK came close to winning the Open Championship, but his dream of becoming Sweden's first Major winner hasn't yet been fulfilled.

(where Parnevik had his first win in the US). He has also launched a vitamin company, and has led the way in fairway fashions thanks to the Swedish designer J. Lindeberg. He also once missed a 2 ft (60 cm) putt at Loch Lomond while thinking about how much extra rope it would take to encircle the world on 3 ft (1 m) high stakes. He has a wandering mind. He also took up magic.

But Parnevik can play golf. He almost won the Open at Turnberry in 1994, but did not look at the leaderboard on the 18th tee. Thinking he needed a birdie, he bogeyed instead; Nick Price eagled the 17th and claimed victory. At Troon in 1997 Parnevik led by two with a round to play, but lost to Justin Leonard. His best chance, he believed, came a year later at Birkdale, when he finished two strokes outside the playoff won by Mark O'Meara.

Retief Goosen

ONE OF THE BEST GOLFERS TO EMERGE IN RECENT YEARS from the rich breeding ground of South Africa, Retief Goosen overcame extreme circumstances to win the US Open in 2001 and 2004. His liking for tough conditions, and ability to stay calm, make him well suited to the most mentally demanding Major championship. This, after all, is a man who survived being hit by lightning.

GOOSEN HAS NO MEMORY OF THE INCIDENT. He thought the storm had passed as he returned to the 12th green at Pietersburg Golf Club. His playing partner was also knocked to the ground but found Goosen unconscious. The lightning bolt had hit a tree before striking the youngster, just a few days away from his 16th birthday. His clothes had been burned away and his rubber shoes had melted. Goosen simply remembers waking up in the hospital "feeling sore and covered in skin burns. There is nothing left of it now, but at the time I was a bit of a mess." There were related health issues for a time, and his mother, Annie, believes that it left him more introverted than he had been before.

Nevertheless, Goosen was one of South Africa's best amateurs, and after winning on his home circuit, he won the European Tour Qualifying School in 1992. Since 1996 he has been a regular winner in Europe and the US. A man of few words, he admits to becoming less intense after marrying English wife Tracy and becoming a family man. On the course he was initially over-long and displayed a bit of a temper. He successfully reined in both, and became supreme at plotting his way around the most difficult courses, while maintaining a calm equilibrium.

In the 2001 US Open at Southern Hills he had two putts from 12 ft (4 m) to win at the last, but missed from 18 inches for the victory, in what commentator Johnny Miller called the "worst three-putt in the history of golf." Contrary to expectation, and thanks to help from his then sports psychologist Jos Vantisphout, Goosen did not crumble after the miss and won an 18-hole playoff the next day against Mark Brookes. Three years later, on the baked-out, glassy greens of Shinnecock Hills, Goosen put on a brilliant display of putting and overcame a New York crowd desperate for a Phil Mickelson win, to claim the title again. He has also won the European Order of Merit in 2001 and 2002.

A QUIET ACHIEVER, Retief Goosen's low-key personality has not stopped him winning some of the game's biggest prizes, on both the European and the PGA Tours.

> Who knows what it would have been like if I didn't win the U.S. Open, but you know, my life has gone down this way now and I've done pretty well.

RETIEF GOOSEN

TWICE GOOSEN HAS TRIUMPHED at the US Open, with his second win coming at Shinnecock Hills in 2004.

David Duval

FOR A BRIEF PERIOD, DAVID DUVAL WAS THE BEST PLAYER IN THE WORLD. He won prolifically, shooting 59 to claim one title, topped the world rankings, and he claimed a three-shot victory, and his first Major championship title at the 130th Open at Royal Lytham & St. Annes. Then he lost his swing, due to injuries, and seemingly his passion for the game. For Duval, life, not golf, took center stage.

PLAYER STATS

BORN November 9, 1971; Jacksonville, Florida
HEIGHT 6 ft (1.83 m)
TURNED PRO 1993

DEBUT WIN Michelob Championship 1997
TOUR WINS 19
PGA TOUR: 13
OTHER: 6

MAJORS 1
MASTERS: 2nd 1998/T2nd 2001
US OPEN: T7th 1998, 1999
THE OPEN: Won 2001
USPGA: T10th 1999, 2001

HONORS
PGA Tour Money Winner: 1998
Vardon Trophy Winner: 1998
Ryder Cup Team: 1999, 2002
Presidents Cup Team: 1996, 1998, 2000

THE WRAP-AROUND SHADES were indicative of a man who showed little emotion on the golf course.

DAVID DUVAL overtook Tiger Woods as the world's best player in 1999 and the success continued when he won the 2001 Open.

GOLF SEEMED TO BE DAVID DUVAL'S SALVATION. A star in college golf, Duval was not out of the top 11 on the money list in his first seven seasons in the US. But at first, the wins would not come; he was a runner-up seven times and third on four other occasions before his first victory. Then, having shown great belief in himself, he found the way to win, taking 11 victories between 1997 and 1999. He won four times early in 1999, including the Bob Hope Chrysler Classic when he shot a 59 in the final round. Having started it seven strokes off the lead, he made 11 birdies, and an eagle at the final hole. None of the putts holed were over 10 ft (3 m); he missed from 12 ft (4 m) and 15 ft (5 m) for birdies.

His was the third official 59 in the US, but the first to win a tournament on the last day. Two months later, on the same day his father won on the Seniors Tour, he won the Players Championship in his home town of Jacksonville.

But early in 2000 he suffered a ligament sprain in his back that would lead to years of problems on the course. Initially overweight when he arrived on tour, Duval had slimmed down with a relentless exercise regime. After a number of near misses at the Majors, a 65 in the third round put him in contention for the 2001 Open at Royal Lytham, and he swept imperiously to victory with a closing 67 and a 10-under par total. Often perceived as a cold, prickly character of few words, he removed his hat and wraparound sunglasses at the prize giving, and smiled, finally allowing his personality to shine through.

"My existential moment was right there," he said. However, he won only once more, in Japan later that year; winning a Major was not the life-changing moment he imagined. The injuries caused him to lose confidence and revamp his swing and his game fell away, but after splitting from his fiancée, he found happiness with a new partner, and settled into family life.

Darren Clarke

A GOLF CAREER THAT HAD SEEN HIM WIN more than 15 times on the European Tour paled in significance to what he went through in 2006, and touched many far outside the golfing world. That August his wife Heather lost her four-and-a-half year battle with breast cancer. Six weeks later Clarke performed with such fortitude in the Ryder Cup that the drama will long be remembered.

PLAYER STATS

BORN August 14, 1968; Dungannon, Northern Ireland
HEIGHT 6 ft 2 in (1.88 m)
TURNED PRO 1990

DEBUT WIN 1993 Alfred Dunhill Open
TOUR WINS 17
EUROPEAN TOUR: 10
OTHER: 7

MAJORS 0
MASTERS: T8th 1998
US OPEN: T10th 1999
THE OPEN: T2nd 1997
USPGA: T9th 2000

HONORS:
Ryder Cup Team: 1997, 1999, 2002, 2004, 2006

CLARKE GREW UP IN NORTHERN IRELAND and learned his golf at such mighty Ulster courses as Royal Portrush. He was always highly talented: in his second year on the European Tour, he shot a round of 60 at Monte Carlo, a feat he would repeat—no one else in Europe has had two rounds of 60—at the more difficult K Club in 1999. His first win came in 1993, and from 1996 he won almost every year until 2003; then in 2001 he became the first Irishman to win on home soil for 19 years (also at the K Club). Another landmark year was 2003. He became only the second player, after Tiger Woods, to win two World Golf Championships. His first had been the Matchplay at La Costa in 2001, when he had defeated Woods, a friend, in the 36-hole final. Major success, however, proved elusive—there was a second and a third place at the Open—but nonetheless, Clarke always enjoyed the trappings that came with the big checks: fast cars, cigars, and well-tailored clothes.

TRAPPINGS OF SUCCESS

Clarke has always had a penchant for the finer things in life. He drives fast cars and drinks expensive wine. His trousers are handmade by a tailor on London's Saville Row, and it is estimated he spends around $50,000 per year on the finest Cuban cigars.

■ Darren Clarke—life in the fast lane

IRISH HERO

In 2003 his wife Heather discovered her cancer had worsened. Splitting his time between caring for her and their two sons, and playing tournaments, Clarke maintained a remarkably high standard of play given the circumstances. It was Heather's wish that Clarke play in the 2006 Ryder Cup, so he accepted a wild card from captain Ian Woosnam.

On the first morning, Clarke had demonstrated remarkable composure—and technique, given that Tiger Woods had just hooked his ball into a lake—with his opening tee shot, after the nerve-tingling reception he received from the Irish crowd on the first tee. He went on to birdie the opening hole. He was successful in two fourball matches with his friend Lee Westwood and in his singles against Zach Johnson. His was not the actual winning putt, but the teary celebrations on the 16th green proved the emotional beginning of Europe's thumping victory.

PLAYING PARTNERS CLARKE (right) and Lee Westwood (left), enjoy Europe's Ryder Cup victory at the K Club in 2007.

Lee Westwood

ALTHOUGH HIS CAREER has had its downs as well as ups since he turned professional, there is no doubting one thing about Lee Westwood: if he is in contention to win a golf tournament, he will probably win it. His well-developed killer instinct also makes him an extremely dangerous Ryder Cup opponent, as the Americans know all too well.

WESTWOOD HAS BECOME a more consistent performer since reconstructing his swing under the guidance of David Leadbetter.

AN ALL-ROUND SPORTSMAN at school and a fan of Greg Norman, Westwood turned professional with a handicap of plus four and immediately earned a place on the European Tour from the Qualifying School. His first couple of seasons were a learning experience and his first win came in Sweden in 1996. In the next four years, he won 14 times in Europe and eight times in other places around the globe, including in New Orleans on the PGA Tour in 1998. In 2000 he won six times in Europe alone and became the European No. 1, ending Colin Montgomerie's seven-year reign as king of the order of merit. At the time Westwood was England's only player in the top 100 on the world rankings, but that was to change, as he subsequently slumped alarmingly.

FINDING FORM

Westwood took a long break over the winter of 2000 and missed the Masters for the birth of his son, Samuel. He always had concerns about his technique, even while he was winning, but once he stopped winning, he lost his swing and his confidence. After working with David Leadbetter in 2003, however, he won twice in quick succession, including at the Dunhill Links Championship. But he still had to wait until May 2007 for his next win, which came in Spain; this was followed later in the year with a victory at the British Masters. No matter how he is playing on the tour, however, he can be relied upon during the Ryder Cup. In 2004 and 2006 he went undefeated, winning 8½ out of 10 points.

> I've always been able to
> ## keep my cool and win tournaments when I've got into contention

LEE WESTWOOD

Karrie Webb

FROM ONE OF THE MOST REMOTE AREAS OF THE WORLD, Karrie Webb emerged to become the best woman golfer in the world. Peter Thomson even suggested she was the best golfer, male or female, with a better swing than Tiger Woods. At the age of 30, Webb joined Thomson and Greg Norman as Australia's representatives in the World Golf Hall of Fame.

I look back at my career sometimes and can't believe how fast everything has gone and how much I've been able to accomplish

KARRIE WEBB ON BEING INDUCTED INTO THE WORLD GOLF HALL OF FAME

WEBB GREW UP IN AYR, around 1,000 miles (1,600 km) from Brisbane, not exactly a hotbed for golf. Most of the town's population of 8,600 are involved either in the production of sugar cane or providing services for it. Webb's parents owned a toy and gift shop, right next door to the corner store.

Kevin Haller, whose parents owned the corner store, used to study the golf magazines and since the local golf club didn't have a professional, he became Webb's coach. Webb turned pro in 1994 and was Rookie of the Year in

Europe. She also won the British Open for the first of three times (the first two did not count as official LPGA Majors). A year later she was Rookie of the Year in the US, becoming the first woman to earn over $1 million in a season. Webb herself does not know where her greatest strength comes from. "I think I was given a gift to play golf and to be mentally strong," she said. "You know, I don't see a sports psychologist. I've somehow just known what to do." Off the course, Webb is uncomfortable in the limelight and happy to let her clubs do the talking.

Her finest spell was between 1999 and 2002 when she won six Majors. She won the US Open in 2000 and 2001 and fellow golfer Meg Mallon said of her, "Sometimes when a player makes it look as easy as she does, it's hard to appreciate how good she is." By winning the British Open at Turnberry in 2002, she became the first player to win all five LPGA Majors, the so-called Super Grand Slam. By 2000 she had earned enough points to be inducted into the World Golf Hall of Fame, but was unable to take up her place until 2005, by which time she had completed her 10th season on the tour.

After a lull, Webb won her seventh Major, the 2006 Kraft Nabisco Championship, in spectacular fashion. She holed a 116-yard shot to eagle the 18th hole and then birdied the same hole in a sudden-death playoff to beat Lorena Ochoa.

WEBB ESCAPES FROM a bunker during the 2000 Women's British Open at Royal Birkdake. She has won the championship three times.

Se Ri Pak

IN 1998, SE RI PAK MADE THE SORT OF SPLASH in the women's game not seen since Nancy Lopez arrived two decades earlier. Pak won two Major championships in her first season on the LPGA tour, including the US Women's Open, and at a stroke signaled the arrival of South Korea, and other less familiar nations, at the top of the women's game.

PLAYER STATS

BORN September 28, 1977; Daejeon, S. Korea
HEIGHT 5 ft 6 in (1.68 m)
TURNED PRO 1996

DEBUT WIN LPGA 1998
TOUR WINS 30
LPGA TOUR: 24
OTHER: 6

MAJORS 5
KRAFT NABISCO: T9th 2002
LPGA CHAMPIONSHIP: Won 1998, 2002, 2006
US WOMEN'S OPEN: Won 1998
DU MAURIER CLASSIC: T7th 2000
WOMEN'S BRITISH OPEN: Won 2001

HONORS
LPGA Tour Rookie of the Year: 1998

PAK WAS NOT THE FIRST PLAYER from South Korea to make it onto the LPGA circuit in the US, but her remarkable rookie season led many more to follow her lead. Her success changed the face of women's golf with players from other non-traditional golfing nations like Mexico and Paraguay enjoying success.

Pak displayed an incredible work ethic when first taking up the game. Although she was a sprinter at school, by at the age of 14, she had turned seriously to golf. Her father, a top amateur golfer, employed training methods perhaps not approved of in other cultures. He had Se Ri running up and down the staircases of their 15-story apartment building at 5:30 in the morning, and sometimes took her to a cemetery in the middle of the night "to develop courage and nerve." He recalled how he "wanted to teach her that to win in golf, she first had to win the battle within herself."

TOO MUCH, TOO SOON

Pak won 30 times as an amateur in Korea, and then as a professional on the Korean Ladies Professional Golf Association (KLPGA) circuit she won six times and was second seven times in her first 14 events. In 1998, she arrived in the US, winning four titles as a 20-year-old.

Her first two wins were Major championships: the LPGA followed by the US Open, which she won after a 20-hole playoff against amateur Jenny Chuasiriporn. At the end of a long season, she returned home to South Korea and was awarded the Order of Merit, the country's highest honor for an athlete. But so exhausting was the attention and fame that she collapsed and spent four days in hospital. Her cool demeanor on the course, compounded by her little English in the early days, masked an emotional character off the course.

PAK HAS LED AN INVASION of talent from South Korea onto the world stage in women's golf.

WINNING THE LPGA CHAMPIONSHIP and the US Women's Open made for a memorable introduction to American golf for Se Ri Pak.

Her first experiences of links golf, in horrid weather, was less than enjoyable, but when the British Open moved to Sunningdale in 2001, she claimed her third Major. In 2005 she suffered from shoulder, neck, back, and finger injuries and took a break from the game, but in 2006 she followed up her 2002 victory by winning her third LPGA crown, beating Karrie Webb in a playoff. In 2007 she surpassed Webb once again by virtue of being the youngest living entrant to be inducted into the World Golf Hall of Fame.

Padraig Harrington

IN 2007 AT CARNOUSTIE, PADRAIG HARRINGTON became the first European to win a Major championship since Paul Lawrie at the same venue eight years before. After a dramatic playoff with Sergio Garcia, Harrington held the Claret Jug and Ireland had their first Open champion since Fred Daly 60 years previously. For Harrington, years of hard work had finally paid off.

PLAYER STATS

BORN August 31, 1971; Dublin, Ireland
HEIGHT 6 ft (1.83 m)
TURNED PRO 1996

DEBUT WIN 1996 Peugeot Spanish Open
TOUR WINS 21
EUROPEAN TOUR: 12
PGA TOUR: 2
OTHER: 7

MAJORS 1
MASTERS: T5th 2002
US OPEN: 5th 2006/T5th 2000
THE OPEN: Won 2007
USPGA: T17th 2002

HONORS
European Tour Order of Merit: 2006
Ryder Cup Team: 1999, 2002, 2004, 2006

▷ **HARRINGTON IS A CONSISTENT** performer. He has finished in the top ten on the European Tour's Order of Merit seven times.

△ **WITH HIS TRIUMPH** at Carnoustie in 2007, Harrington became only the second Irishman ever to win the Open Championship.

AFTER A GLITTERING amateur career, Harrington won the Spanish Open in his first season as a pro. He had to wait until 2000 for his next victory, but all the time, he was improving his game, having started work with the legendary coach Bob Torrance. Harrington has never stopped trying to better himself, combining the work ethic of a Vijay Singh with the discipline and management skills of a Bernhard Langer.

So often Harrington would finish as a runner-up, occasionally because he had a chance to win and slipped up, but more often it was due to a stronger finish from others. From 2000, however, he began to win regularly, including twice in the US in 2005, and in 2006 he won the Dunhill Links Championship for the second time. This victory helped him to win the European Tour's Order of Merit, although it only arrived due to the combination of a strong finish at Valderrama and Garcia's bogey on the last hole. In 2007 he won what he called his "fifth Major," the Irish Open. If the celebrations were great then, they were nothing compared to what was to follow in July at the Open, when Harrington beat Sergio Garcia by one shot in a four-hole playoff.

> I would have settled for being a journeyman when I turned professional, **but I started so well** that I always had the focus to improve and see how good I could become.

PADRAIG HARRINGTON

Sergio Garcia

SERGIO GARCIA BURST ONTO THE GOLFING SCENE in such a whirlwind of energy that it seemed inevitable he would become Spain's next great player. He still awaits a Major championship, after several near misses, but his brilliant record in the Ryder Cup has continued the magnificent tradition of Seve Ballesteros and José Maria Olazábal for the European team.

PLAYER STATS

BORN January 9, 1980; Castellón, Spain
HEIGHT 5 ft 10 in (1.78 m)
TURNED PRO 1999

DEBUT WIN 1999 Murphy's Irish Open
TOUR WINS 16
EUROPEAN TOUR: 6
PGA TOUR: 6
OTHER: 4

MAJORS 0
MASTERS: T4th 2004
US OPEN: T3rd 2005
THE OPEN: 2nd 2007
USPGA: 2nd 1999

HONORS
Ryder Cup Team: 1999, 2002, 2004, 2006
The Amateur: 1998

AT CARNOUSTIE IN THE 2007 Open Championship, Garcia produced a brilliant display of ball-striking on the fearsome course to lead for each of the first three days. But as has so often happened in recent years, his putting was not quite as confident on the final day, and in thrilling circumstances, he was pipped by Padraig Harrington after a four-hole playoff. The disappointment of missing the chance to win his first Major was palpable but he needed only to look at the Irishman's example to learn how such an experience can lead to future glory.

Garcia started playing golf at the age of three, guided by his father, Victor, a professional himself. Nicknamed El Niño, he won heavily as an amateur, including the British Amateur at Muirfield in 1998. He was the leading amateur at the Open in 1996 and at the Masters in 1999, after which he turned professional. In only his third start on the European Tour, he won the Irish Open. Then, at that year's USPGA Championship at Medinah, he lost only narrowly to Tiger Woods. At the 16th hole he played an extraordinary shot—Seve-esque—from behind a tree, and then sprinted and jumped his way down the fairway to see the ball land on the green.

MATCHPLAY MASTER

He showed the same energy in making his Ryder Cup debut at the age of 19 at Brookline later that season, and immediately formed a brilliant partnership with Swede Jesper Parnevik. His tears at the end of the contest encapsulated the pain of defeat for the European team (see pp.236). Throughout his Ryder Cup career, where he has won 14 and lost four of his 20 matches, his putting has been brilliant and his whole enthusiasm irrepressible. Here he is once more the young kid who emerged so gloriously at the end of the 1990s.

However, despite wins in both the US and Europe, he has suffered problems with his technique. Firstly, he had to overcome a loop in his swing (refined so well he became one of the longest and straightest hitters in the game); and secondly, a nervous regripping before taking the club back. He is still afflicted with poor putting, however. When his touch on the greens returns, he will once more challenge for the biggest prizes in golf.

LIKE HIS COMPATRIOTS Ballesteros and Olazábal, Garcia has a tremendous short game around the greens.

GARCIA HAS COME CLOSE TO WINNING a major title, with his playoff defeat to Padraig Harrington in the 2007 Open at Carnoustie being his most disappointing near miss.

△ ALONE WITH HIS THOUGHTS at the 2003 USPGA at Oak Hill, as another Major championship slips away before his breakthrough at Augusta.

△ WINNING THE USPGA CHAMPIONSHIP at Baltusrol in 2005 gave Mickelson a second Major title in the space of two years.

◁ MICKELSON JUMPS FOR JOY after winning a breathtaking duel with Ernie Els to claim his first Masters title in 2004.

Phil Mickelson

FOR MANY YEARS THE ONLY THING MISSING from Phil Mickelson's career was a Major championship. Then at the 2004 Masters, the left-hander finally clinched a green jacket. He won the USPGA in 2005 and the Masters for the second time in 2006. Hugely talented, and wildly popular in the US, he had to temper his aggressive style before succeeding at the highest level.

PLAYER STATS

BORN June 16, 1970; San Diego, California
HEIGHT 6 ft 3 in (1.91 m)
TURNED PRO 1992

DEBUT WIN 1991 Northern Telecom Open
TOUR WINS 38
PGA TOUR: 32
OTHER: 6

MAJORS 3
MASTERS: Won 2004, 2006
US OPEN: 2nd 1999, 2002, 2004/T2nd 2006
THE OPEN: 3rd 2004
USPGA: Won 2005

HONORS
Presidents Cup Team: 1994, 1996, 1998, 2000, 2003, 2005, 2007
Ryder Cup Team: 1995, 1997, 1999, 2002, 2004, 2006
US Amateur Champion: 1990

MICKELSON WAS ALWAYS supremely talented. He grew up in San Diego, the son of a pilot, and it was watching his father play, mirroring his motion while standing alongside him, that Phil started to play the game left-handed. He is naturally right-handed and his father tried to turn him around, but the youngster refused. By the age of six, he was playing all day at a par-3 course and it was there and in his back yard that he developed a stellar range of short-game skills.

At the age of 20 Mickelson became the US Amateur champion. He was the National College Champion three years out of four, and even before he turned professional he won the Northern Telecom Open in Tucson in 1991, the first amateur to win on the US Tour since Scott Verplank's victory six years beforehand.

The victories mounted, but so did the near-misses at the Majors: in his first 46 Majors, he was runner-up twice at the US Open, once at the USPGA, and was third three times at the Masters. "The frustrating part is not that I

MICKELSON BECAME THE THIRD left-handed golfer to win a Major championship, after Bob Charles and Mike Weir.

> He is even more talented than I thought, and I knew he was exceptionally talented

BUTCH HARMON

am trying to win a Major, I'm trying to win a bunch of them," he said. At Augusta in 2004, he adjusted his game slightly, by shortening up his swing, and reining in his all-out aggression. It still produced birdies—in the final round, he birdied five of the last seven holes and shot a 31, to beat Ernie Els in a classic contest (see far left).

Two months later he lost out to Retief Goosen at the US Open, but suddenly he was putting himself in contention. His

MICKELSON IS HELPED into his green jacket by his rival Tiger Woods after his second victory in three years at Augusta.

new preparation routine was paying off. He would go to the tournament site and spend hours and hours studying the course alongside his short-game guru and one-time NASA scientist, Dave Pelz. He won the USPGA in 2005 and the very next major, the 2006 Masters. He was on a roll, but at the US Open that year, at Winged Foot, his driving let him down throughout the week, most disastrously on the 72nd hole where a double bogey six cost him a third Major in a row.

In a bid to tighten up his driving, Mickelson left his long term coach Rick Smith and turned to Tiger Woods's old teacher, Butch Harmon. The partnership was an immediate success, with Mickelson winning the 2007 Players Championship at Sawgrass.

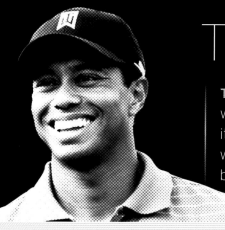

Tiger Woods

TIGER WOODS BECAME A CULTURAL AND SPORTING phenomenon when he won the 1997 Masters at Augusta (see pp. 232–33). It was not just how he did it, winning by 12 strokes, but who was doing it, the first ever golfing superstar with an ethnic background. His influence on how the game is perceived has been immense, but Tiger has simply got on with becoming the best golfer ever.

> **TIGER TAKES A MOMENT** to savor victory at the 2006 Open Championship, an emotional time after the death of his father.

< **A TYPICAL TIGER WOODS** celebration, at the 1998 Johnnie Walker Classic in Thailand, after a stirring comeback against Ernie Els.

He has this uncanny ability, when someone gets close to him, to turn it up to another level

CHRIS DIMARCO, RUNNER-UP TO WOODS IN TWO MAJORS

WHEN, ON THE FINAL GREEN at Southern Hills in the second round of the 2007 USPGA, Tiger's birdie putt defied gravity and the full force of the Woods's will—which bends most golfing things his way—he had to settle for only tying the Major championship record for a single round. It was not the first 62, but the 23rd round of 63 in a Major. It mattered little when it came to winning the USPGA for the fourth time, and his 13th Major championship. It was also the 13th time out of 13 that he had led going into the final round and gone on to win. As a front runner, he is unsurpassed. When he is good, he is so far ahead he cannot be caught. When he is behind, and up to then he had never won a Major from behind, he is not on top of his game.

Tiger learned the game from his high chair, watching his father play with a plastic club, before climbing down one day and having a go himself. At the age of three, he won a pitch-and-putt competition for 10- and 11-year-olds. He was soon on TV shows, including *The Mike Douglas Show*, with Bob Hope and James Stewart, and *That's Incredible*. On the latter, at the age of five, he said of his future, "I want to win all the big tournaments ... and beat all the pros."

IMMEDIATE SUCCESS

First he had to beat the amateurs. Woods became the first person to win three consecutive US Junior Amateur titles, before going on to win three consecutive US Amateurs. Bobby Jones won five in six years, but Tiger became the youngest ever winner at the age of 18. After winning the third Amateur title, Woods turned professional in 1996. He won his fifth tournament as a professional, beating Davis Love in a playoff at the Las Vegas Invitational. He won again that year, and from only eight starts, became the Rookie of the Year.

CHILD PRODIGY

Winning trophies became a habit for Tiger Woods very early in his life. Blessed with natural talent and encouraged by his father, at the age of three he scored 48 over nine holes at the Navy Golf Club in Cypress, and he was soon regularly beating children much older than he was. It wasn't long before television companies took an interest in his exploits.

■ The young cub with his father in January 1989

PROUD PARENTS

Tiger once described himself as "cablinasian," an ethnic mix of Caucasian, black, Indian, and Asian. His mother, Kultida, is from Thailand, and remains as strong an influence in his life as his father, Earl, was on his golf. Earl Woods was a lieutenant colonel in the Green Berets and served two terms in Vietnam. On the second of them, he became friends with Colonel Vuong Dang Phong, who Earl called Tiger, and they went on to save each other's lives. Kultida named her son Eldrick, a name she had made up, but Earl always used the nickname Tiger. Later, Tiger changed his name by deed poll to include his father's nickname. Colonel Vuong was captured by the Vietcong, was imprisoned and died in 1976, unaware that his nickname would become that of the planet's most famous sportsman.

Earl Woods oversaw every aspect of his son's golfing education, including making him the most mentally resilient golfer of his generation. As well as having power to spare, Tiger generally out-thinks his opponents as well. In 1997 he played in his first Major as a professional at the Masters and went to the turn on the first morning in 40. But he came home in 30, with an eagle and four birdies, and after that blew away the field (see pp. 232–33). He had simply overpowered the Augusta course, but in the following years, he and his coach Butch Harmon reined in his swing so that he had both precision and power, when necessary. The result was perhaps the most accomplished golf ever seen.

REACHING NEW HEIGHTS

At the 2000 US Open, he won by 15 strokes with a record score of 12-under par (see pp. 238–39). On the fast greens of Pebble Beach, he never took a three-putt. A month later, on the Old Course at St. Andrews, Woods never went in any of its treacherous bunkers. He won by eight strokes with a record score in the Open at St. Andrews. At the USPGA he beat the relatively unknown Bob May in a playoff and then went to the 2001 Masters

▷ **WITH A FLAIR FOR THE DRAMATIC,** Tiger has produced many wondrous shots, including this chip in for eagle at Valderrama in 1999.

1992
At the age of 16, Tiger plays in his first professional tournament–the Nissan Los Angeles Open–and in three other PGA Tour events.

1994
Tiger enters Stanford University in California, and in two years he wins 10 collegiate events. He also wins the US Amateur.

1995
Plays his first Majors, making the 36-hole cuts in the Masters and the Open Championship, but withdraws from the US Open because of an injured wrist.

1996
Turns professional on August 27, bringing to an end an amateur career in which he won six USGA national championships, plus the coveted NCAA title.

1997
Tiger wins his first Major, the Masters, and breaks a multitude of records in the process, not least the lowest ever four-round total.

TIGER HAS ENJOYED A LONG and successful partnership with his caddie Steve Williams, a New Zealander who drives stock cars in his spare time.

looking for the "Tiger Slam"—his fourth consecutive victory. He held off the challenge of David Duval and Phil Mickelson to make more history.

CHANGING TIMES

The years of 2003 and 2004 were significant for Tiger not winning a Major. He changed coach to Hank Haney and at Augusta, in 2005, won his fourth Masters title. In 2006 at Hoylake, he won the Open for the second year running and the third time in all with an awesome display of iron-play. It was his first win since the death of his father and the most emotional he had been on the course. "I miss my dad so much," he said. "This win is so special." The following year gave way to different emotions as Tiger's wife, Elin, gave birth to their first child, a daughter, Sam Alexis. Maturing as a person in the public gaze cannot have been easy, but it seems only to have made him an even stronger competitor on the course.

1999	2000	2001	2005	2007
Tiger's second Ryder Cup appearance, at the Brookline Country Club, ends in a controversial win for the US. Tiger contributes two points.	In winning the Open Championship, Woods becomes the youngest player to complete the career Grand Slam of professional Majors and only the fifth player ever to do so.	With his second Masters victory, Tiger becomes the first person to hold all four Major championships at the same time.	Woods's wins the 2005 Open Championship, making him only the second golfer (after Jack Nicklaus) to have won all four Majors more than once.	At the USPGA Championship at Southern Hills, Tiger shoots a 63– the equal lowest ever score in a Major championship–on his way to winning the title.

Stars of the Men's Tour

NOTHING SUMS UP THE CHANGING PROFILE OF GOLF better than the recent run of overseas winners at the US Open. Once it was strictly the preserve of US champions, but between 2004 and 2007, the title was claimed by players from South Africa, New Zealand, Australia, and Argentina respectively. That these golfers were all from the southern hemisphere may be a coincidence, but it certainly reflects the truly international nature of the modern game at the highest level.

LUKE DONALD has won on both the European and US Tours, and was a winning member of the 2004 and 2006 Ryder Cup teams.

FOR BRITAIN AND EUROPE, the future looks bright. In 2007 Padraig Harrington became the first European winner of a Major since Paul Lawrie (also at Carnoustie) in 1999, and behind Harrington, a supremely talented bunch of golfers is poised to step forward. Not since the glory days of Ballesteros, Faldo, Langer, Lyle, and Woosnam has Europe had so many potential Major winners. In England, especially, a wave of talent has broken through on to both the European and US Tours.

Luke Donald and Paul Casey were both stars of the college circuit in the US—Donald at Northwestern in Chicago and Casey at Arizona State, where he broke records set by the likes of Phil Mickelson. Having been members of victorious Walker Cup teams, both made their debuts in the 2004 Ryder Cup, and then played vital roles in the European success of 2006. On tour, Donald has won in the US, while Casey has been more successful in Europe and Asia.

BLOOMING ROSE

Then there is Justin Rose. What a career he has already had. As an 17-year-old amateur, he chipped in at the last hole at Birkdale to finish fourth in the 1998 Open. He turned professional but then missed his first 21 cuts. He recovered from what might have been a permanent setback to win four times in 2002, including at the British Masters. The death of his father later that year was another blow. When the wins did not follow, he took the decision to base himself in the US, where he has steadily climbed up leaderboards, including at the Majors. He was one of the few to make the cut in all four in 2007, and his consistent year was capped when he won the Volvo Masters at Valderrama to become the No 1 on the European Tour by topping the order of merit.

EUROPEAN CHALLENGE

Henrik Stenson, the tall Swede, won the Benson & Hedges International Open in Britain during his rookie season, but then his swing fell apart. It took him three years to recover, but in February 2007, he beat Tiger Woods and Ernie Els to win the Dubai Desert Classic, before becoming the Accenture World Match Play champion. Sweden still awaits a Major champion, but Stenson, or the feisty Niclas Fasth, could make the grade.

Although Sergio Garcia remains one of the most talented players in the world striving to win a first Major, Spain unearthed another brilliantly gifted player in Pablo Martin. In 2007, while still at college in the US, Martin won the Portuguese Open, becoming

▷ **AFTER AN INCONSISTENT START** as a professional, Justin Rose established himself on both sides of the Atlantic and won the 2007 European Order of Merit.

YOUNG BLOOD

Rory McIlroy, from Northern Ireland, is surely a star of the future. At the age of just 17, he came to the wider public's attention by ending the first day at the 2007 Open in 3rd place. Just four months after his 18th birthday, he turned professional and soon earned his first tour card with a 3rd place at the Alfred Dunhill Links Championship and a 4th at the Madrid Open.

■ McIlroy acknowledges the crowd at the 2007 Open

> There's no give-up in Rosey and **no limit to what he can achieve**

NICK FALDO, TALKING ABOUT JUSTIN ROSE

The foreign tours out there are producing more talent, and are playing at a higher level than they have ever played

ERNIE ELS

the first amateur ever to win on the European Tour. It was a remarkably mature performance from the 20-year-old and promised much.

SOUTHERN STARS

Geoff Ogilvy probably never thought he would be the first of a new breed of Australian player to win a Major, as he did at Winged Foot at the 2006 US Open. His talented contemporaries include Robert Allenby, Stuart Appleby, Aaron Baddeley, and Adam Scott. Baddeley had the distinction of winning the Australian Open as an amateur and then retaining the title as a professional. He had to wait until 2006 for his breakthrough on the US Tour and then he won again the following year. After winning in Europe on a regular basis, Adam Scott went to the US and won the 2004 Players Championship —the next biggest title to a Major—and the US Tour

Championship title two years later. Coached by Butch Harmon, Tiger Woods' former coach, he has a swing eerily reminiscent of Woods in 2001.

Trevor Immelman is thought to be of the same caliber of talent as Bobby Locke, Gary Player, Ernie Els, and Retief Goosen. He twice won the South African Open, was victorious at the European Players Championship in 2004, and then again at the 2006 Western Open in the US, holding off Tiger Woods in the process. Charl Schwartzel is another South African to watch, having won consecutive South African Order of Merit honors, and two European Tour titles.

YOUNG AMERICANS

Inspired by Angel Cabrera's win at Oakmont in the 2007 US Open, Andres Romero suddenly burst onto the scene in July 2007. The 26-year-old Argentinian came close to winning the Open at Carnoustie with an inspired final round which contained 10 birdies. Leading by two strokes on the 17th, his second shot hit the wall of a burn and went out of bounds, causing him to miss out on the playoff by one stroke. However, he won the Deutsche Bank Players Championship by three strokes the following week for his maiden win on the European Tour, in only his second season.

In the US, players seem to come through later as they struggle to shrug off the shadow of Woods. Charles Howell III has been a noted pretender for a few years and got back to winning ways in 2007. Lucas Glover is another talented and consistent player who made his Presidents Cup debut in 2007. He played alongside Hunter Mahan, a 25-year-old who suddenly turned on the heat in the summer of 2007, winning his maiden title and reaching the semi-final of the HSBC World Match Play at Wentworth.

Asia, where the game is growing at an astonishing rate, will probably be the next big breeding ground for new talent, with challengers taking over from Vijay Singh and Korea's K.J. Choi. However, beating Tiger Woods remains the task for all the challengers, no matter how old they are, or where they are from.

ARGENTINIAN ANDRES ROMERO burst on to the scene at the 2007 Open, and the following week, he won his first European Tour title.

COLLEGIATE STARS

The US collegiate circuit has proved a fertile breeding ground for professional stars, including Phil Mickelson and Tiger Woods. But there has been a growing trend of Europeans traveling to the US on sports scholarships to further their golfing ambitions.

■ Arizona State's Phil Mickelson

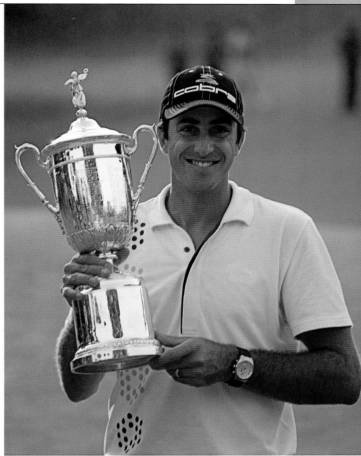

△ **AUSTRALIAN GEOFF OGILVY** won two PGA titles in 2006, one of them the US Open at Winged Foot, where he defeated Phil Mickleson.

◁ **PAUL CASEY ATTENDED** Arizona State University on a sports scholarship, and played on the winning European Ryder Cup teams of 2004 and 2006.

△ **HENRIK STENSON BECAME** the world's highest ranked European golfer–number eight–by winning the 2007 Dubai Desert Classic.

◁ **EVERGREEN JIM FURYK** remains one of golf's most consistent performers. He won the 2003 US Open, and finished second on the PGA Tour money list in 2006.

△ **COLUMBIAN FITNESS FANATIC** Camilo Villegas is one of the game's big-hitters. Since turning professional in 2004 he has already won on the US Tour.

◁ **ENGLISHMAN IAN POULTER** is one of the more flamboyant personalities on the European Tour. He now splits his time between the European and US Tours.

◁ **AARON BADDELEY** won the Australasia Order of Merit in 2001. His first PGA victory was the Verizon Heritage in 2006.

▽ **SOUTH AFRICAN TREVOR IMMELMAN** won his country's Sunshine Tour Order of Merit in 2003, and was named PGA Rookie of the Year in 2006.

△ **ADAM SCOTT OF AUSTRALIA** has won five PGA titles and 12 championships since turning professional. His biggest win was the 2004 Players Championship.

▽ **MIKE WEIR** became the first Canadian to win a Major when he won the 2003 Masters. At the 2007 President's Cup, he defeated Tiger Woods in the final day's singles.

Stars of the Women's Tour

AT THE 2007 WOMEN'S BRITISH OPEN, Lorena Ochoa became the first Mexican to win a Major championship and, in doing so, confirmed her position as the new No. 1 in the women's game. The 25-year-old headed a list of highly talented young players from all around the globe, that included Michelle Wie—the most famous and the wealthiest female golfer, but not yet the most successful.

AFTER A STELLAR CAREER in US college golf, and as an amateur, Lorena Ochoa soon became a popular figure in Mexico, despite the sport not being particularly popular. Her charming personality has brought her many friends on tour, and she is always happy to be photographed with her fans. She was the Rookie of the Year in 2003, won three times in 2004–05, but enjoyed her big breakthrough in 2006 when she won six times on the tour, and was named Player of the Year. She overtook Annika Sorenstam (see pp.178–79) as the No. 1 in the world that year, and in 2007 added a first Major to her list of successes, when the first professional women's event was played on the Old Course at St. Andrews.

HEALTHY RIVALRY
If any more proof were needed of the rivalry in the women's game, there were four first-time winners in the Majors in 2007, with Norway's Suzann Pettersen taking the LPGA Championship, Cristie Kerr winning the US Women's Open, and Morgan Pressel claiming the Kraft Nabisco Championship at the age of 19. Pressel, who is coached by her grandfather, had first qualified for the US Open at the age of 12 and almost won it at the age of 17 as an amateur. Paula Creamer won twice in her rookie season in 2005 at the age of 19 and beat Laura Davies (see p.171) 7&5 in the Solheim Cup. Natalie Gulbis, who models for her own calendar, won the Evian Masters in 2007, proving herself a star both on, and off the course.

YOUNG PRETENDERS
Having won the US Women's Public Links Championship at the age of 13, at 14 Michelle Wie hit the headlines by missing the cut by just one stroke at the men's Sony Open in her home state of Hawaii. She turned professional in 2005, aged 16, with much fanfare and with millions in the bank (see right), and the following year increased her tally of top-five finishes in the women's Majors to six. However, Wie's presence in men's PGA Tour events through sponsors' exemptions has drawn criticism, as has her sense of fashion.

Other talented young women have emerged from all over the world. Ai Miyazato helped Japan to win the World Cup in 2005 at the age of 19. Julieta Granada, from Paraguay, became the first woman from her country to win a tournament when she took the $1 million prize at the 2006 ADT Championship. Ashleigh Simon won four times on the South African tour when she was an amateur and then won on her fourth start as a pro at the 2007 Catalan Open. In Britain, Melissa Ried claimed the silver salver as the low amateur in the 2007 Women's British Open, while Carly Booth shocked golf clubs around Scotland by starting to win club championships at the age of just 12. Certainly, the future of the women's game appears as bright as it has ever been (see pp.32–33).

LORENA OCHOA tees off during the 2007 Women's British Open at St. Andrews. She won the championship with a four-under par 287.

BIG MONEY DEALS

Big hitters like Nike and Sony did not wait for Wie to win on the women's professional tour before signing her up. Both companies were more than willing to hand her multi-million dollar sponsorship deals at the start of her career. Only time will tell if she will become the new face of modern golf.

■ Wie keeps her eyes on the prize

SUZANN PETTERSEN of Norway celebrates winning her first Major, the 2007 McDonalds LPGA Championship at Bulle Rock Golf Course in Maryland.

Her poise is unbelievable. Either you've got it or you don't. And this girl's got it

TOM LEHMAN, DESCRIBING MICHELLE WIE

MORGAN PRESSEL turned professional in 2006 when she was 17, and the following year became the youngest winner of a Major.

▷ **ASHLEIGH SIMON** won the South African Open in 2004 when she was 14, and won it on two further occasions while still an amateur.

▷▷ **HAVING WON 19** amateur titles, Paula Creamer won twice in her first year on tour and was named Rookie of the Year in 2005.

△△ **A POPULAR COVER GIRL,** Nathalie Gulbis celebrates winning the 2007 Evian Masters. It was her first victory as a professional.

△ **CHRISTIE KERR** is only 5 ft 3 in, but she packs a punch. She was a professional for over 10 years before she won her first Major.

▷ **$1 MILLION GOLFER** Julieta Granada of Paraguay celebrates on her way to winning the ADT Championship in 2006.

4 GOLFING LANDMARKS

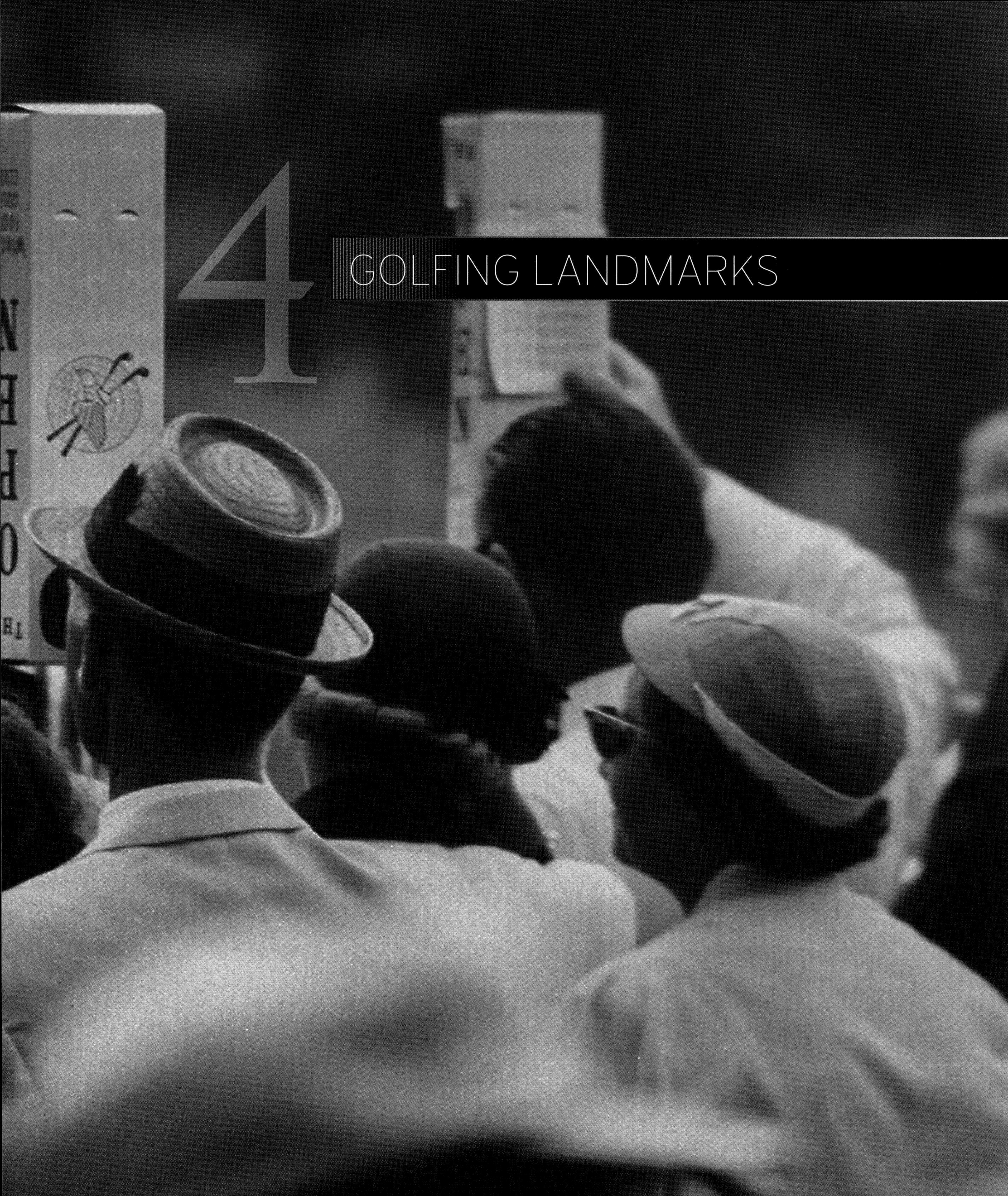

■ Willie Park (far left) and assorted professionals in the 1860s.

THE EARLIEST ORIGINS of the game of golf are, despite the best efforts of generations of historical experts and scholars, sketchy at best. We can say without hesitation, however, that by the middle of the 15th century, golf in Scotland had grown in popularity to such an extent that the powers-that-be felt it had become an unwelcome distraction. By the mid-18th century, the game had its first set of written rules. And a century later, in 1860, it had its first championship—what we now regard as golf's first Major.

Probably the main reason for staging this event was to establish the identity of the "new" best golfer after the recent death of Allan Robertson—the undisputed No.1 of the time and the first man to break 80 for a round of the Old Course at St. Andrews. The tournament was staged for the leading professionals, although for reasons unknown only eight players took part. And some of the golf was shocking even by the erratic standards of the day—one competitor took 21 strokes on one hole.

However, on Wednesday, October 17, 1860, on the windswept links of Prestwick on the west coast of Scotland, Major championship golf was born. Old Tom Morris, who held the position we would now know as greenkeeper at Prestwick, was the local favorite and expected to win, but it was Willie Park who won with a three-round aggregate of 174.

Morris atoned for the disappointment of losing the first ever Open by winning four of the next seven, thus cementing his place in history. His son, young Tom Morris, would go on to emulate that feat and win four Opens himself between 1868 and 1872.

There are three other Majors now—the Masters, US Open, and USPGA—but 1860 is still recognized as the year when it all started. The Open will always be the oldest, the greatest, and by most people's judgment, the most prized championship in the sport.

Major birth at Prestwick

OLD TOM MORRIS (left), Allan Robertson
(4th from left), and St. Andrews Captain
Hay Wemyss (right).

■ Bobby Jones with the US Open trophy in July 1930.

DESPITE NEVER TURNING professional, Bobby Jones dominated the game between 1923 and 1930, during that time winning 13 of the 21 majors in which he competed. Some consider him to be the greatest golfer who ever lived. Jones achieved much in his short, glittering career, but everything is overshadowed by his achievements in the 1930 season, when he won what was then considered the Grand Slam of championship golf.

One could have gained a measure of Jones' intentions that season from his first-round match in the Amateur Championship at St. Andrews, the first leg of that Grand Slam. Sidney Roper was his opponent that day and he was in fine form, but Jones started his round on the formidable Old Course with a birdie, then a par, followed by another birdie, an eagle and another birdie. Jones was five-under par for the first five holes. Poor Roper must have known it was not to be his day!

Jones followed that victory by claiming the Open Championship at Royal Liverpool and later that summer the US Open at Interlachen, Florida, where a sublime third-round 68 game him a five-shot lead going into the final day. Finally, he completed the Grand Slam in the US Amateur at Merion, Pennsylvania, in September, winning the final by the overwhelming margin of 8&7 and confirming his status as a national hero.

No golfer has ever won the modern-day Grand Slam—all four majors in a single season—but Jones completing the "Impregnable Quadrilateral," as it was dubbed by one New York journalist at the time, is probably the next best thing.

"Bobby Slam" for Jones

BOBBY JONES RECEIVES a hero's welcome in New York after returning from Britain with the Amateur and Open Championship titles.

■ Come April, and another year's Masters, Augusta is awash with color.

GOLF WITHOUT AUGUSTA NATIONAL, without the Masters, is as unthinkable as tennis without Wimbledon. We have Bobby Jones to thank that it was created in the first place.

Jones had the golfing world at his feet when he retired at the age of 28, and although his decision was a huge loss to the competitive golfing scene, it would prove to be a shrewd move for him personally. He soon found himself overwhelmed by an avalanche of commercial offers.

Jones had his own agenda, though. In the years since his retirement, he had found it increasingly difficult to venture on to a course without a huge gallery shadowing his every move; he appreciated the support, but at the same time he yearned to play golf in private with just his friends for company. One such friend was businessman Clifford Roberts and together, they formulated the idea of a private members' golf course. A plot of land, the Fruitlands Nursery in Augusta, Georgia, was earmarked as perfect.

Bobby Jones would later recall his first ever visit to the site. "When I walked out on the grass terrace under the big trees behind the house and looked down over the property, the experience was unforgettable. It seemed that this land had been lying here for years just waiting for someone to lay a golf course upon it."

To lay this golf course, Jones and Roberts enlisted the services of the great golf course architect Dr. Alister Mackenzie and together they created Augusta National, a golf course that would be playable for golfers of all standards, but at the same time represent the ultimate test of strategic golf.

It is the most beautiful and manicured golf course in the world and it is home to the Masters Tournament. That was Jones' idea, too. The man was touched by genius, both on and off the golf course.

Masterclass of course design

AN AERIAL VIEW of the newly completed Augusta National, taken in January 1933, shortly before its official opening.

Nelson's golfing achievements in 1945 will never be equalled.

BLESSED WITH AN ELEGANT SWING, Byron Nelson was a sublime ballstriker, and a great champion.

John Jacobs, top coach and former Ryder Cup player and captain, knew Nelson. He remembers a conversation with the great man, during which they were discussing the swing changes Nelson had made in the winter of 1944. "I could win with my old swing," he said, "but I could also miss the cut. Once I'd changed my swing, though, I knew I would never play badly again." It was an extraordinary statement and it was also prophetic.

The following year Nelson won 11 consecutive tournaments on the American Tour and 18 in total; he went five months without losing a golf tournament.

His run started in January at the Phoenix Open; starting with rounds of 68 and 65, he then coasted to a two-shot victory. In his next tournament, the Corpus Christie Open, he shot 66, 63, and 65 to blow the rest of the field apart. He did the same again in the New Orleans Open. Then as the PGA Tour season progressed, Nelson won the Charlotte Open by four shots, the Greensboro Open by eight shots, the Atlanta Open by nine, the Montreal Open by 10, the Chicago Victory Open by seven, the Tam O'Shanter Open by 11, the Knoxville Invitational by 10, the Esmeralda Open by seven, and the Seattle Open by 13!

This was, and still is, the most extraordinary run of dominance in the history of the game. His stroke average that season was 68.33, lower than Tiger Woods manages most years on Tour.

A bit like Bobby Jones before him, Nelson retired when he was at the top of his game, aged 34. However, a handful of years later, he had a brief change of heart. While on vacation with his wife, he decided to enter the 1955 French Open. He won it, of course. This was Byron Nelson. Old habits die hard.

"Lord" Byron sets the standard

ED DUDLEY (CENTER), president of the USPGA, with Sam Byrd (left), present Byron Nelson with the USPGA Championship trophy at Morraine Country Club in Dayton, Ohio, on July 15, 1945.

■ Hagen wins his third USPGA Championship, in September 1925.

WALTER HAGEN WAS AN extraordinary character: a man's man; ladies' man; man about town; showman. He once proclaimed that he didn't want to be a millionaire, rather to just live like one. He achieved both.

But there was more to Hagen than showy gestures and a champagne lifestyle. Above all, he was a champion golfer with a rare and exquisite array of skills. He was known to walk on the 1st tee and say, "Who's going to finish second, then?"

For a while Hagen's bold pronouncement was prophetic. In the 1920s when the USPGA Championship was a matchplay event, Hagen made it to the final six times in seven years, winning five, including four in succession from 1924–27. The man was virtually unbeatable, as four fine challengers would testify. Jim Barnes pushed Hagen to the limit at French Lick in 1924, but ultimately went down by two holes. Will Mehlhorn took a 6&4 hammering at Olympia Fields in the following year's final and Leo Diegel was trounced 4&3 at Salisbury in 1926. J. Turnesa stood in the way of Hagen's fourth consecutive win at Dallas in 1927 and, despite putting up a good fight, lost on the last hole.

During that period Hagen also managed to win four Open Championships. Bizarre, then, that he seems remembered now not so much for his golfing prowess, but more for his witty turn of phrase, his flamboyant lifestyle, and the unbridled joie de vivre that characterized everything he did. In so doing we risk overlooking what an incredible golfer he was. The man won 11 major championships at a time when there were only three majors to play for, not four as there are today. Hagen was a legend for all the right reasons.

Walter walks on air

WALTER HAGEN PRACTICING his swing on the roof of the Savoy Hotel, London, in June 1922, prior to that year's Ryder Cup matches.

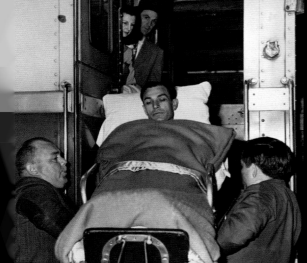

Hogan being transferred home after his car crash, on April 7, 1949.

BEN HOGAN'S CAR CRASH, in February 1949, is the stuff of legend. Hogan crashed head-on into a Greyhound bus that was passing a truck, and suffered horrific multiple injuries.

Few dared entertain the thought that he might be able to play golf again—a local newspaper even published his obituary—but they hadn't reckoned with Hogan's steely resolve. This was a man who was known to practice until his hands bled. Just 18 months after the accident, he won his second US Open.

In 1953 he played golf of a standard which may never again be equaled. He entered six tournaments that year and won five of them. Three were majors.

At the Masters he smashed the tournament record by five strokes, closing with rounds of 69, 66, and 69 to win by a handful of shots.

The US Open was played at Oakmont in Pennsylvania, a golf course with a fearsome reputation. But Hogan brought it to its knees. After the first round, Skip Alexander, a fellow competitor playing in the group behind Hogan, pronounced that he knew how to shoot 67 on this golf course. "You hit every goddamn fairway and every green about 10 feet from the hole, just like Hogan did." Hogan's round contained 13 pars, 5 birdies, and no bogeys. It set the standard, and he went on to win by six shots.

The Open Championship at Carnoustie was next. Hogan had never played in the Open; he hated the traveling. He arrived two weeks early to get accustomed to the smaller British golf ball and to study the course and formulate his strategy. No one stood a chance. Hogan broke the course record on the last day and won by four shots.

He never played in the Open again.

Hogan's triumph over tragedy

HOGAN SHOWS OFF his signature driver after another scorching shot straight down the middle.

Tiger Woods seals the Grand Slam with victory at St.Andrews in 2000.

THE GRAND SLAM WINNERS' CLUB is the most exclusive clique that exists in the game of golf. Gaining membership requires the player to win all four majors, a feat that only five players—Gene Sarazen, Ben Hogan, Gary Player, Jack Nicklaus, and Tiger Woods—have achieved.

Others have come close. Sam Snead won more tournaments on the PGA Tour than any other player in history, but the US Open escaped him; for Arnold Palmer and Tom Watson, it was the USPGA.

The founding member, Sarazen, had already won three legs of the Grand Slam when he turned up at Augusta National to play in his first US Masters in 1935. He didn't just win the tournament; he also hit probably the most famous golf shot in history—holing a 5-wood on the 15th for an albatross-two.

Ben Hogan was next to win the Grand Slam, sealing it with his one and only visit to the Open at Carnoustie in 1953.

Gary Player beat his great rival Jack Nicklaus to the Slam by almost a full calendar year. Player won his first major championship in the 1959 Open at Muirfield and completed the quadruple six years later at the US Open. Jack Nicklaus followed Player into the Grand Slam Winners club in 1966 when he won the Open Championship. Nicklaus would go on to win more major championships than any other golfer—18 in all. By most people's reckoning it was a record that would stand forever ... but then along came Tiger Woods.

Woods won his first major, the 1997 Masters, by a remarkable 12 strokes—just nine months after turning professional. Three years later, he had the full set of majors to his name. He was in the club. And now he's chasing Jack's tally of 18.

Golf's most exclusive club

■ McCormack and IMG changed the face of sports marketing.

MARK MCCORMACK was a visionary. He opened the door for riches that were beyond anything any sportsperson could have dreamed of and in so doing became the king of sports marketing. Today's mega-rich golf stars should tip their visors to the great man.

McCormack's first smart move was signing up Arnold Palmer as his first client in 1960. Palmer was like no other golfer. He had extraordinary charisma, raw appeal and a crash-bang-wallop style of play that transformed the world of professional golf.

McCormack saw the commercial value in someone like Palmer. His energy and entrepreneurial skills enabled him to become the architect of a burgeoning new industry. It wasn't long before McCormack had also signed up a talented young South African called Gary Player, and also a chubby young American with a crew cut; his name was Jack Nicklaus.

McCormack had golf's undisputed "Big Three" on his books. Between 1958 and 1975, the three of them shared the spoils in 29 of the 72 major championships played in that period, a 40 percent strike rate over the rest of the world's top golfers.

McCormack's relationship with the "Big Three" was the foundation of his International Management Group (IMG) company. He became hugely rich, but then so did his clients. Over the years IMG managed other top people in the world of sport, including Rod Laver, Bjorn Borg, Martina Navratilova, Nick Faldo, Greg Norman, Colin Montgomerie, and now Tiger Woods.

McCormack created an extraordinary empire. He deserved all the plaudits he received before he passed away in 2003, aged 73.

McCormack's "Big Three"

LEGENDS IN THE MAKING. Player, Palmer, and Nicklaus during the World Series of Golf in Akron, Ohio, in September 1962.

Seve with the Claret Jug in 1979—the first of his five majors.

EUROPEAN GOLF was in the doldrums in the early to mid-1970s. Then along came a dashing, handsome young Spaniard called Seve Ballesteros.

Aged just 19, Seve almost won the Open at Royal Birkdale in 1976, thwarted on the last day by Johnny Miller. But by finishing tied-second with Jack Nicklaus, Seve had signaled his intentions to the world. Here was a major champion in waiting.

Seve was Europe's No.1 money winner three years in a row following his emergence at Birkdale, and he arrived at Royal Lytham & St. Annes for the 1979 Open as one of the pre-tournament favorites, with a win and a second-place finish in his previous two tournaments. He was still only 22.

A brilliant second-round 65 thrust him to the head of the field and he never looked back. The last round was a rollercoaster affair. Seve used his driver nine times and hit just one fairway. He was subsequently labeled by some critics the "parking lot champion" on account of driving his ball into a temporary parking lot on the 16th hole.

But he had a strategy that day which is largely overlooked. It was windy and the fairways were baked hard. Seve figured that by hitting a driver he could at least take some of the dangerous fairway bunkers out of play. And he could also use his power and length off the tee to his advantage, a pre-meditated strategy which yielded relatively straightforward approach shots into the greens. It was a great win which owed nothing to luck.

The following year Seve won his first Masters and would go on to win 70 tournaments all over the world and on all types of golf course. And it all started that day at Lytham on July 21, 1979.

Seve starts it all

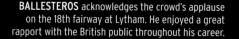

BALLESTEROS acknowledges the crowd's applause on the 18th fairway at Lytham. He enjoyed a great rapport with the British public throughout his career.

Nicklaus and Watson show mutual respect at Turnberry in 1977.

THE INTENSE RIVALRY between Jack Nicklaus and Tom Watson started at the 1977 Open Championship at Turnberry. The pair had shot identical scores in the first three rounds—68, 70, 65—and in the final round, in blazing hot sunshine, the pair continued to play sublime golf. As they strode toward the 18th tee, Nicklaus was trailing Watson by one shot, 10-under par plays 11-under par.

After a solid 1-iron, Watson hit a towering 7-iron to 30 in (75 cm). Nicklaus tried to go for the green, but pushed it right into the fringes of a gorse bush, from where he muscled a shot to the edge of the green, some 30 ft (9 m) from the hole. Before Watson could hole his putt, Nicklaus rolled in his. The crowd were ecstatic. Watson's expression didn't change at all. He calmly placed his ball back down on its spot and rapped in the putt to win by one shot. As they walked off the green, Nicklaus said to Watson, "I gave you my best shot and it just wasn't good enough. You were better." The greatest winner who ever lived was also the best loser.

Just as well, because Nicklaus suffered again in the 1982 US Open at Pebble Beach. Big Jack started the final round three strokes in arrears, but a run of five straight birdies helped his cause, and, as Watson came to the tough par-3 17th (with Nicklaus in the clubhouse) they were tied for the lead on four-under par.

Watson missed the green to the left where his ball buried itself in ankle-deep rough. It looked like an impossible situation, but he produced an outrageous stroke of genius, holing his chip for a birdie-two and a one shot lead. Victory was effectively his.

Always the gentleman, Nicklaus was there on the 18th green to congratulate the winner.

Golfing gladiators

TOM WATSON SINKS his birdie putt on the 15th to move into a tie with Jack Nicklaus during a dramatic final day at Pebble Beach.

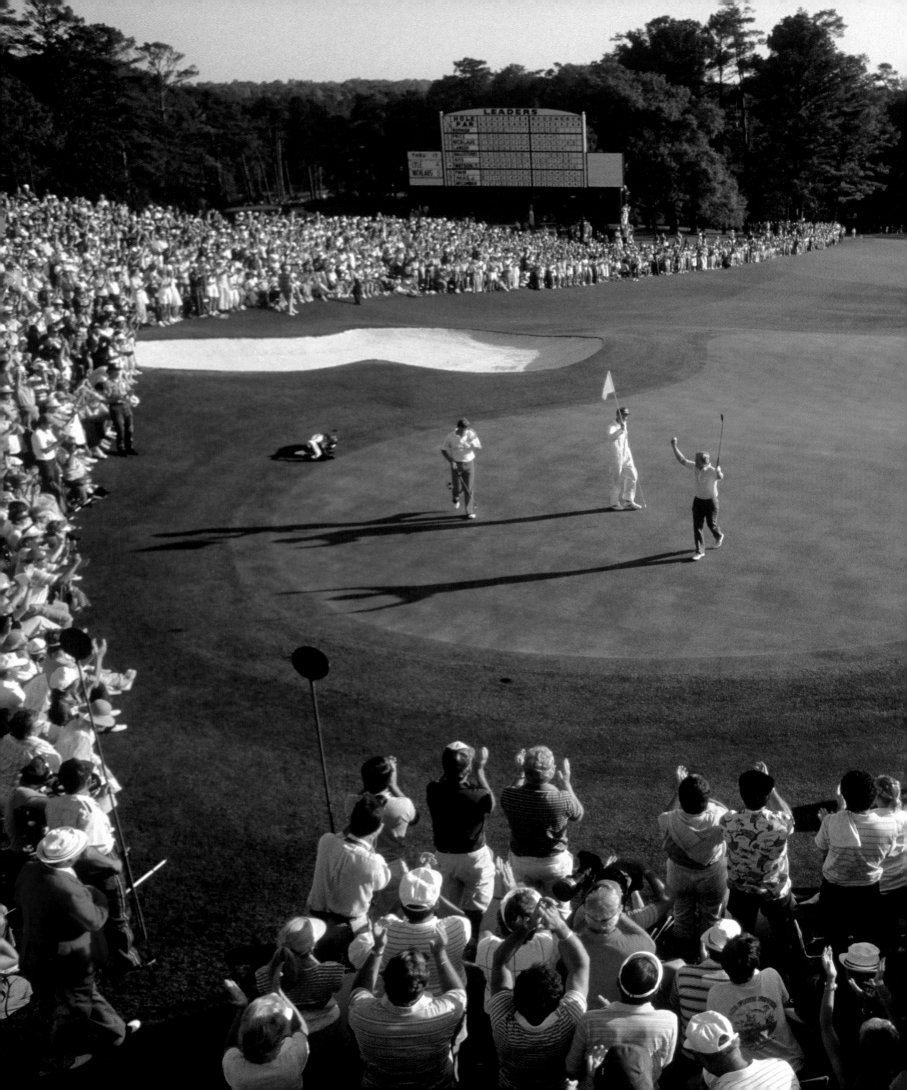

■ Nicklaus is helped into his sixth Green Jacket by Bernhard Langer.

JACK NICKLAUS WINNING his sixth Green Jacket, and the last of his 18 major championships, is one of the greatest days in the history of the sport.

By 1986 everyone thought Jack was past it. He was 46, he hadn't won a golf tournament in over two years and his last major win was six years earlier in the US Open. A local newspaper even ran an article during the build-up to that week's Masters saying that Jack was "done, through, washed-up, and finished."

It was all the motivation he needed.

After fairly modest rounds of 74, 71, and 69 Jack wasn't even on the radar as far as most commentators were concerned. They were all expecting Greg Norman to win; he had a four-shot lead. And should he stumble, there were others—Seve Ballesteros, Tom Watson, Nick Price, and Tom Kite—ready to pounce. The young lions were circling, but a Golden Bear muscled in on the party with one of the greatest charges in the history of the game.

After a methodical first eight holes, Jack birdied the 9th, 10th, and 11th. He stumbled at the 12th with a bogey, but recovered to birdie the par-5 13th and then eagled the 15th after a majestic 4-iron to 10 ft (3 m). At the 16th, he struck an imperious 6-iron and, as the ball was in the air, turned to his son Jackie who was caddying, and winked. The ball came down 3 ft (1 m) from the hole. He holed that, too. He sunk a snaking 10 ft (3 m) putt on the 17th for another birdie; then, just as Jack always had done throughout his heyday, he secured a safe par on the 18th ... where he really needed it.

Jack had played the last 10 holes at Augusta in just 33 strokes to shoot 65. It was like the old days—Jack playing his own game to the end; rivals crumbling around him. "It was the most gratifying win of my career," said Jack.

He remains the tournament's oldest winner.

Big Jack's final charge

Tiger with his proud parents, Kutilda (left) and Earl in 1996.

TIGER WOODS WAS FAMOUS long before he turned professional at the end of August 1996. He had won three consecutive US Junior Amateur titles—no other golfer had ever won it more than once. Then he won three consecutive US Amateur titles from 1994—not even the greatest amateur of them all, Bobby Jones, had achieved that astonishing feat.

After making the cut in his first tournament as a pro, the Greater Milwaukee Open, Tiger then finished 11th, tied-5th, and tied-3rd in his next three events. He won his next tournament, the Las Vegas Invitational, finished second the week after that, and then won again the week after. Despite starting his season effectively eight months after everyone else, he won more than $700,000 in prize money and finished 24th on the year-end Money List.

The following season he got ready to tee up in the 1997 Masters, his first major championship as a professional. Things started badly. Playing in the company of the previous year's champion Nick Faldo, Tiger was four-over par for his first nine holes.

Things then started to go a lot better. He played the remaining 63 holes in a mind-boggling 22-under par and won the tournament by 12 shots. Records fell like nine-pins. He was the youngest ever winner; it was the lowest ever winning score and the biggest ever winning margin; he was the most shots under par for Augusta's back nine (16-under); he had the lowest middle 36 holes (131); he had the lowest first 54 holes and the largest 54-hole lead; and he had more threes than anyone had ever had at Augusta.

Tiger has continued to break records ever since. He is the only player of the last 30 years who has looked like even having a remote chance of approaching Jack Nicklaus' tally of 18 Major victories. Indeed, Tiger looks odds-on now to surpass that number.

Tiger roars to major victory

TIGER SINKS THE FINAL PUTT on the 18th green at Augusta to win the Masters with a record low score of 18 under par, and signal his arrival as the new force in Major championship golf.

An elated Bernhard Langer holes a chip shot on Day One.

UP UNTIL THE 1980s, Ryder Cup matches on US soil were very one-sided affairs—the Great Britain & Ireland team were always heavily beaten. In 1983 the US came close to losing for the first time on home turf, and after a resounding victory at The Belfry, England, in 1985 the European team traveled to Muirfield Village in Ohio two years later with hopes of an overseas win higher-than-ever.

This was Europe's dream team, captained by Tony Jacklin but led in many ways by Seve Ballesteros, at that time a winner of four Major championships and a Ryder Cup colossus. Nick Faldo had just won his first Open Championship; Sandy Lyle had won it two years earlier and would go on to win the Masters; Bernhard Langer had won his first Masters already. This was a team with serious talent, and even more serious intent.

Honors were even after the morning foursomes on Day One, but in the afternoon fourballs Europe produced a clean sweep. By the end of Day Two, Europe had a five-point advantage.

The Americans came out all-guns blazing in the final day singles, claiming five victories and a half in the first seven matches. But the Europeans countered strongly. Eamonn Darcy ensured Europe could not lose by holing a slippery-quick 6 ft (2 m) putt on the 18th green to defeat Ben Crenshaw.

Fittingly it was Seve, the talisman and inspiration of the team—the man who in many ways revitalized European golf—who delivered the knockout blow minutes later, beating Curtis Strange on the 17th green. It was the first time the US had lost on home soil and it would prove to be the first in a run of eight epic, close contests between the two teams.

Europe's Ryder Cup raid

EUROPE'S HEROES, with Tony Jacklin center stage, dance with joy after winning the Ryder Cup for the first time on US soil.

A tearful Sergio Garcia (center) finds defeat hard to take.

IT WAS THE GREATEST COMEBACK in the history of team golf. Ben Crenshaw's US team had taken quite a pounding on the first two days of the 1999 Ryder Cup at Brookline Country Club, Boston, and were trailing Europe by the hefty margin of 6 points to 10 going into the last day's singles matches.

The US put its big guns in the top half of the draw and the results were truly explosive. They quickly built big leads, won the first six matches, and set in motion an unstoppable momentum. On an afternoon of high drama and quite deafening crowd noise, this Ryder Cup contest would hinge on the result of American Justin Leonard's match against José Maria Olazábal.

Leonard had been four down with just seven holes to play, but he somehow won four holes in quick succession and arrived at the 17th all-square and with everything—not just his match, but the Cup itself—to play for. Both players found the green in regulation and faced birdie putts, Leonard from 50 ft (15 m) away, Olazábal from about half that distance.

Leonard to putt first, then. He hit it sweetly, if a little hard, and the line looked perfect. Then, bang, the ball hit the back of the hole and in it went. Leonard went bananas. The US team then invaded the green to congratulate him, but in the process, stampeded over the line of José Maria Olazábal's putt. Such exuberance was understandable, but it gave Olazábal little chance of composing himself for his now vital putt. He missed it, inevitably, and the US was guaranteed the half-point they needed.

When the dust had settled, it was impossible to deny the Americans due credit for a phenomenal fight-back. It was a deserving victory and rightly goes down as the greatest Ryder Cup comeback ever. Of equal significance, this Ryder Cup also taught the two teams and the fans a salutary lesson; that the spirit of the game of golf should always be upheld and that in terms of celebrations and on-course conduct, there is a line that is best not crossed.

The Battle of Brookline

JUSTIN LEONARD'S birdie on the 17th green sparks scenes of unbridled celebration in the US camp.

Woods tops the leaderboard

IT IS HARD TO THINK of an equivalent margin of victory in any other sport at the highest level to compare with Tiger Woods' win in the US Open at Pebble Beach in 2000. Equally, it is hard to imagine that one of golf's Major championships will ever again be won by a margin of 15 shots.

That single week was the perfect measure of how utterly superior Tiger's golf was that year. *Golf World* magazine ran a cover line with an image of Tiger acknowledging the crowd, his right arm raised to the air. The strap-line read, "Greetings Earthlings." That was about the sum of it. Tiger was on another planet from everyone else that year.

The US Open is arguably the most grueling, demanding, and plain toughest of all the Major championships. The greens are hard and fast, the pins are tucked away in inaccessible places, the fairways are typically narrower than at any other tournament, and the rough is thick and clinging. By way of its actions the USGA, who run the US Open, sends a clear message to all competitors—hit a stray shot and you will be severely, although in its view fairly, punished.

Tiger Woods made it look ridiculously easy. He opened with a blistering round of 65 to lead by one shot. After two rounds he led by six shots; after three rounds he had increased his lead to 10 shots and, at the end, the margin was an incredible 15 shots. He was the only player under par; 12-under par, to be precise. Tied for second, on three-over, were Miguel Angel Jimenez and two-time US Open champion Ernie Els.

"If you want to watch a guy win the US Open playing perfectly, you've just seen it," said Els, graciously. It was true. Every other competitor that week averaged five bogeys a round; Tiger had only six bogeys in total. Moreover, he did not three-putt once, an astonishing feat in any Major, let alone a US Open.

Woods in a class of his own

WOODS TEES OFF on the 14th hole in the final round at Pebble Beach. This was the 100th US Open and the USGA was presented with a golfing showcase from Woods to mark the centenary.

■ Sorenstam wins the ANZ Masters, one of 13 victories in 2002.

IN THE EARLY 2000s, one could debate endlessly who was the most dominant player on their respective tour, Tiger Woods or Annika Sorenstam. That the answer was even in question, given the standard of play achieved by Tiger in that period, says everything about Sorenstam's talent.

Annika drove the ball long and straight, her judgement of distance on approach shots was sublime, and she could putt like an angel. She was blessed with an ice-cool temperament and a fierce will to win.

Her 2001 season was special enough. She won eight tournaments, became the only female golfer in history to shoot 59, and the first LPGA golfer to top $2 million in prize money in a season. Her great rival Karrie Webb remarked in an interview at the end of that year that she would "eat her hat" if Annika won eight times again in 2002.

Yet she did more than that; much more. In 2002, she played a season's golf to almost rival that of Byron Nelson's epic streak in 1945. She won 11 LPGA tournaments in a single season, beating all records. Annika won her fourth Major at the Kraft Nabisco and set a scoring record at the Kellogg-Keebler Classic where she won by 11 shots. During the course of the season she also became the first female golfer to pass the $9 million, $10 million, and $11 million in LPGA career earnings.

Not content with trouncing the opposition in the US, Annika traveled abroad to conquer other territories, too. She won the ANZ Ladies Masters in Australia and the Compaq Open in Sweden. All in all, she competed in 26 events and won 13 of them. She had 20 top-10 finishes and by the end of the season her stroke average was an incredible 68.70, another new record, and secured her place in the LPGA Hall of Fame. She also pocketed $2.8 million in prize money, smashing her own record that she had set the previous year.

Sorenstam reigns supreme

ANNIKA SORENSTAM (left) reacts as she nearly holes in one at the 2005 Solheim Cup, watched by Suzann Pettersen (center), and European captain Catrin Nilsmark.

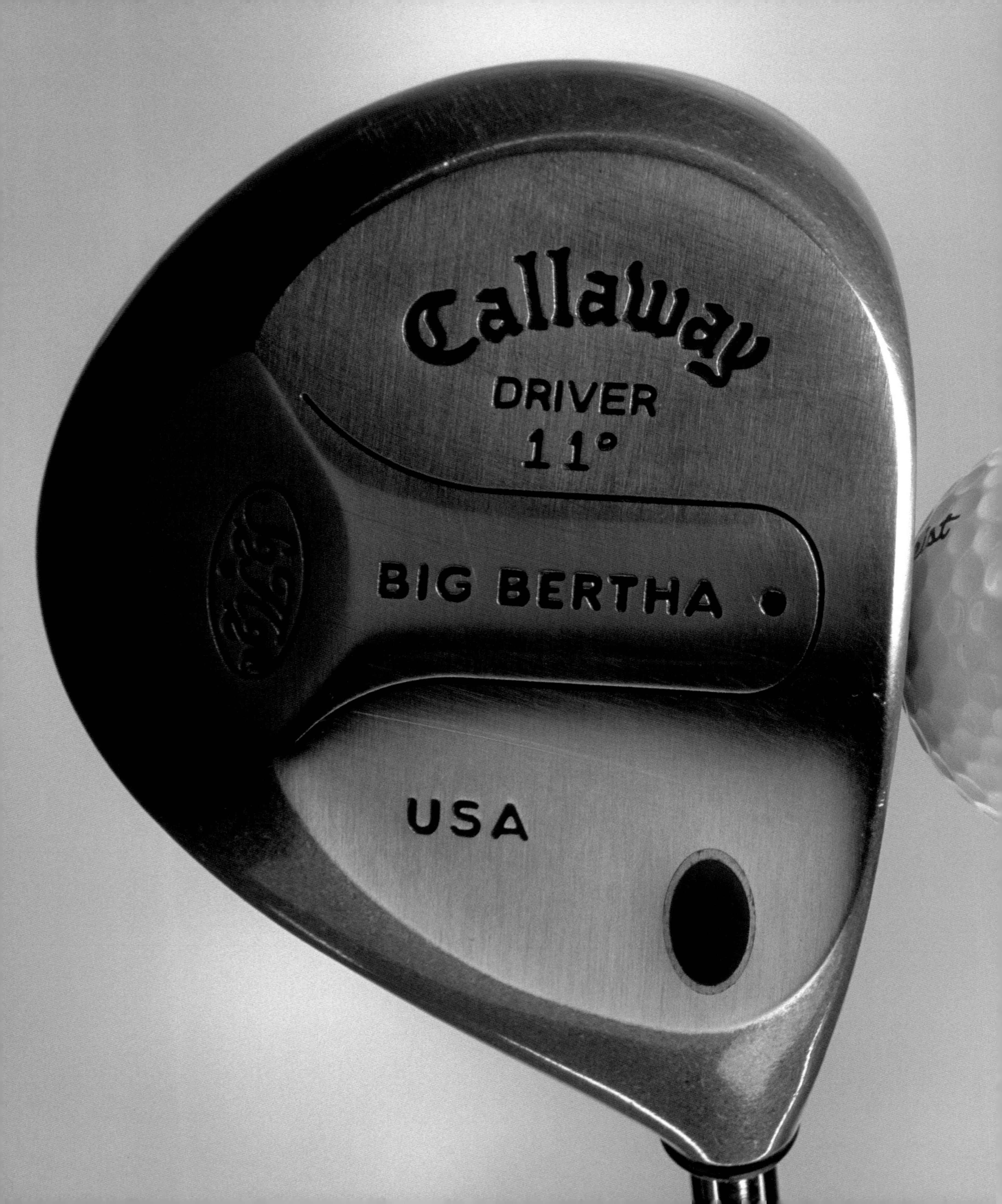
Callaway
DRIVER
11°
BIG BERTHA
USA

■ Ely Callaway in January 2001 with the clubs that made his name.

THE GAME OF GOLF was destined to change forever when millionaire businessman Ely Callaway walked into a pro shop in Palm Springs in 1982. So impressed was Ely with a particular pitching-wedge that he saw for sale on the shelf that he not only bought the club, but with it half the company.

It wasn't pitching-wedges that made the Callaway company what it is, of course. It was drivers, metal drivers. And it wasn't that long before Callaway was the club of choice. By the end of the 20th century, Ely's company had become a giant in the world of golf clubs, utterly dominating the driver market.

Ely Callaway was typical of that rare breed of super-entrepreneurs with a vision to do things differently. And like all successful people, he had the courage of his convictions. When he launched the company's iconic Big Bertha, the world's first over-sized steel-headed driver, he was so confident of its success that he pre-ordered 300,000 heads, and charged top dollar for it, too.

It was a massive hit. For many golfers the transition from persimmon-headed drivers to metal-headed drivers was not without its difficulties—the metal clubs looked, felt, and sounded different. But no one could deny the effectiveness of this new technology in terms of game improvement.

The company continues to make great golf clubs that pioneered a new era in the game of golf and genuinely made the game more enjoyable for the average golfer. "Until we came along, the driver was the most feared club in the bag," Ely told *Golf World* magazine in an interview in 2001, not long before his death. "Today it is probably the most popular."

He was right. That is Ely Callaway's legacy.

Big Bertha arrives

CALLAWAY'S OVERSIZED steel-headed drivers enabled players of all levels to hit the ball straighter and further than ever before.

Nick Faldo (left) studies plans for a new course, in 2004.

THERE WAS A TIME WHEN when the demarcation was clear: players played golf courses, designers designed golf courses. Gone are those days of seminal golf course architects like Dr. Alister Mackenzie, Donald Ross, and Harry Colt.

Nowadays, developers know that if they want immediate credibility and recognition for their new golf course, the best way to do it is enlist the services of one of the world's best players. Most of the top players are in on the act: Jack Nicklaus, Gary Player, Greg Norman, Phil Mickelson, Ernie Els, Ben Crenshaw, Annika Sorenstam, Sergio Garcia, Vijay Singh, José Maria Olazábal, Davis Love III, Colin Montgomerie, and even Tiger Woods–they have all embraced the world of golf course design.

Arnold Palmer was in many ways the trailblazer. "When I started building golf courses," he remembers, "there were only a few golfers who were architects. Today just about everybody who plays or plays well has become an architect."

One can see the attraction. Although golfers enjoy longer playing careers than any other sportsperson, they are only at their peak for so long. This is a way of seamlessly stepping into a new career, a way of staying involved with the game of golf when their best playing days are behind them.

"I wanted to be young enough to just flip over (to full-time course design) when I'm done playing; I didn't want to start doing this at age 50," says Ernie Els, whose design company is building many golf courses in the Far East, Middle East, and India.

There is big money in this business, too. Golfers can make seven-figure sums for designing a single golf course. It has changed everything and one of the benefits is that it has brought to the fore the art of golf course design, whereas 75 years ago it was a mystery. That has to be a good thing.

Golfers' grand designs

JOSÉ MARIA OLAZÁBAL plays what will become the par-5 15th hole of his eponymous course at Mission Hills, China, in March 2003 .

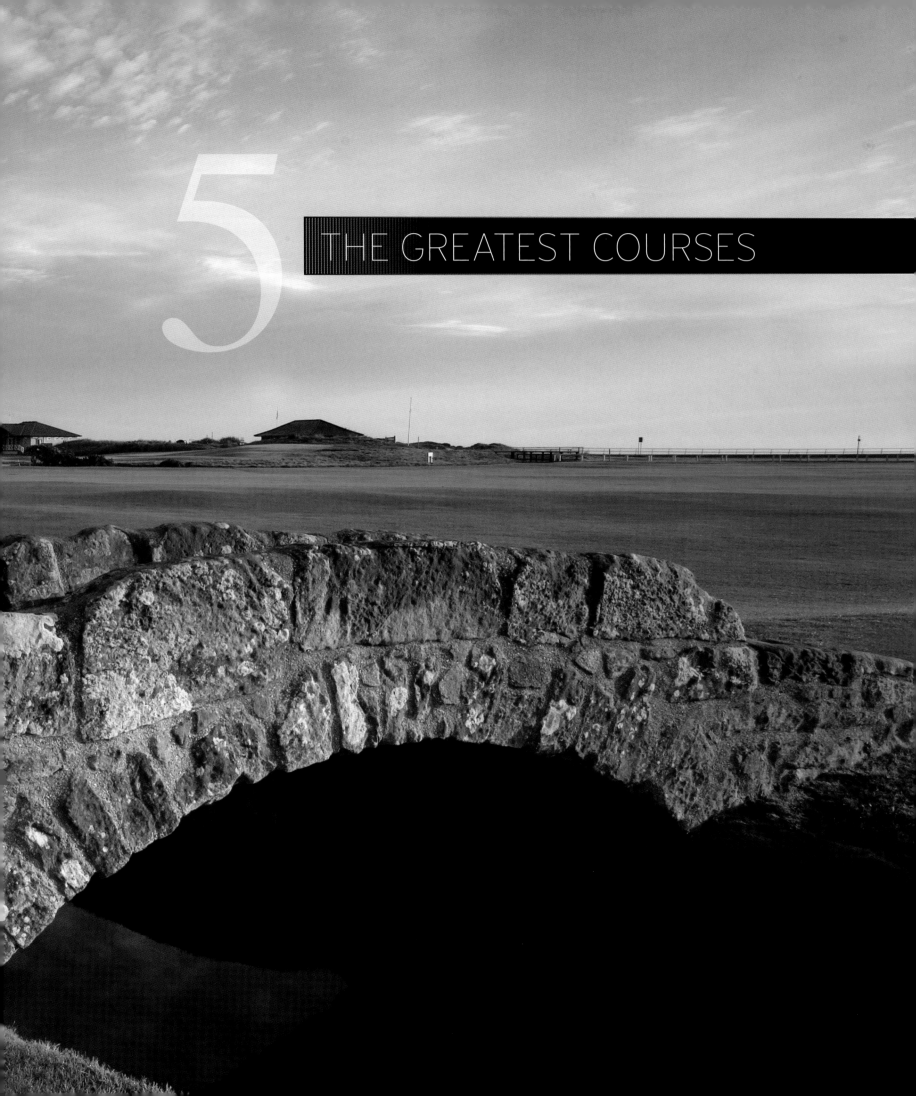

5

Links courses

WHILE THE TRUE ORIGINS OF GOLF ARE MUDDLED in the mists of time, one fact is not in dispute—the sport evolved on the sandy coastal wastes of Scotland and England. For centuries links golf dominated the game. The creased landscapes and changeable weather make for the ultimate and most original golfing test.

△ **THE LINKS COURSE** at Royal County Down stands beside the sweep of Dundrum Bay in Northern Ireland.

◁◁ **WATERVILLE** golf course in Ireland faces the Atlantic Ocean and is the most westerly great links in Europe.

◁ **THE LINKS OF** the Ailsa Course at Turnberry in Scotland enjoys one of the most beautiful settings in the world of golf.

Unpredictability is the watchword, both in the weather conditions and in the fate of your ball that trusts to fortune as it lands and bounces on the hard, hummocked ground. But purists would not have it any other way

IT SEEMED NATURAL to the early intrepid golfers to practice their pastime on the land between the sea and more fertile fields inland, as its crumpled and grassy features were not much good for anything aside from kite flying and walking. Hence the name "links" was coined—the land connecting pasture and sea.

A links challenge is unique, where a golfer who has been schooled purely on the modern high ball game will struggle at first with the features and the methods needed to conquer them. The inevitable winds that can whip across a links have not only created the dunescape you play on, but test a golfer's shotmaking skills.

A links asks for special shots to be played—often ones to punch low through the breeze as well as delicate running pitches that use the natural contours of the ground.

NATURAL COURSE

Fairways tend to find their natural route through the valleys between the humps and hollows, and they are punctured by signature pot bunkers that have been gradually groomed and shaped from age-old pits of sand into what we know today. Traditionally, links were left to fend for themselves against the elements, so although the fairways, tees, and greens were tended to,

DOONBEG ON THE WEST COAST of Ireland is one of the few links to have been built in recent times. Designed by Greg Norman, the holes weave through massive dunes that are synonymous with linksland on the west-but not the east-of the British Isles.

they have always been firm and fast. In hot summers, it is no surprise to see the dry turf turn a light shade of brown. The fine blend of seaside grasses is only kept alive by the combination of nature's sea frets—damp, drizzly sea fogs—and by a greenkeeper's careful hand. Water is only used sparingly so not to bring on rogue grasses and to preserve the unique links characteristics.

Many old links also follow a similar pattern in their layout because of the narrow nature of the linksland they sit on. The holes move away from the clubhouse until they reach a point when they need to turn around and make their way back to

INLAND SISTERS mimic the characteristics of a true links, except for the sea! Two of the best in Europe are The Montgomerie at Carton House near Dublin and The Faldo Course in Berlin. They were designed by the golfers that bear their name along with architect Stan Eby.

the sanctuary of the clubhouse. It is not uncommon that you might work with the wind on the way out only to return into the teeth.

There are times, however, that an unlucky golfer battles the wind going out, only to find that the turning tide has caused the breeze to swing around and so they have to fight the elements coming home, too. That is the beauty of a links course. Unpredictability is the watchword, both in the weather conditions and in the fate of your ball that trusts to fortune as it lands and bounces on the hard, hummocked ground. Purists would not have it any other way.

INLAND LINKS

Despite its historic significance and continuing fame, links golf is a rarity today. Fewer than 250 true links exist, with the vast majority flirting with the cool seas around

FANCOURT GOLF COURSE in South Africa was designed by Gary Player and is one of the new breed of inland links courses.

the British Isles. Forever it will be so too, with coastal strips around the world now protected, and getting a permit to create a new links is increasingly difficult.

Luckily for links enthusiasts, the foibles of this particular style of course will continue through the building of so called "inland links." Although the fickle sea breezes are not there to test a golfer's skills, clever designers are fashioning the same kind of challenges as a true links course, but often not even within a whiff of the ocean. They will never be like the real thing, but when so few can now be added to the brilliant pedigree of our most historic courses, the new breed of "links" are a welcome next best

BUNKER HELL

Links bunkers are deep and shell-like by default so the sand in their depths is not as easily gouged out by the winds. Yet wind erosion is a problem for the faces of these dastardly traps and therefore a special way of building them has evolved over the years. Revetting, as it is known, is the practice of making firm, stable, and imposingly steep faces by layering slices of turf on top of each other. In effect it builds a wall of turf. Not only does it maintain the bunker shape, it poses very difficult questions for the golfer who finds the sand. A turf nursery helps to provide the thousands of strips of grass needed to revet all St. Andrews' bunkers, including the infamous "Road Hole" bunker and "Hell" bunker, a massive cross trap up to 10 feet (3 meters) deep.

■ The massive "Hell" bunker on the 14th at St. Andrews

Waterville, IRELAND

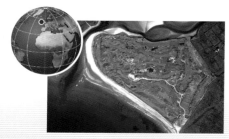

FROM THE WORD GO, WATERVILLE IS A BIG, POWERFUL, mean, and magnificent challenge in a wonderfully remote and inspiring setting on the Ring of Kerry. Waterville is Europe's most westerly great links and because of that has a unique transatlantic bond. According to Henry Cotton, Waterville is "one of the greatest courses ever built. If it were located in Britain, it would undoubtedly be a venue for the British Open."

SPIRIT OF STEWART

Triple Major champion Payne Stewart was a flamboyant and likeable man, who loved the links, the village, and its people. The feeling was mutual. He had just agreed to become Waterville's honorary captain for the year 2000 when he died in a plane crash, only months after winning his second US Open. His memory lives on through a bronze statue behind the 9th green– he can be seen from the clubhouse windows in his trademark plus fours leaning on his putter.

Stewart's statue and his wife Tracey

WATERVILLE IS KNOWN for its unforgiving links—the 1st is called "Last Easy"—but its reputation is not based solely on the bravado needed to tackle it. The course is much more than that. For one, Waterville rambles over a sensational corner of duneland, flanked on one side by the breaking Atlantic waters of Ballinskelligs Bay and on another by the estuary of the Inny River. A glance at the panorama away from the waters reveals the dark, brooding hills of the Magillicuddy Reeks. Second, it is a charming, romantic links despite its brutality, and deserves praise for its wonderfully creative design.

DRAMA IN EVERY HOLE

The roots of the course go back to the late 1800s when the curious village was transformed by a cable station, which linked it to the United States via an undersea communications line. Golf found a home nearby for the workers.

Over time the links fell into disrepair until an Irish American named John A. Mulcahy rekindled its fire and in the early 1970s set about creating a benchmark modern links course fit to test the best. It was a roaring success, attracting and wooing visitors from all over the world, but it has been made even greater since 2003.

Tom Fazio, responsible for many superb new courses and renovations of some the world's greatest, was asked to put drama into every hole. Waterville has always been known for its stupendous back nine and a few stunners on the front, but Fazio made them all memorable. He included two new holes and even improved on the most renowned. All holes are edged with tumbling dunes and dotted with grassy-banked, shell-like bunkers. Each tee shot needs to be thought out and committed to, because big numbers await a wayward golfer. Some holes are scary, others gripping and thrilling in their beauty.

Stand on any par-3 hole here and you are struck by their sensational look. Then reality sets in and you see the danger and difficulty. The 4th is played off a windy elevated tee by the estuary to a long green flanked by encroaching banks. At the 6th a downhill tee shot must find the green. Miss it right and a burn lurks; miss left or long and your ball rolls away down a slippery slope.

At the 12th you must play over an ancient dell where Mass once took place. Finally, the 17th is pure exhilaration. Mulcahy's Peak, as it is known, is the largest dune on the course and sitting atop its wilderness is an isolated tee from which you can spy the whole course. The ocean is on the right and, almost 200 yards (183 meters) away, lies a green surrounded by trouble. One solitary deep bunker and grassy swales guard the front left. Around the back snagging mounds wait for a miss-club, and tantalizingly close to the right is the drop-off to the beach.

Heart-in-the-mouth shots are not just limited to the short holes. Both greens at the par-4 2nd and 3rd holes are startlingly close to the river. A snaking burn down the right of 7 swallows many drives. Massive dunes line the par-5 11th, once described by a writer as "like walking through Manhattan," so enclosing are the sandhills. And the drives on 15 and 16 are awesome in a wind.

The course is equal to any famous British links, yet its remoteness excludes it from attracting a top class tournament. Still, the world's finest test their mettle here, particularly before the Open—Tiger Woods, Mark O'Meara, Jim Furyk, and Payne Stewart have been regular visitors. They love the solitude as well as the no-nonsense, demanding, and ultimately thrilling course.

KNOWN AS LIAM'S ACE, the 16th is prone to offshore winds as it follows the curve of the dunes where the estuary of the Inny River meets the sea.

It's tough, exhilarating, and I love coming back to savor her charms. She is a wondrous challenge, but **a fair maiden** nonetheless

JOE CARR, PAST CAPTAIN OF THE ROYAL & ANCIENT GOLF CLUB

THE COURSE

Brushed by stiff Atlantic winds, this awesome links in an idyllic setting is demanding from the off and never lets up. Tumultuous dunes, wispy rough, and scooped-out bunkers make every shot an adventure. To beat it, nothing but nerveless and pure striking will do.

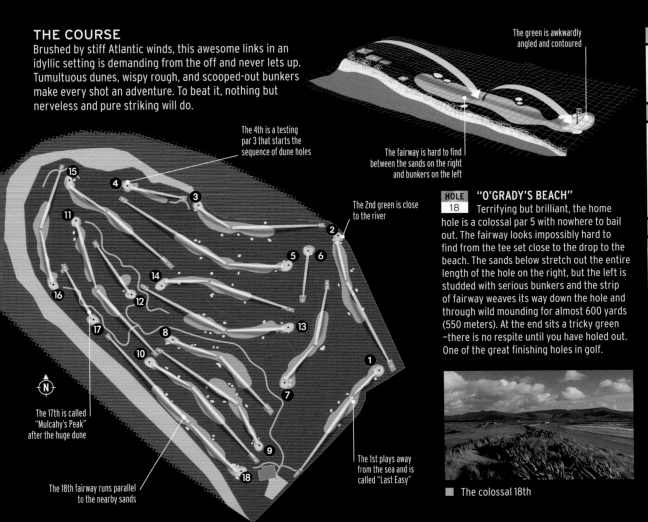

The green is awkwardly angled and contoured

The fairway is hard to find between the sands on the right and bunkers on the left

The 4th is a testing par 3 that starts the sequence of dune holes

The 2nd green is close to the river

The 17th is called "Mulcahy's Peak" after the huge dune

The 1st plays away from the sea and is called "Last Easy"

The 18th fairway runs parallel to the nearby sands

HOLE 18 "O'GRADY'S BEACH"

Terrifying but brilliant, the home hole is a colossal par 5 with nowhere to bail out. The fairway looks impossibly hard to find from the tee set close to the drop to the beach. The sands below stretch out the entire length of the hole on the right, but the left is studded with serious bunkers and the strip of fairway weaves its way down the hole and through wild mounding for almost 600 yards (550 meters). At the end sits a tricky green —there is no respite until you have holed out. One of the great finishing holes in golf.

■ The colossal 18th

WATERVILLE

WATERVILLE GOLF LINKS, WATERVILLE, CO. KERRY, IRELAND
www.watervillegolflinks.ie

THE COURSE

FOUNDED 1889	**DESIGNERS**
LENGTH 7,325 yards (6,698 meters)	John A. Mulcahy, Eddie Hackett,
PAR 72	Claude Harmon,
COURSE RECORD 67	Tom Fazio
Liam Higgins (1977)	

SELECTED CHAMPIONS

KERRYGOLD INTERNATIONAL CLASSIC George Burns (1975); Tony Jacklin (1976); Liam Higgins (1977)

CARD OF THE COURSE

THE FRONT NINE			THE BACK NINE		
HOLE	YARDS	PAR	HOLE	YARDS	PAR
1	430	4	10	470	4
2	464	4	11	506	5
3	425	4	12	200	3
4	185	3	13	488	5
5	595	5	14	456	4
6	194	3	15	428	4
7	424	4	16	386	4
8	436	4	17	194	3
9	445	4	18	594	5
OUT	3,598	35	IN	3,727	37

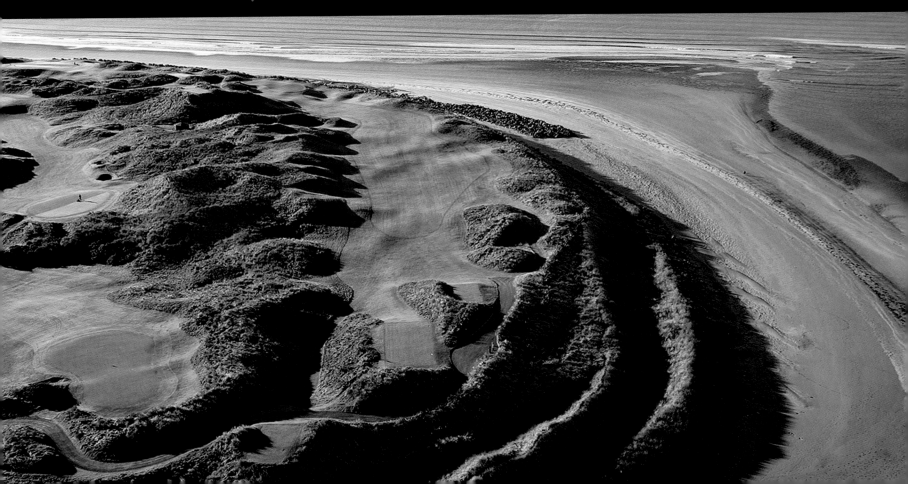

Ballybunion, IRELAND

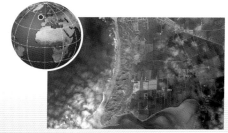

AS EYE-POPPING LINKS GO, THE OLD COURSE at Ballybunion is right up there with the best. It is a swooping course that rides over and around some vast, hairy dunes beside the dramatic waters of the Atlantic Ocean. Arguably it also boasts the greatest par-4 hole on a links course—the terraced yet bunkerless 11th. A bit like St. Andrews, it has been seen as a mecca for golfers searching for the ultimate links experience.

THE GREEN ON THE PAR-3 15th hole nestles among the extensive dunes on the Old Course at Ballybunion Golf Club.

BALLYBUNION LEAVES NO ONE UNDECIDED about its merits. Set hard by the Shannon River Estuary on the west coast of Ireland, most golfers who walk the fairways fall in love with its quirkiness and demanding nature. A few are exasperated by its reliance on "Lady Luck" and its raised greens and snagging rough— usually those who have had a bad day.

Even in its infancy, back in the late 19th century, Ballybunion courted controversy and golfers were divided. A report in the *Irish Times* of 1897 laid into its peculiarities and described it as, "a rabbit warren below the village, where a golfer requires limitless patience and an inexhaustible supply of golf balls." A harsh verdict on a brilliant course, although it is still true today that a cool nerve is needed not to lose your head and a stack of balls among the dunes.

Walking onto the 1st tee for your maiden outing is an exciting moment, yet the anticipation can turn into intrigue as you stare down the fairway and catch sight of the town's cemetery over a stone wall just to the right. Even with the morbid start, the opener is a relatively gentle introduction to a course that gets tougher and

The Old Course in Ballybunion ... is one of the best and most beautiful tests of links golf anywhere in the world

TOM WATSON, FIVE TIMES OPEN CHAMPION

BALLYBUNION

SANDHILL ROAD, BALLYBUNION,
COUNTY KERRY, IRELAND
www.ballybuniongolfclub.ie

THE OLD COURSE

FOUNDED 1893	**DESIGNERS**	
LENGTH 6,684 yards	James McKenna,	
(6,112 meters)	Tom Simpson,	
PAR 71	Tom Watson	

SELECTED CHAMPIONS

IRISH PROFESSIONAL CHAMPIONSHIP Harry
Bradshaw (1957)
MURPHY'S IRISH OPEN Patrick Sjoland (2000)
PALMER CUP (UNIVERSITIES CUP) Europe (2004)

CARD OF THE COURSE

THE FRONT NINE			THE BACK NINE		
HOLE	YARDS	PAR	HOLE	YARDS	PAR
1	403	4	10	361	4
2	439	4	11	451	4
3	220	3	12	200	3
4	529	5	13	486	5
5	552	5	14	135	3
6	382	4	15	212	3
7	420	4	16	499	5
8	154	3	17	376	4
9	456	4	18	379	4
OUT	3,555	36	IN	3,129	35

THE COURSE

Sharp contours on both the fairways and the greens are distinctive features of the Old Course, where there are no trees to negotiate but play is forever at the mercy of the offshore winds and breezes. There are few blind shots and the course demands that you play accurate shots onto the green.

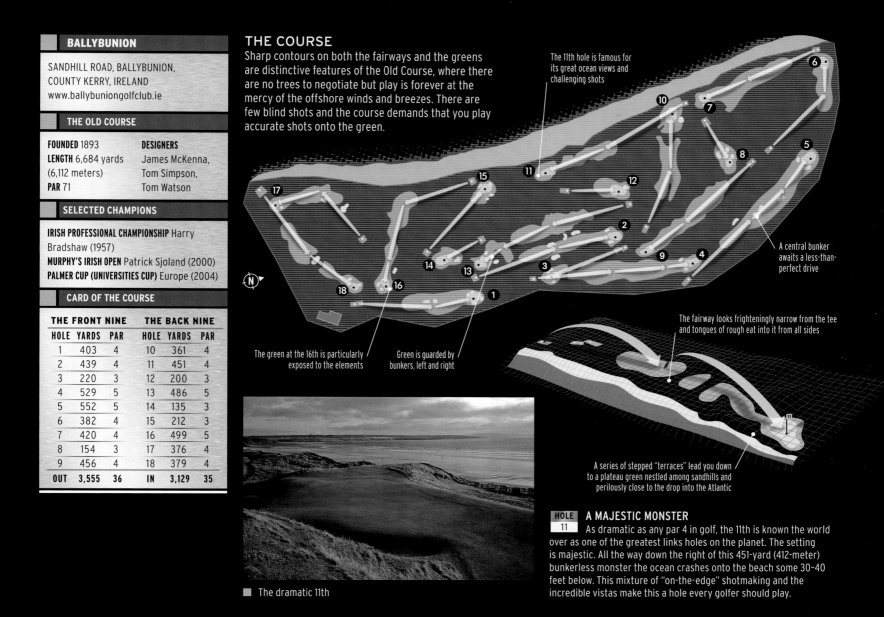

The 11th hole is famous for its great ocean views and challenging shots

A central bunker awaits a less-than-perfect drive

The green at the 16th is particularly exposed to the elements

Green is guarded by bunkers, left and right

The fairway looks frighteningly narrow from the tee and tongues of rough eat into it from all sides

A series of stepped "terraces" lead you down to a plateau green nestled among sandhills and perilously close to the drop into the Atlantic

■ The dramatic 11th

HOLE 11 A MAJESTIC MONSTER
As dramatic as any par 4 in golf, the 11th is known the world over as one of the greatest links holes on the planet. The setting is majestic. All the way down the right of this 451-yard (412-meter) bunkerless monster the ocean crashes onto the beach some 30–40 feet below. This mixture of "on-the-edge" shotmaking and the incredible vistas make this a hole every golfer should play.

tougher. The rollercoaster nature of the fairways can take their toll on a game, as rarely do you play off a truly flat lie. Approach shots are often played from these hanging lies into greens that perch on a raised area of ground with drop offs into grassy swales. Exact striking is always needed at Ballybunion.

A TRULY ENJOYABLE RIDE

The Old Course is best known for its 11th hole (see above), its five par 3s, and the last three holes that all skirt right to left around huge dunes and flirt with the sea. The short holes are truly spectacular, and, quirkily, three of them are found within a four-hole stretch on the back nine. Probably the pick of the par 3s is the 15th, which plays downhill toward the ocean. Its green is long and two-tiered, set down in the dunes and studded with four bunkers. With the wind in your face off the ocean, it can be a hellish shot in.

With a decent score going the last three holes can make or break a round. A birdie is definitely on at the 16th, but so is much worse, as the tee-shot fired from hard by the beach causes trouble. It is semi-blind and you have to decide how much of the dogleg to bite off before striking up a dune-lined valley to the green that is particularly exposed to the elements.

The 17th is another severe dogleg, this time played back down toward the beach and then around to the left along the shoreline. Finally, the home hole is a brute of an uphill par 4. Its fairway is split in two by a yawning bunker and the green is surrounded by steep, grassy banks and three pot bunkers.

Ballybunion's Old Course is a truly enjoyable ride over a dramatic landscape. It is also very challenging, especially in a hard breeze, and in parts alarmingly idiosyncratic. But its holes stand alone as memorable and fun despite their difficulty.

CLINTON PLAYS A ROUND

In 1998, President Bill Clinton played a round of golf on the Old Course at the end of his official visit to Ireland. A life-size bronze statue of the president, ready to tee off, stands in the center of town as a commemoration of the visit.

■ Distinguished visitor

Royal County Down, NORTHERN IRELAND

AN EXHILARATING RIDE OVER UNTAMED COUNTRY, Royal County Down is many golfers' idea of heaven and hell together—a marriage best described as a brutal beauty. With many fairways framed by thick gorse and boasting 130 distinctive bunkers, the course has many quirks and idiosyncracies that are both enthralling and punishing. Yet despite these ultra traditional nuances, this unique links has become a favorite the world over.

THE COURSE
Backed by the imposing fells of the Mountains of Mourne and skirting close to the Irish Sea, this rugged and uncompromising links is both delightful and exasperating in its traditional style. Blind shots and fortuitous bounces play with the head as well as the game.

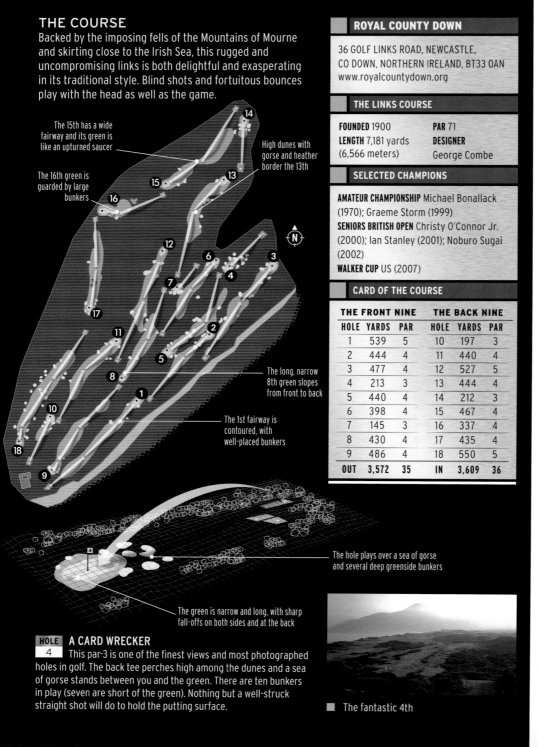

The 15th has a wide fairway and its green is like an upturned saucer

High dunes with gorse and heather border the 13th

The 16th green is guarded by large bunkers

The long, narrow 8th green slopes from front to back

The 1st fairway is contoured, with well-placed bunkers

The hole plays over a sea of gorse and several deep greenside bunkers

The green is narrow and long, with sharp fall-offs on both sides and at the back

HOLE 4 A CARD WRECKER
This par-3 is one of the finest views and most photographed holes in golf. The back tee perches high among the dunes and a sea of gorse stands between you and the green. There are ten bunkers in play (seven are short of the green). Nothing but a well-struck straight shot will do to hold the putting surface.

■ The fantastic 4th

ROYAL COUNTY DOWN

36 GOLF LINKS ROAD, NEWCASTLE, CO DOWN, NORTHERN IRELAND, BT33 0AN
www.royalcountydown.org

THE LINKS COURSE

FOUNDED 1900		**PAR** 71	
LENGTH 7,181 yards		**DESIGNER**	
(6,566 meters)		George Combe	

SELECTED CHAMPIONS

AMATEUR CHAMPIONSHIP Michael Bonallack (1970); Graeme Storm (1999)
SENIORS BRITISH OPEN Christy O'Connor Jr. (2000); Ian Stanley (2001); Noburo Sugai (2002)
WALKER CUP US (2007)

CARD OF THE COURSE

THE FRONT NINE			THE BACK NINE		
HOLE	YARDS	PAR	HOLE	YARDS	PAR
1	539	5	10	197	3
2	444	4	11	440	4
3	477	4	12	527	5
4	213	3	13	444	4
5	440	4	14	212	3
6	398	4	15	467	4
7	145	3	16	337	4
8	430	4	17	435	4
9	486	4	18	550	5
OUT	3,572	35	IN	3,609	36

GOLF NEVER HAS BEEN FAIR, especially when its pioneers took to the links. Yet over the years, we've tried to iron out the traditional idiosyncrasies many modern players find infuriating. That fortune always plays a part in golf has never been truer than at Royal County Down. Of all the finest links, this has to be the one that is the most outrageously trusted to fortune and skill combined.

A SENSE OF THE UNKNOWN
Old Tom Morris was originally credited with its design, but little of his layout remains. Member George Combe shifted the holes from the flatter part of the coastal strip into the wilder, more crumpled dunes nearby. In 1900 when he began, he had no earthmovers, only men and horses, so the holes took on the towering sandhills head first. His trademark blind holes remain in abundance.

A golfer stands on many a tee with a marker post or white stone on the horizon as a guide for caressing a drive. Not knowing what is over the top can cause timid players to sweat, but the sense of the unknown can also be a joy. Sometimes there's nothing finer than to nail one over the marker, walk to the brow of the hill, and spot your ball smack bang in the middle of the fairway. It is more important for that to happen here than just about anywhere, as the trouble you can find is nasty indeed.

ACROSS THE WHOLE LINKS a tumble of dunes erupts boldly, covered in gnarled grasses, vast tracts of gorse, and heather.

The bunkers are deep and thoughtfully placed, with an almost disheveled look, where neat faces are replaced by grasping fronds of grass and patches of heather. This deliberately natural state adds to the mystique of the place, especially compared with the beautifully kept fairways and emerald greens.

As opening holes go, the 1st has just about everything. A potential two-shot par 5 makes you think of a birdie, but it is fraught with danger. The waters of Dundrum Bay hug the right side just over the top of the dunes while snagging banks line the left. Anything pitching short of the slightly sunken green is liable to bound away. But at least you can see where you are going.

This cannot be said of several of the ensuing holes. At the 5th, for example, the hole swings from left to right and a bright white rock gleams at you on the rise in an attempt to show you the way. Long hitters may want to hit over it with a fade or fire just right of it as the hole bends that way. However, overdo it and gorse will snaffle your drive. You'll have a shorter shot to the green if you take the bolder route, but perhaps the cagey way is to

take less club and go down the left. The dangers around this green are typical of the course: fringed bunkers, run-offs, and banks at the back with heather and rough. The safe miss is short and straight, as with nearly all the greens here. Overclubbing brings nothing but trouble.

The 8th green has big drops into trouble around it (which you can't see from the fairway). The long par-4 9th has a disconcerting blind drive, and if it wasn't for some work Harry Colt did in the 1920s, the second shot would still be blind too. This is County Down's most famous hole, along with the Colt-inspired 4th.

THE RUN FOR HOME

Although the front nine is the more heralded—Tom Watson called it "as fine a nine holes as I have ever played"—the run for home also has much to admire. It has two cracking par 3s, some monstrous two shotters, with the 13th particularly acclaimed, and a guts-or-glory par-5 home hole that features 24 devilish bunkers. It all adds up to a rare, formidable, heart-in-the-mouth challenge in the most superb of surroundings.

THE 10TH IS FULL OF CHARACTER, with the tee beside the clubhouse window and a large green guarded by bunkers.

OPEN FOR BUSINESS

Technically, Royal County Down could host The Open as it is part of the UK, and it certainly has the pedigree. But politics have been the main reason it has never been granted the honor. With Northern Ireland thought to be too much of a security risk, the Open has only once been played there—at Royal Portrush in 1951. However, in recent times, the Royal & Ancient Golf Club of St. Andrews, the game's governing body and organizer of British championships, has taken the Seniors British Open to County Down, meaning the names so synonymous with The Open, like Jack Nicklaus and Tom Watson, have been able to enjoy her delights.

Turnberry, SCOTLAND

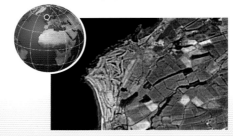

CLASSY, ELEGANT, AND ENJOYABLE, the Ailsa Course at Turnberry in Ayrshire boasts one of the most beautiful settings in golf. Overlooking the Irish Sea, with the Isle of Arran and the granite dome of Ailsa Craig dominating the seaward horizon and an old lighthouse hovering on the headland, its remarkable holes provide a dramatic challenge that has always produced great champions.

SCENERY THIS GOOD can overshadow a mediocre course. But at Turnberry, the gentle fall of the land taking the holes all the way down to the craggy rocks on the sea's edge enhances an already dazzling links.

Golf has been played on this jagged coastline stretch since the turn of the 20th century, but the sport took a back seat during the World Wars when the fairways were flattened and tarmac was laid to create an airfield. Golf was almost abandoned until Frank Hole, owner of the nearby opulent whitewashed hotel, insisted the course should be resurrected. It was left to Mackenzie Ross to make the place look natural again and in 1951, after intensive work, it reopened. And what a course it became.

TURNING UP THE HEAT

The 1st hole is a short four that breaks you in gently, but then the heat is immediately turned up on your game. After two tough two-shotters, the course runs north and close to the shoreline for five holes that test your driving in particular. The golf can often be into and across the wind, making this string of holes one to tough out rather than burn up.

The 8th green is only a few feet from the rocky oblivion on the left, but the walk to the 9th—named Bruce's Castle and Turnberry's most famous hole (see left)—will capture your attention most. The 10th hugs the beach and is high in shot values. Its new tee in front of the lighthouse requires a carry of 220 yards (200 meters) over water and rocks to reach the fairway and from there you often need a piercing long iron to find the green.

After the pretty 11th, played from a tee close to the sea, the course turns inland and tacks back over the gorse spattered and heavily grassed dunes. On every hole coming home, there is at least one heart-stopping shot: the pick of the knee-knockers are probably the drive-dangerous 13th, the tee shot at the hit-and-hope par-3 15th, the approach over the burn on 16 and the drive between dunes at the 17th.

THE CHAMPIONSHIP TEE FOR THE 9TH teeters on a rocky promontory, with the lighthouse on the left, a rugged inlet in front, and a distant cairn indicating the fairway.

The Open Championship returns for its fourth visit in 2009 and much work has been done to toughen up the course. Even though the Ailsa Course could always be a challenge in a wind, on a calm day it lacked a true fear factor. Many of the fairway bunkers were becoming too easy to miss; others were not a stern enough test. But today, thanks to the work done in conjunction with the Royal & Ancient, the course has been lengthened and tightened, bringing far more pressure shots than before. Seventeen new fairway bunkers were added and four more on approaches.

Perhaps a great champion will win as they have on the previous three tournaments: Tom Watson was up with the best when he outlasted Jack Nicklaus in 1977; Greg Norman shot a 63 in 1986 as the rest of the field floundered; and in 1994 Nick Price came home in only 31 shots on Sunday, including a monster eagle at the 17th.

A WONDERFUL CHALLENGE

Turnberry's fairness and variety means a golfer needs all the shots and a great brain to conquer it. You need to shape drives, hit bump-and-runs, and be imaginative around the greens that are generous in size and vary greatly in their shaping. It is no surprise that all three Open winners were fantastic putters, too.

It is very rare indeed to find a golfer who has visited Turnberry and not wanted to return, because the Ailsa Course ticks all the boxes. It's simply a wonderful challenge in the most glorious of surroundings.

DUEL IN THE SUN

A celebrated head-to-head between Jack Nicklaus and Tom Watson (see pp. 228-29) was played out at Turnberry in 1977. As Tom led by one going down the last, he stroked a 7-iron toward the pin. Jack gouged a 7-iron out of thick grass, found the green, then grabbed a birdie. But Tom kept his nerve to win and the hole was named "Duel in the Sun."

Tom Watson and Jack Nicklaus go head-to-head

THE COURSE

A breathtaking beauty set hard to the crashing waves of the Irish Sea. It is a demure, tranquil links where bunkers are used sparingly but cleverly and its subtle lines and constant change of pace mean finesse and power have to be used hand in hand.

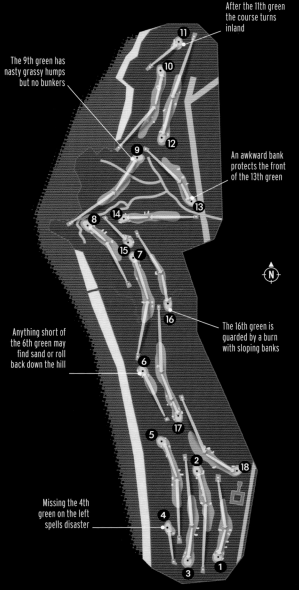

After the 11th green the course turns inland

The 9th green has nasty grassy humps but no bunkers

An awkward bank protects the front of the 13th green

Anything short of the 6th green may find sand or roll back down the hill

The 16th green is guarded by a burn with sloping banks

Missing the 4th green on the left spells disaster

HOLE 16 — "WEE BURN"

The name of the hole "Wee Burn" undersells the 16th. Yes, the channel of water meandering across the front and right of the green is small, but the banks that slope down to it are not. Virtually any ball pitching short or right of the putting surface will struggle to keep dry as a huge rounded bank dips steeply down to Wilson's Burn, dragging underhit shots into trouble. Yet a bolder shot designed to take the burn out of play can struggle to hold the green, too—especially downwind—often leaving either a delicate chip or a deft putt from the back. The hole is 50 yards (46 meters) longer than it was in 1994 and doglegs left to right, making the approach even more difficult.

THE AILSA COURSE

FOUNDED 1946	**DESIGNER**
LENGTH 7,224 yards	Mackenzie Ross
(6,605 meters)	**COURSE RECORD** 63
PAR 70	Greg Norman (1986)

SELECTED CHAMPIONS

OPEN CHAMPIONSHIP Tom Watson (1977); Greg Norman (1986); Nick Price (1994)
WOMEN'S BRITISH OPEN Karrie Webb (2002)
SENIORS BRITISH OPEN Tom Watson (2003); Loren Roberts (2006)

CARD OF THE COURSE

THE FRONT NINE			THE BACK NINE		
HOLE	YARDS	PAR	HOLE	YARDS	PAR
1	358	4	10	458	4
2	430	4	11	174	3
3	489	4	12	446	4
4	165	3	13	412	4
5	476	4	14	449	4
6	231	3	15	209	3
7	538	5	16	458	4
8	454	4	17	558	5
9	454	4	18	465	4
OUT	**3,595**	**35**	**IN**	**3,629**	**35**

The bridge at the 16th

The new doglegged fairway makes the approach even more dangerous

Anything short or right will be sucked into the burn by steep, smooth sides

Kingsbarns, SCOTLAND

ONE OF THE FEW LINKS TO HAVE BEEN BUILT in modern times, Kingsbarns is as much a feat of civil engineering as it is a brilliant piece of course design. While many of the holes unashamedly pay homage to other links courses, such as St. Andrews, Turnberry, and Carnoustie, Kingsbarns is a spectacular addition to links culture and robustly holds its own against the more vaunted links several miles away at the "Home of Golf."

KINGSBARNS HAS A REMARKABLE tale to tell. This hamlet a few miles southeast of St. Andrews has had a fluctuating love affair with golf since the late 1700s. The original links was plowed over in 1850 by the tenant farmer, and golf did not return to the sweep of linksland above Kingsbarns Bay until 1922, when St. Andrews professional Willie Auchterlonie laid out nine new holes. Yet again it suffered with the onset of war and was mined as part of the coastal defenses.

It took another five decades until the rather flat pasture would see golf again. And what a transformation. Before the earth movers rolled in to craft this genius of a links, the land simply fell gradually toward the sea, only split by a natural terrace. There were no dunes to speak of, just easy pasture that farm machinery could run smoothly over.

Then Americans Mark Parsinen and Kyle Phillips got hold of the prime piece of seaside above the dark crusty rocks of the North Sea, and turned their dreams into a links wonder. After thousands of hours of manipulating the land to build natural-looking dunes, a course rose from the levels and now no one can tell that this higgledy-piggledy land has not been like this for centuries.

STRATEGY AND GUILE

Their team methodically formed the features that the holes would weave into. They thought of every detail and their inspiration was drawn from all the great links courses. They are unabashed when they say a little piece of St. Andrews is there, along with strategic influences from Carnoustie and others, right down to the sympathetic mimicking of Turnberry's ball-gobbling burn at the 16th, which appears at Kingsbarns's home hole. These are not copies, but rather a homage to the great links, for Kingsbarns stands alone in its own right.

Every hole is fun as well as an individual. No two holes are alike, yet the course comes together as a group wonderfully well. The par 3s are a varied test—the 15th

is the star with its green delightfully placed over a rocky inlet. Most courses have a few humdrum slogs of par 4s, but at Kingsbarns they go in for strategy and guile rather than out and out length. And all par 5s are risk-and-reward chances, reachable for some, but with trouble lurking for the brave.

Every hole gives you a choice—either safety first or the brave line. The more bold the drive, the easier the approach tends to be, and for every pin position, there is a preferred line off the tee to take.

A BREATHTAKING GAMBLE

There is no let up on the greens either, as most are quick and heavily contoured. Again, it would have been easy to lay down mundane putting surfaces, but instead they were bold and looked for inspiration from some of the more ancient links such as Prestwick. A few greens border on the unfair, but that, in its way, is what is so distinctive about Kingsbarns, and there is no denying you will remember them. Kingsbarns was a breathtaking gamble, but the attention to detail and bold features mean it has come off superbly and will stand the test of time.

INFAMOUS GREEN

Kingsbarns is notorious for its green designs, and none are more infamous then the 9th. After just one year of play, it was recontoured and had a foot shaved off the height of the middle shelf. It remains a very difficult target with a raised and shallow plateau running across the green, and many wicked pin positions are possible.

■ The shelved green at the 9th

QUICK AND CHALLENGING GREENS, such as the 5th, lie in wait amid the evening shadows cast across the low-lying artificial dunes beside Kingsbarns Bay.

THE COURSE

This modern great is brilliant in its variety and is a very fair test despite some vast rolling greens. It has been made to look so natural and the gnarled dunes have been cleverly groomed and the bunkers placed to create a strategic gem.

■ The sloping 12th green

Loosely based on the 18th at Pebble Beach, the hole curves gracefully from right to left around the rocks

The sloping green is narrow and about 70 yards (64 meters) long

A bold drive over the bunker on the 4th leaves the easiest approach

The best tee shot is down the left of the 5th fairway

A burn protects the 18th green

Right-to-left contours dominate the 7th fairway

The 15th green is located over a rocky inlet

The large bunker guards the 12th green

HOLE 12	STAGGERING SCENERY

Scenically, this is the stand-out hole at Kingsbarns. If you can tear your eyes off the staggering view of the crashing waters on the arc of rocks, you will see a master hole to go with the beauty. A big drive down the left side will leave a tempting second to the long sloping green. The safe route is to lay the second up to the right of the fairway, then pitch down the length of the green. Birdies and double bogies galore.

KINGSBARNS

KINGSBARNS, ST. ANDREWS, FIFE, SCOTLAND, KY16 8QD
www.kingsbarns.com

THE COURSE

FOUNDED 2000
LENGTH 7,126 yards (6,516 meters)
PAR 70
DESIGNERS Mark Parsinen, Kyle Phillips
COURSE RECORD 62
Lee Westwood (2003)

SELECTED CHAMPIONS

DUNHILL LINKS CHAMPIONSHIP (WITH ST. ANDREWS AND CARNOUSTIE) Paul Lawrie (2001); Padraig Harrington (2002, 2006); Lee Westwood (2003); Stephen Gallacher (2004); Colin Montgomerie (2005); Nick Dougherty (2007)

CARD OF THE COURSE

THE FRONT NINE			THE BACK NINE		
HOLE	YARDS	PAR	HOLE	YARDS	PAR
1	414	4	10	387	4
2	200	3	11	455	4
3	516	5	12	606	5
4	408	4	13	148	3
5	398	4	14	366	4
6	337	4	15	212	3
7	470	4	16	565	5
8	168	3	17	474	4
9	558	5	18	444	4
OUT	3,469	36	IN	3,657	36

Royal Birkdale, ENGLAND

ETCHED INTO THE LARGE SAND DUNES overlooking the Irish Sea, Royal Birkdale is a rough-and-tumble challenge with a fantastic array of varied holes. With a reputation for being hard but fair, it is often ranked as the best course in England. Located on the west coast of Lancashire, it sits on the greatest stretch of linksland in the country, which definitely gives it the "wow" factor that all golfers love.

4TH TIME LUCKY

24-year-old Peter Thomson of Australia won the Open Championship at Royal Birkdale in 1954 with a final round of 71. Thomson had made three previous attempts to win the Open, but went on to win it four more times—in 1955, 1956, 1958, and 1965. This last victory was also at Royal Birkdale.

■ Thomson and the trophy

THE BIG WEST COAST DUNESCAPE piled up by the prevailing westerly wind over thousands of years was the perfect place to create a "stadium" style links, where fairways and greens are watched over by huge piles of sand swaying with wild grasses. Over the fence to the south lie two more golf clubs—Hillside and Southport & Ainsdale—which are both magnificent tests sharing the same terrain. But Royal Birkdale stands out for its boldness and escapism.

AN EVOLVING COURSE

Modern course builders can only dream of having such a brilliant piece of land to work with, but it still needs a clever eye to get the best out of it and lay out a golf course to drool over. Despite the club being formed in 1889, it wasn't until the 1930s that a pair of talented designers was commissioned to update the course and get the best out of the linksland.

THE CRUMPLED DUNES of England's west coast cradle Birkdale's brilliant holes, yet despite their gnarled appearance they are perfectly fair.

Five-time Open champion J. H. Taylor and his architect partner Fredrick Hawtree routed the fairways through natural valleys between the dunes and sited the greens superbly—many nestled in the sandhills, creating mini-amphitheaters. Because they used the valley floors, rather than riding the mounds, the fairways were not excessively contoured and Birkdale's reputation for fairness was born.

After Arnold Palmer's slaying of the course in the 1961 Open, it was thought crucial to update the links, both in terms of difficulty and spectator viewing. Hawtree's son Fred was asked to add bite, and among his changes was a brand new hole in the farthest reach of the course. One of the most celebrated short holes in golf, the par-3 12th can't be improved on. It is beautiful to the eye and the

THE COURSE

In a huge dunescape, the holes weave down the valleys between the sandhills. Big carries over crumpled ground, angled fairways, devious bunkering, and subtle greens make this a fair but bruising encounter in a wind.

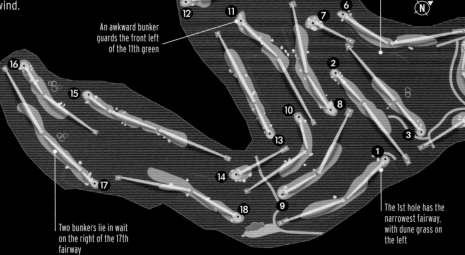

A small channel runs along the left of the 6th fairway

An awkward bunker guards the front left of the 11th green

The 1st hole has the narrowest fairway, with dune grass on the left

Two bunkers lie in wait on the right of the 17th fairway

The hole plays as a slight dogleg, more so from the back tee

The pear-shaped green is guarded by two front bunkers

■ The Art Deco clubhouse

green perches above a shaved apron across a wasteland of scrub surrounded on three sides by tall, fearful dunes. The front corners are studded with pot bunkers and it takes an extremely well-struck long iron to hit it.

In preparation for the 2008 Open, Martin Hawtree, son of Fred Jr., removed 12 fairway bunkers and added 16 new ones. Six new championship tees not only add length but have changed the lines of play on many holes, making the course a tougher test, but still wonderfully honest.

THE MANLY FIGHT

The world's best golfers have always contended with long carries over wild space from small, secluded tees. But now the fairways are harder to find and need long, shaped shots, not just big, straight blasts. And when you reach the greens here, you face subtly undulating surfaces rather than ridiculously severe slopes.

The art of green reading is such an important factor at Birkdale. One famous example saw the emergence of a modern genius. In the dry and dusty 1976 Open, the shot that Severiano Ballesteros played on the final hole to secure his runner-up spot has gone down in folklore. He'd missed the 18th green, then produced a piece of magic to thread a running chip from the rough between two bunkers and down to the hole to save his par.

If you survive the manly fight, especially the run-in from the 15th, you are greeted by the landmark white Art Deco clubhouse, reminiscent of an ocean liner. And whatever a golfer scores here, they will know that they have been on a beautiful walk on the wild side.

FEW GOLFERS are privileged to have a plaque on any course for a historic feat, yet Arnold Palmer has one at Royal Birkdale on the 16th. It marks a spot just off the right edge of the fairway among the willow scrub from where, in the 1961 Open, he smashed a 6-iron onto the green in the second round. It astounded onlookers and the fearsome blow had to be commemorated.

ROYAL BIRKDALE

ROYAL BIRKDALE GOLF CLUB, WATERLOO ROAD, SOUTHPORT, ENGLAND, PR8 2LX
www.royalbirkdale.com

THE COURSE

FOUNDED 1889	Fred Hawtree Sr. &
LENGTH 7,180 yards	Jr., Martin Hawtree
(6,565 meters)	**COURSE RECORD** 65
PAR 70	Tiger Woods (1998),
DESIGNERS J H Taylor,	John Huston (1998)

SELECTED CHAMPIONS

OPEN CHAMPIONSHIP Peter Thomson (1954, 1965); Arnold Palmer (1961); Lee Trevino (1971); Johnny Miller (1976); Tom Watson (1983); Ian Baker-Finch (1991); Mark O'Meara (1998)
RYDER CUP US (1965); GB&I tied with US.

CARD OF THE COURSE

THE FRONT NINE			THE BACK NINE		
HOLE	YARDS	PAR	HOLE	YARDS	PAR
1	450	4	10	412	4
2	421	4	11	434	4
3	450	4	12	183	3
4	203	3	13	498	4
5	346	4	14	201	3
6	509	4	15	544	5
7	177	3	16	439	4
8	458	4	17	572	5
9	411	4	18	472	4
OUT	3,425	34	IN	3,755	36

MOMENTOUS HOLE

HOLE 18 The scene of many great shots and moments, the home hole is very demanding. There is a bunker in the middle of the split fairway at about 230 yards (210 meters) from the tee, which should only pose problems into the wind. Instead the thick rough and gorse on the right are more of a threat. Once on the fairway, a long iron will be needed to thread between two front bunkers to find the pear-shaped green. In the 1965 Ryder Cup, Arnold Palmer issued the coup de grace to the Great Britain and Ireland team by cracking a 3-wood to 4 feet. Tom Watson also hit a mind-blowing shot here in the 1983 Open, firing a 2-iron from 213 yards (195 meters) out through the narrow 15-yard (14-meter) entrance to 18 feet (5.5 meters). He calmly took two putts and won by one shot from Hale Irwin and Andy Bean.

■ The pear-shaped 18th green

Muirfield, SCOTLAND

HOME TO THE OLDEST GOLF CLUB IN THE WORLD–The Honourable Company of Edinburgh Golfers–this links overlooks the Firth of Forth near Edinburgh. It is often rated the finest course in the British Isles and among the top 10 in the world. In 1744, members of the golf club drew up the game's first official rules, "The 13 Articles and Laws at Playing at Golf," to be followed during that year's inaugural golf competition, which was won by Gordon Rattray.

IT IS HARD TO ARGUE with the experts who rate this course so highly. Muirfield is a stupendous design, not because it is the most dramatic course, or even the toughest, but because it is clever and ultimately the fairest of all the great links. In the scheme of links history, this demure course is not all that old, coming into existence in 1891, almost 150 years after the club was formed in 1744. But since that day, it has been at the forefront of golf, wooing all who are lucky enough to have walked its fairways.

In 1836, The Honourable Company moved, because of overcrowding, from the Leith Links, where they played on only five holes, to the nine holes of the Old Course at Musselburgh. Then they moved again to the present location to the east of Edinburgh and laid out their own course on the far from wild open fields just a few hundred yards from the sea.

Not blessed with tumultuous dunes, the course design team, led by Old Tom Morris, relied more on the particular placing of the deep bunkers to test both strategy and ball-striking. But more than that, they brilliantly devised a way of constantly changing the directions of the holes. The outward nine runs in a clockwise direction and hugs the perimeter of the site. Then, cunningly, the holes reverse and run counterclockwise within the outer nine.

A CEREBRAL TEST

A golfer must contend with 13 changes of direction— only the 3rd, 4th, and 5th can be called a stretch of holes running the same way. On every tee the wind has to be thought about, and it is these subtle changes, combined with the brilliant bunkering, that makes Muirfield a cerebral test. So good was the original layout that the great Harry Colt was able to keep it roughly the same when he added some bite in 1922. And if you glance down the list of Open Championship winners, it seems the cream always rises to the top.

THE GREEN AT THE PAR-3 13TH is narrow, slopes from back to front, and is protected by three bunkers on the right and two on the left.

NICK FALDO FINALLY fulfilled his promise and won his first major title at Muirfield in 1987 with a perfect 18. But he had to do it the hard way. Starting the final round level with David Frost and one behind Paul Azinger, Faldo strung together a remarkable 18 pars in a row. His mix of pure striking, thoughtful play, and scrambling culminated in a nervy 4-foot putt at the last.

ERNIE ELS'S SHOT OF THE YEAR came at the tough par-3 13th where severe bunkers eat into the putting surface like trenches. He found a bunker on the left of the green on the final round of the 2002 Open. Els recalls: "The ball was tight against the face of the bunker and just getting it out—never mind close—would be a reasonable result I thought. I pulled out my 59 degree sand wedge and I said to my caddie, 'I'm going to hit this as hard as I can.' I was amazed. I got it out and almost holed it! It was a really, really good save and helped me win the Open." It was voted European Tour Shot of the Year.

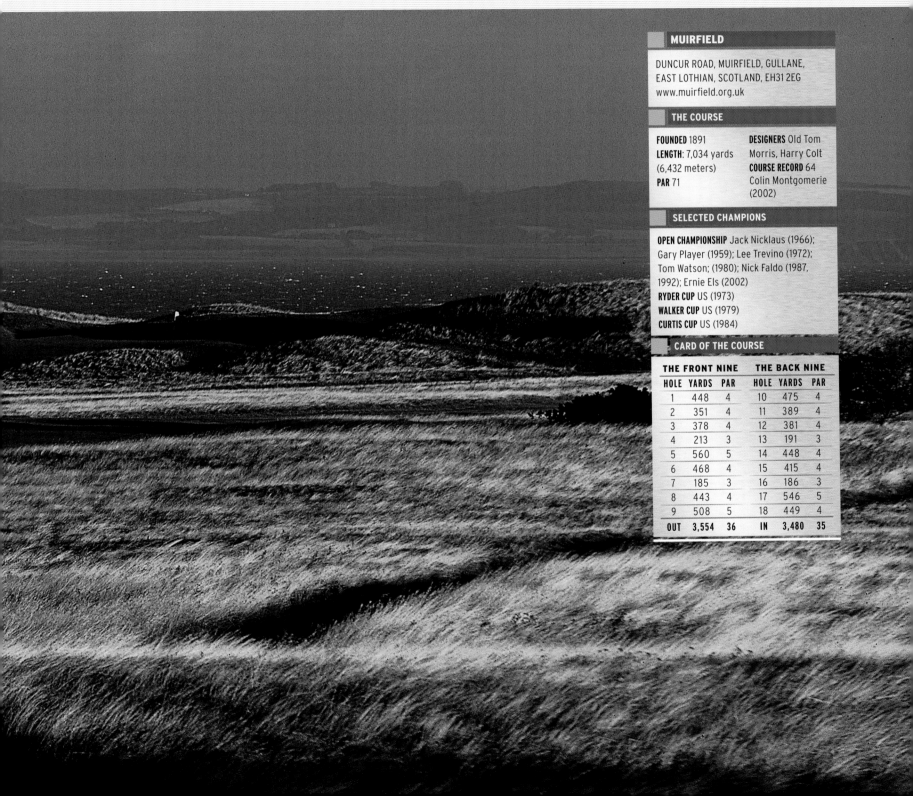

MUIRFIELD

DUNCUR ROAD, MUIRFIELD, GULLANE, EAST LOTHIAN, SCOTLAND, EH31 2EG
www.muirfield.org.uk

THE COURSE

FOUNDED 1891
LENGTH: 7,034 yards (6,432 meters)
PAR 71

DESIGNERS Old Tom Morris, Harry Colt
COURSE RECORD 64 Colin Montgomerie (2002)

SELECTED CHAMPIONS

OPEN CHAMPIONSHIP Jack Nicklaus (1966); Gary Player (1959); Lee Trevino (1972); Tom Watson; (1980); Nick Faldo (1987, 1992); Ernie Els (2002)
RYDER CUP US (1973)
WALKER CUP US (1979)
CURTIS CUP US (1984)

CARD OF THE COURSE

THE FRONT NINE			THE BACK NINE		
HOLE	YARDS	PAR	HOLE	YARDS	PAR
1	448	4	10	475	4
2	351	4	11	389	4
3	378	4	12	381	4
4	213	3	13	191	3
5	560	5	14	448	4
6	468	4	15	415	4
7	185	3	16	186	3
8	443	4	17	546	5
9	508	5	18	449	4
OUT	3,554	36	IN	3,480	35

■ The raised green at the 3rd   ■ The comfortable locker room   ■ The expansive 10th hole

THE COURSE

Known as the fairest links of them all, Muirfield is an honest but tough examination on a gently sloping "meadow." Deep bunkering, subtle changes of direction, and cambered greens make it a strategic beauty.

THE FRONT NINE ❶ A tough start with a C-shaped trap down the left and thick rough both sides. ❷ Straightforward par 4, but a tricky green guarded front right by a nest of traps. ❸ Two large sandhills pinch the fairway and can obstruct the view to the green beyond. ❹ Although bunkers patrol the front the green has run-offs all around. ❺ Drive over the fairway traps on the right for the best line in. ❻ Four traps in the lee of the dogleg have to be avoided for any chance at par. ❼ Difficult to judge the club as the green sits level with your eyeline and with nothing beyond. ❽ A nasty collection of sand sits in the corner of the dogleg right. ❾ A great par 5 that needs careful plotting.

THE BACK NINE ❿ A semiblind approach thanks to two large cross bunkers. ⓫ The only true blind shot with a drive over a large saddle. ⓬ The best line to the green is from the left side toward the bunker. ⓭ A raised and angled green deviously bunkered both sides. ⓮ Three traps on the left and a solo bunker on the right patrol the drive. ⓯ Thirteen bunkers taunt you the length of the hole. Precision is key. ⓰ Classy three with several deep traps and a steep drop off the left side. ⓱ Reachable in two and the green sits in a natural amphitheater. ⓲ Exacting finish needing a great strike to find the green and avoid the ring bunker on the right.

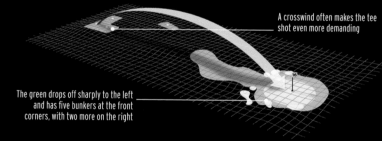

The flat, moundless green sits only yards from the boundary wall

The fairway has a large bunker on the left at 260 yards (238 meters) out and a diagonal string of five bunkers

HOLE 9 — FEARSOME AND HAZARDOUS

Though not long for a modern par 5, the 9th is dangerous. The tee shot can be fearsome, especially into the wind, with an Out of Bounds stone wall all along the left of the hole and thick rough on the right. After avoiding these hazards and the large fairway bunker, it's decision time: a lay-up or a go at the green. The long approach is trickily angled and the more you go right to avoid the wall, the more the string of bunkers comes into play. Many feel this is a birdie hole, but it has entrapped the best, too.

The tee shot at the 16th must avoid the bunkers around the green

The long approach to the 9th green must avoid a string of bunkers

Approach shots can fall prey to the bunkers around the 11th green

Bunkers congregate where tee shots land on the 5th fairway

A crosswind often makes the tee shot even more demanding

The green drops off sharply to the left and has five bunkers at the front corners, with two more on the right

HOLE 16 — ABSOLUTE PRECISION

A brilliant one-shotter that requires absolute precision with a mid-to-long iron depending on the wind. Going long may seem preferable, but the green tilts slightly from the back and to the front right, making putting quite tricky from beyond the hole.

The banks around the green can act as a ball gatherer

A cluster of bunkers cross the hole at around 110 yards (100 meters) short of the green

HOLE 17 — STRATEGIC THINKING

This hole can turn fortunes as it is a reachable in two par 5, given a favorable wind. However, such is the severity of the bunkers up the left and also short of the green, that a par has to be earned with good strategy and precise striking. The banks around the green make for an awkward chip if the ball stays up in the grass.

The angled and well-protected 13th green

TV crew above the 16th green in 2007

Harold Hilton won the first of Muirfield's Opens in 1892, and from then on, the list of winners includes many of the greatest names in golf: Harry Vardon, James Braid, Walter Hagen, Henry Cotton, Gary Player, Lee Trevino, Tom Watson, Jack Nicklaus, Nick Faldo, and Ernie Els. The course also holds the distinction as the only course to have held the Open and The Amateur as well as all three of the transatlantic team contests—The Ryder, Walker, and Curtis Cups.

A REPUTATION FOR HONESTY

Those golfers fortunate to have played in these various championships are always impressed by Muirfield's honesty. Holes glide through golden knee-high rough and very few have an up-and-down nature. There is only one truly blind shot—the drive at the 11th—but generally what you see is what you get.

Fairways are predominantly straight but several of them dogleg almost imperceptibly and nests of traps patrol the corners. Because it lies on quite flat land, the fairways, along with Royal Birkdale's, are probably the least contoured of all on the Open course list. It means that the best ball strikers aren't compromised by fortune so much and can get the best out of their game. All a golfer needs to do is to avoid the devilish bunkers—easier said than done since there are over 150 eager to devour even a slightly off-line shot.

They are particularly gruesome on the short holes where missing the green is not a savory option. Seven deep traps are entrenched around the 16th and coming in the home stretch as it does, its 186 uphill yards become a potential card wrecker. But even if you avoid the

numerous traps on any of Muirfield's holes and find the greens, the work is not done—far from it. Although not lightning fast, they are almost always firm and slopey, and tend to filter off shots that land close to the edges. Putting is an art here.

Muirfield is hard to fault golfwise as it tests the all-around quality of a game like few others. The only slight quibble from some who like to be truly wowed is the lack of real drama in its landscape. Unassuming and reserved rather than eye-popping and spectacular, to walk Muirfield's holes is a more serene experience than at other more rough-and-tumble links. But it is a special place to play because of that. It is a thinking man's course not necessarily for cavaliers—and pure and simply, it is a cracking challenge.

THE DISTINCTIVE RING BUNKER to the right of the 18th green, and in front of the clubhouse, presents players with a demanding challenge at the end of their round.

St. Andrews, SCOTLAND

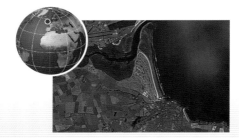

THE OLD COURSE IS KNOWN AS "THE HOME OF GOLF," and for centuries, every champion that has ever played the game, has done so here. The game of golf was nurtured on this strange links–with its multitude of bunkers and double greens–and for that reason alone, there is no place like it. As Jack Nicklaus declared, "I fell in love with it the first day I played it. There's just no other golf course that is even remotely close."

THE ST. ANDREWS STORY is an extraordinary one. No one really knows whether this is the oldest golf course in the world, but it is said that the sport has been played on the town's links since around 1400. The earliest written proof was when King James IV bought clubs in the town in 1502. But whenever it was first played, it is true to say that it is the most famous course in the world, and one that every golfer must aspire to play.

The Old Course (there are five, soon to be six, other courses) started out as 22 holes—11 out and 11 back. But in 1764 when some of the holes were deemed too short, they amalgamated a few to become 18 holes, and that is why we have that standard number today.

The Royal and Ancient Golf Club of St. Andrews is the governing body of world golf (except for the US) and runs the national championships of the UK as well as being responsible for the Rules of Golf. However, despite its prominent position on the course, it does not own the links, but is just one of a number of golf clubs that are allowed to play on the town's courses. The links are public and run by a trust. No play is allowed on Sundays on the Old Course except for major tournaments.

DOUBLE GREENS AND SINGULAR NAMES

Until the late 1890s when Old Tom Morris tinkered with the course, a golfer played out and back to the same holes. But Old Tom widened the fairways through the gorse and made the greens bigger so they could hold two flags. That is why St. Andrews has seven huge double greens even to this day and only the 1st, 9th, 17th, and 18th holes have their own green. This configuration is also responsible for the way the bunkers come into play, as they were designed to be a hazard whether you were going out or coming back. Many are hidden to the eye and it comes as a shock to the first timer to find their ball in sand from a seemingly perfect drive. Even an experienced campaigner will do well to avoid a fairway bunker in a round, so cunning are their placement.

THE SUN SETS OVER THE 18TH, the most famous finishing hole in golf. Old Tom Morris considered it to be his finest work.

KEY MOMENTS

THE FIRST OF JACK NICKLAUS' two Opens at St. Andrews in 1970 was the most memorable, but probably for the wrong reason. American Doug Sanders needed two putts at the 72nd hole to win. His first stopped three feet shy of the hole. Nervously and famously he pushed his second wide to put him in an 18-hole play-off with Nicklaus. One ahead on the last, The Golden Bear drove to the back of the green, chipped down from the rough, and holed out for a winning birdie.

TIGER WOODS HAS PLAYED two Opens at The Old Course as a professional, and has won both. His first, at the 2000 championship, saw him demolish the field by 8 strokes and establish a record score of 269 (19 under par). It also meant that, at the age of 24, he became the youngest player to win the career Grand Slam (win all four majors)—only the fifth golfer to do so. In 2005 (left), he won by a mere 5 strokes from Colin Montgomerie, and registered the 10th Major of his career.

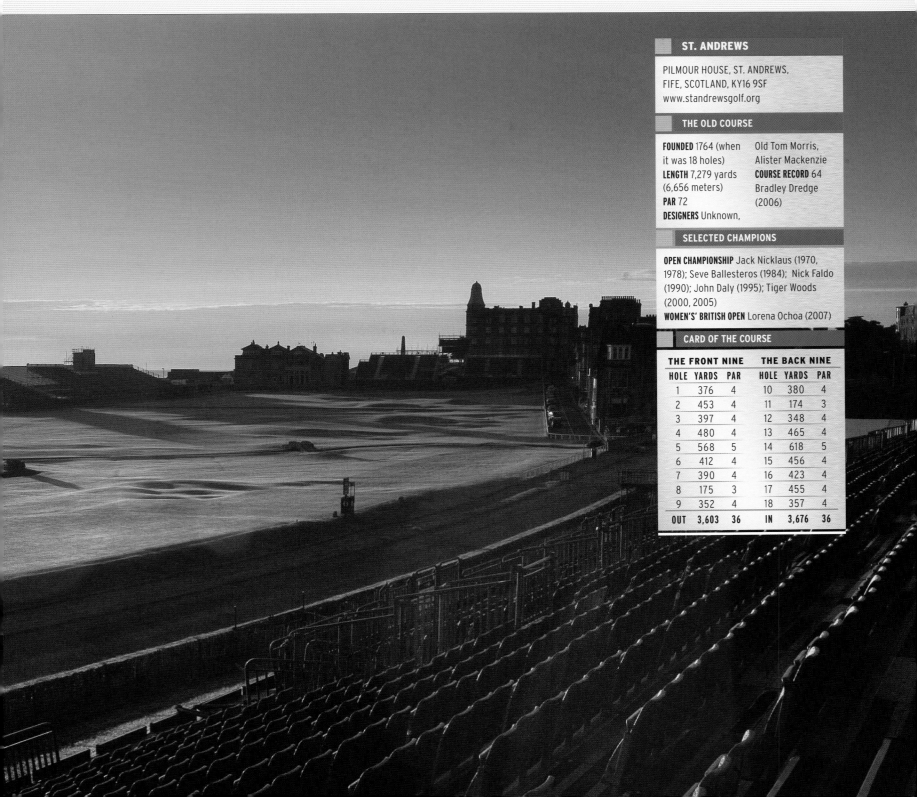

ST. ANDREWS

PILMOUR HOUSE, ST. ANDREWS,
FIFE, SCOTLAND, KY16 9SF
www.standrewsgolf.org

THE OLD COURSE

FOUNDED 1764 (when it was 18 holes)
LENGTH 7,279 yards (6,656 meters)
PAR 72
DESIGNERS Unknown, Old Tom Morris, Alister Mackenzie
COURSE RECORD 64 Bradley Dredge (2006)

SELECTED CHAMPIONS

OPEN CHAMPIONSHIP Jack Nicklaus (1970, 1978); Seve Ballesteros (1984); Nick Faldo (1990); John Daly (1995); Tiger Woods (2000, 2005)
WOMEN'S BRITISH OPEN Lorena Ochoa (2007)

CARD OF THE COURSE

THE FRONT NINE			THE BACK NINE		
HOLE	YARDS	PAR	HOLE	YARDS	PAR
1	376	4	10	380	4
2	453	4	11	174	3
3	397	4	12	348	4
4	480	4	13	465	4
5	568	5	14	618	5
6	412	4	15	456	4
7	390	4	16	423	4
8	175	3	17	455	4
9	352	4	18	357	4
OUT	3,603	36	IN	3,676	36

HELL BUNKER is the largest bunker on the Old Course. This monster trap lies around 100 yards (91 meters) from the green on the par-5 14th and should be avoided at all costs.

that runs in front of the first green is the most photographed feature in golf. Everyone who is anyone has strode across it and felt pride, in the same way that every debutant feels nervous excitement on the 1st tee.

Despite the historic fame of this quirky course, the actual golf still has to live up to the billing. Fairways, often hidden from full view off the tee by banks of gorse and scrub are almost ludicrously rippled and seamlessly run into many of the greens which are also tantalizingly cambered. The art is to weigh up the wind, then know which line to take off the tee for the best chance of maneuvering the ball toward the flag. It takes many rounds to know how the ball will skip in and be affected by the slopes, and where to miss if you are going to.

Many of these deep pits of sand, some way over head high, have acquired singularly appropriate names, such as the ominous "Hell," "Principal's Nose," "Pulpit," "The Beardies," "Coffins," "Lion's Mouth," and "Cat's Trap."

The titles of other features are also recognizable the world over: "Miss Grainger's Bosoms" appear as mounds either side of the 15th; "The Elysian Fields" are the flat part of the 14th fairway; the "Valley of Sin" is the deep-shaved swale below the 18th green. But probably the two most notable in golf are the "Swilcan Bridge" and the "Road Hole." The ancient stone bridge over the burn

Once on the greens, you could be faced with an extraordinarily long putt. Most have huge putting surfaces—the 5th and 13th joint green is 100 yards (91 meters) long, with an area of 1½ acres (0.6 hectares). The Open has been held here 27 times since 1873, and you will find that most champions are the ones who avoid the bunkers and three-putt the least.

The Old Course is not to everyone's liking, simply because it is so hard to read. Even if you have done your homework, Lady Luck can turn against you. Yet it is the very fact that nature built this unparalleled course that St. Andrews will always be cherished.

> ## The reason why the Road Hole at St. Andrews is such a great par-four **is because it's a par-five!**
>
> BEN CRENSHAW, SUMMING UP THE DIFFICULTY OF THIS HOLE

■ St. Andrews and the Eden Estuary   ■ The world-renowned Swilcan Bridge   ■ The infamous "Road Hole" bunker on the 17th

THE COURSE

This is a bizarre links with its naturally rippled ground, quirky layout with shared fairways and greens, and its devious bunkering. It takes a long time to get to know, but it is the "must play" experience in world golf. There is nothing like it on earth.

THE FRONT NINE ❶ Possibly the widest fairway in golf, but still a nerve-wracking experience due to the weight of history. ❷ Semiblind drive over gorse. Anything landing short of the green is prone to a bad bounce. ❸ The safer line down the left leaves an approach that flirts with a large bunker. ❹ There is plenty of room down the left side, but a large mound defends the front of the green. ❺ Reachable in two downwind, but the green is 100 yards long, often leaving monstrous putts. ❻ A dip at the front of the green dictates your strategy. Go aerial or run it through. ❼ Difficult ridges run through the green, making putting tricky. ❽ One of only two short holes. Avoid the two front pots. ❾ Driveable for the longest hitters, but gorse left and two small traps await.

THE BACK NINE ❿ A cut drive can find one of three bunkers, from which par is tough. ⓫ The dastardly "Strath" bunker is a card wrecker and guards a wickedly sloping green. ⓬ Difficult to plot through the bunkers on the drive, and a running approach may be needed to this shelf green. ⓭ Finding the "Coffins" bunkers down the left will leave you dead. ⓮ A real birdie chance if you can avoid Out of Bounds on the right and "Hell" bunker on the second. ⓯ Aim at the steeple in the distance for the best line. ⓰ The safe line is down the left but leaves a tougher approach. A steep bank crosses the front. ⓱ The safe play is to aim for the front right of the green to avoid the "Road Hole" bunker. ⓲ Best to aim for the clubhouse clock left, then pitch in over the "Valley of Sin."

The green at the 7th has a view of the Eden Estuary

The 11th features the nasty "Strath" bunker

The 5th fairway has a pair of bunkers called the "Spectacles"

"Hell" bunker lurks on the 14th

"Cartgate" bunker guards the joint 3rd and 15th green

A burn crosses in front of the 1st green

"Hell" bunker is a gargantuan pit waiting to trap you

An Out of Bounds wall runs down the right side

Aim your drive over a green shed and avoid the stone wall

The most severe and most famous bunker in golf awaits on the left

The large green slopes quite sharply from back to front

A road crosses the fairway between "Swilcan Bridge" and the green

HOLE 14 "LONG'
One of only two par 5s on the course and a brief respite before the rigors of the home stretch. The landing area from the drive is generous. Into the wind a player has to decide how to take on "Hell" bunker. Downwind many can reach the green, but a steep bank at the front can play havoc even with seemingly perfect shots.

HOLE 17 "ROAD HOLE"
As strange a hole as you will find on a championship course, the Road Hole has peculiarities at every turn. If you have found the fairway, you must run a long shot up onto the green, avoiding the bunker on the left but not overcooking the approach as it will fall off the back and either end up on a paved road or worse against the stone wall beyond.

HOLE 18 "TOM MORRIS"
Aim for the clock on the R&A clubhouse and give it a good crack so it clears the road. A deep crease eats into the front left edge of the green. You can either hit a low running shot through it and up onto the green, or try to fly it and hope for some spin. Most people finish beyond the hole (having avoided the "Valley of Sin"), leaving a slippery putt to the hole.

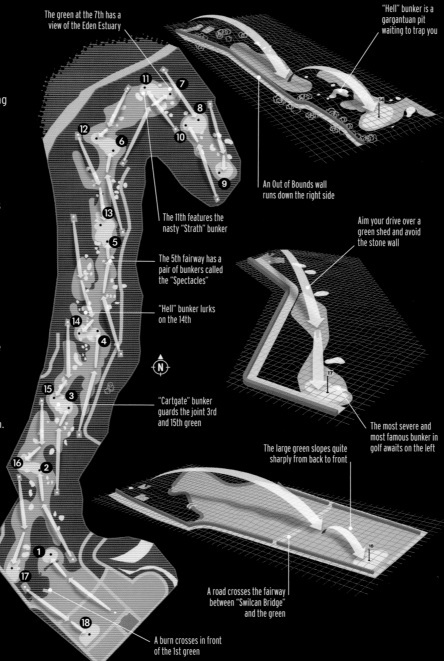

An aerial view of the double green shared by the 2nd and 16th

The Royal & Ancient clubhouse

Royal St. George's, ENGLAND

OFTEN KNOWN AS SANDWICH, named after the quaint town nearby, Royal St. George's is a powerhouse of variety set over a vast 400 acres (160 hectares) of wonderful linksland on the Kent coast in southeast England. It was the first English club to host the Open Championship back in 1894. A massive area of duneland boasts examples of rare flora as well as a mind-blowing, precocious links that offers a complete golfing examination.

THE COURSE

A massive piece of wild ground houses a course of tremendous variety and power. Large dunes at one end of the course gradually level out to a gently undulating test at the other. Many fairways are humpbacked and rolling and the greens have awkward run-offs and are studded with bunkers. Fortune plays a big part at St. George's.

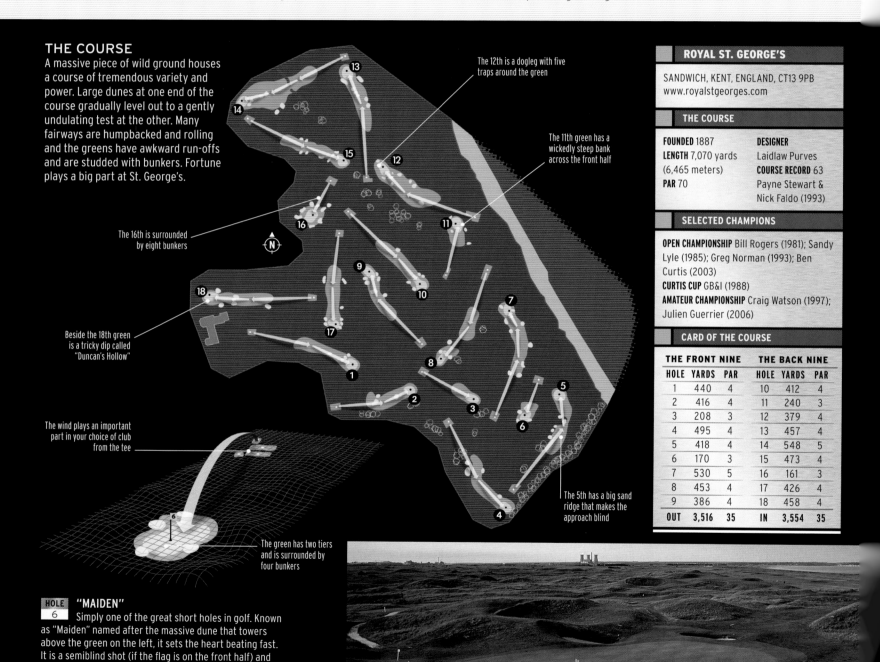

The 12th is a dogleg with five traps around the green

The 11th green has a wickedly steep bank across the front half

The 16th is surrounded by eight bunkers

Beside the 18th green is a tricky dip called "Duncan's Hollow"

The wind plays an important part in your choice of club from the tee

The green has two tiers and is surrounded by four bunkers

The 5th has a big sand ridge that makes the approach blind

ROYAL ST. GEORGE'S

SANDWICH, KENT, ENGLAND, CT13 9PB
www.royalstgeorges.com

THE COURSE

FOUNDED 1887	**DESIGNER**
LENGTH 7,070 yards	Laidlaw Purves
(6,465 meters)	**COURSE RECORD** 63
PAR 70	Payne Stewart &
	Nick Faldo (1993)

SELECTED CHAMPIONS

OPEN CHAMPIONSHIP Bill Rogers (1981); Sandy Lyle (1985); Greg Norman (1993); Ben Curtis (2003)
CURTIS CUP GB&I (1988)
AMATEUR CHAMPIONSHIP Craig Watson (1997); Julien Guerrier (2006)

CARD OF THE COURSE

THE FRONT NINE			THE BACK NINE		
HOLE	YARDS	PAR	HOLE	YARDS	PAR
1	440	4	10	412	4
2	416	4	11	240	3
3	208	3	12	379	4
4	495	4	13	457	4
5	418	4	14	548	5
6	170	3	15	473	4
7	530	5	16	161	3
8	453	4	17	426	4
9	386	4	18	458	4
OUT	**3,516**	**35**	**IN**	**3,554**	**35**

HOLE 6 "MAIDEN"

Simply one of the great short holes in golf. Known as "Maiden" named after the massive dune that towers above the green on the left, it sets the heart beating fast. It is a semiblind shot (if the flag is on the front half) and four venomous bunkers surround it. Two patrol the front right corner, which means you have to take enough club to clear them, but have to have enough control to stop it from skipping through or worse, turning left into another trap.

THE GENIUS RESPONSIBLE for the course, way back in 1887, was Laidlaw Purves. He was lucky to have so much elbow room to give the golfer a feeling of seclusion and cherry pick the best parts of the land overlooking Pegwell Bay. Nonetheless he did a splendid job.

Play changes direction on virtually every tee. Given the mix of holes, it is no wonder that all your skills are needed. There is an 80-yard (73-meter) range between the four brilliant short holes. Depending on the wind, some par 4s are unreachable in 2, yet a couple are on the edge of being driveable. And the only two par fives play in opposite directions, meaning one usually plays a good deal harder than the other. Rarely will someone put the flag back in the hole on the difficult 18th and not have used nearly all the clubs in their bag—a true mark of a legendary test.

LUCK PLAYS A PART

The course starts with a bang, as Tiger Woods knows only to well. On his opening hole of the 2003 Open, he cut his driver right into the rough and lost a ball for the first time in his professional career. Tiger also found out how luck plays a part at Sandwich—something that some professionals don't like about the course. Many of the fairways are humpbacked and kick balls off even if you have hit one straight down the middle—the 17th is probably the hardest to hit.

The greens can do similar things, too. The 4th green, which sits at the end of an extreme par 4, is monstrously shaped. A huge upslope rises from the front left and it also dips away severely off on the right. Likewise the 10th, which in a wind is just about the hardest to hit and hold, even with a wedge in your hand. The putting surface is a tilting plateau a good 15 feet above the level of your approach shot, and consequently it has huge drop-offs, either into very deep traps or down into rough.

Unfavorable bounces, frustratingly awkward bunkers, and vile rough are not the only obstacles a golfer has to contend with. There are upward of 10 totally or semiblind shots on the course, although none are truly perplexing. What you think is the line, generally is the right one, although the drive at the 4th should really take on the huge bunker rather than go left of it to find the heart of the fairway. Incidentally, it is the 2nd highest bunker in golf (behind the Himalaya bunker at St. Enodoc) and does prey on your drive.

THE FAMOUS FIVE

If Royal St. George's is famous for one stretch of holes it is the final five, although the par 3s as a set are as good as anywhere. From the 14th in, you are faced with some palpitating shots. Standing on the par-5 14th tee is very nerve-wracking: a noticeable out-of-bounds fence just yards from you runs all the way down the hole on the right. The hole is also is dissected by a wide ditch called

THE UNDULATING CARPET OF THE 17TH fairway has every player praying for a favorable bounce, particularly if they drive too far. The raised green is well-guarded on both sides

"Suez" which, depending on the breeze, can trouble the drive or the second. The 15th is a slog and the green is guarded across the front by bunkers and should not be missed left. The 16th is a magnificent short hole, scene of the first televised hole-in-one and the collapse of Thomas Bjorn in 2003 when he took three to get out of the right greenside bunker and lost the Open by one.

Cross your fingers for a favorable bounce at the 17th, and even the best find it hard to hit the green at the 18th in two. If the wind stays away, the course is supremely serene. If it doesn't, then you can be thankful that after your inevitable fight, you can find sanctuary in one of the most convivial clubhouses in Britain.

SANDY LYLE'S VICTORY

Sandy Lyle famously sunk to his knees and thumped his club into the ground after a chip on his final hole at the 1985 Open came back to his feet. Luckily he composed himself and went on to win by one from Payne Stewart.

■ Sandy Lyle wins the Open

Fancourt, SOUTH AFRICA

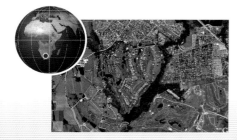

DESIGNED BY ONE OF THE GAME'S GREATS and hometown favorite Gary Player, The Links at Fancourt is one of the new breed of inland courses built to resemble a seaside masterpiece. Located near the town of George on South Africa's scenic Garden Route, it is one of four courses at Fancourt. Although the dunes are artificially created and water comes into play, this demanding and surreal test boasts many true links characteristics.

BUNKERS SET INTO LARGE HUMPS and a nasty water hazard left of the green make the 12th the hardest hole on the course.

MOTHER NATURE DID MOST to build our greatest links courses, with original landscapes merely tinkered with by a golf architect. Yet here in deepest South Africa, bulldozers rather than wind and waves have shaped the course. Fancourt was already an established golf venue, with two excellent and beautifully lush courses, when in 2000 they added a third 18 holes which quickly became the star of Africa. It is called The Links for a reason.

A flat airfield site and adjoining farmland was taken over and transformed into a gnarled artificial dunescape, where holes rock and roll over gently rippled ground and are flanked by shaped sandhills. Most characteristics of a links course are in evidence—isolated tees, creased fairways, deep and strategic bunkers, fast and firm greens with swales and roll offs, and tangly hummocks of grass. It may be a little greener than some of the best-known links, but it still plays like one. The only give-aways to its pretender status are the network of lakes that come into play on several holes, including the 15th which has a peninsula green, and the impressive Outeniqua Mountains that rise majestically behind the course. Otherwise you could easily be beside the sea.

Gary Player, an expert links exponent having won the Open Championship three times, used his knowledge of

Links golf is how the game originated and at The Links we take golfers back to the roots of golf—and they can play a "British Open" all of their own!

GARY PLAYER, COURSE DESIGNER

THE COURSE

Totally manmade but shaped to look like natural rippled linksland, it is a big, strong course that true links experts thrive on. Because of its design, it needs to be tackled with an imaginative mind and a shotmaker's skill. The bunkers can be evil (deep and cleverly placed), but the wild grasses flanking the fairways are equally tough.

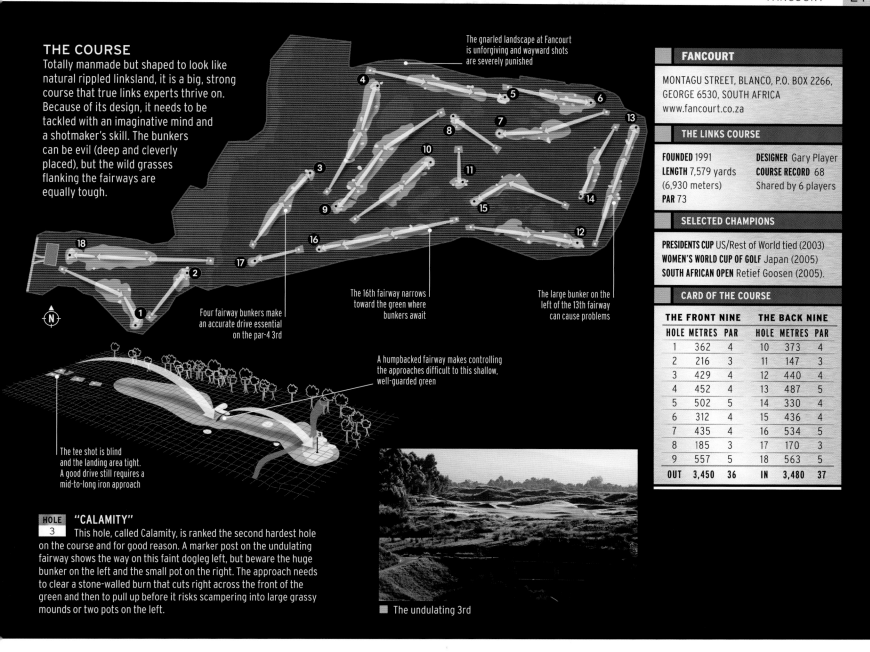

The gnarled landscape at Fancourt is unforgiving and wayward shots are severely punished

The 16th fairway narrows toward the green where bunkers await

The large bunker on the left of the 13th fairway can cause problems

A humpbacked fairway makes controlling the approaches difficult to this shallow, well-guarded green

Four fairway bunkers make an accurate drive essential on the par-4 3rd

The tee shot is blind and the landing area tight. A good drive still requires a mid-to-long iron approach

HOLE 3 "CALAMITY"
This hole, called Calamity, is ranked the second hardest hole on the course and for good reason. A marker post on the undulating fairway shows the way on this faint dogleg left, but beware the huge bunker on the left and the small pot on the right. The approach needs to clear a stone-walled burn that cuts right across the front of the green and then to pull up before it risks scampering into large grassy mounds or two pots on the left.

■ The undulating 3rd

FANCOURT

MONTAGU STREET, BLANCO, P.O. BOX 2266, GEORGE 6530, SOUTH AFRICA
www.fancourt.co.za

THE LINKS COURSE

FOUNDED 1991		**DESIGNER** Gary Player	
LENGTH 7,579 yards		**COURSE RECORD** 68	
(6,930 meters)		Shared by 6 players	
PAR 73			

SELECTED CHAMPIONS

PRESIDENTS CUP US/Rest of World tied (2003)
WOMEN'S WORLD CUP OF GOLF Japan (2005)
SOUTH AFRICAN OPEN Retief Goosen (2005).

CARD OF THE COURSE

THE FRONT NINE			THE BACK NINE		
HOLE	METRES	PAR	HOLE	METRES	PAR
1	362	4	10	373	4
2	216	3	11	147	3
3	429	4	12	440	4
4	452	4	13	487	5
5	502	5	14	330	4
6	312	4	15	436	4
7	435	4	16	534	5
8	185	3	17	170	3
9	557	5	18	563	5
OUT	3,450	36	IN	3,480	37

the great courses of the world to manufacture a natural-looking landscape of windswept hillocks. An incredible 500,000 cubic yards of earth were dug, moved, pushed and scraped to form the many contours, and 25 acres (10 hectares) of wetlands also sprang to life.

Then, painstakingly, the mounds were hand-planted with links grasses. Instead of the wispier European fescue grasses, the unkempt rough here consists of the more robust savanna types, able to withstand the fierce southern African climate. The wild amber-tinged rough grasses, so reminiscent of true links courses, frame wonderfully the immaculately kept fairways, but also are a punishing hazard.

AN AWESOME CHALLENGE

As in real links fashion, the fairways are far from flat. Player created a wavy effect and even if you strike a perfect drive, luck does play its part in keeping the ball on the short grass. Although it is possible to get an awkward lie on the fairways because of the slopes, usually a ball trickles off the slopes into the hollows making life a little easier for the next shot.

Throw the bunkers into the mix (many are scooped out of the manmade hills), and the fact that it is a modern links stretching out to almost 7,655 yards (7,000 meters) off the championship tees, and you have an awesome challenge to contend with. A glance down the scorecard reveals holes called "Calamity," "Sheer Murrrder," "Wee Wrecker," and "Prayer"—clearly an indication of its brutality.

It may be long and extremely testing, but it is fair and tameable: the best ball strikers tend to come out on top. Retief Goosen birdied the last two holes to defeat fellow South African and Fancourt homeowner Ernie Els in 2005 to win his country's Open Championship with a score of 10 under par 282. Definitely a case of classy striker winning on a classy golf course.

ALL THE PRESIDENT'S MEN

In the 2003 Presidents Cup, a biennial team event between the US and the Rest of the World, the teams tied at 17 all. Captains Jack Nicklaus and Gary Player chose Tiger Woods and Ernie Els for the play-off. They parred three extra holes but darkness intervened so the captains agreed to share the cup.

■ Thabo Mbeki presents the cup

Kiawah Island, US

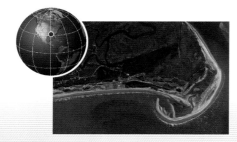

REMEMBERED FOR ONE OF THE MOST PULSATING Ryder Cups in history, Kiawah Island's Ocean Course is brutal and unforgiving but a beautiful place to play golf. The waves of the Atlantic Ocean are in view from every hole. Perhaps not a traditional links because of a "target golf" element and a sign that says "Caution: Alligators Are Dangerous," yet the closeness of the ocean and the sandy wastes provide a unique links experience.

INFESTED WATERS

The waterways threading through the holes of the Ocean Course are a natural habitat for dozens of alligators. They rarely attack humans, but can be very dangerous if provoked. Stay clear.

An alligator lurks in the water

You can't just have **one battle plan** as you never quite know what the wind will be doing

HALE IRWIN, THREE TIMES US OPEN CHAMPION

SET IN THE LOW COUNTRY of South Carolina, the Ocean Course has no towering dunes, so holes skip over the scrubland and skirt the marshes rather than follow natural valleys. Instead of creating large dunes, architect Pete Dye, famed for his bruising designs, relied on building up the tees, fairways, and greens to raise them slightly off the scrubland that butts up to the ocean.

The raised fairways drop off into sandy waste areas where the line between the deliberately unkempt and the more shaped bunkering is blurred. So that no one is left in any doubt where the real hazards begin, players are allowed to ground their clubs in the sand. Water comes into play on many holes, either as a marsh or an inland seawater channel.

DANGERS AND DIFFICULTIES

When Pete Dye and his wife Alice came to develop the site, the course had already been chosen to host the 1991 Ryder Cup, so the pressure was on. Unpredictable wind blew quite consistently from both east and west. Dye's solution was ingenious: to build two loops of nine, one designed to play with an easterly and the other would be friendlier in a westerly. Great in theory, but sometimes it blows so hard that neither nine offers any respite.

Kiawah's style creates dangers and difficulties for a golfer. Tees and fairways are like small islands surrounded by sand and marsh. Grasses can be chest high and squat trees edge in tight. The greens are often incredibly hard to hit and hold; balls are tossed off down wicked slopes, leaving tough chip shots. Ideally, golfers would like to play linkslike shots—like a low runner to combat the wind—and skip the ball up to the green, but they can't. Bermuda grass (totally alien to a true links) is the only strain that can thrive. Its coarse grain snags a ball like Velcro and pitch and runs are virtually ruled out.

PLAYERS AND THE CROWD celebrate a US victory in the 1991 Ryder Cup at Kiawah Island, after an intense cliffhanger on a tough course that became known as the "War on the Shore."

Just about every tee shot on the Ocean Course is a heart-pounding affair. Even the par-3s can put the frighteners on. The humpbacked green of the 14th sits way over head height above the surrounding wastes. If you miss the green, the only safe place is short right on the closely mown run off. Even from here, a par is difficult.

The 17th is fronted by a lake and the angled green looks intimidatingly hard to find. Anywhere short or right will be wet, and going left will find sand or worse. Even the best can fall foul of this course. There is no doubting its beauty and its clever design, but it is certainly one of the toughest courses in the world.

AT KIAWAH ISLAND'S OCEAN COURSE the holes are raised slightly above the marsh and scrubland, and the South Carolina climate is both hot and humid.

THE COURSE

Stunning yet brutal, the holes saunter over sandy scrub and are buffeted by the Atlantic winds that sometimes scream in from the ocean. Most of its trouble comes in the form of the haphazard natural bunkering and the channels of seawater and marsh. It takes power and bravery to combat Kiawah's daunting challenge.

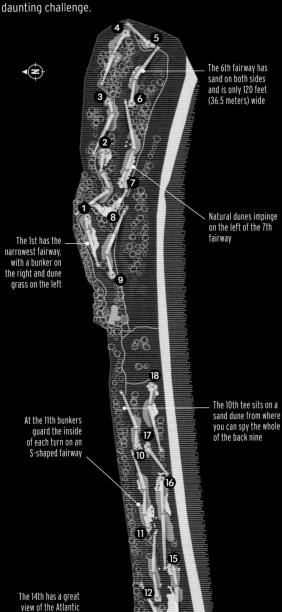

The 6th fairway has sand on both sides and is only 120 feet (36.5 meters) wide

The 1st has the narrowest fairway, with a bunker on the right and dune grass on the left

Natural dunes impinge on the left of the 7th fairway

At the 11th bunkers guard the inside of each turn on an S-shaped fairway

The 10th tee sits on a sand dune from where you can spy the whole of the back nine

The 14th has a great view of the Atlantic Ocean, as players turn back to the east

KIAWAH ISLAND

ONE SANCTUARY BEACH DRIVE,
KIAWAH ISLAND, SOUTH CAROLINA 29455
www.kiawahresort.com

THE OCEAN COURSE

FOUNDED 1991	**DESIGNER** Pete Dye
LENGTH 7,356 yards	**COURSE RECORD** 67
(6,726 meters)	Tom Kite (2006)
PAR 72	

SELECTED CHAMPIONS

RYDER CUP US (1991)
WORLD CUP OF GOLF Ireland–Padraig Harrington & Paul McGinley (1997); South Africa–Trevor Immelman & Rory Sabbatini (2003)
SENIORS PGA Denis Watson (2007)

CARD OF THE COURSE

THE FRONT NINE			THE BACK NINE		
HOLE	YARDS	PAR	HOLE	YARDS	PAR
1	395	4	10	439	4
2	543	5	11	562	5
3	390	4	12	466	4
4	453	4	13	404	4
5	207	3	14	194	3
6	455	4	15	421	4
7	527	5	16	579	5
8	197	3	17	221	3
9	464	4	18	439	4
OUT	**3,631**	**36**	**IN**	**3,725**	**36**

■ The angled 18th green

HOLE 18 — STRONG PAR 4

The tee sits up and plays across a waste area to a fairway that features a saddle that takes the ball away to the right. A large waste bunker patrols the right side. From the crest the green sits slightly below you. For the best line into the angled green aim for the right of the fairway if you dare. A nasty complex of bunkers eats into the front left and grassy scrub flanks the right.

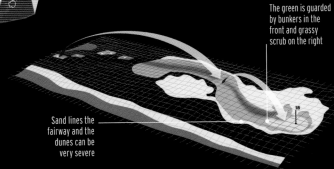

The green is guarded by bunkers in the front and grassy scrub on the right

Sand lines the fairway and the dunes can be very severe

Shinnecock Hills, UNITED STATES

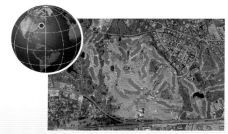

IF WE ARE HAPPY TO CATEGORIZE Shinnecock Hills as a links, then there is probably no finer outside of Great Britain and Ireland. Sweeping over 260 acres (105 hectares) of old Native American Reservation land near Peconic Bay on Long Island, it is a tranquil gem. One of America's founding fathers in golf terms, Shinnecock belonged to the group of five clubs that formed the United States Golf Association back in 1894.

THERE IS A REAL SENSE of freedom at Shinnecock Hills. Stand in the middle of this vast space and the meandering course delivers a 360-degree panorama of nothing but gently swaying sandy pasture and the odd stand of trees, watched over from on high by the oldest clubhouse in the US. A privileged air washes over you.

The original links has melted away with time and has been replaced by the masterful creation of Toomey and Flynn which came into play in 1931. Only a few holes remain from an earlier course, including the tricky par-3 7th, a "Redan" hole based on the original type of raised tilting green seen at North Berwick in Scotland.

All the other holes are superbly routed around it and nine of the par 4s dogleg, leaving a golfer to think about the wind twice on each hole. The holes were crafted by a 150-strong contingent of local Shinnecock Indians, who were part of the Algonquin tribe that still reside close by today.

Although the site, not far from the Atlantic Ocean, doesn't feature piles of dunes like many seaside courses, it does pitch and roll, especially on the back nine, making it a slightly unusual area for a links. It is more Muirfield than Royal Birkdale, meaning it is more demure and strategic than big and bold, and flirts with wild dunes.

Plenty of bunkers, many in clusters, patrol the corners of the doglegs. They are shallower than their transatlantic

It is probably **the best course** in the world. It naturally changes tack continually— that is the genius of the layout. It's a special place.

RAY FLOYD, WINNER OF 1986 US OPEN AT SHINNECOCK

SHOT OF THE YEAR

The diminutive Corey Pavin came to the awkward 18th on the final day of the 1995 US Open thinking a par might be good enough to see off the chasing pack. He hit a great tee shot to the right edge of the dogleg left uphill hole. He knew if he hit his next shot onto the green and two-putted for par that he would probably win. As it was a little uphill and the wind was blowing right to left, he took a 4-wood and knew the second he hit it, it was going to be good. It finished 4 feet away from the pin and, although he missed his birdie chance, his solid par sealed victory.

■ Corey Pavin with the trophy

counterparts and have few really steep faces. They give you a chance, unlike the rough, which can get knee-high and sways with the customary golden hues.

FAST-RUNNING SURFACE

As modern greens go, they are small. Today, you have to cope with their size from further out off the championship tees where there are six par 4s over 440 yards (400 meters) long. Most of the surfaces are quick, contoured, and have smooth run-offs. If you don't hit the heart of them, you can slide away down a nasty bank. The problem deepens when they allow the course to become fast-running. It became a controversy in the 2004 US Open when the course was borderline playable in a strong wind. Out of 66 players in the final round, 28 failed to break 80. Retief Goosen won with an amazing 71. But to do that, he had to single putt 12 times (24 putts in total) because he only hit six greens in regulation. That is Shinnecock's defense.

Shinneock Hills thrills the best with its ever-changing paths, firm, thoughtfully-angled fairways and heart-wrenching greens. It is a cracker, and neighbor to two other fine links—The National Links of America and Southampton Golf Club—making this part of Long Island a golfer's paradise.

THE PAR-4 18TH HOLE exemplifies the wide open spaces of Shinnecock Hills, seen here during the third round of the 104th US Open.

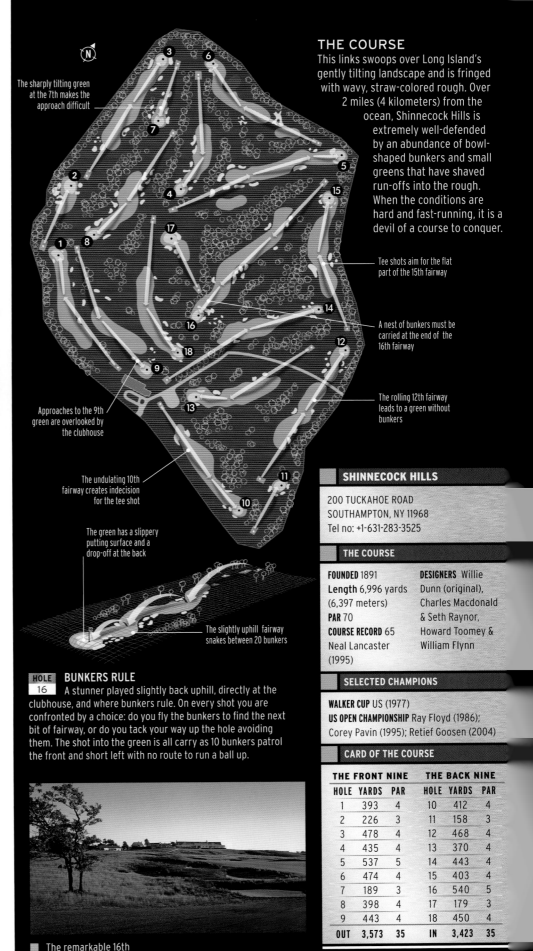

THE COURSE

This links swoops over Long Island's gently tilting landscape and is fringed with wavy, straw-colored rough. Over 2 miles (4 kilometers) from the ocean, Shinnecock Hills is extremely well-defended by an abundance of bowl-shaped bunkers and small greens that have shaved run-offs into the rough. When the conditions are hard and fast-running, it is a devil of a course to conquer.

The sharply tilting green at the 7th makes the approach difficult

Tee shots aim for the flat part of the 15th fairway

A nest of bunkers must be carried at the end of the 16th fairway

The rolling 12th fairway leads to a green without bunkers

Approaches to the 9th green are overlooked by the clubhouse

The undulating 10th fairway creates indecision for the tee shot

The green has a slippery putting surface and a drop-off at the back

The slightly uphill fairway snakes between 20 bunkers

HOLE 16 — BUNKERS RULE

A stunner played slightly back uphill, directly at the clubhouse, and where bunkers rule. On every shot you are confronted by a choice: do you fly the bunkers to find the next bit of fairway, or do you tack your way up the hole avoiding them? The shot into the green is all carry as 10 bunkers patrol the front and short left with no route to run a ball up.

■ The remarkable 16th

SHINNECOCK HILLS

200 TUCKAHOE ROAD
SOUTHAMPTON, NY 11968
Tel no: +1-631-283-3525

THE COURSE

FOUNDED 1891	**DESIGNERS** Willie
Length 6,996 yards	Dunn (original),
(6,397 meters)	Charles Macdonald
PAR 70	& Seth Raynor,
COURSE RECORD 65	Howard Toomey &
Neal Lancaster	William Flynn
(1995)	

SELECTED CHAMPIONS

WALKER CUP US (1977)
US OPEN CHAMPIONSHIP Ray Floyd (1986);
Corey Pavin (1995); Retief Goosen (2004)

CARD OF THE COURSE

THE FRONT NINE			THE BACK NINE		
HOLE	YARDS	PAR	HOLE	YARDS	PAR
1	393	4	10	412	4
2	226	3	11	158	3
3	478	4	12	468	4
4	435	4	13	370	4
5	537	5	14	443	4
6	474	4	15	403	4
7	189	3	16	540	5
8	398	4	17	179	3
9	443	4	18	450	4
OUT	**3,573**	**35**	**IN**	**3,423**	**35**

Parkland courses

GOLF CONTINUES TO BOOM AROUND THE PLANET. There are more than 35,000 courses, and still counting. Of these, the vast majority are parkland courses. Parkland is a slightly vague term covering similar styles—including forest layouts—that depend on components such as topography, kinds of trees, the use of bunkers and water, as well as the prevailing winds.

◁◁◁ **PARIS INTERNATIONAL** to the north of Paris was designed by Jack Nicklaus and opened in 1991. ◁◁ **THE BRABAZON COURSE** at The Belfry in England has hosted the Ryder Cup four times. ◁ **MERION GOLF CLUB** is located in the suburbs of Ardmore in Pennsylvania. ▽ **LES BORDES**, surrounded by forest in the Loire Valley in France, has been described as a "floating golf course."

WHY ARE PARKLAND COURSES so prevalent around the world? To answer this you have to consider the pure geography of our planet. Centers of population have usually grown and multiplied near an area of fresh water—whether it is a lake or a river—and tend to avoid inhospitable places wherever and whenever possible. Except for the rare links courses that sit on the sandy coastal strips and the few hundred desert and mountain courses, we tend to build most of our courses among the pastures, fields, woodlands, and forests, that are easily accessible to the bulk of golfers.

Parkland courses tend to be lusher than any other style, as often they are not exposed to the coastal

THE TWO COURSES AR WINGED FOOT were created in pastures and woodland near Mamaroneck, north of New York City.

winds experienced by a links or the searing temperatures that a desert course has to bear. And trees play a vital role too, giving shade and protection from the elements. The soil is also more fertile than a sandy heath or links and therefore even grass coverage is easier to cultivate.

TOPOGRAPHY AND TREES

Trouble usually comes in various forms. Fairways are tree-lined and so they often lead to doglegging. Bunkering becomes strategic rather than deep and menacing as they are called upon to protect landing areas and greensides. The rough beside the fairways is often verdant, thick, and ankle-deep. Parkland courses vary greatly in their topography. Some, such as Augusta National, swoop and climb, while others simply wend their way around large specimen trees on a flat pasture.

The variety of tree is also endless. Broad-leaf deciduous trees are much more abundant in the mid-European nations and Northeastern US, while the forest layouts of Canada and Scandinavia tend to be lined with softwood coniferous species, such as pines and firs. Go further south in Europe to warmer climes, such as the Mediterranean conditions you find in Spain, and umbrella pines, eucalyptus, and cork oaks can provide the woodland canopy.

Each style makes for different challenges. Often, a course threaded through pine forest gives a golfer a chance to escape the trees with a low accurate punch, as the canopy tends to be higher and the trunks more slender than say, a wood of broad-trunked oaks and beech. In the latter case a golfer has to be able to shape the ball around trouble, as going through it is less of an option.

COPING WITH WIND

Wind plays a big part on parkland courses. Whereas on a links the wind tends to blow, sometimes quite hard admittedly, from the same direction, on a parkland course, it can swirl and be dragged into the holes by the tall canopies of trees. Sometimes you can look at the skitting clouds moving serenely one way and the flag on the green is blowing the other. Club selection then can become taxing. As a general rule, you should trust more to the direction in which the clouds are moving, or how the treetops are behaving, than the flag.

FLYING HIGH

As the parkland fairways tend to be slower running, and often bunkers can patrol the fronts of greens, the high ball game is needed more than on a heathland or links course, when you are able to bounce the ball short and let it run onto the green.

OAK HILL golf course, designed by Donald Ross, was created out of farmland near Rochester in upstate New York.

From the parkland tee you cannot rely on getting a huge amount of run, so golfers tend to favor long, bombing carries, especially on the US-style parklands where the ground staff are likely to water the courses more freely.

Firing into greens, too, can mean going the aerial route to fly the trouble rather than skip past it on the floor. However, it is also wise to think about the wind. Because you can be protected from the full force of it on a blustery day, it can be best to try to hit lower shots to avoid flying above the canopy.

On most parklands, the bunkers are relatively shallow, because there is no wind erosion to worry about, and so the art of the long bunker shot, especially from a fairway trap, needs to be in the golfer's armory. Splashing out sideways is rare on the majority of parklands.

LINNA GOLF COURSE is set among the tall, spindly evergreen pines and deciduous birch trees north of Helsinki in the heart of Finland. The undulating course, which opened in 2005, features rocky outcrops and the chance to play at midnight in the summer!

A wooded course can be a stunning place to play, especially as the seasons change. Playing over a green rolling landscape as leaves turn an autumnal brown, yellow, and orange can be a magical experience.

Merion, UNITED STATES

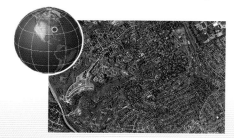

THE PROVERB "THE BEST THINGS COME IN SMALL PARCELS" is very true of Merion. Squeezed into only 126 acres (50 hectares) of woodland, its clever design makes the most of a leafy suburban site in Pennsylvania. The course is simply a classic, and Merion's history adds to the atmosphere. Every great player has walked the hallowed turf and the stories that come from its numerous national championships are written in golfing folklore.

AROUND THE TURN of the 19th century, cricket and tennis were all the rage in smart neighborhoods of Philadelphia, and Merion Cricket Club, founded in 1865, was at the heart of sporting affairs. But as golf was also coming into the mainstream, these sports' clubs realized that a golf course would make a fine and popular addition to their facilities. The Philadelphia Cricket Club took the lead and even hosted the US Open in 1907 and 1910. Merion, which had had a short course (The West Course) since 1896, wanted something grander so that they, too, could hold such illustrious championships.

The members met together and chose one of their own—a 32-year-old golfing Scottish expat called Hugh Wilson—to design a course. In 1910 he journeyed back to his native lands for seven months to take inspiration from the great links and heaths, returning with vigor to set about designing Merion Cricket Club's East Course.

Wilson was given a small but wonderfully wooded site in the Main Line suburbs of the city, and what he produced was a compact but magnificent gem in the shape of an L. Eleven of the holes (from the 2nd to the 12th) are located across Ardmore Avenue in one half of the L, while holes 1 and 13 to 18 are on the clubhouse side. Because the course was short, its defenses had to be strong and that is still true today, although in the last few years 400 yards (366 meters) have been added to bring it into the modern day.

WHITE FACES

Wilson may have been an amateur architect, but his routeing and bunkering were exquisite. The course he devised uses the natural gifts well. Mature trees dot the entire landscape and stony creeks snake through it. Areas of rocky, broken ground and enough gentle elevation changes make life interesting. The bunkering is superb and yawning. Many of the 120 bunkers are jagged-edged and their steep faces are fringed with grasses—someone described them as having eyebrows. Their look led Chick Evans, the winner here of the 1916 US Amateur, to call them the "White Faces of Merion."

RED WICKER BASKETS instead of flags sit on top of Merion's pins. They give no clue as to which way the wind is blowing.

HOGAN'S WONDER SHOT

After a horrific car crash in 1949 Ben Hogan, the pre-eminent golfer of his time, fought back to semi-fitness and came to Merion a year later to take a tilt at the US Open once more. During 36 demanding holes on the final day, he tired and his lead dwindled. He stood on the 18th fairway with a 1-iron in hand, needing a par to get himself in a play-off. He raked a long-iron wonder shot into the heart of the green and secured his play-off place, going on to win it the next day.

■ Ben Hogan on the 18th at Merion in 1950

The greens need to do their defensive job, too. Precision rather than power is the name of the game at Merion, as the greens are cunningly cambered and small. Some have quite distinct levels and if golfers are to score well, their approaches must be controlled and distance perfect.

A course's short holes are often a telltale sign of its quality and Merion has four to savor. The 3rd is uphill and dotted with half a dozen traps. At the 9th you play downhill to a kidney-shaped green fronted by a stream and pond. Over the road at the pretty 13th, the green is tiny and surrounded by sand. The 17th is a brute over an old quarry and measures 246 yards (225 meters) off the back. And it is all carry. Lee Trevino once described it as "the shortest par 4 in Open history."

GREAT PLAYERS

The legendary Bobby Jones is inextricably linked with Merion. He first played the US Amateur here in 1916 at the age of 14, and got through to the quarter finals. He won it here in 1924 and then again in 1930. What made this feat so remarkable was he had already won the US Open, British Amateur, and Open in the same year, and so his quartet of titles became known as the Grand Slam (see pp.212–13). He won his 36-hole final on the 11th green and a plaque stands there today to commemorate his feat. He gave up competitive golf a few months later.

Merion is a true classic and, now that its compact charms have been updated, it can welcome great players once again. It is set to host the US Open in 2013, 32 years after its last visit. The best are sure of a fantastic challenge.

SUNSET OVER THE 4TH GREEN highlights the putting surface that slopes from back left to front right. Five grass-fringed bunkers lie in wait for any wayward shots.

THE COURSE

Compact but intricate, this historic parkland features small, sloping greens and gaping deep bunkers that draw the eye and mercilessly gobble up balls. Strategy, imagination, and control, rather than power and bravery, are needed to conquer Merion's superb variety of holes.

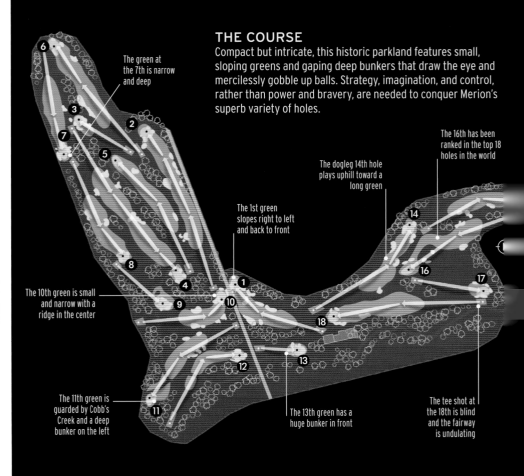

The green at the 7th is narrow and deep

The 16th has been ranked in the top 18 holes in the world

The dogleg 14th hole plays uphill toward a long green

The 1st green slopes right to left and back to front

The 10th green is small and narrow with a ridge in the center

The 11th green is guarded by Cobb's Creek and a deep bunker on the left

The 13th green has a huge bunker in front

The tee shot at the 18th is blind and the fairway is undulating

■ The quarry at the 16th hole

HOLE 16 — THE "QUARRY"
The 16th is known as the quarry hole for obvious reasons. The bold player must first find the fairway, then decide whether to take on the sunken rock and sand waste area right in front of the green. From the end of the fairway it is 100 yards (91 meters) to the front of the green, but many players come from much further back.

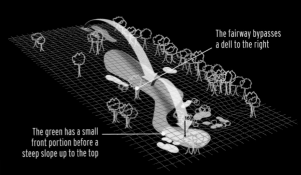

The fairway bypasses a dell to the right

The green has a small front portion before a steep slope up to the top

MERION

450 ARDMORE AVENUE
ARDMORE, PENNSYLVANIA 19003
www.meriongolfclub.com

THE EAST COURSE

FOUNDED 1912	**PAR** 70
LENGTH 6,846 yards	**DESIGNER**
(6,260 meters)	Hugh Wilson

SELECTED CHAMPIONS

US AMATEUR Bobby Jones (1924, 1930); Eduardo Molinari (2005)
US OPEN Ben Hogan (1950); Lee Trevino (1971); David Graham (1981)
CURTIS CUP US (1954)

CARD OF THE COURSE

THE FRONT NINE			THE BACK NINE		
HOLE	YARDS	PAR	HOLE	YARDS	PAR
1	350	4	10	303	4
2	556	5	11	367	4
3	219	3	12	403	4
4	597	5	13	120	3
5	504	4	14	438	4
6	487	4	15	411	4
7	345	4	16	430	4
8	359	4	17	246	3
9	206	3	18	505	5
OUT	3,623	36	IN	3,223	34

Les Bordes, FRANCE

SECLUDED, REFINED, AND BRILLIANTLY BOLD, Les Bordes is a tranquil haven in a wondrously natural woodland setting. Deep in the heart of the Sologne, a lake-strewn forest area in the Loire Valley, it is a mammoth but beautiful challenge where there are so many thrilling shots to be played. Although no championships have been played here, many good players have tasted her charms, but none have conquered her.

AGONY OF A MISSED PUTT

A gigantic putting green—the largest in Europe—doubles as a sculpture garden. In a small island of grass sits a sculpture by Rodin of a naked man clasping his forehead. Baron Bich thought it perfect for the spot as he saw it depicting the agony of a missed three-foot putt.

Rodin's sculpture of a naked man

RARELY CAN YOU DESCRIBE a course as eclectic, but Les Bordes is exactly that. Predominantly forested, it has smatterings of a heath and a US-style water course. Opened in 1986, it was originally a private course for two rich families. Baron Marcel Bich—of Bic pen and razor fame—and his Japanese business partner Yoshiaki Sakurai enlisted the expertise of American Robert Von Hagge to turn Bich's hunting estate into a world-class golf course.

Design-wise, it has everything. Frightening carries, doglegs, plenty of risk-and-reward shots to contemplate, mounds instead of bunkers, sleepered greens next to water, snaking white fairway bunkers, some sadistic greens, open-your-shoulder drives, and even an island green. Quite a mix, but they work perfectly.

There are only 44 bunkers on the course and a few of these are nastily deep, but that doesn't tell the full story. Hole 1 is a dead-straight par 4 with only one bunker, but it almost entirely circles the green. More monster traps flank the 6th, 12th, and 15th fairways. In any case, the fairways dart through such dense forest in places that no bunkers are needed to make a golfer feel claustrophobic and jittery on their drive. Only five traps feature in the last four holes, but it is undoubtedly as tough a finishing stretch as you will find anywhere.

Von Hagge doesn't seem to do simple, gentle doglegs. Nearly all of the six swinging holes are seriously curved. The pulsating 7th is a full 90 degrees and the second shot must fire over a huge pond to reach the green. He has created three par 3s that are absolute crackers over water and one plainly difficult uphill hole. Of the three over ponds, the 4th green is buttressed with timber sleepers and the 13th is perhaps the toughest. From the back tee it is a carry of 174 yards (158 meters) to the front edge of the green. In a wind, the strike had better be pure.

Then, just when you think you might be over the worst, the 14th confronts you. Water is everywhere. You must carry it from the tee and avoid it on the right and left with your second, before hitting over some more to an island green reminiscent of the 17th at Sawgrass (see pp.364–67). A five here is treasured.

Yet for all Les Bordes' challenges through the most picturesque countryside, it is fair. If a golfer is humble and chooses the right tee for his or her ability, then this graceful yet powerful course will charm all comers.

SURROUNDED BY MISTY WATER the extraordinary island green at the 14th hole is reached by a footbridge where you can see Koi carp swimming beneath you.

THE COURSE

Full of on-the-edge shots, Les Bordes meanders through mature forest, and its fairways and greens flirt with several graceful lakes. Sand is used sparingly but, where it does come into play, it's both confrontational and bold. Because of its power and dangers, Les Bordes a very trough proposition, even for the best golfers.

Only a well-struck shot will make the carry over water to the 13th green

The final approach on the 18th is to a seriously ridged green

HOLE 6 — NATURAL AND CLEVER

The 6th looks very natural despite its two massive bunkers: one hugs the driving area on the right, while the other starts just a few more yards on and patrols the front and right of the green. The fairway is cleverly raised so that the fall-offs into the traps are quite deep but not jarring to the eyes, and wild grassy banks frame the hole too. A big swale mid-right means your approach must be precise and thereafter your putting, too.

An island green at the 14th hole makes for some nervous approaches, even with a wedge

The 7th hole turns through a full 90 degrees

One bunker almost surrounds the 1st green

A huge oak stands serenely by the green on the left

A huge stretch of sand protects the right side of the fairway

A bunker almost 120 yards (110 meters) long waits beside the fairway

LES BORDES

41220 SAINT-LAURENT-NOUAN, FRANCE
www.lesbordes.com

THE COURSE

FOUNDED 1986		**DESIGNER**	
LENGTH 7,009 yards		Robert von Hagge	
(6,409 meters)		**COURSE RECORD** 71	
PAR 72		Jean Van de Velde	

CARD OF THE COURSE

THE FRONT NINE			THE BACK NINE		
HOLE	YARDS	PAR	HOLE	YARDS	PAR
1	439	4	10	511	5
2	521	5	11	399	4
3	388	4	12	413	4
4	165	3	13	184	3
5	435	4	14	557	5
6	384	4	15	437	4
7	507	5	16	215	3
8	156	3	17	453	4
9	390	4	18	447	4
OUT	**3,388**	**36**	**IN**	**3,620**	**36**

■ The genteel-looking 6th

Valderrama, SPAIN

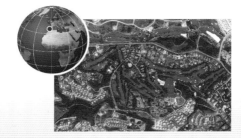

CONSISTENTLY RANKED THE NUMBER ONE COURSE in Continental Europe, Valderrama in southern Spain is not for the faint-hearted. For several years the home of the European Tour's flagship event, the Volvo Masters, this is no easy challenge and even the greats have been humiliated at times. It is brilliant but has so many almost frightening shots that it is a test for the spirit as much as for the game. There is so much drama in Valderrama.

LOVE HAS BEEN POURED onto Valderrama in the pursuit of perfection. Creating uncompromising but graceful holes through the forest of bent cork oaks and olives has been the passion of Valderrama's owner ever since he bought the original Los Aves course in 1984. Jaime Ortiz-Patino took an average course, and with the talents of architect Robert Trent Jones, masterminded a rebuild of epic proportions. It went from little known to highly acclaimed in a few short years, thanks to countless millions thrown at it, a mind-boggling amount of earth moved, and thousands of trees planted, moved, and chopped. Even to this day, Patino's quest for the best does not idle, and he is constantly trying to improve on the already outstanding golf course.

An abundance of drives, approaches, even chips and putts are on the edge. At every turn you must take a deep breath and trust your game to pull you through. The terrain and design make it tough. Trees hem in the fairways; dazzling white bunkers, banks of wiry rough and yet more trees defend the greens. Two greens—the 4th and 17th—are notoriously guarded by water, and all have super slick putting surfaces that tilt steeply in places.

ACCURACY AND CONTROL

Accuracy off the tees is the number one priority, simply because the trees encroach on the landing areas and their canopies kill even a slight miss-hit. Advancing a ball from the squat and gnarled trees is possible but tricky—you have to fire out low to escape. Often, a bended recovery is needed. But with bunkers guarding green entrances and the fairways not rolling fast, it is hard to run an escape shot up onto the green.

Even if fairways are found, control is still vital on approaches as missing greens causes severe problems. Anyone going long at, say, the brilliant par-3 12th will have a nightmare bunker shot back onto a green that slopes viciously away from them. The crux of the matter is: whether you hit or miss a green, make sure you're in

THE LEAST PARKLAND IN NATURE, the 17th is definitely Valderrama's most notorious hole, with a lake and a trio of bunkers guarding its green.

KEY MOMENTS

THE 17TH HOLE produces dramatic moments like no other. Tiger Woods found water here in the last round of the 1999 American Express Championship with a seemingly perfect pitch and took a triple bogey 8, but still went on to win in a play-off. However, Woods was one of only three players to finish under par.

IN 1997, VALDERRAMA hosted the first Ryder Cup on mainland Europe, and Seve Ballesteros was non-playing captain. On the final afternoon, Europe led by five points going into the singles. Only three Europeans won their matches, including Colin Montgomerie, whose stonewall par 4 on the nasty 18th sealed victory.

VALDERRAMA

11310 SOTOGRANDE, PROV DE CADIZ, SPAIN
www.valderrama.com

THE COURSE

FOUNDED 1974
LENGTH 6,356 meters (6,959 yards)
PAR 71

DESIGNER Robert Trent Jones, Sr.
COURSE RECORD 62 Bernhard Langer (1994)

SELECTED CHAMPIONS

RYDER CUP Europe (1997)
AMERICAN EXPRESS WORLD GOLF CHAMPIONSHIP Tiger Woods (1999); Mike Weir (2000)
VOLVO MASTERS Colin Montgomerie/Bernhard Langer (2002); Fredrik Jacobson (2003); Ian Poulter (2004); Paul McGinley (2005); Jeev Milka Singh (2006); Justin Rose (2007)

CARD OF THE COURSE

THE FRONT NINE			THE BACK NINE		
HOLE	METRES	PAR	HOLE	METRES	PAR
1	356	4	10	356	4
2	385	4	11	500	5
3	179	3	12	194	3
4	515	5	13	368	4
5	348	4	14	338	4
6	149	3	15	206	3
7	448	4	16	386	4
8	320	4	17	490	5
9	403	4	18	415	4
OUT	3,103	35	IN	3,253	36

THE COURSE

Ancient cork oaks and olives crowd the emerald fairways and shadow some of the table-top greens. Blindingly white bunkers filled with crushed, locally sourced marble hug the fringes and the odd water hazard puts a premium on accuracy.

THE FRONT NINE
❶ Left side of the fairway leaves the best line into the shady green. **❷** A huge oak sits in the middle of fairway. If you are long, you may get past it. **❸** Better to be short than long or left as violent slopes can take the ball into trouble. **❹** Best to play it as a genuine three-shotter, as the lake by the green shows no mercy. **❺** No need for a driver off the tee, better to play for position on this dogleg left. **❻** Great downhill short hole. Try to be short right of the flag to leave uphill putt. **❼** Needs two big smacks to get home, but well-guarded by huge bunkers. **❽** Must find the fairway as there is no chance of chasing one on to the green from the trees. **❾** Dead straight and flat, making judging approach tricky.

THE BACK NINE
❿ Shaping left to right around a pond, the green is a sloping devil. **⓫** Although approach is semiblind up a hill, it is a birdie chance. **⓬** Amazing par-3 over a small valley to a back-to-front tilting green. **⓭** No bunkers but very narrow as flanked by trees down both sides. **⓮** Very hard to judge approach as green sits way above fairway. **⓯** Daunting par-3 over valley of scrub. Aim for left side of green. **⓰** Let tilting fairway feed your drive left as it leaves the best line into green. **⓱** It takes guts to go for this in two. Anything short will be swallowed by a lake. **⓲** A kink in fairway means you being creative to keep out of trouble.

HOLE 8	"EL BUNKER"

Short but dangerous, this slight dogleg left is dominated by trees either side of the fairway and a large bunker that arcs its way all around the front of the green. If you miss the fairway, you cannot fire out low under the branches and expect to skip it through the sand on to the green.

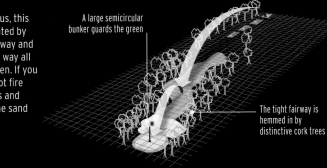

A large semicircular bunker guards the green

The tight fairway is hemmed in by distinctive cork trees

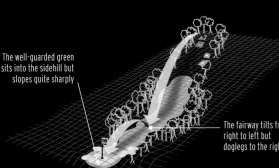

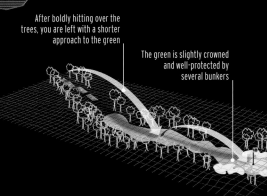

After boldly hitting over the trees, you are left with a shorter approach to the green

The green is slightly crowned and well-protected by several bunkers

The well-guarded green sits into the sidehill but slopes quite sharply

The fairway tilts from right to left but doglegs to the right

HOLE 16	"MUY DIFÍCIL"

The perfect line flirts with the trees down the right and the ball should feed down to the left, leaving a clear sight of the green that sits downhill of the landing area. Left is best. An awkward driving hole plus putting is a trial. No wonder this hole is called Muy Difícil (Very Difficult).

HOLE 18	"CASA CLUB"

A finishing hole where anything can happen, there are two ways to play the 18th. Play safe and hit straight into the corner, leaving a long, raking shot that may need to bend around some trees. Play boldly and hit blindly over the trees on the left, hoping to find the narrow fairway which doglegs left.

The lake at the 4th

The huge bunker at the 8th

Bunkers guarding the 7th green

the richness of the landscape and wildlife ... means that each player completes his round challenged by the layout and enriched by the beauty of nature

JAIME ORTIZ-PATINO, OWNER AND PRESIDENT

the right place. Being beyond a pin at Valderrama makes putting so much harder. Always aim to leave your ball below the cup. As Christy O'Connor Jr. says, "You will sweat tears if you miss the greens here."

The wind doesn't make it any easier. Close to the ocean, but up in the hills, Valderrama is prone to fickle winds. The Poniente wind blows hot air from the inland north; the Levante is a cooler breeze coming in off the sea to the south. Depending which is blowing and how hard, the course can be a different animal from day to day.

NO EASY HOLES

Valderrama tests a golfer's skills and patience from the off. At the 1st you can find the fairway and still not see the green clearly. A shaped shot around, or a strike over, tall trees is needed if the drive finishes up the right side. At the 2nd there's a huge cork oak in the middle of the fairway, 284 yards (260 meters) from the back tee. It forces a decision for both the drive and approach. And so it goes on. Not one hole can be seen as a pushover.

Perhaps the 11th, an elevated par 5, is one of the few genuine birdie chances. Another par 5, the 4th, features an astonishing green complex. Tucked away behind a lake and waterfall in the shadow of a large oak, it may look stunning, but there is real danger. The tiny green is at the end of a long hole. It has two distinct levels and the top plateau, although flat, is extremely hard to get at.

Many golfers do find the water there, but more will sink at the infamous 17th. For a chance of reaching the green in two, you must avoid the gaping fairway bunker on the left, and then make a decision. If you are in

range, do you go for it over the water to the small slopey green, or simply lay up and trust your short game? Because the banks of the green are shaved tightly, only the most precise shots will hold the surface.

The world's touring professionals have a love-hate relationship with Valderrama. While they sometimes find that luck plays a big part, they also know that great golf brings rewards. What they love most is the sensational conditioning of the course: fairways are like carpets, the bunkers of crushed white marble are firm and just the consistency they like for control, and the greens are unbelievably smooth and true. It might be as taxing a course as there is in Europe, but it is a supreme venue and a wondrous test for the best.

VALDERRAMA'S BUNKERS are a trademark feature and are filled with crushed white marble instead of sand. Not only do the coarse grains have a bright sparkling appearance, they make for a great surface to play from. It compacts well and so the ball lies superbly and means a skillful golfer can spin the ball for better control.

The 15th and the Serranía de Ronda in background

The beautiful setting of the 16th green

Hirono, JAPAN

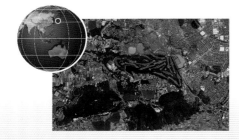

EVER SINCE HIRONO OPENED IN 1932, it has been acclaimed the best course in Japan, which is no mean feat considering there are almost 2,500 courses crammed into the islands. Ranked among the Top 50 in the world and part of a private members' club, Hirono is located in a pine-lined parkland, but has a character more associated with the great heathland courses of the Surrey sandbelt in England.

THE COURSE

The best-ranked course in Japan has a heathland feel to add to its pine-flanked holes, but rocky ravines and winding lakes and streams also add to its intrigue and bite. Hirono may be a traditional test, but it has lost none of its early vigour over the years.

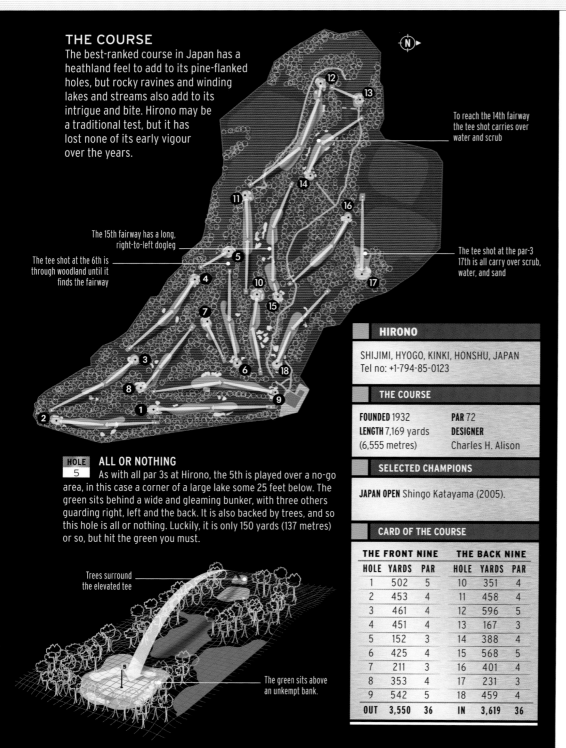

The 15th fairway has a long, right-to-left dogleg

The tee shot at the 6th is through woodland until it finds the fairway

To reach the 14th fairway the tee shot carries over water and scrub

The tee shot at the par-3 17th is all carry over scrub, water, and sand

HOLE 5	**ALL OR NOTHING**

As with all par 3s at Hirono, the 5th is played over a no-go area, in this case a corner of a large lake some 25 feet below. The green sits behind a wide and gleaming bunker, with three others guarding right, left and the back. It is also backed by trees, and so this hole is all or nothing. Luckily, it is only 150 yards (137 metres) or so, but hit the green you must.

Trees surround the elevated tee

The green sits above an unkempt bank.

HIRONO

SHIJIMI, HYOGO, KINKI, HONSHU, JAPAN
Tel no: +1-794-85-0123

THE COURSE

FOUNDED 1932		**PAR** 72	
LENGTH 7,169 yards (6,555 metres)		**DESIGNER** Charles H. Alison	

SELECTED CHAMPIONS

JAPAN OPEN Shingo Katayama (2005).

CARD OF THE COURSE

THE FRONT NINE			THE BACK NINE		
HOLE	YARDS	PAR	HOLE	YARDS	PAR
1	502	5	10	351	4
2	453	4	11	458	4
3	461	4	12	596	5
4	451	4	13	167	3
5	152	3	14	388	4
6	425	4	15	568	5
7	211	3	16	401	4
8	353	4	17	231	3
9	542	5	18	459	4
OUT	**3,550**	**36**	**IN**	**3,619**	**36**

VISCOUNT KUKI WAS A FEUDAL WARLORD and keen golfer who wanted a course built on his estate. He asked Charles Alison, one half of the famous Colt and Alison partnership, to design him a course while he was touring Japan in the early 1930s.

When he arrived at the site 12 miles (19 kilometres) northwest of Kobe, Alison was impressed with the range of natural gifts he was given. The land over which he would design Hirono was gently undulating and featured a great number of pines as well as thick, jungle-like undergrowth and several lakes, streams, valleys, and rough ravines. He spent some days walking the site and sketching holes before checking into a suite in the Oriental Hotel near the train station in Kobe. A week later he emerged with his brilliant routeing, and many special holes, and was paid a handsome fee of £1,500.

WONDERFUL EFFECT

While in England, Alison had been involved in creating many great heathland courses. He used his experience of them and their visual tricks to wonderful effect at Hirono. The fairway bunkers he built are large expanses set into mounding, which makes them a big target for off-line drives. Those beside the greens are set into raised plateaus, effectively making them deeper and more menacing than otherwise. The greens have fall-offs into dips or into the surrounding bunkers, and their putting surfaces are tilting and tricky to hold. A handful of greens are almost completely encircled by sand traps, but all have narrow entrances.

In 1932, when the course opened, Alison remarked: "In America Pine Valley is more tightly bunkered and definitely more brutal, but Hirono comes up well to the first-class standard of the United States, and will afford much pleasant excitement, and perhaps a little pain, to players from that country".

Alison used the natural terrain superbly and several tee shots have to fire over wastelands or water. Three of the four par 3s are played over lakes to greens guarded by bunkers. They include the 17th, which is 231 yards (211 metres) in length and can ruin a good scorecard in a heartbeat. Some carries are long on the par 4s, too.

THE GRAND PARKLAND DESIGN and intensely private nature of the course at Hirono is epitomized by the lush wooodland and glorious fairway of the long 9th hole.

Off the championship tee on the 14th you must fire first over an inlet of water and then over more scrub to reach the fairway just over 200 yards (183 metres) away. Next comes the most notable hole on the course – the par-5 15th, which has been ranked among the world's top 500 golf holes. It is famous for a huge, very old Kuromatsu (black) pine that sits in the crook of the long, right-to-left dogleg. Without it the hole would be much shorter, and therefore easier. In fact, the pine is so important to

the hole that the club has insured it for 5 million yen. Sadly, netting now protects it from the battering it gets from those who either try to cut the corner or fail to bend around it. This hole is also famous for a shot Jack Nicklaus hit in an exhibition match of 1963 (see right).

Hirono is old school, including the wood panelled clubhouse adorned with the kind of gold-lettered honours' boards that feature in traditional golf clubs the world over. It is a very private club, so the mysticism of the course is heightened by its exclusivity. Nonetheless, Alison did a fine job in bringing a little bit of classic golf design to this once secluded corner of Japan, and created a temptress of a course for the privileged few.

JACK'S PURE POWER

During an exhibition match in 1963, Jack Nicklaus stood on the 15th fairway after hitting a big drive and with 250 yards to go. The club captain told him that no-one had ever reached the green in two. Nicklaus smiled and said "I'll try". With his persimmon 3-wood he smacked it with pure power. It rose high over the pine, pitching over the bunker at the front of the green and rolling up to the flag on the back right.

Whether for a blood match from the back tee or a gamble among the portly ... I can name no superior among British inland courses.

CHARLES ALISON, ARCHITECT

■ The power of Jack Nicklaus

Muirfield Village, UNITED STATES

KNOWN AS "THE COURSE THAT JACK BUILT"–Nicklaus that is–Muirfield Village is a parkland in Ohio, close to where he grew up. A rolling setting intersected by streams, this course oozes class–like its founder. Each year between the Masters and the US Open, Muirfield hosts the Memorial Tournament, an invitation-only event that is often referred to as the fifth Major.

UNTIL TIGER WOODS BURST on to the scene and started winning Majors hand over fist, it was always assumed that Jack Nicklaus was the greatest player the world has ever seen. Many people think it should stay that way, at least until Tiger passes the 18 Major mark that Jack reached. But whatever the outcome of the argument, when Jack Nicklaus sets out to create himself a golf course, you can be sure that it will be a special place and as brilliant as the man himself.

Muirfield Village is unashamedly Augusta-esque. It was while sitting in the Augusta National clubhouse back in 1966, that Nicklaus had the idea to build a course near his home town that would be fit to host an annual PGA Tour championship. Ivor Young, a real-estate friend, was sitting with him at the time and he went back to Columbus, Ohio, and identified 10 sites that could potentially be up to it. Nicklaus plumped for the first he saw, a neat 160-acre (65-hectare) undulating woodland site that was filled with an array of trees and winding streams.

A THRILLING EXAMINATION

Nicklaus' intention was to give it the feel of exclusivity, prepare it faultlessly, and make it into a course where the cream would rise to the top. He and Desmond Muirhead designed a thrilling examination, one which would see the best shots rewarded and poor ones cruelly dealt with. It looked superb, too.

As Nicklaus commented later: "I set out to build not only an outstanding golf course for every level of player, but a magnificent course for watching a tournament... I thought the Masters was a great thing for golf and that I'd like to do the same thing in Columbus."

The course opened in 1974 and was named in honor of Jack's victory in the Open Championship at the original Muirfield in Scotland in 1966, the year this project was conceived. Besides the name, the two courses share only one trait, whether deliberate or not.

MEANDERING CREEKS AND STREAMS, many of them hugging the side of a fairway, are an important feature of the hazardous nature of the golf at Muirfield Village.

MUIRFIELD VILLAGE

5750 MEMORIAL DRIVE
DUBLIN, OH 43017
Tel no: 614-889-6740

THE COURSE

FOUNDED 1974		**PAR** 72	
LENGTH 7,366 yards (6,735 meters)		**DESIGNER** Jack Nicklaus, Desmond	

SELECTED CHAMPIONS

RYDER CUP Europe (1987). **US AMATEUR** Justin Leonard (1992) **SOLHEIM CUP** US (1998). **MEMORIAL TOURNAMENT** Tiger Woods (1999, 2000, 2001); Jim Furyk (2002); Kenny Perry (2003); Ernie Els (2004); Bart Bryant (2005); Carl Pettersson (2006); KJ Choi (2007).

CARD OF THE COURSE

THE FRONT NINE			THE BACK NINE		
HOLE	YARDS	PAR	HOLE	YARDS	PAR
1	470	4	10	471	4
2	455	4	11	567	5
3	401	4	12	184	3
4	200	3	13	455	4
5	527	5	14	363	4
6	447	4	15	529	5
7	563	5	16	215	3
8	185	3	17	478	4
9	412	4	18	444	4
OUT	3,660	36	IN	3,706	36

THE COURSE

Holes swoop down wooded hillsides and many fairways are intersected cleverly by snaking streams that can play havoc with a wayward golfer. Its style and conditioning are deliberately reminiscent of Augusta National.

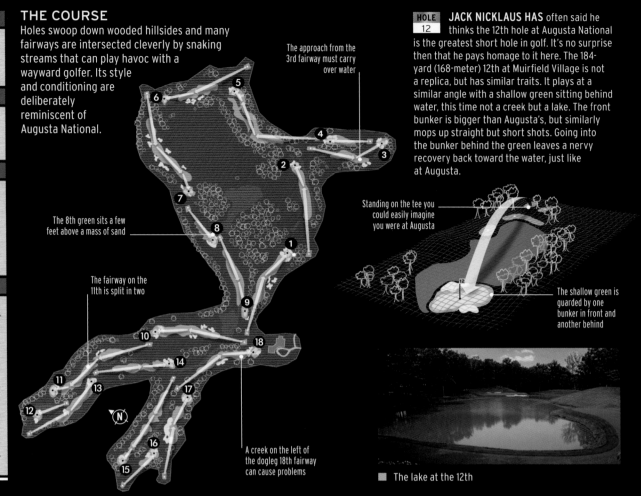

The approach from the 3rd fairway must carry over water

The 8th green sits a few feet above a mass of sand

The fairway on the 11th is split in two

A creek on the left of the dogleg 18th fairway can cause problems

HOLE 12

JACK NICKLAUS HAS often said he thinks the 12th hole at Augusta National is the greatest short hole in golf. It's no surprise then that he pays homage to it here. The 184-yard (168-meter) 12th at Muirfield Village is not a replica, but has similar traits. It plays at a similar angle with a shallow green sitting behind water, this time not a creek but a lake. The front bunker is bigger than Augusta's, but similarly mops up straight but short shots. Going into the bunker behind the green leaves a nervy recovery back toward the water, just like at Augusta.

Standing on the tee you could easily imagine you were at Augusta

The shallow green is guarded by one bunker in front and another behind

■ The lake at the 12th

The Muirfield runs in two loops of nine, one running clockwise while the back nine loop runs counterclockwise. Muirfield Village has a rough configuration of two loops, but both run counterclockwise.

Nicklaus was not afraid to be brutal in parts and design on-the-edge holes where a slight miss-hit would surely be punished. Water comes into play on 11 of the holes. Lakes or a widened creek sit dauntingly in front of a few greens—namely the 3rd, 6th, 9th, and 12th—but the snaking streams pose just as many problems on several more holes.

UNIQUE CREEKS

Almost uniquely in world golf, the creeks hug a side of the fairway. Some cut across them, dangerously splitting the landing areas in two. The stream then plays havoc with wayward shots near the green. The split fairway holes are the 5th, 11th, and 14th, and your strategy is tested just as much as your ball striking.

The most unusual of these holes is the par-5 5th, which is 527 yards (482 meters)long. The drive fires downhill into a secluded wooded valley and, at around the 300-yard (274-meter) mark, the creek appears from the left edge to cut into the fairway. It then meanders

down the middle of the hole all the way to the green before swinging left and hugging the green edge. The lay up shot into the split fairway is a tricky one as you can go either side of the water. Cunning and beautiful at the same time.

THE DO-OR-DIE 15TH

The course uses the elevation changes wonderfully well too, with fairways diving down hills and rumbling over humps and through valleys. Probably one hole more than any other epitomizes the course's nature and spirit though, and that is the do-or-die par-5 hole at the 15th. It is dead straight and flanked on both sides by gorgeous mature oaks, pines, and beeches. A rocky stream runs down the left side before swerving across the hole in a deep channel some 40 yards (36 meters) shy of the green. The fairway is cut across by a grassy dell at about halfway. It is a perfect risk-and-reward hole. The big boys can reach in two, but danger lurks.

The hole sums up Muirfield Village, where the best players in the world come to each year for the Memorial Tournament hosted by Jack Nicklaus. The setting is eye-catching and the golf is clever, rewarding the bold but punishing mistakes.

EUROPE'S DAY

In 1987, the European Ryder Cup team came to Muirfield Village as holders of the trophy, but no team from across the Atlantic had ever won on American soil. As Jack Nicklaus was US captain on his home course, the unthinkable couldn't happen—but it did. Europe played inspired golf for the first two days and withstood the inevitable US fightback in the Sunday singles. Seve Ballesteros, the master of the Ryder Cup, holed the winning putt and ruined Jack's day. The score finished Europe 15, US 13.

■ Eamonn Darcy wins on the 18th

Augusta National, UNITED STATES

IF THERE IS ONE COURSE IN THE WORLD that every golfer aspires to play, it is Augusta National. The thirst stems from watching the world's elite golfers testing themselves every April in The Masters Tournament. It is a course that can't be beaten for beauty and drama. A sacred place on the golfing map, it is an exclusive, even mysterious club that has an exquisitely prepared and remarkable golf course to swoon over.

AUGUSTA WAS A LATE STARTER in the annals of golfing history, even though today the course is woven inextricably into them. In 1930, when the late great amateur Bobby Jones had the idea to build a course that could host an annual tournament for the prominent players of the day, Augusta was still a tree and flower nursery. Jones and designer Alister Mackenzie set about turning the swooping site—then known as Fruitlands—into the most recognisable golf course in the world.

ELEVATION CHANGES

The setting was already blessed with many trees, most notably 80 year-old pines that now tower above the areas around the 10th. Many more were planted along with 30 species of azalea and dogwoods. Despite its natural potential, it wasn't an easy site to work with, largely because of the massive elevation changes. The old clubhouse, built as a plantation home in the 1850s, overlooks the course from on high. In front, the course drops some 200 feet (61 meters) beyond the trees and away to the furthest point of the course by Rae's Creek.

The slope is most noticeable on the 10th and 18th, which arc together side by side. From the 10th tee, the fairway is blind, falling away and around a corner until it reaches a green 120 feet (37 meters) below. The rise from the 18th tee is equally severe, although the hole starts further up the slope. At the end of a tiring day, the uphill battle tests stamina as well as technique.

ATTENTION TO DETAIL

Today, the condition of the course is unsurpassed; the attention to detail by the army of greenkeepers is second to none. Barely a blade of grass is out of place: come Masters time, the edges of the bunkers may even be trimmed with a pair of scissors. It wasn't always so from the beginning when Bermuda grass was sown on the

THE IMMACULATE GREEN of the 12th hole, known as "Golden Bell," lies among the flowers and trees of Augusta National's trademark parkland setting.

KEY MOMENTS

A BRIGHT GREEN JACKET is awarded to the winner of The Masters and is presented by the previous year's champion. Here, Phil Mickelson presents the jacket to Zach Johnson in 2007. Sam Snead received one first, in 1949. All champions and members keep their jackets in the clubhouse. Only the current champion can take it off site, but cannot display it in public.

AT THE FINAL HOLE in the 1988 Masters, Sandy Lyle drove into a gaping fairway bunker on the left, leaving a 160-yard (146-meter) uphill shot. With a 7-iron he muscled the ball up and out, pitching it 20 feet (6 meters) behind the pin. The ball wobbled slightly, then slowly fed back down the slope to within 10 feet (3 meters), from where he calmly holed for birdie and the title.

AUGUSTA NATIONAL

2604 WASHINGTON ROAD
AUGUSTA, GEORGIA 30904
www.masters.org   www.augusta.com

THE MASTERS COURSE

FOUNDED 1933
LENGTH 7,445 yards
(6,808 meters)
PAR 72

DESIGNER
Alister Mackenzie
COURSE RECORD 63
Nick Price (1986)
Greg Norman (1996)

SELECTED MASTERS CHAMPIONS

Nick Faldo (1996); Tiger Woods (1997, 2001, 2002, 2005); Mark O'Meara (1998); José Maria Olazábal (1999); Vijay Singh (2000); Mike Weir (2003); Phil Mickelson (2004, 2006); Zach Johnson (2007)

CARD OF THE COURSE

THE FRONT NINE			THE BACK NINE		
HOLE	YARDS	PAR	HOLE	YARDS	PAR
1	455	4	10	495	4
2	575	5	11	505	4
3	350	4	12	155	3
4	240	3	13	510	5
5	455	4	14	440	4
6	180	3	15	530	5
7	450	4	16	170	3
8	570	5	17	440	4
9	460	4	18	465	4
OUT	3,735	36	IN	3,710	36

Flowers adorn the path on the 6th, 1981 ■ The well-guarded 12th green ■ Caddies wait in the "Caddie Shack", 1989

THE CHAMPIONS DINNER

On the eve of The Masters, all former winners gather for dinner in the clubhouse and the current champion chooses the menu. Previous featured dishes include: haggis, neeps, and tatties (Sandy Lyle); Texas BBQ (Ben Crenshaw); fish and chips (Nick Faldo); cheeseburger and fries (Tiger Woods); chicken Panang curry (Vijay Singh).

■ Nick Faldo eats his chips

fairway to combat the sticky heat of the Deep South. Yet today the course is closed for the summer and then resown with finer grasses for winter play.

Historically, there was no rough, just vast areas of immaculate lawns that seamlessly joined up with the fairways. The only trouble if you hit the ball wide were the trees and shrubs (and the manicured bark below), and the water on holes 11 to 16 (except for the 14th). Rough is now a feature after Tiger Woods' record 12-shot win in 1997 (see pp.232–33). Some called the toughening of the course "Tiger proofing," with the aim to curb the monster hitting of the top pros. Since then tees have been pushed back and a semirough grown which affects ball control.

SLIPPERY GREENS

Ultimately, the skill needed most at Augusta is the ability to hit controlled approaches. As driving has been made harder, firing into the greens and what happens after is now the crunch.

Augusta's putting surfaces are notoriously contoured and extremely quick. A slight error of judgment on the approach can see a ball swept away to another part of the green—or worse, taken off the green to find sand, water or simply a resting place in an awkward spot down a bank from where chipping is painfully tough. Few courses have such a fine line between success and failure.

Even if a ball finds the green quite close to the hole, severe slopes

THIS SOUVENIR ENTRY TICKET was for the 1937 Augusta National Invitation Tournament, the forerunner of The Masters.

AUGUSTA NATIONAL GOLF CLUB. 3109

AUGUSTA NATIONAL INVITATION TOURNAMENT
Fourth Round Tournament
SUNDAY, APRIL 4th
PRICE $2.00—TAX 20c
TOTAL
$2.20

mean that putting is loaded with danger, especially if the ball finishes above the hole leaving a downhill putt. For Masters week the greens run at 13 on the stimpmeter (used to measure the speed of greens), which is frighteningly slippery.

UNMISSABLE THEATER

Such an "on-the-edge" set-up means the course throws up spellbinding drama. Watchers know the course inside out because The Masters is always played here. No wonder then that the greatest names in golf have blessed the honors boards since the first tournament in 1934. Ben Hogan, Sam Snead, Arnold Palmer, Gary Player, Jack Nicklaus, Seve Ballesteros, Nick Faldo, and Tiger Woods are all multiple winners. They have all dealt with the pressure of the course when other players have crumbled.

The back nine is filled with do-or-die holes, where eagles, birdies, and double bogies are commonplace. The two par 5s at 13 and 15 are brilliantly conceived, offering the brave a chance of something special, but also serving up potential for disaster. Likewise the short holes at 12 and 16. Probably the most famed par 3 in golf, the 12th is a devilish test, with its angled and slender green perched above Rae's Creek and backed by sand and colorful shrubs. Anything goes here, as clubbing in the swirling wind is bewildering even to the best.

Yet at every turn, golfers need to strike the ball purely and precisely to avoid a scramble for par, and one's sanity. Augusta National is not afraid to change to cope with today's masterful players, but it will always be an incredibly evocative and dazzling place and the one course on the planet that all golfers would love to play.

I love going to that golf course. I fell in love with it watching it on TV. It's one of the greatest places we can ever play

TIGER WOODS

■ "Gang mowers" trim the 15th

■ Ticket collection of a Masters' fan

■ Augusta's famous clubhouse

THE COURSE

Immaculately prepared and enticing in its beauty and danger, Augusta swoops through lofty pines and skirts banks of shrubs and encroaching water. Every facet of the game is tested to the limit, as a golfer faces extreme challenges at every corner. Its greens are legendary for their speed and slope.

A steep ridge on the 5th green makes putting from front to back very tough

AMEN CORNER

The 11th, 12th, and 13th holes have become know as Amen Corner. Writer Herb Warren Wind coined the phrase after the 1958 Masters. He thought it described the stretch of the course that was critical to the outcome of the tournament. It stuck, as these three holes are demanding, stunning, and risk-ridden.

Successfully negotiating the dogleg is the key to success on the 13th

The wide 4th green gives plenty of opportunities for long putts

The 8th green sits in an amphitheatre of grassy mounds

N

Bunkers await on the left of the steeply rising 18th fairway

The tee shot on the 11th is through a long corridor to an open fairway

THE FRONT NINE
❶ A gaping bunker on the dogleg confronts you. It can be carried, but it takes a mighty strike. ❷ Reachable in two for the longest hitters, but bunkers virtually surround the green. ❸ A plateau green with sharp run-offs teases even the best. ❹ A monster par-3 where three putts are common as the green is severe. ❺ Another green where it is difficult to get the ball close. It is huge and slopey. ❻ The hole drops down over a bank of shrubs to a back-to-front tilting green. ❼ The fairway is hemmed in by pines and you need a very precise approach to find the shallow green. ❽ Uphill and turning left, a birdie is definitely on if you avoid the yawning fairway trap. ❾ Danger looms on the approach. Too short and the ball will run back down the hill. Too long and putting is a nightmare.

THE BACK NINE
❿ A downhill sweeping hole from right-to-left shadowed by staggering pines. ⓫ Heart-in-the-mouth second shot with water guarding the left. A bale out right still spells danger. ⓬ Nothing but a pure strike will do, as water awaits at the front and banked traps at the back. ⓭ An arcing dogleg to a green defended by a rocky stream. Anything is possible—eagles and doubles. ⓮ Bunkerless, but a humpbacked green awaits. Miss it and chipping close is almost impossible. ⓯ Find the right side of the fairway and you can go for the green in two. Anything short though gets wet. ⓰ A ridge in the green can be your friend as it might feed the ball to the hole, but it can also make putting tough. ⓱ "Eisenhower's tree" looms large on your drive. Avoid it for any chance at par. ⓲ Judging distance up to the flag is tricky as the hole plays incredibly steeply uphill.

Slopes and a bunker guard the right of the green

The approach is dangerous, with a lake to the left and Rae's Creek flowing behind

The green is guarded by Rae's Creek, a bunker in front and two at the rear

The bridge spanning Rae's Creek is named after Ben Hogan, who won the Masters in 1951 and 1953

A rocky creek guards the green across the front and right

The bend in the dogleg is many players' target off the tee

| HOLE 11 | "WHITE DOGWOOD" |

This is the first par 4 at Augusta to be longer than 500 yards (457 meters) and the first of the water holes. Accuracy off the tee is important.

| HOLE 12 | "GOLDEN BELL" |

The 12th is a mid-iron over water, and the legendary Jack Nicklaus was so respectful of its dangers that he used to aim for the middle of the green wherever the flag was.

| HOLE 13 | "AZALEA" |

You need a big draw around the corner. Then, if going for it in two, a long-iron or wood off a hanging lie to the green.

Oakmont, UNITED STATES

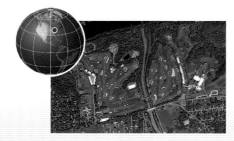

ONE OF AMERICA'S MOST HISTORIC COURSES, Oakmont is revered the world over for its uncompromising design and immaculate conditioning. It has hosted more US Open Championships than any other course, eight times so far and most recently in 2007. Only a few hundred yards from the Allegheny River that flows through the city of Pittsburgh, Oakmont is a beautifully lush, rolling wonder that packs a real punch.

OAKMONT IS A DIFFICULT COURSE to categorize. Is it a parkland or is it an inland links? Certainly, when it was founded in 1903, there was a distinct lack of trees on the pastureland and it was said that 17 of the 18 flags could be seen from the clubhouse porch. But a huge tree-planting scheme in the 1950s altered the look and feel of the course and many of the fairways became tree-lined like a classic parkland test.

Over the last few years, however, almost 5,000 trees have been removed so that the original open feel has returned. What hasn't changed, though, is its unique and demanding nature. The course is neatly packed into 170 acres (69 hectares) and split into two by the Pennsylvania turnpike road. All those who drive through her gates enter with trepidation, as Oakmont has a reputation for being one of the toughest classic tests in the United States. Perhaps it is *the* classic test.

PENAL BUNKERS AND SPECIAL GREENS

Founder and architect Henry Fownes knew exactly what philosophy would be applied to his creation as he was famously quoted as saying: "a poor shot should be a shot irrevocably lost." His thinking applies to every part of the course from tee to green. Tightly-mown fairways that swoop and pitch are hemmed in by strings of very deep bunkers—there are 180 in all. The sand traps come in strange formations: some are in rows of five or six, while others are grouped together in clusters. A couple appear as long strips, such as the aptly named Sahara bunker on the 8th, which is 100 yards (91 meters) long.

The Church Pews bunker is a massive area of sand between the 3rd and 4th holes. It is split into sections by strips of grassy banks some 3 feet (0.9 meters) high and covered in hairy grass. It originally had seven "pews," but for the 2007 US Open, it was extended and now has 12. Now over 130 yards (119 meters) long, it isn't just for show, as it catches many golfers' drives on both holes, and they find it very hard to advance the ball far from it.

MIST HANGS OVER THE COURSE AT OAKMONT where the greens are fast and challenging, and nearly all the bunkers are cut very tightly to the edges of the fairways and greens.

KEY MOMENTS

FLAMBOYANT AMERICAN
Johnny Miller put together a blistering round of 63 in the 1973 US Open. Many experts consider it the finest round of golf ever. It broke the major scoring record, enabling him to win the first of his two majors. He came from behind to beat Arnold Palmer and Jack Nicklaus through the purity of his striking.

THE ROUND OF THE YEAR in world golf came from Paul Casey on day two of the 2007 US Open. On a day when only three players out of 156 shot par or better, and the scoring average soared to 76.9, Paul Casey's round of 66 was truly remarkable. With only one bogey despite the buffeting wind, it catapulted him from 104th to inside the top 15.

THE SPEED OF A GREEN can be measured by a Stimpmeter, invented by Edward Stimpson after he watched the 1935 US Open at Oakmont. A track like a yardstick is held at an angle until a ball is released from a notch. The distance traveled by the ball in feet is the speed of the green. For example, 10 feet equals a green speed of 10 on the Stimpmeter.

OAKMONT

1233 HULTON ROAD
OAKMONT, PA 15139-1199
www.oakmont-countryclub.org

THE COURSE

FOUNDED: 1903
LENGTH: 7,230 yards
(6,611 meters)
PAR: 70

DESIGNER
Henry Fownes

COURSE RECORD 66
Paul Casey (2007)

SELECTED CHAMPIONS

US PGA CHAMPIONSHIP Sam Snead (1951); John Mahaffey (1978).
US OPEN Ben Hogan (1953); Jack Nicklaus (1962); Johnny Miller (1973); Larry Nelson (1983); Ernie Els (1994); Angel Cabrera (2007).
US WOMEN'S OPEN Patty Sheehan (1992).

CARD OF THE COURSE

THE FRONT NINE			THE BACK NINE		
HOLE	YARDS	PAR	HOLE	YARDS	PAR
1	482	4	10	435	4
2	341	4	11	379	4
3	428	4	12	667	5
4	609	5	13	183	3
5	382	4	14	358	4
6	194	3	15	500	4
7	479	4	16	231	3
8	288	3	17	313	4
9	477	4	18	484	4
OUT	3,680	35	IN	3,550	35

THE COURSE

Incredibly tough but a pleasant beauty nonetheless, Oakmont is famed for its diving fairways, diabolical bunkering, and wicked greens that sweep and dip like a sea swell. An awesome test for even the best golfers.

THE FRONT NINE ❶ A beast of a start where the approach is semiblind to a green that tilts away. ❷ The landing area is tight with 6 bunkers right and a ditch on the left. ❸ The first encounter with the massive Church Pews bunker on the left. ❹ A big swinging par-5, where the Church Pews and 5 deep traps right must be avoided. ❺ A hole needing precision, most crucially on the approach to this rolling green. ❻ Tightly guarded par-3 with a right-to-left sloping green. Missing right is trouble. ❼ Tough long 4. A narrow entrance and tilting green make it hard to get the ball close. ❽ The ideal shot is a draw into this huge par-3 but the

long Sahara bunker awaits. ❾ A well-bunkered fairway leads to an almost rectangular and awkwardly rippled green.

THE BACK NINE ❿ Downhill but testing because the green slopes away and to the back left. ⓫ Aim to reach the plateau portion of the fairway from where a short iron is left. ⓬ Unreachable for most, it is one to plot carefully to miss the 20 bunkers. ⓭ A long, narrow, well-guarded green puts a premium on accuracy. Try to stay below the hole. ⓮ Luckily it is a short par-4 as 10 deep bunkers patrol the landing area, so an iron from the tee will do. ⓯ Pray you hit the fairway and avoid the nasty bunker ruts left, as it is a monster par-4. ⓰ Big short-hole where left-to-right shot may be needed to get at the flag. ⓱ Driveable semi-blind par-4, but fraught with danger. A nest of bunkers have to be carried and the greenside traps are deep. ⓲ Awesome finish, whose crowning glory is the wickedly undulating green, where a three putt can ruin the day.

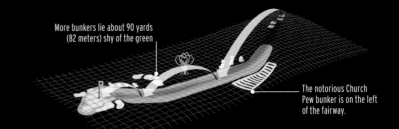
More bunkers lie about 90 yards (82 meters) shy of the green

The notorious Church Pew bunker is on the left of the fairway.

HOLE 4   THE CHURCH PEWS bunker starts on the left of the fairway at about 245 yards (224 meters) from the back tee and hugs the right-turning hole for 100 yards (91 meters) or so. A cluster of deep traps is in the corner opposite. If a drive finds any of these bunkers, reaching the par-5 green in three is a very tough proposition. As the fairway kinks further right around some more traps, it is hard to get at the hole wherever you are coming in from.

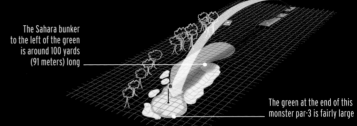
The Sahara bunker to the left of the green is around 100 yards (91 meters) long

The green at the end of this monster par-3 is fairly large

HOLE 8   STANDING ON the tee, the view is dominated by the wide strip of sand on the left called Sahara. From the back tee, it's a carry of 200 yards (182 meters) to clear the corner of it directly in front of the green, preferably with a right-to-left shape so the ball can run up the length of the green. Anyone erring to the right or hitting too straight will find one of the four other traps. It is a huge one-shotter and one that a par-3 should be treasured on.

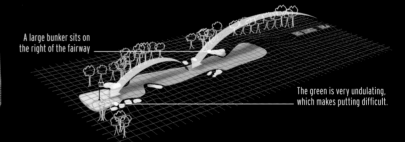
A large bunker sits on the right of the fairway

The green is very undulating, which makes putting difficult.

HOLE 18   NOT FOR THE FAINT of heart, this challenge is scary. Although the tee shot is down-hill, the bunker on the right and two pairs of traps either side further up will catch anything not perfectly struck. They are all deep and make finding the green unreachable in regulation. The approach is uphill to a rolling green. Many balls finish short of the putting surface and roll back down a slope from where an up-and-down is extremely difficult.

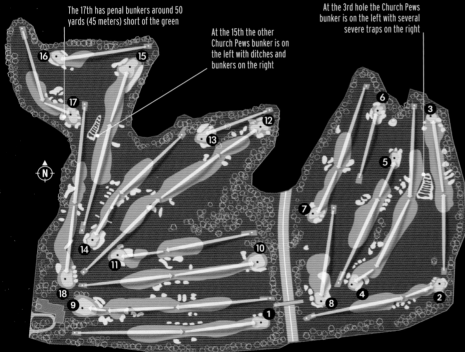

The 17th has penal bunkers around 50 yards (45 meters) short of the green

At the 15th the other Church Pews bunker is on the left with ditches and bunkers on the right

At the 3rd hole the Church Pews bunker is on the left with several severe traps on the right

The 6th hole

The 9th tee and clubhouse

The 18th hole

The putting surfaces mark Oakmont out as somewhere special. Today, many run-of-the-mill designers build standard back-to-front sloping greens where the golfers' choices are far too predictable. Not so at Oakmont. Many defy design logic and feature terrifying slopes, terraces, and dips. Some also very definitely slope from front to back, like the 10th, which makes getting near a flag here incredibly difficult. Because the fairways are firm and fast, a ball sometimes has to land well short of the green, then be allowed to trickle out down the slope onto the putting surface, trusting as much to luck than to judgment.

All greens feature something out of the ordinary. The 9th is almost rectangular and the 18th resembles a sea swell with the slopes rolling down the green like waves. To make the course even tougher, the speed of the greens can measure up to 14 on the Stimpmeter (see pp.301), which is searingly fast for such slopey surfaces.

THE 2007 US OPEN

As if this is not penal enough, the course for the 2007 US Open Championship was pushed up to 7,230 yards (6,611 meters)—the second longest in US Open history —and the rough was like wire. The course featured the longest hole in major history—the 667-yard (610-meter) par-5 12th—plus four par-3s that averaged 224 yards (205 meters) in length, including the monster 8th which was 288 yards (263 meters) long. No wonder, then, that only 31 sub-par rounds have ever been achieved in the 8 US Opens that Oakmont has held. Remarkably, two of these were claimed by Argentine Angel Cabrera, who was the eventual winner in 2007.

Oakmont thrives on its individuality, and although highly demanding, it is thought by the best to be as much a true test of patience as skill, a place where it is best to go in with a safety-first game plan.

THE CHURCH PEWS BUNKER between the 3rd and 4th holes has strips of grass and is one of the most famous sand traps in world

■ The clubhouse clock

■ The 5th hole

■ The entrance to Oakmont

Heathland courses

RATHER LIKE A LINKS COURSE, a true heathland is quite a rarity. As with their seaside cousins, the greatest heaths are mainly found in the British Isles, although there are less celebrated pockets elsewhere in northern France, Belgium, Denmark, and Holland, as well as some in the northeastern United States, Asia and South Africa.

△ **GLENEAGLES** boasts three championship courses located among the sweeping landscapes of Perthshire, Scotland.

◁◁ **ALWOODLEY**, set in natural moorland in Yorkshire, England, was the first course that Dr. Alister Mackenzie designed.

◁ **BOAT OF GARTEN** golf course was fashioned from a birch forest and set in the Cairngorms National Park, south of Inverness, Scotland.

A TRUE HEATH HAS to have—and be able to sustain—the growth of heather. This is a low, ground-covering, evergreen shrub that has small usually pink or purple, bell-shaped flowers at certain times of the year. Heathers thrive on sandy, acidic soils and are often found on moorlands and in pine forests. A

EYE-CATCHING BUNKERING is a feature of heathland courses. Many bunkers have faces covered with either heather or thick grass. Often, they are just short of the greens which tests distance perception and accuracy.

heathland's characteristics are very similar to the great sandbelt courses of southern Australia, and a few astonishing venues in North America that have no heather to speak of. Because of that, all have been put under one banner in this book.

BRITISH HEATHS
The finest true heathland courses are found in what is known as the Surrey Berkshire sandbelt—a wide corridor of sandy, wooded land running southwest of London in England. Household names such as

Walton Heath, Sunningdale, The Berkshire, Swinley Forest, and Wentworth all share the soil in this sandbelt with less heralded gems, such as St. George's Hill, Woking, and Hankley Common. Many cracking heaths are also found in the heartland of England, such as the courses at Alwoodley near Leeds, Notts Golf Club, Ganton, and the amazing Woodhall Spa. Others can be found on the south coast. The middle of Scotland in Perthshire and Moray is also home to a smattering of terrific heaths

and moorlands—courses include the Boat of Garten, Blairgowrie, Ladybank, and Gleneagles.

AUSTRALIA AND THE US
Further afield from this British nucleus is the Melbourne sandbelt in Australia. The most famous of its several incredible courses is Royal Melbourne, while others include Kingston Heath, Huntingdale, and Metropolitan Golf Club. In the US the number-one ranked course in the world rests in a heathlike setting at Pine Valley.

SOIL AND BUNKERING

What do these heathland courses share? Soil is the answer. Their sandy-based land does two jobs. Firstly, it can create very attractive, natural-looking settings where heather, pines, birch, broom, gorse, grasses, and in some cases flowering shrubs such as rhododendrons, thrive. Secondly, it is naturally excellent draining land, which makes for firm, fast-running courses reminiscent of a links.

As you might suspect with a sand-based course, bunkering is key in their design. The master architects of heathland courses were Harry Colt, Herbert Fowler, James Braid, Tom Dunn, Willie Park, and Alister Mackenzie. They all put great store in the bunkers being real hazards and strategically placed.

Many of the bunkers are deep and fringed with heather or thick grass, and appear in thought-provoking places. Although traps do guard the greenside as you would expect, some are deliberately short of the green by some 10 to 30 yards (9 to 27 meters). It gives the golfer the chance to clear them or land beside them and still be able to run the ball up onto the green if the course is playing fast. A little mistake on judgment, however, and you can find the next shot being a mid-range bunker shot, one that even the pros are not keen on. These bunkers also provide a visual trick and make distance perception deceptive.

Cross-wastes feature on many holes, too, either eating into the fairway or completely splitting them in two. They are a main feature of Pine Valley, although its bunkers are less formal than in the British Isles.

Australia's sandbelt courses have slightly different bunkers, although they are designed by some of the renowned heathland architects. Their traps tend to be shallower, bigger, and more freeform in shape, and tend to come in clusters rather than singles. But all these courses, aside from some holes at Pine Valley, feature a route through the hazards up by the green so that a golfer can play the running ball onto the putting surfaces, which tend to be fast, and contoured.

HEATHER TROUBLE

A heathland's troubles are made worse by the heather itself—in fact, sandbelt-style courses tend to rely on tall grass and sandy wastes as the main source of trouble. Some people consider a sprig of white heather to be a lucky charm, but golfers do not feel fortunate at all if they find it.

Heather is a nightmare to play from and is more punishing than even the thickest rough. Its wiry, woody stems grab your club as you try to strike the ball. Normally, you would use a wedge or a short iron and attack the ball steeply to ensure as little contact as possible with the heather. It's worth remembering that the clubface almost always closes through impact as it snags on the woody stems.

As a general rule you should take your medicine and play out with a lofted club back to the safety of the fairway, rather than try a miraculous shot.

WHEN THE HEATHER IS IN BLOOM and the sun is shining, a heath can be one of the most alluring settings in the world of golf. Many courses feature heather as a hazard and, even though it is colorful and beautiful, it can also be a troublesome experience if you stray from the straight and narrow.

AIRING THE HEATHS

Some heaths are trying to return to their real roots by "opening up" the landscape again. Hankley Common, to the southwest of London, undertook a massive tree clearance program to give the heath some "air" and bring it back to how it would have looked in 1895 when it was first laid out. The wind now has more effect on the golf and the heather grows more virulent than ever.

■ Hankley Common

A heathland's troubles are made worse by the heather itself... Some people consider a sprig of **white heather to be a lucky charm,** but golfers do not feel fortunate at all if they find it

Sunningdale, ENGLAND

THE ARCHETYPAL HEATHLAND COURSE, Sunningdale mixes old-world charm and grace with demanding golf in a delightful corner of England. Hemmed in by mature woodland, the Old Course is also a pleasure to walk around, and you can scarcely believe that it is only 25 miles (40 kilometers) from central London. Each year, Sunningdale plays host to a number of professional and amateur tournaments.

SUNNINGDALE'S POTENTIAL was recognized in 1900 by two golfing brothers who asked Willie Park Jr. to design a course for the club's 100 or so members who each put up a £100 bond. What Park saw over a century ago is somewhat different to today's landscape, but what he laid out is essentially the same course, although Harry Colt added to its prowess in the 1920s.

Heather is abundant and noticeable, especially on the carries from the sheltered tees and flanking the fairways. It also cuts across in front of the 6th and 7th greens, but is not so brutal around the fringes of the excellent bunkering as it is at, say, Walton Heath. The Old Course is less taxing than other heaths and is short by modern standards. Yet it has a wonderful subtlety to its predominantly straight holes. Any doglegs that do occur are only gently offset, but just that simple change of direction can make the angles for attacking the greens cleverly cunning.

CRITICAL LINES OF PLAY

Strategy plays a huge part in defeating Sunningdale. It is typically firm and bouncy, and must be plotted around rather than bludgeoned. The bunkering is thoughtful and hampers every shot on the course, except for drives at the 1st, 2nd, and 6th. Archetypal heathland tricks are used with traps set close to the line of play but some yards shy of the greens to catch a slightly misdirected approach intended to be run in. On the 12th, 16th, and 18th, a string of traps runs across the entire width of the fairway, very much a Willie Park trademark and a wonderfully provocative feature.

Lines of play are critical to counteract the influence of the traps hovering near and next to the subtle greens, but the perfect line often has to flirt with other hazards. A superb example of thinking golf comes at the 7th, where placement of the tee shot is vital to have the best line into the green.

There are plenty of birdie chances, which adds to the feelgood factor of this divine heath. Nothing makes a golfer feel better than starting with a birdie—a definite possibility as the opener is a short par 5 at 492 yards (450 meters). However, with trees right and heather down the left, it's a confident strike that finds the fairway.

THE TEE OF THE LONG, swooping, par-4 10th hole lies close to the back of the 9th green, and invites a big, booming drive down the hill.

STUNNING START

It was the most dramatic beginning to any round in major championship history. At the 2004 Weetabix Women's British Open, England's Karen Stupples was one shot behind leaders Heather Bowie and Rachel Teske with a round to go. Stupples grabbed an eagle three at the 1st, then holed a 5-iron from 205 yards (187 meters) for an albatross two at the 2nd. She added five more birdies to finish on 64 and win by five shots. Finland's Minea Blomqvist fired a 62 to set a record score for a major championship, for both men and women, in the third round.

■ Karen Stupples waves to the crowd

Sunningdale's finish is a classic challenge and the last quartet is the toughest stretch on the course. At the 15th you fire out from trees over a daunting expanse of purple heather to a green patrolled by four bunkers. The 16th has a bunker smack bang in the middle of the fairway to taunt the drive, then your approach is cracked over a necklace of deep traps up to a raised green, which makes distance hard to judge.

The last two are pure golf holes that need precise drives and perfectly struck approaches—downhill to the 17th, uphill to the 18th. Once you have walked off the final hole and repaired to the elegant and traditional clubhouse, you can reflect on what is a graceful, shrewd, and timeless test in lovely, soothing surroundings. Sunningdale is the quintessential heathland experience.

THE GREENS AND FAIRWAYS AT SUNNINGDALE are shaded by an eruption of pines, oaks, and birch as they rise and fall over the sweeping sandy ground owned by St. John's College, Cambridge.

THE COURSE

Short by modern standards, the Old Course relies on its subtle design, strategic bunkering, fast firm ground, and the brutality of its clinging heather for its defenses. Its beauty is enhanced by the stands of pine, oaks, and birches that flank all holes in some way. A classic test.

HOLE 18 — THE HOME HOLE

The 18th has been the scene for many fine victories from some of the game's great players: James Braid, Harry Vardon, Bobby Jones, Bob Charles, Gary Player, Nick Faldo, and Greg Norman, as well as one of the greatest lady golfers of all time, Nancy Lopez. After your uphill tee shot has avoided bunkers right and left, your approach is again uphill over a diagonal run of bunkers to the green and beneath Sunningdale's massive famed oak tree, which doubles as the club's emblem. If a flag is cut back right, as it often is on championship days, a player can use the left-to-right slope to feed the ball around to the cup.

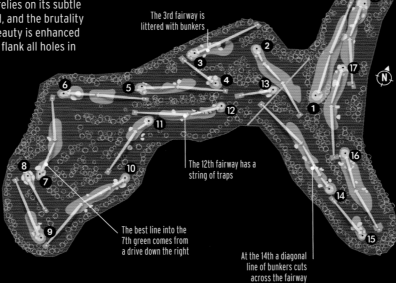

The 3rd fairway is littered with bunkers

The 12th fairway has a string of traps

The best line into the 7th green comes from a drive down the right

At the 14th a diagonal line of bunkers cuts across the fairway

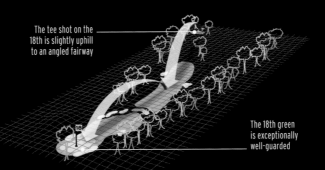

The tee shot on the 18th is slightly uphill to an angled fairway

The 18th green is exceptionally well-guarded

Heather-fringed bunkers cross the 18th fairway

SUNNINGDALE

RIDGEMOUNT ROAD
SUNNINGDALE, BERKSHIRE SL5 9RR, UK
www.sunningdale-golfclub.co.uk

THE OLD COURSE

FOUNDED 1901		PAR 70	
LENGTH 6,627 yards		DESIGNER	
(6,060 meters)		Willie Park Jnr	

SELECTED CHAMPIONS

EUROPEAN OPEN Bernhard Langer (1985); Greg Norman (1986); Ian Woosnam (1988); Peter Senior (1990); Nick Faldo (1992)
WOMEN'S BRITISH OPEN Karrie Webb (1997); Se Ri Pak (2001); Karen Stupples (2004)
WALKER CUP US (1987) US 16, GB&I 7.
SEVE TROPHY Continental Europe (2000)

CARD OF THE COURSE

THE FRONT NINE			THE BACK NINE		
HOLE	YARDS	PAR	HOLE	YARDS	PAR
1	492	5	10	475	4
2	489	4	11	322	4
3	318	4	12	442	4
4	156	3	13	185	3
5	419	4	14	503	5
6	433	4	15	239	3
7	406	4	16	434	4
8	193	3	17	425	4
9	273	4	18	423	4
OUT	3,179	35	IN	3,448	35

Woodhall Spa, ENGLAND

INTIMIDATING CARRIES, DISHEARTENINGLY DEEP BUNKERS, and riots of gorse and heather make the Hotchkin Course at Woodhall Spa the most daunting pure heathland test in the world. Set in a remote, wooded haven in rural England, it is worth the trip just to sample her alluring menace. A thoroughbred heath in every way, Woodhall displays a pedigree that often has it ranked as the finest inland course in the British Isles.

APPROACHING THE ENVIRONS, of this quaint, slightly time-warped town in middle England does not prepare you for the oasis of Woodhall Spa. Here, open farmland quickly turns to woodland within yards and the sandy soil under the canopies of the pines, oaks, and birch is heaven for prolific heather, bracken, gorse, and broom. By any yardstick, the Hotchkin Course is an extraordinary golf links. Its endless variety of holes can charm and humiliate in equal measure.

Golfers played on a nine-hole course in the town as early as 1890, but it wasn't until 1905 that a proper 18 was hewn from the heath by Harry Vardon. It was tinkered with soon after by J.H. Taylor and later modified over a period of years by Harry Colt. Then the landowner Colonel Stafford Hotchkin added his style to the masterpiece. The course has remained very much the same for 70 or so years, except for adding new tees to combat ongoing technological advances.

NOTORIOUS BUNKERS

Four influences, one unique course. Playing Woodhall for the first time is an enlightening experience. Golfers may have heard stories about the notorious bunkering, but nothing quite prepares you for the reality. Some say the course once had a bunker for every day of the year, but now a mere 110 remain. But what bunkers they are. Anyone tugging their drive at the difficult 2nd can find the cavernous bunker dug deep into the heath sand shaded by a heavy stand of birch and gorse. Any hope of reaching the green is long gone and it takes some skill to splash out. But that is just a fairway bunker; compared to some of the greenside traps, it's a baby.

Most golfers give up trying to knock the ball close out of the greenside bunkers at the 4th and 5th. Just getting the ball onto the green is a feat. The short 5th is a prime example of the punishment fitting the crime though, as the green should be hit from the tee.

HOME OF THE ENGLISH GAME

In 1995, Colonel Hotchkin's son Neil sold Woodhall Spa to the English Golf Union (EGU) to provide it with a thriving home, while safeguarding the future of this magnificent heath. The EGU have since built another course, The Bracken, and a state of the art academy to help develop homegrown talent.

■ The 16th on The Bracken course

For unparalleled theater, you must go deeper into the course and admire the mid-length 12th, where five ludicrously deep traps surround a green only 18 yards (16 meters) across at its widest. The trap front right and the simply gargantuan pit on the left could lay claim to being the toughest bunkers to get out of in world golf. Such traps ruin perfectly good rounds, with golfers merrily hacking away for several shots before emerging.

DEMANDING BUT FAIR

The pressure the bunkering puts golfers under can turn a normally reliable and solid swing into a nervy heave. This has never been truer than from the tees when you also have to contend with long carries over heather and gorse, with more heather and trees hugging the fairways. In all honesty, the tee shots are demanding but fair. Good striking will be rewarded with a good look at the green, and there are very few tricky angles to deal with.

The 2nd to the 10th holes are in more open heath, but from 11 onward, the holes enter a dense tree-lined section and the golf becomes increasingly claustrophobic. Yet every hole is distinct and you finish with one of the most intimidating drives in England. Two sets of tees are on offer. One is set back by the 17th green and from the back tee a drive must carry 210 yards (192 meters) to reach the bony fairway. The other, set deep in the forest, gives you a more direct line to the fairway, but it is down the narrowest of channels between the walls of trees, which go on for over 150 yards (137 meters).

Yet that is Woodhall in a nutshell. It will ask ultra challenging questions at every turn, but like at the reachable par-5 home hole, it gives you opportunities to score if you can hold your nerve and game together. It is inspired but dangerous golf.

THE REMARKABLE 12TH GREEN on the Hotchkin Course is a small gem, but it is guarded by particularly deep bunkers that drive golfers to distraction as they try to escape.

WOODHALL SPA

THE BROADWAY, WOODHALL SPA, LINCOLNSHIRE LN10 6PU, UK
www.woodhallspagolf.com

THE HOTCHKIN COURSE

FOUNDED 1905
LENGTH 7,080 yards (6,474 meters)
DESIGNERS Harry Colt, Harry Vardon, JH Taylor, Col. Hotchkin

SELECTED CHAMPIONS

ENGLISH AMATEUR David Gilford (1984); Ian Garbutt (1990); Mark Sanders (1998)
BRABAZON TROPHY (ENGLISH STROKEPLAY) Jochen Lupprian (2000)
HOME INTERNATIONALS (MEN) England (2001)

CARD OF THE COURSE

THE FRONT NINE			THE BACK NINE		
HOLE	YARDS	PAR	HOLE	YARDS	PAR
1	361	4	10	338	4
2	442	4	11	437	4
3	415	4	12	172	3
4	414	4	13	451	4
5	148	3	14	521	5
6	526	5	15	321	4
7	470	4	16	395	4
8	209	3	17	336	3
9	584	5	18	540	5
OUT	3,569	36	IN	3,511	37

The cross bunker and heather on the 11th

HOLE 11 — NERVE-RACKING BRUTE

Often chosen as the pick of the par 4s, the 11th is a brute, especially into the prevailing westerly wind. Standing on the back tee is nerve-racking, even though the fairway framed by tall pines is generous enough. In the distance you can just spy the green beyond a gently rising fairway. Your second is slightly downhill over a wide stretch of rough grass, heather, and a large cross bunker to a green backed by tall trees. The real dilemma occurs if you have found rough off the tee or are a long way back, as it takes a brave man to go for the carry over the waste. If you do not make it, a big score beckons.

THE COURSE

This is probably the most ruthless pure heathla world, where the cavernous bunkers, banks of c broom, and claustrophobic fairways hemmed in and birch are extremely intimidating to all. Woo variety is legendary and it is not for the faint-h

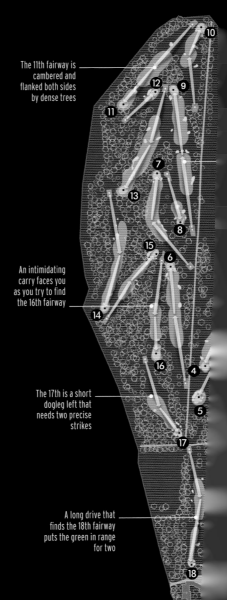

The 11th fairway is cambered and flanked both sides by dense trees

An intimidating carry faces you as you try to find the 16th fairway

The 17th is a short dogleg left that needs two precise strikes

A long drive that finds the 18th fairway puts the green in range for two

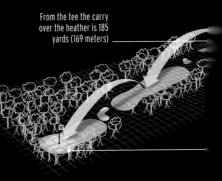

From the tee the carry over the heather is 185 yards (169 meters)

Royal Melbourne, AUSTRALIA

THE FAMED SANDBELT AROUND AUSTRALIA'S second city houses several amazing courses, but Royal Melbourne stands out from the crowd. Set in gently rolling landscape, the terrain could be described as a blend of heathland and linksland. The Composite Course is ranked the best course in the Southern Hemisphere, and has been host to prestigious championships, such as the World Cup, the Presidents Cup, the Heineken Classic, and many Australian Opens.

IF THERE WAS EVER an area so perfect for golf, then the Melbourne sandbelt is it. Gracefully undulating sandy ground covered in native bushscrub and shadowed by eucalyptus and acacia trees, it is an ideal setting for one of the world's great courses.

Melbourne's club was founded in 1891 and given its royal moniker in 1895 by Queen Victoria. But it wasn't until 1931, after two moves from other sites, that its famous West Course was opened, designed by Dr. Alister Mackenzie. The East Course soon followed and today the two courses are mixed come tournament time to create a wonderful test of golf.

Twelve holes from the more heralded West course and six from the East make up what is known as the Composite Course. The two courses were melded together for two reasons. Firstly, to keep all the holes on one side of the property and not split into two by a road, easing the flow of spectators. Secondly, to give the course extra length and bite. The Composite is just over 7,000 yards (6,400 meters), whereas the West and East are only 6,589 and 6,566 yards (6,025 and 6,004 meters) respectively.

A PUSSYCAT ON PAPER

Royal Melbourne's sandy soil makes for fast rolling playing surfaces, and coupled with generous-looking fairways, it appears a bit of a pussycat on paper. Yet being on top of your game is essential if you are to score well, because the course has so many subtleties that you can be caught out very easily.

Mackenzie liked to give the player options, and that is why the fairways are wide in parts. There is always the choice for a player to play safe, but rarely will they beat their handicap unless they take on the tighter lines. The difference between the two routes can mean someone playing a 4-iron in or an 8-iron. And given the way the greens and their encroaching bunkering is designed, there is a big advantage going in with less club. Standing

PROTECTED BY CLUSTERS OF BUNKERS, the large and inviting green on the long 18th offers birdie chances in a welcome finish, especially to accurate hitters who have safely negotiated the fairway bunkers.

KEY MOMENTS

IN THE 2004 Heineken Classic, Ernie Els came within a whisker of shooting the magic number of 59–only rarely achieved in competitions. In his first round, he was 12 under with four holes to play, then caught a flier at the 15th and bogeyed. Two birdies put him back on track. Needing a birdie at the last his putt slipped by and he had to settle for a course record 60. The next day he scored 66 to be 18 under, and then went on to win by a stroke.

DR. ALISTER MACKENZIE'S 12-week visit to Australia in 1926 led him to have a hand in designing 18 golf courses, many of which bear his trademark wavy-edged sweeps of sand. The shapes of his bunkers mean that every player can glimpse the sand, which helps them with their perception and strategy, but also puts pressure on their game. Mackenzie never saw his finished work at Royal Melbourne and instead entrusted the final shaping of the course to his partner Alex Russell.

ROYAL MELBOURNE

CHELTENHAM ROAD, BLACK ROCK,
VICTORIA, AUSTRALIA 3193
www.royalmelbourne.com.au

THE COMPOSITE COURSE

FOUNDED 1891
LENGTH 7,002 yards
(6,403 meters)
PAR 72

DESIGNERS
Alister Mackenzie,
Alex Russell
COURSE RECORD 60
Ernie Els (2004)

SELECTED CHAMPIONS

WORLD CUP US–Ben Crenshaw &
Mark McCumber (1988)
PRESIDENTS CUP International Team (1998)
HEINEKEN CLASSIC Ernie Els (2002, 2003,
2004); Craig Parry (2005)

CARD OF THE COURSE

THE FRONT NINE			THE BACK NINE		
HOLE	YARDS	PAR	HOLE	YARDS	PAR
1	429	4	10	465	4
2	480	5	11	439	4
3	333	4	12	433	4
4	440	4	13	354	4
5	176	3	14	509	5
6	451	4	15	383	4
7	148	3	16	201	3
8	305	4	17	558	5
9	455	4	18	443	4
OUT	3,217	35	IN	3,785	37

Royal Melbourne is Mackenzie's masterpiece. By any judgment it must have strong claim to **equal anything on earth**

PETER THOMSON, FIVE TIMES OPEN WINNER

LOCAL BOY PETER THOMSON hits a screamer during the Canada Cup (which later became the World Cup) at Royal Melbourne in 1959, when the Composite Course was used for the first time. Thomson, who had won four Open Championships, teamed up with Kel Nagle and they destroyed the field by 10 shots.

on any tee, what you see before you is obvious. There are no hidden tricks. Eyes are drawn to the large spreading bunkers with white sand and tongues of grass. Some you must take on and fly, others must be carefully skirted. Fearless, skilful drivers are rewarded with better positions than those more timid or slightly less precise.

Booming driving has to be backed up by exacting and imaginative iron play: you either have to bounce a shot through narrow entrances or shape it to get at tightly cut pin positions on the enormous and rippled greens. The putting surfaces are famously smooth-rolling and lightning fast with slopes that can intimidate the less confident. Putting becomes like a game within the game. Top players can hit the greens relatively easily, but because the course is fast-running, an approach can finish many yards away, from where keeping a three-putt off the card is an art in itself.

DECEPTIVE BUNKERS

If a green is missed, the shot is likely to find sand or run away into a scrubby lie. Often, the bunkering comes in clusters. The bunkers are shaped like deformed clover leaves and their sweeping sand faces tend to feed the ball down into the center of the trap. Many are cut sharply next to the putting surface. They are not the most

fearsome depth-wise and getting spin from them is easy. But they are deceptive when combined with the slopey and speedy greens, and splashing out close to a flag is often difficult. Some days you seem to be always facing tricky six footers for par, even if you have hit the green.

RISKS, REWARDS, AND PUNISHMENTS

Mackenzie and his sidekick Alex Russell, who designed the East, built a very fair test nonetheless. You can score well despite its difficulties. The par 5s are reachable with two exacting shots and brave golfers can thrive on the few short par 4s. The 8th (the 10th on the West Course) is a terrific do-or-die hole at only 305 yards (279 meters). You have to take on a gaping bunker in the lee of the slight dogleg left if you are to go for the green. But tug the drive left and it will find bushes. Hit it too straight and it might run across the fairway into more bunkers or worse into thick undergrowth on the far side. An easy birdie chance can quickly become a double bogey.

That is testament to the designers. The routeing and shaping of the holes are brilliant and tempt a golfer into taking risks, but the punishments can be great too. The risk-and-reward element is evident at the three short holes on the Composite Course. A skilful golfer can go for the flags, using slopes and a shaped shot to get the ball close to a pin. But the trouble, should you miss the target, is severe because of the large spreads of sand or rough grass and bushes.

Both courses are marvelous tests of ball striking in a wonderfully natural setting where the wind can also play havoc. Put together as the Composite Course, they lose little in charm and style, but gain in pure golfing terms. Little wonder it is the greatest course south of the equator.

The Royal Melbourne clubhouse

The tricky 5th green on the West Course

THE COURSE

Royal Melbourne's Composite Championship Course is an amalgam of the best holes from its two world-beating 18s. Holes weave gracefully over sandy terrain and flit past vast sweeping bunkers and native scrub, and the course plays firm and fast. Such is the strategic nature of the course that it nearly always identifies the best golfers.

THE FRONT NINE ❶ A gentle opener that features just one bunker up by the green. **❷** Once the vast fairway bunker is flown, a birdie is a definite possibility. **❸** A short par-4 but an awkward sloping green tests wedge play. **❹** The raised green tests club selection as much as ball striking. **❺** Benchmark short hole, with dangers on all sides, and a very slopey green. **❻** Long dogleg right. Take on the carry over the traps to leave shorter shot in. **❼** An uphill beauty where most of the trouble is right of the green. **❽** Great risk-and-reward hole—big hitters can take the corner bunker on. **❾** A dogleg left where a drive that flirts with the fairway traps leaves the best line in.

THE BACK NINE ❿ A very tough, long par-4, where a bunker just short of the green catches many. **⓫** A nest of bunkers to the right of the green toy with the eyeline from the right side of the fairway. **⓬** Taking on the massive cluster of sand in the dogleg makes for a much shorter shot in. **⓭** A well-placed long-iron to the corner will leave a good birdie chance. **⓮** Fly the traps and the ball bounds down a hill. A reachable par-5. **⓯** The green is brilliantly guarded at the front by sand. **⓰** A cracking long par-3, where a right-to-left shot is best to get at the flag. **⓱** A line of traps short of the green dictate your strategy—go for it or lay-up. **⓲** Generous off the tee, but a mass of sand surrounds the green. A top finish.

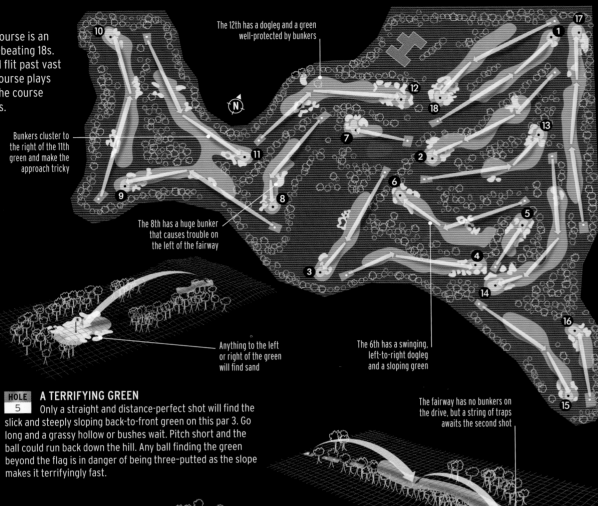

The 12th has a dogleg and a green well-protected by bunkers

Bunkers cluster to the right of the 11th green and make the approach tricky

The 8th has a huge bunker that causes trouble on the left of the fairway

The 6th has a swinging, left-to-right dogleg and a sloping green

Anything to the left or right of the green will find sand

The fairway has no bunkers on the drive, but a string of traps awaits the second shot

HOLE 5 — A TERRIFYING GREEN

Only a straight and distance-perfect shot will find the slick and steeply sloping back-to-front green on this par 3. Go long and a grassy hollow or bushes wait. Pitch short and the ball could run back down the hill. Any ball finding the green beyond the flag is in danger of being three-putted as the slope makes it terrifyingly fast.

Bunkers lie on the right of the dogleg on the fairway

HOLE 12 — A CLEVER DESIGN

This hole typifies Melbourne's clever design. First you have to decide how much of the dogleg you want to cut off. Big hitters can take a direct line over the bunkers on the right and get a kick down the hill, leaving a much shorter shot than someone who has played safe will face. Swathes of sand focus your attention on the approach, which can be flown high or run in through a narrow entrance.

Swathes of sand focus the golfer's attention on the approach

HOLE 17 — A TRICKY DILEMMA

If the drive is long and straight then a golfer faces a dilemma: either go for the green in two by taking on the sand or lay up to leave a short pitch in. The left side of the green is the place to miss, as going right spells real danger, with bunkers, bushes, and Out of Bounds guarding that side.

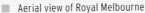
Aerial view of Royal Melbourne

The 7th hole on the West Course

Pinehurst, US

RAMBLING OVER THE FORESTED SANDHILLS of North Carolina, the No. 2 Course at Pinehurst is a design benchmark. Both fun and exasperating, it tests the short game like few other courses in the world. Pinehurst Resort boasts eight terrific 18 holers, but the No. 2 Course wins all the plaudits. Sam Snead once said, "No. 2 has always been number one with me." It is a classic and one from which golf course designers the world over take inspiration.

THE GREEN COMPLEXES at the celebrated No. 2 Course at Pinehurst are a constant source of frustration and a persistent challenge to the imagination.

THE NO. 2 COURSE IS THE HANDIWORK of Donald Ross, a Scotsman who came to live among the tall shady trees of Pinehurst in 1900. By 1907 he had redesigned the fledgling course that was there already, built the No. 2 Course and was on his way to creating the imaginatively named No. 3 and No. 4 courses. For Ross, his "baby" would always be the No. 2 and it became a labor of love.

ROSS'S GIFT TO GOLF

This course has no gimmicky par 3s, no manicured flowerbeds as backdrops, no waterfalls or manmade streams. Simply a collection of excellent and cohesively designed holes that come together to provide golfers with a thorough test. When it finally got grass greens in 1935, in readiness for the 1936 PGA Championship, the course was already up to 6,879 yards (6,290 meters) long, way ahead of its time in length terms. Players could cope with that length because it was fast-running. Little has changed

today, except for adding another few hundred yards, because its defenses are as good and as relevant as ever.

Trouble comes in the form of sandy waste areas, thick Bermuda rough, pine straw on the ground under the lofty pines, and the odd, more formal bunker edged with native wire grass. But fairways are generous, allowing a bit of leeway from the tee. Yet if a golfer is to conquer this course, drives must find the correct side of the fairway so they can attack the flags from the right place. Coming in from the wrong angle makes life hard, as the green complexes can make grown men weep.

The greens and their surrounds are Ross's gift to the world of golf. Most of the greens are raised with mounds and dips all around. They are also studded with bunkers. The greens invite both a low running ball and a high stopping shot, but if the approach is not well executed, shots are tossed away down a shaved bank or fed to a different part of the green.

THE COURSE

Many golf course architects come and study No. 2's intracacies, and players think of it as a mecca too, thanks to its shady nature, gently turning holes and its amazing green complexes that tease allcomers. No one can come to Pinehurst and expect to score well without their "A" short game, such is the severity of the slopes on and around the greens.

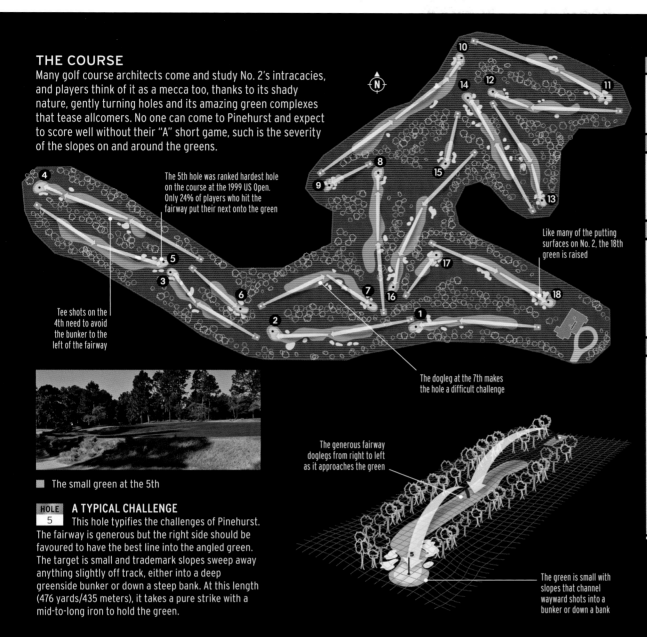

The 5th hole was ranked hardest hole on the course at the 1999 US Open. Only 24% of players who hit the fairway put their next onto the green

Tee shots on the 4th need to avoid the bunker to the left of the fairway

Like many of the putting surfaces on No. 2, the 18th green is raised

The dogleg at the 7th makes the hole a difficult challenge

The generous fairway doglegs from right to left as it approaches the green

The green is small with slopes that channel wayward shots into a bunker or down a bank

The small green at the 5th

HOLE 5 — A TYPICAL CHALLENGE

This hole typifies the challenges of Pinehurst. The fairway is generous but the right side should be favoured to have the best line into the angled green. The target is small and trademark slopes sweep away anything slightly off track, either into a deep greenside bunker or down a steep bank. At this length (476 yards/435 meters), it takes a pure strike with a mid-to-long iron to hold the green.

PINEHURST

1 CAROLINA VISTA DRIVE, VILLAGE OF PINEHURST, NORTH CAROLINA 28374
www.pinehurst.com

THE NO. 2 COURSE

FOUNDED 1907
LENGTH 7,335 yards (6,707 meters)
PAR 70
DESIGNER Donald Ross
COURSE RECORD 66 Peter Hedblom (2005)

SELECTED CHAMPIONS

USPGA CHAMPIONSHIP Densmore Shute (1936).
RYDER CUP US (1951)
TOUR CHAMPIONSHIP Craig Stadler (1991); Paul Azinger (1992)
US OPEN Payne Stewart (1999); Michael Campbell (2005)

CARD OF THE COURSE

THE FRONT NINE			THE BACK NINE		
HOLE	YARDS	PAR	HOLE	YARDS	PAR
1	405	4	10	611	5
2	472	4	11	478	4
3	384	4	12	451	4
4	568	5	13	380	4
5	476	4	14	471	4
6	224	3	15	206	3
7	407	4	16	510	4
8	467	4	17	190	3
9	190	3	18	445	4
OUT	3,593	35	IN	3,742	35

PIN BADGES were worn by members of the Silver Foils, an exclusive club formed by women golfers at Pinehurst in 1909 to fight for equal treatment with the men.

Donald Ross's philosophy is made clear by his 1935 quote after he'd just rebuilt the greens: "This mounding makes possible an infinite variety of nasty short shots that no other form of hazard can call for. Competitors whose second shots have wandered a bit will be disturbed by these innocent appearing slopes and by the shot they will have to invent to recover."

AN ALL-ROUND GAME

As Ross had hoped, the arts of pitching, chipping, and putting are never more challenged than on No. 2. If you have missed one of these "upturned saucer" greens and rolled away down a slippery slope, there are usually three ways to play the next. The high tariff shot is the lob, but get it wrong, and you could be way past the hole or down the other side. You can try the bump and run, which skips up the bank. Or you can take the putter as the slopes around the greens are so closely mown.

Pinehurst's No. 2 Course favors great iron players who have the skill to hit the precise shot into the green, but they must also be great chippers and putters. If you look down the honors boards, a list of legends leaps out at you. Walter Hagen, Ben Hogan, Sam Snead, Byron Nelson, and Jack Nicklaus have all won here.

The best players in the world love No. 2's balance and the fact that for once, the premium is on an all-round game, not just on power and keeping the ball out of the rough. Despite the advance of technology, this brilliant sandbelt course will go on teasing all-comers for years to come. No. 2 is a masterpiece.

KIWI BEATS TIGER

Michael Campbell won the 2005 US Open at Pinehurst by two strokes over Tiger Woods. He used his heath knowledge brilliantly to hold the world's best at bay. He became the second New Zealander, after Bob Charles, to win a Major.

Campbell holds the US Open trophy

Pine Valley, UNITED STATES

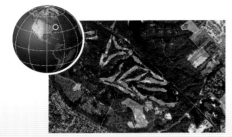

AN OASIS OF CALM AND BEAUTY just 15 miles (24 kilometers) southeast of downtown Philadelphia, Pine Valley is rightly rated the best golf course in the world—an amazing fact when you consider it was the designer's one and only golf course. A punishing mixture of sand, scrub, and pine forest, the course has little room to host Major championships and is home to a private club, so few golfers are able to sample its delights.

A STAGGERING COURSE in every way, Pine Valley came into existence in 1914 thanks to a group of golf-mad businessmen from Philadelphia, one of whom was hotelier George Crump. They chose a wondrous 184-acre (75-hectare) wilderness site in pine-scented sandhills for its natural beauty and obvious golf course potential. Crump was the main mover behind it and he even sold his hotel to help build his dream.

Crump had a noble design philosophy—if at all possible, no consecutive holes should run parallel to each other or play in the same direction. Nor should another hole be seen from the one that was being played. It works brilliantly here. Although Crump died in 1918 before holes 12 to 15 were complete, he had laid down a course of unspeakable splendor, and without doubt a monumental challenge.

BEAUTY AND THE BEAST

The heaving landscape of unkempt sandy scrub houses holes that sweep majestically through the wasteland. There is no margin for error as the scrub acts as the rough that both flanks the fairways and often cuts spectacularly across them, so dividing the holes into islands of green. From the back tees, there is a carry of at least 120 yards (110 meters) to reach safety on every hole, either over the wastes or a shimmering lake. The cross wastes in the fairways are intimidating, too—for example, at the 7th, called "Hell's Half-Acre," the fiendish scrub stretches for over 100 yards (91 meters) and makes reaching this monster par-5 in two a virtual impossibility, given there is another tranche of waste shy of the green.

Undoubtedly Pine Valley's trademark, the waste areas are stunning in their natural devilish state, but are also a huge psychological barrier. Three-time British Walker Cup player Edward Storey summed up the beauty and beast element of the course when he saw the gorgeous and daunting 2nd for the first time: "Tell me, do you chaps play this hole, or do we just photograph it?."

EVERY HOLE AT PINE VALLEY seems to be cut off from every other by quite inpenetrable trees, wasteland, or water. Conquering the greens at some holes is like unlocking the code of a closely guarded secret.

KEY MOMENTS

THE WALKER CUP OF 1936 saw Francis Ouimet, one of America's finest amateurs and the 1913 US Open champion, as non-playing captain. He'd played in the first 8 encounters and led his US side to a record 9th victory in a row against Great Britain and Ireland, winning 10 1/2 to 1 1/2. The second-day singles was a mauling, with GB&I gaining a solitary half point out of the 8 matches.

THE 1985 WALKER CUP was a tight affair until the young Davis Love III beat Peter McEvoy in the singles, winning by 5&4 to put daylight between the two teams. As Love III didn't carry a wood, and hit his 1-iron everywhere, it proved that Pine Valley can be plotted around, not just overpowered. The US won 13-11.

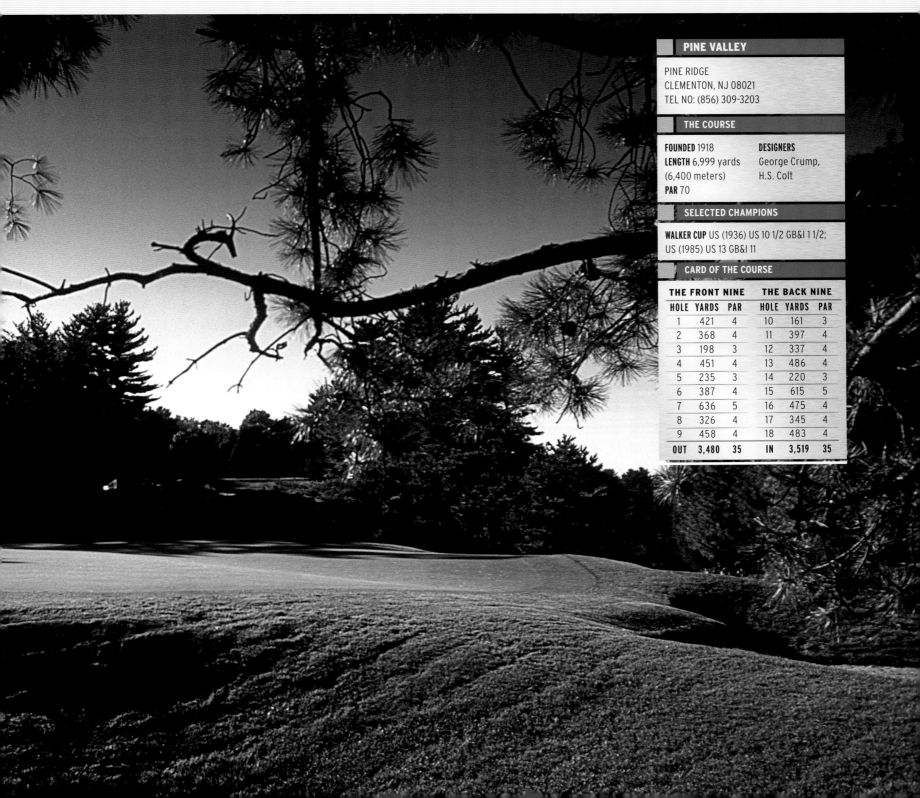

PINE VALLEY

PINE RIDGE
CLEMENTON, NJ 08021
TEL NO: (856) 309-3203

THE COURSE

FOUNDED 1918	**DESIGNERS**
LENGTH 6,999 yards	George Crump,
(6,400 meters)	H.S. Colt
PAR 70	

SELECTED CHAMPIONS

WALKER CUP US (1936) US 10 1/2 GB&I 1 1/2;
US (1985) US 13 GB&I 11

CARD OF THE COURSE

THE FRONT NINE			THE BACK NINE		
HOLE	YARDS	PAR	HOLE	YARDS	PAR
1	421	4	10	161	3
2	368	4	11	397	4
3	198	3	12	337	4
4	451	4	13	486	4
5	235	3	14	220	3
6	387	4	15	615	5
7	636	5	16	475	4
8	326	4	17	345	4
9	458	4	18	483	4
OUT	**3,480**	**35**	**IN**	**3,519**	**35**

▪ The lake at the 14th ▪ The view to the 17th green

▪ The tree-lined 13th green

THE COURSE

Once open scrubland but now shrouded by a dense forest of pines, Pine Valley is an immense challenge, with its tees, fairways, and greens virtual islands amid sandy wastes. A few serene lakes add to its ambience and bite.

The 10th green is small and heavily contoured

The 18th green is large and sloping

3rd green is on the right

An unusual series of sandy ruts line both sides of the fairway

A huge rippled green ensures the terror is not over even if you find it

HOLE 2 — TYPICALLY DANGEROUS

A short but demanding par 4 that typifies Pine Valley's dangers. If you miss the fairway, you can't reach the green in two as a 50-yard (46 meters) stretch of sandy waste sits in front, therefore the approach is all carry. If you find the green, three or even four putts are common.

The 12th is a pitch-and-run hole with a sharp left turn

The 8th fairway is sloping and leads to a tiny green

The 6th fairway doglegs to the right

The 14th green is just about the flattest on the course

The elevated tees are set back in the trees

HOLE 14 — FEARSOME PAR 3

This hole is as difficult as it looks. Anything short will find the lake or, if you are lucky, the sandy "beach" beyond. A strong pull might bound to the back left into the reappearing lake or get tangled in the pines. It is simply a case of finding the green or potentially racking up a big score.

THE FRONT NINE ① A dogleg right with huge traps that hug the inside line. ② Dead straight par 4, with a long row of rutlike bunkers on both sides. ③ A sea of sand makes the green of this par 3 into an island in the wilderness. ④ Fairway cross bunkers force everyone to have at least 150 yards (137 meters) in. ⑤ Terrifying one-shotter over a lake to a green flanked by trouble. ⑥ Great dogleg right, which rewards a bold drive over the waste. ⑦ "Hell's Half-Acre" bunker splitting the fairway in two makes this a genuine three-shot hole. ⑧ Short but awkward hole as the wedge approach needs to be played from a hanging lie. ⑨ Looks intimidating from the tee, but this hole has the widest fairway on course, and the dual green only adds to the intrigue.

THE BACK NINE ⑩ Features a nasty small pot bunker at the front, and more sand nearly all the way around. ⑪ The fairway twists and narrows up by the elevated green. ⑫ A sharp dogleg left. The further you drive down the hole, the more the green opens up. ⑬ Often a swinging right-to-left approach is needed to find the green tucked around a corner. ⑭ Another scary par 3, with water at the front and back left, trees and sand everywhere else. ⑮ A gradually narrowing long uphill par 5 flanked by trees. ⑯ Bolder drives down the right leave the more direct route to the wicked green by a lake. ⑰ A 60-yard (55-meter) sandy waste stretches back from the green so finding the fairway is vital. ⑱ Magnificent finish, with an approach over waste, water, and bunkers.

The green's putting surface is 42 yards (38 meters) long and 34 yards (31 meters) wide

The tee shot demands a carry over scrubland

HOLE 18 — A SPIRITED FINISH

A finishing hole epitomizing Pine Valley's dangers and spirit. The tee shot is generous but potentially horrible if you stray off the short grass as trees, bunkers, and wastes await. The approach is long over a wide stream and a nest of bunkers to a raised and sloping green. The putting surface is large and so finishing with a three putt is always on the cards.

Water hazard along the fairway at the 15th | The elevated green at the one-shot 5th | The small, well-protected 10th green

Although the holes are scary to look at and the trouble is extremely penal, the fairways are generally spacious from the tee—up to 60 yards (55 meters) wide. This doesn't tell the full story, though. To play the holes properly, a golfer has always to decide the best side for approaching the green.

RISKS AND DANGERS

The par-4 6th brilliantly illustrates another decision about how much of a dogleg to chew off. The hole bends right and a waste area hugs the corner. Play the safe drive into the heart of the fairway and the approach is longer than if a bolder line had been taken over the scrub. Risk-and-reward golf at its best. Nearly always the perfect line sails closer to the trouble than the safe way.

Danger envelops the holes all the way up to and around the greens. Nine of the holes feature scrub or bunkers directly in front of the putting surfaces, and a handful are almost completely surrounded by fiendish sand. Those that are not have more formal bunkers around their fringes or, like the 1st, have very steep slopes dropping off into impenetrable trees and shrubs. The only saving grace is that the putting surfaces are huge, but they are deviously contoured, making three-putting a definite possibility.

A FINE MIX OF HOLES

Short, tricky par 4s (although none driveable), long sweeping doglegs, a set of par 3s that will need anything from a 9-iron to a driver to conquer, and two stunning par 5s: Pine Valley has a fine mix of holes, none of which is even remotely weak.

Possibly the only drawback of this mix is that neither of the par-5s are reachable in two. The 7th is 636 yards (582 meters) long and is split by the "Hell's Half-Acre"

waste area, while the 15th hole at 615 yards (562 meters) features a carry over water and a gradually narrowing uphill fairway to a green that sits over 30 feet (9 meters) higher than the tee box.

Perhaps it possesses the most brilliant set of short holes in the world, both scenically and playing wise. Sandy wastes surround the 198-yard (181-meter) 3rd, and the 5th hole is daunting in the extreme, playing a mammoth 235 yards (215 meters) over a pond and scrub to a green that has no safety net.

The 10th hole only requires a short to mid-iron, but the green is small and heavily contoured, with nasty bunkers to protect it. One tiny pot right at the front is so punishing it is called the "Devil's Ass-hole." And finally the 14th, another long par-3 over water and scrub where a carry of about 200 yards (183 meters) is needed to find the front edge of the green.

ONLY THE BEST SURVIVE

It has been said that Pine Valley is an easy course for players to make bogies because many holes are endowed with a safety-first route. Pars and better are much harder to come by because of the risks of a more attacking game. For many years the members bet all newcomers they couldn't break 80 at their first attempt. They made good money, as nearly everyone failed. One notable exception was a fresh-faced Arnold Palmer who visited after winning the 1954 US Amateur. He took on more bets than he could afford, but that spurred him on to shoot a dazzling 68.

Only the best survive the torment, mental anguish, and the pressure placed on the golf game. Great store has been put on the strategic element of the game as well as ball striking, and it is all played out on one of the most glorious but dangerous settings in golf.

SNAPPER SOUP

SEVERAL LAKES FEATURE at Pine Valley —for example, at the 5th, 15th, 16th, and 18th holes. At the 14th the water is as much of an obstacle as sand. Pine Valley's network of lakes not only provides golfers with a challenge on a few holes, but they also teem with turtles. Locals go "snappering," a term for catching them, to make the famous Snapper Soup which is served in the clubhouse.

A turtle in the water

> We build them [bunkers] so high that dub golfers would all break their necks. This is a course for champions and **they never get into trouble**

GEORGE CRUMP, FOUNDER AND DESIGNER

Ocean courses

DRAMATIC, EXHILARATING, AND OFTEN CHALLENGING, ocean courses are a departure from the conventional and excite the senses like almost no other style of course. The sight and sound of crashing waves, the smell of the salty sea, and an emerald fairway leading to a green perched above the foaming waters is a winning combination for every golfer.

◁◁ **PEBBLE BEACH**, which overlooks the Pacific Ocean on the Monterey Peninsula in California, has been the scene of many dramatic tournaments. ◁ **THE SHORE COURSE** at the Monterey Peninsula Country Club near Pebble Beach has a beautiful ocean-front design and was built in 1961 ▽ **THE 11TH HOLE** on the Shore Course at Monterey Peninsula Country Club is exposed to the wind from the Pacific Ocean.

THE FEATURED COURSES in this chapter are categorized as ocean layouts because they are not strictly links courses, even though they are located close to the sea—sometimes perilously so. Aside from Cypress Point on the Monterey Peninsula in California, whose inland holes wind through a sandy waste, these coastal courses feature holes that teeter on the very ocean's edge, most sitting atop rocky cliffs rather than playing through dunes and tall grass. Their playing surfaces, too, are unlike a pure links. Bone-hard fairways are less common and, instead, are usually lusher and more suited to the high ball game.

However, because of their proximity to the open seas, they share one thing with a true links, and that is their susceptibility to the raging ocean winds. When the offshore winds play havoc with the air above the course, the links-style game can come in handy as golfers attempt to keep the ball under the breeze and stop it from careering away.

A STEADY MIND
But it is not just the swing that has to be under control to play these cliffside treats. A golfer's mind must be tuned in to the job in hand to prevent it from succumbing to the waves. Imagine standing beside a rocky precipice with a driver at the ready and standing before you is a craggy inlet of spuming water and the fairway beyond runs tight to the cliff edge. It might look stunning, but it can be intimidating, too. And a wary golfer is not necessarily the best golfer. Negative thoughts creep into your game and can destroy even the best swing.

Ocean holes must be treated with respect, especially if a wind is blowing, but they must be taken on with a positive frame of mind. By all means a golfer should admire the view—for, ultimately, enjoyment of the surroundings is one of the major reasons why we play—but, come action time, the scenery should be put firmly to the back of the mind. Concentration is key.

GREAT HOLES
Of course, top designers cannot just rely on the landscape to do all the talking. They still have to produce great golf holes to back up the drama. But get it right and some holes on ocean courses become the most spectacular and sought-after experiences in golf.

The courses featured in this chapter—from Cape Kidnappers in New Zealand and Casa de Campo in the Dominican Republic to Pebble Beach and Cypress Point in

Imagine standing beside a rocky precipice with a driver at the ready and standing before you is a craggy inlet of spuming water. It might look stunning, but it can be intimidating, too

The Challenge Course at Manele is exactly that—a clifftop spectacular on the tiny island of Lanai in Hawaii, which was once known solely for its vast pineapple fields. Manele's diving fairways were designed by Jack Nicklaus and opened for play in 1993. Bill Gates of Microsoft fame was married on the 12th green. Three holes use the Pacific Ocean as a hazard and the rest of the course cascades over lava outcroppings. The course is raw, wild, and without a single sand dune.

■ Clifftop holes at Manele

VALE DO LOBO golf course has undulating fairways with eucalytpus and pine trees, and stands beside the waters of the Atlantic Ocean in the central Algarve region of Portugal.

California—are all brilliant examples of golfing design. There are world famous challenges throughout their holes, not just on the ones—such as the classic 16th at Cypress Point— that grapple with the ocean's edge.

VARIETY OF STYLE

Stylistically, virtually anything goes, unlike a heathland or a links course. Bunkering does not follow set patterns, the type of rough depends entirely on the native surroundings and the more inland holes interact with many different types of flora. The soil is not necessarily sandy and therefore not hard-running, so the holes can be designed to be more target style. This rich variety of style, mixed in with the undoubted charm of a seaside setting, makes ocean golf a spine-tingling and uplifting test.

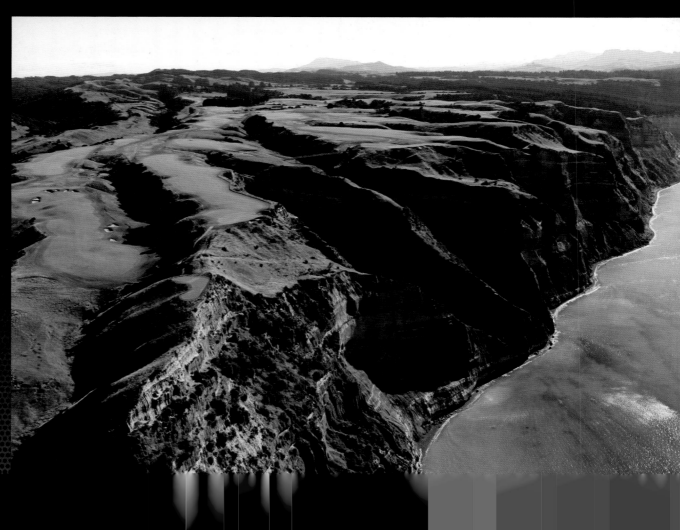

CRAGGY FINGERS OF ROCK above the ocean at Cape Kidnappers in New Zealand provide a weather-beaten location for some of the most dramatic holes in golf.

Cape Kidnappers, NEW ZEALAND

IT IS RARE THAT A MODERN COURSE built within the last decade makes such an impact, but Cape Kidnappers has made so many waves that it has already crashed into the top 30 courses in the world. The course is located on seven craggy, weather-beaten fingers of rock that jut out over Hawkes Bay on the east of New Zealand's North Island, and the holes rock and roll along the spines between the ravines.

SEVERAL HOLES at Cape Kidnappers sit on top of long fingers of land where the cliffs play host to an enormous gannet colony.

"HEADY" AND "INTOXICATING" describe the golf on the Cape Kidnappers course, and not just because some of the holes teeter heroically on the edge of precipitous cliffs or because a 400-feet (122-meter) drop into the Southern Ocean awaits a wayward shot.

The course is brilliant from start to finish, and while the landscape speaks for itself, the design also does some serious talking. It was the brainchild of Julian Robertson, an American hedge fund manager who also owns New Zealand's other star course, Kauri Cliffs in the north. While he was playing golf at Pacific Dunes in Oregon, he was so taken with the course's use of the natural terrain that he enlisted its architect, Tom Doak, to create Cape Kidnappers on his behalf.

OCEANSIDE DRAMA

While some might think that you couldn't go wrong with a property like this, Doak drew the best out of the gnarled terrain and created a variety of holes that not only challenge and excite, but draw wide smiles from all who play them. It opened to wild acclaim in 2003.

It cannot be said that the course starts gently, as a dipping 440-yard (400-meter) par 4 opens up the journey. But in terms of pure oceanside drama, the course only starts to thrill at the 4th, where you play down a winding fairway toward the ocean. The excellently strategic 5th takes you even closer, and then you hit the dangerous 6th, a breathtaking par 3 over a deep gully. To your left is a drop down to the beach way below. A bridge takes you

THE 13TH IS THE SHORTEST HOLE on the course, but its small green right next to the cliffs makes it a little devil. For once, the bunkers on the left are not a bad place to be, considering the alternative.

to the other side and to a green you will have done well to find some 225 yards (206 meters) away.

While the superb and varied front nine only toys with the ocean, the back nine confronts the clifftops sensationally. The 12th hole is aptly named Infinity. Although the cliffs are not directly in play, the green seemingly sits on the very edge of the Earth, as all you can see is the putting surface framed by the glistening waters of the sea and distant hills on the horizon beyond.

A HIGH-CLASS EXAMINATION

Next comes a little beauty, but a stomach churner, too. At only 130 yards (119 meters), the 13th looks like a pushover on paper until you stand on the tee and look left and down and down to the surf way below. Wind is a major factor at Cape Kidnappers, and playing a precise short iron here in a stiff breeze is awkward. Just hope if the shot is heading left it gets down quickly enough to catch one of the four pot bunkers before it joins the whales.

After a deliciously devious short four, the 15th, called Pirate's Plank, comes at you to test nerve and skill to the limit. A long sliver of fairway tiptoes along a flat ridge toward a perilous green 650 yards (594 meters) away. On the right a ravine 60-feet (18-meter) deep awaits a slice. On the left is oblivion. Doak reckons that if a ball disappears over the fence up by the green, it will hit water some 10 seconds later, so precipitous is the drop. Unless you walk to the edge, which is not recommended for those of a nervous disposition, you can't really get a sense of the precarious nature of your position.

Throughout this amazing walk, a golfer encounters all manner of shots, a testament to the designer's skills. Booming drives, long raking irons, knockdown pitches, and imaginative chips that use the significant contours on the greens to filter the ball close—all are part and parcel of the game here. Some bunkers are dastardly and so strategy plays its part, too. It all adds up to a high-class examination of the game, in possibly the world's most spectacular golf setting.

THE COURSE

Laid out on one of golf's most glorious sites and teetering 400 feet (122 meters) above the South Pacific Ocean on rocky promontories, this is escapist golf at its finest. It is as much a sensual journey as it is an exacting modern test which encompasses many unique challenges.

CAPE KIDNAPPERS

448 CLIFTON ROAD, TE AWANGA,
HAWKE'S BAY, NEW ZEALAND
www.capekidnappers.com

THE COURSE

FOUNDED 2003	**PAR** 71
LENGTH 7,137 yards (6,526 meters)	**DESIGNER** Tom Doak

CARD OF THE COURSE

THE FRONT NINE			THE BACK NINE		
HOLE	YARDS	PAR	HOLE	YARDS	PAR
1	440	4	10	470	4
2	540	5	11	224	3
3	205	3	12	460	4
4	544	5	13	130	3
5	420	4	14	348	4
6	225	3	15	650	5
7	453	4	16	500	5
8	182	3	17	463	4
9	403	4	18	480	4
OUT	3,412	35	IN	3,725	36

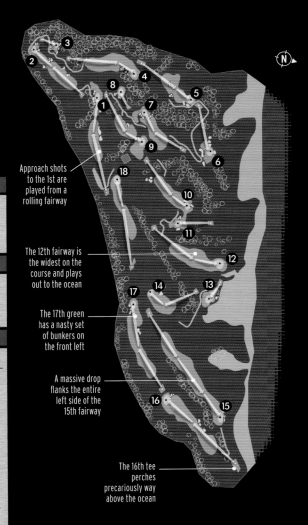

Approach shots to the 1st are played from a rolling fairway

The 12th fairway is the widest on the course and plays out to the ocean

The 17th green has a nasty set of bunkers on the front left

A massive drop flanks the entire left side of the 15th fairway

The 16th tee perches precariously way above the ocean

■ The 7th green on a crest

HOLE 7 — "14 FLAGS"

From the elevated tee with the ocean behind, you can spy 14 greens (the name of the hole is "14 Flags"), but not one of them is the 7th! A heart-in-the-mouth drive over a deep wooded crease to a humpbacked fairway needs all your concentration. A really big drive can reach the summit and tumble down the fairway making the approach much shorter. The green sits on a crest below the level of the fairway and over a manicured gully. A ball going right or long will bound away into trouble.

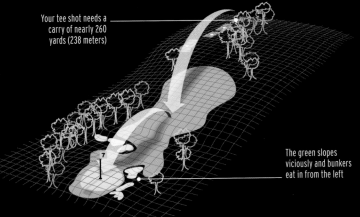

Your tee shot needs a carry of nearly 260 yards (238 meters)

The green slopes viciously and bunkers eat in from the left

Cypress Point, UNITED STATES

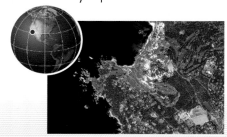

CARVED OUT OF SPARSE WOODLANDS AND DUNES, Cypress Point on California's Monterey Peninsula has been called the "Sistine Chapel of Golf." The course has a certain mystique: before you step onto the springy turf for the first time, adrenalin surges around your body in anticipation for the meeting with golfing heaven. If there's a faint sea mist veiling the crooked cypress trees, then the eerie calm just adds to the expectancy.

CYPRESS POINT OFFERS other-wordly golf on a majestic piece of land jutting out into the Pacific. Many holes tack through stands of cypress trees and dunes that bear whiter-than-white sand. Two holes, the 13th and 14th, sniff the seaside before leading you down to the three most celebrated ocean holes on the planet, played over impossibly beautiful rock-strewn inlets.

Dr. Alister Mackenzie, aided by Marian Hollins, the 1921 US Amateur champion, created the drama and laid out a course that became an emotional journey and a fantastic challenge. Their masterpiece was finished in 1928. Away from the sea, Mackenzie routed the holes superbly using natural sand heaps to funnel the fairways and provide backdrops for his greens, with wavy-edged and white sandy bunkers seemingly climbing up their faces. The bunkering is brilliant—always in the eye line and making a golfer think on every shot.

There is a rugged natural beauty to the inner holes, many ambling over a wooded hillside. Mackenzie's use of sandy waste areas eating into and narrowing fairways is clever and pleasing to the eye. That tactics always play a part with Mackenzie holes is perfectly illustrated at Cypress Point. Perhaps the only exception here is the first of the amazing ocean side holes.

THE 15TH HOLE, the first of the famous clifftop sequence, offers a taste of what's to come. Sitting beyond a narrow cove, the green is protected by bunkers on each side.

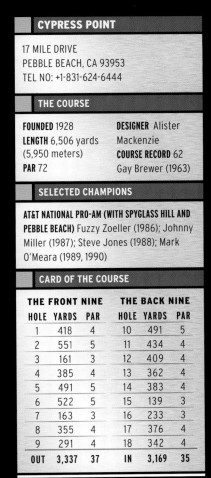

CYPRESS POINT

17 MILE DRIVE
PEBBLE BEACH, CA 93953
TEL NO: +1-831-624-6444

THE COURSE

FOUNDED 1928	**DESIGNER** Alister Mackenzie	
LENGTH 6,506 yards (5,950 meters)	**COURSE RECORD** 62	
PAR 72	Gay Brewer (1963)	

SELECTED CHAMPIONS

AT&T NATIONAL PRO-AM (WITH SPYGLASS HILL AND PEBBLE BEACH) Fuzzy Zoeller (1986); Johnny Miller (1987); Steve Jones (1988); Mark O'Meara (1989, 1990)

CARD OF THE COURSE

THE FRONT NINE			THE BACK NINE		
HOLE	YARDS	PAR	HOLE	YARDS	PAR
1	418	4	10	491	5
2	551	5	11	434	4
3	161	3	12	409	4
4	385	4	13	362	4
5	491	5	14	383	4
6	522	5	15	139	3
7	163	3	16	233	3
8	355	4	17	376	4
9	291	4	18	342	4
OUT	**3,337**	**37**	**IN**	**3,169**	**35**

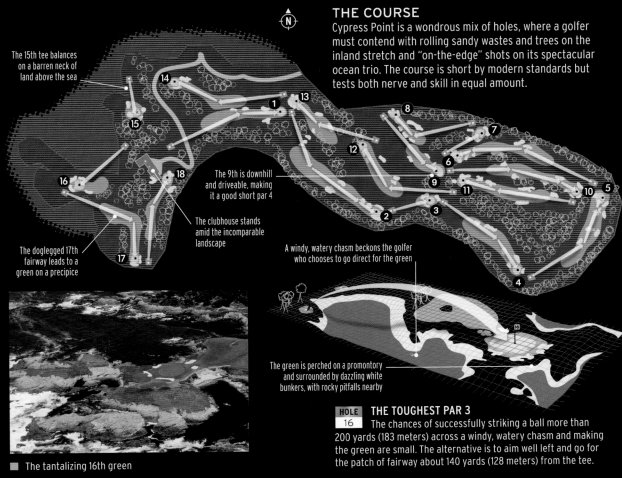

THE COURSE

Cypress Point is a wondrous mix of holes, where a golfer must contend with rolling sandy wastes and trees on the inland stretch and "on-the-edge" shots on its spectacular ocean trio. The course is short by modern standards but tests both nerve and skill in equal amount.

The 15th tee balances on a barren neck of land above the sea

The 9th is downhill and driveable, making it a good short par 4

The clubhouse stands amid the incomparable landscape

The doglegged 17th fairway leads to a green on a precipice

A windy, watery chasm beckons the golfer who chooses to go direct for the green

The green is perched on a promontory and surrounded by dazzling white bunkers, with rocky pitfalls nearby

HOLE 16 THE TOUGHEST PAR 3
The chances of successfully striking a ball more than 200 yards (183 meters) across a windy, watery chasm and making the green are small. The alternative is to aim well left and go for the patch of fairway about 140 yards (128 meters) from the tee.

■ The tantalizing 16th green

Strategy doesn't really come into play at the stunning par-3 15th. You must hit the green or struggle. You need only think of the club, the wind, and the shape of your shot. There's no safe way to play it. The tee balances on a barren neck of land above the turbulent sea; the green nestles over a spiteful, foaming cove, with squiggles of sand all around. Beyond to the right lurk dark, brooding rocks; to the left and beyond, banks of ice plant and twisted cypress taunt you. Both are no-go areas.

What follows is even more frightening. Mackenzie wanted to play the 16th as a two-shotter because of the carry over the cove, but it became a scintillating and dangerous par 3 at Hollins' insistence. Many holes of irrepressible fame are often followed by one that lets you down emotionally. Not so here. Another hole of unspeakable beauty hits you between the eyes.

GNARLED LIMBS AND BUSHY CANOPIES

Among its rocky and sea-swirling charms the 17th is a wonderfully thought-out hole. The tee perches high on a cliff above the waves and the fairway gently arcs around Pacific boulders to a green on a natural promontory. Yet the 17th is dominated by a huddle of gaunt cypresses. Standing proud on the right edge of the fairway some

250 yards (229 meters) from the tee, their gnarled limbs and bushy canopies dictate how the hole is played.

The shortest route to the precarious green is to flirt with the water's edge down the right, but it's dangerous, so most golfers go left to the heart of the fairway. But depending on exactly what line you take and how far the ball has rolled, you are faced with a variety of shots to a green edged with a stone wall and sand. Too safe a line and you face a long shot over the trees. But if the ball runs closer to the trees, blocking the view and line, you must either hit a high one over or shape a shot around the leafy obstacle. Thinking golf at its finest.

After this exhilaration, the 18th is something of an anticlimax. It turns inland and doglegs almost tamely up to the understated wooden clubhouse. But it is a minor blip on an outstanding and unforgettable course.

A LONE WINDSWEPT CYPRESS stands on a cliff overlooking the waters of Monterey Bay. Cypress trees feature throughout most of the holes on the course.

I do not suppose anywhere is there such a **glorious combination** of rocky coast, sand dunes, pine woods, and cypress trees

ALISTER MACKENZIE, COURSE DESIGNER

Pebble Beach, UNITED STATES

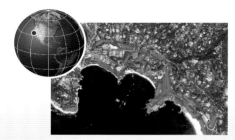

LESS THAN A MILE AWAY FROM CYPRESS POINT as the crow flies, Pebble Beach careers along equally impressive cliffs of the Monterey Peninsula and features nine spellbinding holes that meet head-on the influences of the Pacific. Scene of many heroic tournaments–Jack Nicklaus triumphed here in the club's first US Open in 1972 and Tiger Woods took the 2000 US Open by storm (see pp.238-39)–it holds a special place in the hearts of many golfers.

ANYONE WITH A HANDICAP and a large wallet can play at Pebble Beach, as it is the greatest public course in the world. It was laid out in 1919 by two well-known local amateurs, Jack Neville and Douglas Grant, as part of a major resort complex owned by the Del Monte fruit company. Neville was always modest in his assessment of the course and downplayed his achievement by saying: "It was all there in plain sight. Very little clearing was necessary. The big thing, naturally, was to get as many holes as possible along the bay. It took a little imagination, but not much. Years before it was built, I could see this place as a golf links. Nature had intended it to be nothing else. All we did was cut away a few trees, install a few sprinklers, and sow a little seed."

THE SEASIDE SEQUENCE

It is a testament to how great a job they did that the course remains very much the same to this day. The only major change was a new 5th hole designed by Jack Nicklaus in 1998. For almost 70 years, the owners of a beachfront property had declined to sell so the hole was always played inland. Finally, in 1995, the company managed to acquire the precious land and another superb hole was born. It meant the seaside sequence was now unbroken from the 4th to the 10th. And what a journey those holes are.

The 4th is a short but tricky par-4 with a typically small and sloping green just a few yards from the beach. Nicklaus' 5th hole is a splendid one-shot hole with the beach on the right and pines on the left. It often needs a shaped left-to-right shot in to avoid a front bunker and run up the length of the green. Then you hit the 6th where the old ocean sequence used to start. Lee Trevino once quipped to the gallery on the tee: "If you're five over when you hit this tee, it's the best place in the world to commit suicide." He knew that he was about to begin probably the hardest five-hole run in golf. Even without a wind, the tee shot and second at the

SITTING ON A SMALL ROCKY PROMONTORY just above the waters of the Pacific Ocean, the spectacular green at the famous par-3 7th is surrounded by a ring of bunkers.

KEY MOMENTS

THE GREATEST CHIP EVER came from Tom Watson in the 1982 US Open as he stood just left of the 17th green in ankle-deep rough. He whispered to his caddie, "I'm going to make it," and dropped the clubhead softly in behind the ball. It popped out and rolled gently into the cup for a birdie two. He leaped in the air and ran around the fringe pointing to his caddie mouthing: "I told you." Watson also birdied the last, winning the Championship by two. His incredible chip became known as "The shot that was heard around the world."

TIGER WOODS provided irrefutable evidence at the 2000 US Open that he is one of the best-ever players. His opening 65 was a record for a Pebble Beach US Open. He backed it up with a 69 and a 71, despite a triple bogey, and led after three rounds by 9. Tiger's bogey-free 67 on Sunday blew away the field and he finished at 16 under par and an unbelievable 15 strokes clear–both records for the Championship.

PEBBLE BEACH

17-MILE DRIVE
PEBBLE BEACH, CA 93953
www.pebblebeach.com

THE COURSE

FOUNDED 1919
LENGTH 6,816 yards
(6,232 meters)
PAR 72

DESIGNERS Douglas Grant, Jack Neville
COURSE RECORD 62
David Duval (1997)

SELECTED CHAMPIONS

US OPEN Jack Nicklaus (1972); Tom Watson (1982); Tom Kite (1992); Tiger Woods (2000)
US AMATEUR David Gossett (1999)
AT&T NATIONAL PRO-AM Phil Mickelson (2005, 2007); Arron Oberholser (2006)

CARD OF THE COURSE

THE FRONT NINE			THE BACK NINE		
HOLE	YARDS	PAR	HOLE	YARDS	PAR
1	381	4	10	446	4
2	502	5	11	380	4
3	390	4	12	202	3
4	331	4	13	399	4
5	188	3	14	573	5
6	513	5	15	397	4
7	106	3	16	403	4
8	418	4	17	178	3
9	466	4	18	543	5
OUT	3,295	36	IN	3,521	36

THE CROSBY CLAMBAKE

The AT&T Pebble Beach National ProAm is an annual 72-hole tournament in which 180 professionals pair up with 180 amateurs. Bing Crosby hosted the original event in 1937 at Rancho Santa Fe Golf Club, which is why it is known affectionately as "The Crosby Clambake," or simply "The Crosby." Professionals who have played include Tiger Woods and Phil Mickelson (who won it in 2007), and celebrities include Clint Eastwood and Bill Murray.

■ Celebrity Clint Eastwood

uphill, semiblind and exposed par-5 6th are tough. Any shot veering right will probably disappear over a cliff and sail down to the gushing waters of the Pacific. It does offer birdie chances, but big numbers can be racked up, too. Many would be forgiven for thinking that the tiny par-3 7th is a respite from the rigors of the course, but it has optical properties that make it both dangerous and spectacular (see opposite).

FROM EVIL TO SAVING GRACE

The 8th features a preposterous approach (see panel) and the 9th is equally terrifying and demanding, with a steep cliff down the right side. Anything short or left will probably find the deep gulley, but these are safer options than the ball missing right, which is dead. It is Pebble Beach's most evil hole made harder by the fact that quite often it must be approached with a long iron or wood off a hanging lie.

But just when you think it's got to get easier, the 10th confronts you. Again with ocean cliffs on the right, this time the sloping fairway is patrolled by a large bunker complex on the left at driving distance. There are only 35 yards to play with on the drive and then from another sidehill lie, which wants to push your shots toward the ocean, an approach must avoid the ravine that eats into the front right of the green. The only saving grace is that, if you do go long, a bunker waits at the back to stop the shot from disappearing into a creek.

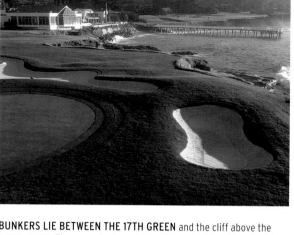

BUNKERS LIE BETWEEN THE 17TH GREEN and the cliff above the ocean waves. The green is shaped like a figure-eight and is a devil to reach when the wind is heading in toward you.

THE JOURNEY HOME

From then on the lush fairways meander through pines and cypress, and it feels a little tame after the thrill of playing above the coastal bluffs. The course reappears by the sea at the quirky-shaped 17th, a par 3 that plays out to the cliffside and the ocean beyond. The angled green is like a narrow figure of 8 that is protected by seven bunkers, including a huge antler-shaped trap across the front. By far and away the most teasing pin position is back left as the cliff awaits a pull just yards away. In 1972, Jack Nicklaus sealed his US Open win with a crunched 1-iron that hit the flagstick and finished inches away.

The risk-and-reward 18th is a great finishing hole (see opposite). Perhaps the most amazing moment it has seen is the miraculous birdie four Hale Irwin made in 1984. He stood one behind leader Jim Nelford at the Bing Crosby Tournament, only to yank his drive left toward the ocean where it hit some rocks and pinged back into play. He reached the play-off, which he duly won.

This is a perfect example of how Pebble Beach toys with emotions. It mixes bravado and brains and taunts you to play the shots of your life.

> If I had **one last round** to play, I would likely **choose Pebble Beach.** I've **loved this course** from the first time I saw it. It's possibly the **best in the world**

JACK NICKLAUS

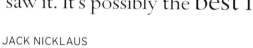

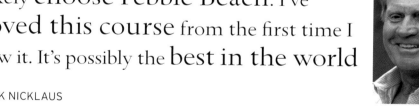

■ The 6th, 7th, and 8th holes on a peninsula

■ The shoreside 10th hole

■ The demanding 9th hole

THE COURSE

Away from the ocean, fairways sweep through pines and cypress trees and are splashed with white sand, but it is the amazing Pacific stretch that draws golfers to its cliffs. Even on a calm day, the seaside holes are tough, but given a stiff ocean wind, they can tear you apart.

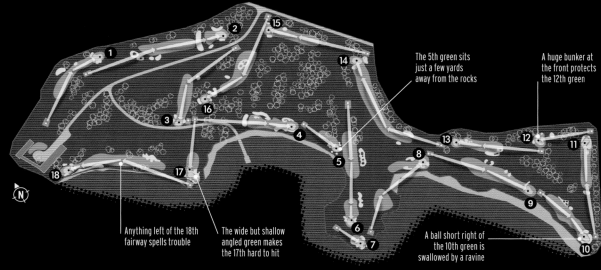

The 5th green sits just a few yards away from the rocks

A huge bunker at the front protects the 12th green

Anything left of the 18th fairway spells trouble

The wide but shallow angled green makes the 17th hard to hit

A ball short right of the 10th green is swallowed by a ravine

THE FRONT NINE ❶ A gentle dogleg right. Aim to drive short of the fairway trap on the left. ❷ Deep gorge 75 yards (68 meters) short of the green dictates strategy. ❸ Right-to-left shot from the tee to hug the contours of this dogleg. ❹ Precise short-iron approach to find small, sand-surrounded green. ❺ To get at a back flag position, a left-to-right shot is best, even though it shapes toward the cliff. ❻ The semiblind second onto the fairway needs total confidence as the ocean awaits right. ❼ Great one-shotter where wind and concentration are key. ❽ Very dramatic approach shot high over an ocean inlet. ❾ Best to aim just inside of the fairway bunker left and let the natural fall of the land move your drive into the center.

THE BACK NINE ❿ Bold approach to carry the ravine eating into the front right of the green. ⓫ Difficult to judge approach on this uphill hole going back inland. ⓬ All carry to a shallow green as a huge bunker front left leaves little room for a run-up shot. ⓭ Very difficult to get approach close as it plays uphill to a seriously sloping and fast green. ⓮ Tempting to carry bunker in the corner of the dogleg right, but best to play it as a three-shotter. ⓯ A decent carry is needed, then a pinpoint approach to green sloping right-to-left. ⓰ Aim directly over bunker in mid-fairway. Hit approaches right of the flag as green is sloping. ⓱ Pray it is not into wind, as it becomes a monster three with a very shallow angled green. ⓲ Best line is just to left of tree in fairway. Play as a three-shotter, as trouble lurks all down the left.

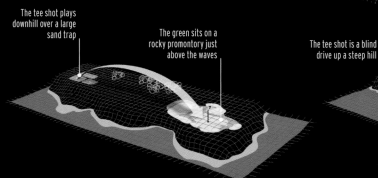

The tee shot plays downhill over a large sand trap

The green sits on a rocky promontory just above the waves

HOLE 7 — A LITTLE DEVIL

This downhill par 3 is a photographer's dream. It's the shortest hole in Major championship golf, but still a little devil. You are wary of hitting too far as all you can see behind the green is ocean, so you may underhit your tee shot. Optical effects can play with the brain and the swing, especially when a wind is blowing. If it's breezy it is best to take more club than you think and swing within yourself to keep the ball lower and under control.

HOLE 18 — A CRACKING DRIVE

It is not time to be greedy on the drive as the ocean hugs the entire left side of the arcing dogleg. But don't be tempted to bail out right either, as Out of Bounds awaits. Aim at the tree in the fairway, and a good crack should see the drive past the obstacle. It is often best to lay quite well back from the green and take your chances with the third. It will also lessen the risk of the huge tree short right of the green coming into play.

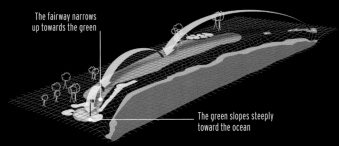

The tee shot is a blind drive up a steep hill

The green has an awkward putting surface that sits 60 feet (18 meters) above the waves

HOLE 8 — A THRILLING PROSPECT

The adrenalin rush you experience as you walk up the hill after your drive is extraordinary, as the sight that greets you is eye-popping. A few yards ahead, the fairway ends then the hole swings sharply right and swoops downward across a steepling cliff to a small green hemmed in by sand. You have to hit the green with a long iron or fairway wood as you can easily face a shot of more than 200 yards (183 meters) from the top fairway.

The fairway narrows up towards the green

The green slopes steeply toward the ocean

■ The dangerous 7th hole

■ The eye-popping 8th hole

■ The ocean-hugging 18th hole

Casa De Campo, DOMINICAN REPUBLIC

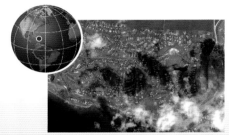

THE LOCALS CALL THE SERRATED CORAL REEFS that sprout from the sea the Dientes del Perro (Teeth of the Dog) because of their jagged and menacing nature. It was the perfect name for this oceanside course that has serious bite and where the golf is heavily influenced by the sea. The Teeth of the Dog is the jewel in the crown of a vast playground on the Dominican Republic and is ranked as the best course in the Caribbean.

A MAMMOTH COURSE

There are two other courses designed by Pete Dye on the site of the Casa de Campo resort, which is set over 7,000 acres (2,833 hectares). These are the Links Course and the Dye Fore Course, which is the latest creation—it measures a mammoth 7,770 yards (7,105 meters) long and follows the Chavon River to where it flows out into the ocean.

■ Course designer Pete Dye

PETE DYE'S TREACHEROUS Teeth of the Dog Course boasts an astonishing seven holes along the jagged water's edge. On each of them, a golfer is so close to the sea and barely above the waves that they can feel the sea spray brushing over them as they play.

It might look like this southern Dominican coastline was born for golf, but when the architect first clapped eyes on this land from the air, he was filled with doubt. It was a barren strip of ground and the sea's edge was just a jumble of encrusted coral. It wasn't until Dye got his feet on terra firma and strode along the shore that he found ready-made inlets and small bays that would be the perfect length for some stunning golf holes. He still maintains to this day that he created 11 holes and "the man upstairs laid out the other seven."

That was in 1969. It took two years to build, mostly by hand. A few tractors trailing heavy metal bars smoothed the jagged coral after it had been pickaxed. Then cartload by cartload of topsoil was brought in from the mountains and painstakingly spread by hand. Three hundred local workers maneuvered the soil to form Dye's trademark mounds and pot bunkers. Tees were built on rocky outcrops and small rippled greens were pushed as close to the ocean as they dare. Even the seed was scattered by hand and palms were planted in strategic positions.

OCEAN HOLES

The inland holes sneak through stands of palm and long patches of sandy waste bunkers flank the fairway. They are great holes in their own right, but it is the ocean holes everyone remembers and craves to play. After four holes to whet the appetite you arrive at the seaside nervous but excited. The 5th is the first of three staggering par 3s by the ocean. It may only be 157 yards (143 metres) but an inlet cuts in between the tee and green and there is

nowhere to go aside from the green. If the wind is whistling in from the ocean on the left, it is a confident golfer who can aim out to sea and hope for the breeze to bring their ball back toward the green.

The same goes at the 6th and the very demanding 7th. At 229 yards (210 meters) from the back tee, the 7th is just about the scariest proposition on the whole course, although an arc of sand rings the left side of the green and catches the slightly wayward shot. Just to add variety, the short 16th plays back along the shore the other way so that the ocean is on the right. Dye was clever here too, placing four magnetic bunkers on the left of the green to catch those players erring too much on the side of caution.

INDIVIDUAL AND MEMORABLE

That is the theme with the ocean holes. All tee shots are intimidating and require a pure strike, but they are not impossible. A properly thought out and well-executed shot will find the short grass, but a wayward shot will find trouble. If you miss the fairways or greens, then the landside of the holes is the lesser of the two evils. But Dye has put in enough danger so that if you land safe but wide of the target, you'll have some tricky escape shots.

It would have been easy for Dye to be repetitive as the ocean terrain is so similar, but he has varied the lengths of the holes and the subtleties of the green complexes and hazards so well that each feels individual and memorable. But then again, no one ever forgets the Teeth of the Dog —it would be impossible. Nowhere in world golf have so many holes been directly influenced by the ocean, which is so close to play as to be disturbing and yet inspiring.

THE WATERS OF THE CARIBBEAN break on an encrusted coral shoreline from which seven holes on the remarkable Teeth of the Dog Course have been fashioned.

This course will come **out of nowhere**, and it will **throw you down** and **stomp on your head**

CASA DE CAMPO

LA ROMANA, DOMINICAN REPUBLIC
www.casadecampo.com.do

TEETH OF THE DOG COURSE

FOUNDED 1969   **PAR** 72
LENGTH 7,471 yards   **DESIGNER** Pete Dye
(6,831 meters)

SELECTED CHAMPIONS

**1974 EISENHOWER TROPHY (WORLD AMATEUR TEAM
CHAMPIONSHIPS)** US (George Burns, Gary
Koch, Jerry Pate, Curtis Strange)
**1974 ESPIRITO SANTO TROPHY (WOMEN'S WORLD
TEAM C'SHIPS)** US (Cynthia Hill, Debbie
Massey, Carol Semple-Thompson)

CARD OF THE COURSE

THE FRONT NINE			THE BACK NINE		
HOLE	YARDS	PAR	HOLE	YARDS	PAR
1	404	4	10	405	4
2	390	4	11	604	5
3	551	5	12	483	4
4	489	4	13	201	3
5	176	3	14	497	5
6	501	4	15	374	4
7	229	3	16	204	3
8	414	4	17	463	4
9	602	5	18	484	4
OUT	3,756	36	IN	3,715	36

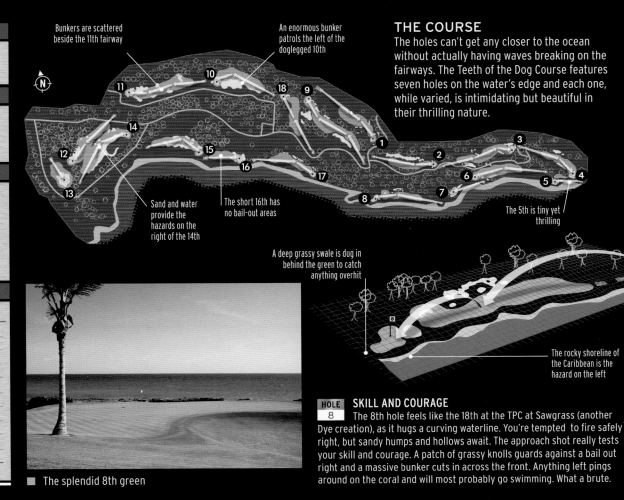

Bunkers are scattered beside the 11th fairway

An enormous bunker patrols the left of the doglegged 10th

Sand and water provide the hazards on the right of the 14th

The short 16th has no bail-out areas

The 5th is tiny yet thrilling

A deep grassy swale is dug in behind the green to catch anything overhit

The rocky shoreline of the Caribbean is the hazard on the left

The splendid 8th green

THE COURSE

The holes can't get any closer to the ocean without actually having waves breaking on the fairways. The Teeth of the Dog Course features seven holes on the water's edge and each one, while varied, is intimidating but beautiful in their thrilling nature.

HOLE 8
SKILL AND COURAGE

The 8th hole feels like the 18th at the TPC at Sawgrass (another Dye creation), as it hugs a curving waterline. You're tempted to fire safely right, but sandy humps and hollows await. The approach shot really tests your skill and courage. A patch of grassy knolls guards against a bail out right and a massive bunker cuts in across the front. Anything left pings around on the coral and will most probably go swimming. What a brute.

Mountain courses

MOUNTAIN GOLF IS INVIGORATING AND BREATHTAKING, quite literally at times, depending on the altitude. Yet golfing in the world's highest places isn't what it seems. It's impossible to craft a course on steep, uncompromising slopes, yet through valleys between peaks or over lofty plateaus is possible, and makes for fabulous golf in staggering surroundings.

△ **KANANASKIS COUNTRY GOLF COURSE** is located in boreal forest high up in the spectacular Rocky Mountains of Canada. ◁◁ **THE LLAO LLAO COURSE** is overlooked by mountains and is framed between two lakes in the Nahuel Huapi National Park in Argentina. ◁ **THE MÉRIBEL GOLF COURSE** is set in an alpine landscape of the Trois Vallée region in France, which is normally associated with skiing.

WHAT VIRTUALLY all "mountain" courses have in common is the beauty or ruggedness of their backdrops. Smacking a drive off an elevated tee that arcs gracefully against the distant pinnacles is a never to be forgotten experience.

The most famous mountain regions for golf include the Alps, where places such as Seefeld Wildmoos and Eichenheim in Austria, Chamonix in France and Crans Sur Sierre in Switzerland. They all provide incredible scenery to go with their courses as they wind through pines and birch and are criss-crossed with streams.

The Rocky Mountains of Canada and the USA hold many superb examples of mountain golf, too – from Whistler in British Columbia through Jasper, Kananaskis, and

Banff in Alberta and all the way down to Colorado, where you will find internationally acclaimed courses such as Redlands Mesa and Castle Pines.

Further off the beaten track, mountain golf excites both locals and intrepid visitors. In Argentine Patagonia tourists delight in the lakeside Llao Llao resort near Bariloche with the steepling Andes behind. And Royal Thimpu in Bhutan, at 2,350 metres (7,710 feet) above sea level, entertains royalty and Buddhist monks alike among the barren Himalayas.

MOUNTAIN CONDITIONS
While these are just a few examples of where mountain golf is played, the terrain is very different. The alpine and Canadian Rockies'

courses disappear under a blanket of snow for 6 months, not just limiting game time but giving the greenkeepers headaches, too. Their playing surfaces tend to be green and lush, and will rarely get dry and fast even in the warmest of summers. While at others further south in the Rockies the air tends to be thin and dry, making the courses run faster. Their conditions are more desert-like, which means the fairways are watered regularly and can provide a stark contrast to the craggy barren surroundings.

Yet wherever you play mountain golf you will find two unique aspects. Firstly, because of the sheer size of the backdrops, judging distance is extremely difficult. Even though many holes are framed by pines and birch, they are dwarfed by the

LUSH JUNGLE VEGETATION, winding ravines, cascading waterfalls, and huge sand bunkers make the Ko'olau Course in Oahu, Hawaii, a breathtaking challenge.

mountain peaks and a sense of scale is hard to achieve. Add to that the fact that some holes change elevation quite dramatically at times so you are playing downhill or off a sidehill lie, clubbing becomes even trickier.

ALTITUDE EFFECTS
However, the single most unique aspect of playing mountain golf is the altitude and the remarkable effect it has on the ball. The air is thin, making the ball travel further – and at high altitudes, much further. As a general rule you should add 10 percent to the distances you hit each club. For example, if you usually strike a 5-iron

THE GLACIER-FED WATERS of the Kananaskis River flow beside the 4th hole on the Mount Kidd Course at Kananaskis Country Golf Club near Calgary, Canada. The spectacular mountain course was designed by Robert Trent Jones. One of the limestone peaks in the stunning mountain backdrop to the course is known appropriately as The Wedge.

160 yards (146 metres), it will travel more like 176 yards (161 metres) at altitude. The difference becomes more marked the longer club you take. For example, a normal 270-yard (247-metre) driver will probably go almost 300 yards (275 metres) with a similar strike.

While that can be quite flattering, it doesn't necessarily mean you will play better. Hitting it further into trouble is not what you want. In any case, course designers are well aware the effect altitude has on shots and build golf holes accordingly. While the par 3s are not made much longer (in relative terms shorter clubs don't go as far) some par 5s are stretched massively to stop them from being overpowered. At Castle Pines in Colorado, home of The International tournament on the PGA Tour, the 1st is 644 yards (590 metres) long on a course that measures a whopping 7,619 yards (6,967 metres) from the professional tees.

As far as hazards go, they can be just about anything, although water tends to feature on many mountain courses. Because valleys are easier than mountainsides to build courses on, you will often encounter snaking rivers and babbling streams as well as lakes. This is particularly true in the glacial regions where seasonal snow and ice melt contributes to the flow. The presence of an icy and rocky river winding through a course only adds to the beauty of the scene, and holes can interplay with the waters wonderfully well.

Mountain golf is a treat. The air is clean and fresh and the scenery undeniably gorgeous. And for once it is gratifying to be able to drive as far as Tiger Woods. It's an uplifting experience all round.

AMID SNOW-CAPPED PEAKS, majestic conifers, and mountain lakes Arnold Palmer designed the distinctive Whistler Course in British Columbia, Canada, and made it into a unique golfing experience.

Banff Springs, CANADA

GOLF COURSES ARE OFTEN CRITICIZED for not harmonizing with the landscape and being an artificial setting–by non-golfers obviously. But here at Banff Springs in the mind-blowing Rocky Mountains, you would have to be hard of heart to disapprove of the golf course and its wondrous setting where elk are allowed to wander the plains and golfers must sometimes wait for a stag and his entourage to pass by before driving.

BANFF SPRINGS OWES its existence to the Canadian Pacific railway. In 1929 the railroad company asked Stanley Thompson to design a golf course fit for the best players in the world. He had already built one for a rival company at Jasper, 150 miles (240 kilometers) away.

Thompson went to extravagant lengths to create this gem at Banff, with the railroad bringing in vast amounts of topsoil to help with the shaping and grooming. It cost the princely sum of $1 million—at the time the most expensive course ever built. But it was worth every cent.

Aside from changing the hole sequences around in the late 1980s to accommodate a new clubhouse, a relaying of the greens, and some bunker work, the course has remained much as it was for almost 80 years.

A STRATEGIC BEAUTY

Since the panorama is so spectacular and the river so captivating, what players should see from the tee looking down each golf hole needs to be eye-catching as well. Thompson did that perfectly. His bunkering style is legendary and similar to Alister Mackenzie's. His freeform wavy-edged traps dominate a player's thinking. Long, lazy sweeps of sand are tucked in at the corner of doglegs, and nests of traps need to be carried to get the best line into the greens. On the par 5s the odd bunker toys with a lay-up shot, and every green is well-guarded, many heavily so. All the trouble is visible. Thompson left nothing to chance and Banff is a strategic beauty.

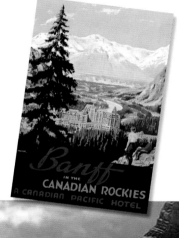

THE GRANDIOSE Scottish baronial style of the Banff Springs Hotel, which was built in 1887/8, set the tone for the golf course.

A LOCAL RULE reads: "Any shot striking an elk may be replayed with no penalty." The advice for players facing a bear looking for food is do not run, but retreat slowly.

The front nine gets its name, Rundle, from the mountain overshadowing it (and the back nine is named after Mt. Sulphur). Thompson's men blasted out rock at the base of it so the holes could play as close as possible to the towering face. The superb one-shot 2nd and the fabulous arcing par-5 3rd play toward the mountainside. So dominating is its sheer presence that correct clubbing is virtually impossible by eye alone. You have to trust the yardage and take the altitude into account.

A CHARMING VARIETY OF HOLES

The holes move further away from the face of Mt. Rundle until gracefully they reach the river at the 8th. Standing just yards away from the impossibly blue waters of Bow River, you must take your eyes off the scene and concentrate on finding the green over a small lake. The next six holes, separated from the river's edge by stands of pine and spruce, are charming in their variety: a reachable par 5 with a green 15 yards (14 meters) from the stream, two juicy par 3s and three very testing par 4s.

The 14th is one of Thompson's finest. The perfect line is to fly the nest of sand on the left, a hit of 255 yards (233 meters) that leaves a clear sight of the green. Going right of the bunkers means a long approach over an imposing set of traps until just shy of the green. A strategic masterpiece, it is a wonderful sight too, as you play directly toward the grand old hotel 130 feet (40 meters) above, framed by the pines of Mt. Sulphur.

Banff's finishing stretch befits a course so at one with nature. They all play toward the distant snow dappled range and the course climaxes with a roaring dogleg par-5. Even if a birdie eludes you, the scenery and the quality of the course leaves everyone thirsting for more.

BANFF SPRINGS NESTLES at the bottom of Bow River Valley and is overshadowed by majestic peaks, including Mt. Rundle and Mt. Sulphur.

THE COURSE

The wondrous Rocky Mountains may dominate the skyline but the course is a star in itself. Flirting with the Bow River and snaking through pines and past clever curving bunkers, Banff Springs is a fabulous walk as well as a fine strategic test of golf. Its many optical illusions are cunning and it's the benchmark mountain course.

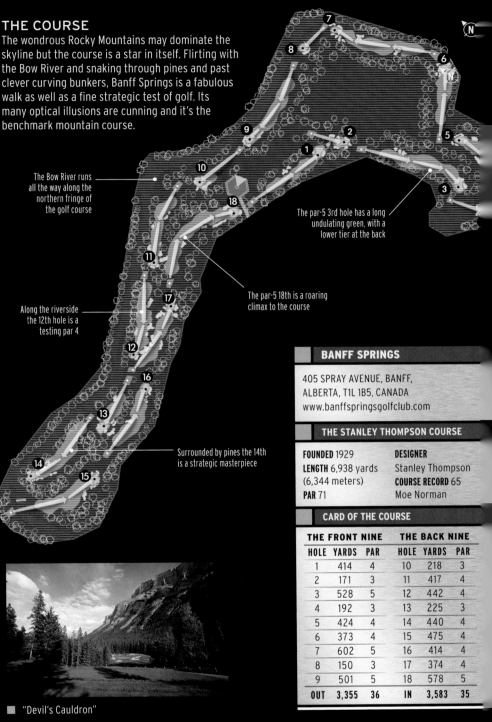

The Bow River runs all the way along the northern fringe of the golf course

The par-5 3rd hole has a long undulating green, with a lower tier at the back

The par-5 18th is a roaring climax to the course

Along the riverside the 12th hole is a testing par 4

Surrounded by pines the 14th is a strategic masterpiece

BANFF SPRINGS
405 SPRAY AVENUE, BANFF, ALBERTA, T1L 1B5, CANADA
www.banffspringsgolfclub.com

THE STANLEY THOMPSON COURSE

FOUNDED 1929	**DESIGNER**
LENGTH 6,938 yards	Stanley Thompson
(6,344 meters)	**COURSE RECORD** 65
PAR 71	Moe Norman

CARD OF THE COURSE

THE FRONT NINE			THE BACK NINE		
HOLE	YARDS	PAR	HOLE	YARDS	PAR
1	414	4	10	218	3
2	171	3	11	417	4
3	528	5	12	442	4
4	192	3	13	225	3
5	424	4	14	440	4
6	373	4	15	475	4
7	602	5	16	414	4
8	150	3	17	374	4
9	501	5	18	578	5
OUT	**3,355**	**36**	**IN**	**3,583**	**35**

"Devil's Cauldron"

HOLE 4 **"DEVIL'S CAULDRON"** Unquestionably in the top 10 most recognizable par 3s in golf, the 4th defies words. The almost sheer face of Mt. Rundle seemingly crashes into the pines directly behind the punchbowl green, which sits behind a glacial lake. The water's eerie mottled look is down to the boulders that litter the bottom of the pond. From the elevated tee it is a wondrous sight if not a little disturbing, because the deep dell is enclosed by trees and is often shadowed by the massive mountain above. It takes an exacting strike with a mid-to-long iron to find the green, and a par is one to cherish.

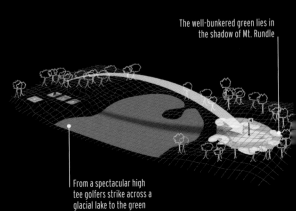

The well-bunkered green lies in the shadow of Mt. Rundle

From a spectacular high tee golfers strike across a glacial lake to the green

Desert courses

AS A RULE DESERT GOLF IS SOME OF THE MOST IMAGINATIVE on the planet, simply because the courses run over a vast nothingness and the designers can run riot with their designs. Some of the scenery is spellbinding and the golf, although inevitably target-style due to the lush manicured surfaces, can be of the highest order.

◁◁◁ **THE GOLF CLUB SCOTTSDALE** lies in the Sonoran Desert in Arizona. ◁◁ **AN EYE-CATCHING** water feature dominates the 18th hole of the Raptor Course at Grayhawk at Scottsdale, Arizona. ◁ **THE COURSE** at Desert Forest at Carefree, Arizona, is one of the first desert designs. ▽ **GRAND SAGUARO CACTI** stand like sentries over the holes at Troon North in the Sonoran Desert in Arizona.

THE FIRST DESERT COURSES, mostly in the Middle East, were rough-and-ready affairs where grass was nowhere to be seen. The greens, or browns as they are known, were leveled out patches of oiled sand that were brushed after a group had been through. A player would either tee up all over the course or carry a

THE WATERBOUND GREEN of the 17th, called "Devil's Drink", is a feature of the Talon Course at Grayhawk Golf Club in Scottsdale, Arizona.

small mat to play from. As water management became increasingly clever, grass courses started to spring up like oases.

Today, there are fantastically lush and beautiful desert golf courses, particularly in California, Nevada, Utah, New Mexico, and Arizona, with a few in Qatar, Bahrain, Egypt, the United Arab Emirates, and Oman. The courses of the Middle East are carved out of shifting sand dunes, but the hundreds of desert courses in the

HEAVILY CONTOURED SAND TRAPS around the 7th hole threaten golfers from all directions on the Faldo Course at the J.W. Desert Ridge Resort near Phoenix, Arizona.

US are laid out over rocky landscapes dotted with native cacti and scrub. All are artificial as soil was brought in and the grass is constantly watered.

No golf course is allowed to have more than 90 acres (36 hectares) of grass. This creates dramatic scenery, where thin ribbons of green are in stark contrast to the inhospitable environment they meander through. Boulders, cacti, and thorny scrub make up the rough, and within the wilderness, "critters" such as coyote, scorpions, and rattlesnakes lurk.

THE WATER ISSUE

Water is a more complex issue in the main desert course areas of the US. In the Greater Phoenix/Scottsdale area of Arizona, probably the most famous desert golf region of the world, there are more than 3 million people and over 150 golf courses.

The average yearly rainfall is 8.3 inches (210 millimeters), so most of the water comes via pipelines and canals from the mountains to the north of the valley, siphoned from the Salt and Verde Rivers that carry the snow melt out to the Gulf of California. Golf courses also have reservoirs, and many pump treated used water onto the courses. But there are strict building regulations to lessen the amount of water needed.

AMERICAN LAYOUTS

The Scottsdale courses ramble through the Sonoran Desert, which is famous for its saguaro cacti. These

spiny, fluted, columnlike growths can reach over 25 feet (7.5 meters) tall and some are 200 years old. They make a bizarre backdrop and hazard for the golfer. The courses at Troon and at Desert Mountain are brilliant examples of Sonoran desert layouts, punctuated by a mass of eerie saguaro and using the rocky and undulating topography superbly.

Elsewhere in the US, where the deserts are far less contoured and have no iconic vegetation, the recent

This creates dramatic scenery. Boulders, cacti, and thorny scrub make up the rough, and within the wilderness, "critters" such as coyote, scorpions, and rattlesnakes lurk

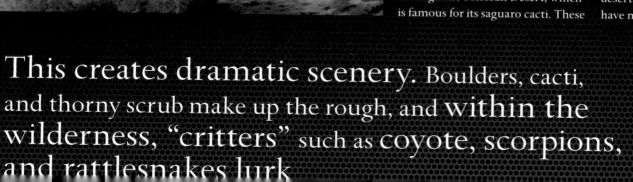

trend has been to build courses like oases. From flat, featureless land designers create lush and exotically landscaped environments.

The two best examples are Shadow Creek and Cascata Golf Clubs outside Las Vegas, Nevada. Both were built by casino groups and no expense was spared. Masses of earth was moved and shaped, allowing the designers to let their imaginations go wild.

The Cascata course cost around $60 million and features a 420-foot (128-meter) long cataract that cascades down the artificial hillside and even runs through the middle of the clubhouse. This is opulence in true Las Vegas style.

GOLFERS ON THIS DESERT COURSE in Namibia can play on grass, but only on the tees and greens, otherwise they have to tee up on the composite clay fairways.

Emirates, DUBAI

HOME OF THE DUBAI DESERT CLASSIC on the European Tour, this desert wonder set the standard for grass courses in the Persian Gulf, when it sprang to life in 1988. Known locally as the "Desert Miracle," it winds its way over sand dunes and through palm trees and spiky grass. Named after the Arabic word for meeting place, the Majlis Course rose from the desert thanks to His Highness General Sheikh Mohammed bin Rashid Al Maktoum.

COURSE SPECIALIST

Ernie Els first played on the Emirates Course in the Dubai Desert Classic of 1993. In his 40 competitive rounds here, he has never signed for an over par score. He is a staggering 157 under par with a stroke average of 68.05. Out of 10 starts, his worst finish is 8th place in 1993. He has 8 top three finishes, including three wins, to his name.

Ernie Els's 2nd shot to the 13th

WHEN ALL AROUND IS AN ENDLESS, scorching desert of wind-whipped sand dunes, and the only water is the saltiness of the Persian Gulf, it is no mean feat to build a world-class golf course. But despite the natural problems surrounding the Emirates Golf Club, they managed to fashion an emerald stunner from the uncompromising landscape.

The Sheikh, who is Crown Prince of Dubai and the Minister of Defense of the UAE, realized there was a niche for a grass golf course and one that his nation would be proud to offer the world. So he asked American architect Karl Litten to build him a pedigree course, the first grass layout in the Gulf.

At first it was a problem finding suitable land, not because there wasn't any desert to build on—there were miles and miles of emptiness—but because each time a particular site was chosen, local Bedouin tribesmen complained that they would be encroaching on ancient camel-grazing routes.

Eventually, the Sheikh himself donated a rectangular parcel of his own land 13 miles (21 kilometers) south west of the Old City and only 2 miles (3.2 kilometers) from the ocean. Its 190 acres (77 hectares) had a solitary tree and large undulating dunes. Nothing was around it, unlike today, now that it has been engulfed by the rapid expansion of the city.

A MILLION GALLONS A DAY

Litten immediately encountered problems. Although given a blank canvas, it seemed like every time his team marked out the holes with poles over the dunes, they had all but disappeared the next day under the shifting sands. So he decided to water them in the hope that they would stabilize. They did exactly that, but there was also a welcome by-product of the irrigation.

Suddenly, as if waiting for centuries to come to life, camel grass, date palms, coconut palms, flame trees and petunias erupted from the desert floor. With some extra

planting, the course took on a magical oasis feel. They used the excess desalinated water from an aluminum plant, and even now more than a million gallons a day are pumped on to the course to keep it in the pristine condition it is known for.

The conditioning is incredible given its geography, but the design is also fabulous with an excellent mix of gently rolling holes. There seems to be a natural balance to the holes that ask different questions at every turn, and no two similar holes follow each other. Water plays a big part on the course, as a network of lakes means that 10 holes feature a shot that contends with a pond. Some holes, however, are more affected than others. Water eats into the right side of the short 4th and makes a real nuisance of itself at the long par-4 9th. Those two, along with the 18th, are probably the most affected.

The pick of the holes on the front nine are the 8th and 9th. The 8th is a desert classic. It swings right and uphill to an elevated green in front of the unusual halfway house. Flanking the fairway is nasty scrub: if a golfer tries for the perfect line up the right side, it only takes a slight miscue to find the camel grass and palms. The desert floor is hard packed, but escaping the scrub from anywhere on the course can be a problem.

PLENTY OF BIRDIE OPPORTUNITIES

The iconic holes on the back nine are the 10th and 18th. Both reachable par 5s, they can define a round. Although the 10th is in range with two huge hits, the green is almost completely ringed by a wiggly-edged bunker, so that the ball has to be flown all the way.

Emirates ends with a risk-and-reward par 5. A long 90-degree dogleg from right to left means that anyone aiming for the green in two has to take the corner on and hope they skip the clinging Bermuda rough onto the fairway. The players then face a long shot in over a glistening lake to a wide but shallow green. There is a fine line between winning and losing the tournament on this hole. In 1996 Colin Montgomerie played the European Tour's Shot of the Year on the 72nd hole with a driver off the fairway over the lake to win the championship. But a year later, needing only a par to win, Ian Woosnam dunked his third-shot wedge into the water and blew his chance.

There is no denying the Majlis is a benchmark desert dune course, and the professionals love it. It is eminently fair and always in immaculate condition, and of course there seems to be plenty of birdie opportunities to excite both the players and spectators. Thomas Bjorn holds the tournament record of 22 under par for four rounds, but every year Europe's best go low on this bizarre but absorbing course. It truly is a "Desert Miracle."

BEHIND THE 9TH AND 18TH GREENS stands the unusual and striking clubhouse, which has been built to resemble a cluster of welcoming Bedouin tents.

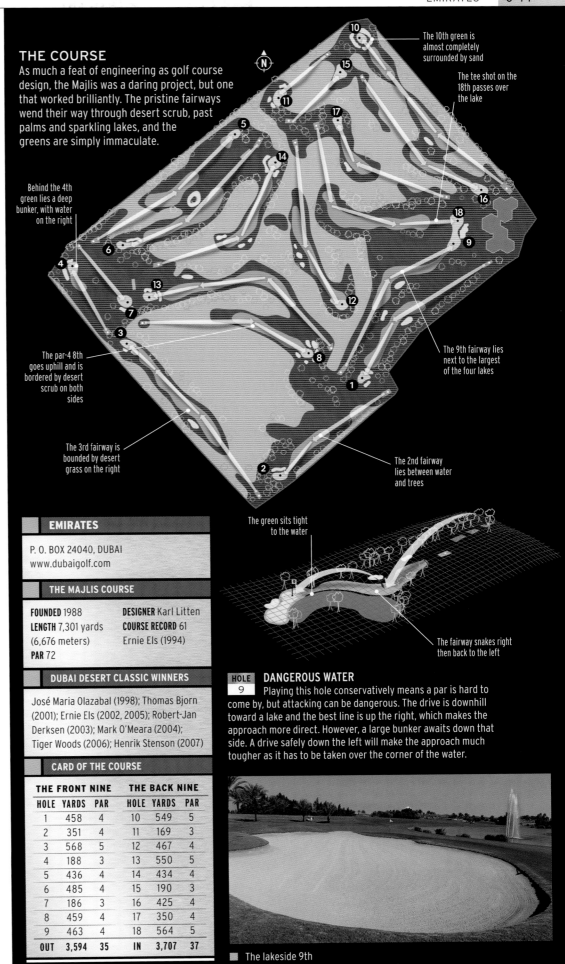

THE COURSE
As much a feat of engineering as golf course design, the Majlis was a daring project, but one that worked brilliantly. The pristine fairways wend their way through desert scrub, past palms and sparkling lakes, and the greens are simply immaculate.

The 10th green is almost completely surrounded by sand

The tee shot on the 18th passes over the lake

Behind the 4th green lies a deep bunker, with water on the right

The 9th fairway lies next to the largest of the four lakes

The par-4 8th goes uphill and is bordered by desert scrub on both sides

The 3rd fairway is bounded by desert grass on the right

The 2nd fairway lies between water and trees

The green sits tight to the water

The fairway snakes right then back to the left

EMIRATES

P. O. BOX 24040, DUBAI
www.dubaigolf.com

THE MAJLIS COURSE

FOUNDED 1988	**DESIGNER** Karl Litten
LENGTH 7,301 yards	**COURSE RECORD** 61
(6,676 meters)	Ernie Els (1994)
PAR 72	

DUBAI DESERT CLASSIC WINNERS

José Maria Olazabal (1998); Thomas Bjorn (2001); Ernie Els (2002, 2005); Robert-Jan Derksen (2003); Mark O'Meara (2004); Tiger Woods (2006); Henrik Stenson (2007)

CARD OF THE COURSE

THE FRONT NINE			THE BACK NINE		
HOLE	YARDS	PAR	HOLE	YARDS	PAR
1	458	4	10	549	5
2	351	4	11	169	3
3	568	5	12	467	4
4	188	3	13	550	5
5	436	4	14	434	4
6	485	4	15	190	3
7	186	3	16	425	4
8	459	4	17	350	4
9	463	4	18	564	5
OUT	**3,594**	**35**	**IN**	**3,707**	**37**

HOLE 9 DANGEROUS WATER

Playing this hole conservatively means a par is hard to come by, but attacking can be dangerous. The drive is downhill toward a lake and the best line is up the right, which makes the approach more direct. However, a large bunker awaits down that side. A drive safely down the left will make the approach much tougher as it has to be taken over the corner of the water.

■ The lakeside 9th

Shadow Creek, UNITED STATES

CREATED A FEW MILES NORTH OF THE WORLD'S most renowned gambling city, casual passers-by might think they have stumbled across a mirage in the Mojave Desert, such is the lush, artificial nature of this amazing course. From the moment it opened, Shadow Creek was hailed as one of the best new courses in the United States. Its reputation has brought it recognition as one of the top 100 courses in the world.

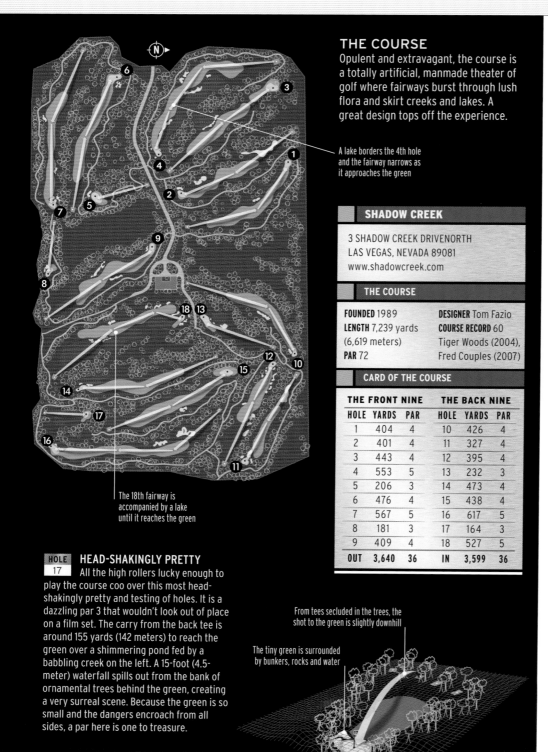

The 18th fairway is accompanied by a lake until it reaches the green

THE COURSE

Opulent and extravagant, the course is a totally artificial, manmade theater of golf where fairways burst through lush flora and skirt creeks and lakes. A great design tops off the experience.

A lake borders the 4th hole and the fairway narrows as it approaches the green

SHADOW CREEK

3 SHADOW CREEK DRIVENORTH
LAS VEGAS, NEVADA 89081
www.shadowcreek.com

THE COURSE

FOUNDED 1989
LENGTH 7,239 yards
(6,619 meters)
PAR 72

DESIGNER Tom Fazio
COURSE RECORD 60
Tiger Woods (2004),
Fred Couples (2007)

CARD OF THE COURSE

THE FRONT NINE			THE BACK NINE		
HOLE	YARDS	PAR	HOLE	YARDS	PAR
1	404	4	10	426	4
2	401	4	11	327	4
3	443	4	12	395	4
4	553	5	13	232	3
5	206	3	14	473	4
6	476	4	15	438	4
7	567	5	16	617	5
8	181	3	17	164	3
9	409	4	18	527	5
OUT	3,640	36	IN	3,599	36

HOLE 17 HEAD-SHAKINGLY PRETTY

All the high rollers lucky enough to play the course coo over this most head-shakingly pretty and testing of holes. It is a dazzling par 3 that wouldn't look out of place on a film set. The carry from the back tee is around 155 yards (142 meters) to reach the green over a shimmering pond fed by a babbling creek on the left. A 15-foot (4.5-meter) waterfall spills out from the bank of ornamental trees behind the green, creating a very surreal scene. Because the green is so small and the dangers encroach from all sides, a par here is one to treasure.

From tees secluded in the trees, the shot to the green is slightly downhill

The tiny green is surrounded by bunkers, rocks and water

LAS VEGAS IS NO STRANGER to the weird and wonderful. To a city that has recreated the Pyramids, the Eiffel Tower, and the canals of Venice, and where people gamble away millions each day, nothing seems a surprise. But back in 1988, when casino magnate Steve Wynn embarked on creating Shadow Creek, thousands of eyebrows were raised.

He set about building one of the most ambitious golf course projects ever seen. On a plain, completely flat desert site 9 miles (14.5 kilometers) north of Las Vegas' famous "Strip," an area of 320 acres (130 hectares) was marked out and the spectacular transformation began under the gaze of the highly respected Tom Fazio. He was given free rein and an astronomical budget. Wynn is a rich man, and legend has it that no expense was spared, with rumors that it cost anywhere between 40 and 60 million dollars. Someone in the know once said about the course: "Steve had an unlimited budget for Shadow Creek and he exceeded it. Whatever it took to make the place special, they did it." Wynn hit the jackpot, for it is a startling landscape.

What Fazio fashioned was not so much a desert golf course, but a golf course in the desert. If someone were to be dropped blindfold in the middle of the course, they would open their eyes and not have a clue that they were standing in the middle of the Mojave Desert. The only giveaways would be the searing heat and the barren backdrop of the Spring Mountains.

A GAMBLER'S DELIGHT

Shadow Creek resembles a tropical parkland despite an annual rainfall in the area that only reaches 4.5 inches (115 millimeters). Fazio imported over 200 plant species and built lakes, rocky creeks, and waterfalls to complement the piles of earth that gave the whole site definition and unexpected elevation changes. It might be described as an ornamental garden setting, with a golf course seamlessly woven in.

THE SPLENDID SETTING of the 9th hole epitomizes the emerald course that Tom Fazio fashioned from the desert at Shadow Creek—an immaculate fairway beside a sparkling creek with fabulous mountains in the background.

All holes are isolated from each other and shaded by the mass of foliage, and they flow beautifully. There are no ridiculously sharp doglegs, but a few of the holes do arc majestically, most notably at the 1st, 4th, 10th, and 16th. The pick of these sweeping holes is the 553-yard (505-meter) 4th, which bends from right-to-left around a twinkling, curvaceous lake edged with strips of sand. As befits a golf course in Las Vegas, it is a gambler's delight, goading a player to risk taking it on.

RISKS AND REWARDS

As a rule, all the par 5s are exceptional risk-and-reward holes, with the finest saved until last. Fazio summed up the design here, bringing all the elements found around the course together into one spectacular hole. At the 18th, tees are elevated and set at different angles to the fairway. Stands of trees and bunkers patrol the left and a series of lakes linked by three waterfalls flow down the right from the green. The final rocky drop cuts across the front of the green, which is reachable in two by the long and brave. Most, however, will face a charming but tricky pitch in over the stream to a shallow green framed by weeping willows, pines, and shrubs.

Other holes of note are two par 3s—the 5th and 13th. The former is a mid-length one shotter that woos the eye as it drops down over a stunning valley of shrubs. But the 13th is a beast of a hole, needing a long iron or fairway wood downhill to an angled green, which is tightly guarded on the right by a small pond and a large bunker. A direct line takes you straight over the corner of the trouble, so it is often best to fade a left-to-right shot in, especially if you have to get at a flag in the back right portion. It is a blow of about 230 yards (210 meters) which frays the nerves, a bit like a gambler watching a roulette wheel spinning.

After it opened, Shadow Creek became the preserve of the rich and famous, and A-list celebrities have always had strong connections. Basketball legend Michael Jordan and actor George Clooney are regulars. And despite the fact that no championships are held here, Shadow Creek has an impressive course record holder—one Tiger Woods who shot a game 60.

Strokeplay will never be a main feature of Shadow Creek—it does not have an official USGA rating. Fazio designed it to be the ultimate matchplay course, where golfers face each other with their poker faces and play for their hard-earned dollars. Unless you have lost a mint against a bandit, then no one will go away from this stunner disappointed. It is surreal golf and a magnificent experience, fitting for a town that is sometimes beyond belief.

PRIVILEGED FEW

Technically, Shadow Creek is a daily fee public course, but it is owned by MGM Mirage and to have any chance of playing, you must register at one of its properties in Las Vegas. Then you must pay $500 for the privilege. The fee includes limousine transfers from the city, your own personal caddie who meets your car at the clubhouse, practice balls, drinks, and snacks.

The MGM Grand Hotel in Las Vegas

The golf course exists for one single reason...to bring pleasure to my guests, **and to hell with everything else**

STEVE WYNN, COURSE FOUNDER AND FORMER OWNER

Troon North, UNITED STATES

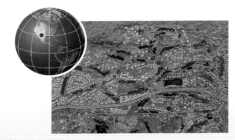

DESERT GOLF DOESN'T COME ANY BETTER THAN THIS. Its combination of vibrant green fairways diving over the boulders and scrub of the Sonoran Desert is a treat for the eyes as much as for tacticians of the game. The original Monument Course at Troon North, watched over by the rubble-clad Pinnacle Peak, is a stunning piece of architecture that uses the dramatic prehistoric landscape to perfection.

A COURSE WITH BITE

The desert floor at Troon North hides two menaces. Rattlesnakes are native to the rock-strewn landscape, but are rarely seen–and it's against Arizona law to kill one. More hazardous is the Jumping Cholla, a magnetic plant that is drawn to humans walking past by the magnesium in their bodies. It has nasty barbs like fishhooks.

■ A rattlesnake on the sand

WHEN ASKED TO PICTURE pure desert golf, most players will conjure images of arid, brown scrub and rocks dotted with tall, spiky "cowboy" cacti surrounding neatly-striped lush islands of green. Troon North may well be the perfect pure desert golf course based on those archetypal thoughts.

The Monument Course, so named after the gigantic boulder in the middle of the 3rd fairway, was created by Tom Weiskopf and Jay Morrish. This "stone" was seen as such an important piece of the desert that the local planning authorities asked specifically for it to stay. And while the design team were worried about having such a vast boulder in play for safety reasons, the city of Scottsdale waived any legal responsibility to the course.

A DISTINCTIVE COURSE

The original course was arranged in two distinct loops of nine holes. The front nine circled counterclockwise on lower ground, and the back nine (now part of its sister course, The Pinnacle, as of November 2007) turned

A SAGUARO CACTUS STANDS TALL beside the 10th hole on the "New" Monument Course at Troon North, adding a calming influence to the travails of playing golf in such a rugged landscape.

clockwise on higher, more sculpted land. New houses have taken away some of the wilderness feel, but they don't detract much from the very enjoyable challenge.

Anytime fairways are edged with sandy, thorny scrub and rough boulders, as they are here, the potential for trouble is great, but the playing areas are generous in size. While they look intimidating—especially when the desert floor creeps across as it does on five holes, most notably on the wonderful 10th—the fairways are wide and rippled, and the greens are large and not hemmed in by the bush. For such a lush, green course, it's surprising to see the ball bound nicely from the tees—this is probably down to the pristine, close-cropped nature of the playing surfaces. With the greens being reasonably firm and quick, it's a delight to be able to use the contours to filter approaches close to tricky flag positions.

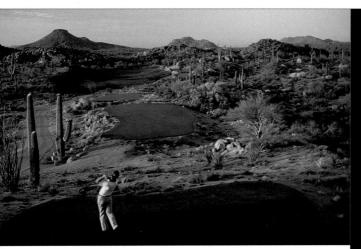

FROM THE TEE AT THE PAR-5 11TH HOLE on the Original Monument Course, the vibrant green of the cambered fairway leads gradually uphill, then swings to the right around rocky terrain.

There are plenty of holes where you can open your shoulders, including all the par 5s. Standing on the 11th tee, staring at the cambered and funneled fairway in the distance, entices you to smack a drive away, hopefully with a touch of left-to-right to mimic the shape. It is one of five holes that don't have any fairway bunkers in the landing area, but you do not miss them because of the clever contouring of the fairways. When fairway traps do come into play, they are a mixture of styles: you must fly some, skip past others, and sensibly lay up short of a few.

One superb hole—a short driveable par 4 that Tom Weiskopf always tries to put into each of his courses— gives a player two of these options. The 6th is 306 yards (280 meters) long and has three bunkers that split the hole in two. One big sweep of a trap patrols the right, and two pots cut off the direct route. If you can carry the drive around 250 yards (228 meters), and avoid another small pot further up, you can find the green or get mighty close. The sensible choice is to play short of the trouble and take your chances with a wedge into the small slopey green.

TANTALIZING THE EYE

The real gift of the course is the way it uses the land and tantalizes the eye. Isolated among the wilderness, the tees are often stepped gradually so you can see all in front of you. The humps and hollows of the undulating land seduce the visual senses and challenge the golfer with an awkward stance on the fairways or a merciless kick to your ball by the green. Troon North is choc full of smooth lines and understated contours and, despite the harsh surroundings, it is as fair as you could wish a course to be.

Just to add to the pleasure of playing both courses here, thousands of saguaro cacti stand defiantly in the undergrowth and somehow have a calming influence on the place. As the sun goes down and an orange blanket of light is thrown over the desert, their ghostly silhouettes are a wondrous sight. Troon North is a treat.

THE COURSE
Ribbons of green cascade over the rocky scrub of the desert floor and invite a golfer to turn on the power and style. The clever routeing and strategic design is watched over by the ancient missilelike cacti that sprout from the earth. A benchmark desert course.

TROON NORTH

10320 EAST DYNAMITE BLVD.
SCOTTSDALE, AZ 85262
www.troonnorthgolf.com

THE ORIGINAL MONUMENT COURSE

FOUNDED 1990
LENGTH 7,028 yards
(6,426 meters)
PAR 72

DESIGNERS
Tom Weiskopf,
Jay Morrish

CARD OF THE COURSE

THE FRONT NINE			THE BACK NINE		
HOLE	YARDS	PAR	HOLE	YARDS	PAR
1	444	4	10	392	4
2	172	3	11	539	5
3	564	5	12	414	4
4	420	4	13	176	3
5	464	4	14	604	5
6	306	4	15	368	4
7	205	3	16	140	3
8	408	4	17	438	4
9	530	5	18	444	4
OUT	3,513	36	IN	3,515	36

The 16th green is protected by a lake front right

A rocky waste cuts the 12th fairway in two

The tee shot on the 11th is best shaped left to right

The desert creeps across the 10th in front of the green

A boulder shaped like an obelisk stands in the dogleg of the 3rd fairway,

The 6th is driveable, but cross bunkers await miss-hits

The dogleg 3rd

HOLE 3 A TRICKY DOGLEG
An obelisklike boulder in the middle of the fairway is the signature of this hole and dictates how it is played. The safest route is to go left of it, but because the hole swings right, going this way means the green is out of range in two, even for the big hitters. The bolder drive right of it, and flirting with a corner of the encroaching desert, gives decent golfers a chance of getting home, but it still takes a great strike slightly downhill to reach the green. One solitary bunker pinches the fairway in about 40 yards (36 meters) short of the green.

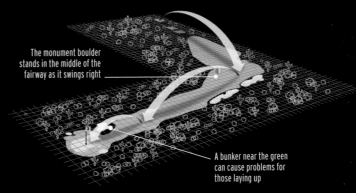

The monument boulder stands in the middle of the fairway as it swings right

A bunker near the green can cause problems for those laying up

Unique courses

WITH THOUSANDS OF GOLF COURSES THE WORLD OVER laid out on all sorts of terrain, it is very difficult to categorize them all into certain styles. Many are an amalgam of styles, or played in such unique surroundings, that you cannot neatly pigeon-hole them. This chapter features some of the most singular examples of such courses.

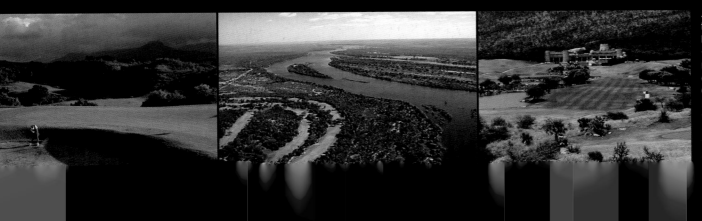

△ **THE DRAMATIC 15TH HOLE** is at the Quarry Course at Black Diamond Ranch near Tampa, Florida. ◁◁◁ **PRINCEVILLE** Golf Course is magnificently placed on the island of Kauai, Hawaii. ◁◁ **THE GOLF COURSE** at Elephant Hills, Zimbabwe, lies beside the Zambezi River and is within earshot of the Victoria Falls. ◁ **THE LOST CITY** course has unique water hazards and belongs to the Sun City complex in South Africa.

WHEN DOES A PARKLAND

become a jungle? What determines an ocean course as opposed to a links. Inevitably, the classification of golf courses has some fuzzy edges because golf is played in such diverse landscapes. When you add various architectural oddities such as island greens, many courses simply do not fit into a category.

As a general rule, heathland must have heather, but how much does it need so that it does not become known as, say, an inland links or simply a parkland?

WHISTLING STRAITS

The category problem is exemplified by Whistling Straits, situated on the shores of Lake Michigan. It is a staggering piece of design by Pete Dye, where there are few trees, tumbling dunes on otherwise flat land, and a ludicrous amount of bunkers—albeit in a haphazard style. The lake is so vast that it looks like an ocean, and the soil is sandy.

But is Whistling Straits a links or an ocean course? Many of its holes have design features that are not necessarily found on a links—for example, some forced carries onto greens and much lusher turf than a real links. This means that it does not play like a true links, although it looks like one.

FROM SWAMP TO BIG GAME

The courses of some of the more traditional areas for golf tend to find themselves within a category, but there are still many examples that don't fit perfectly. For example, in the low country of The Carolinas and Georgia, marshland is ubiquitous and holes weave over wetlands and swamp. Even though they may feature trees, the classic styles cannot be applied.

The problem is exacerbated in other more tropical parts of the world, too. In the Far East, where the vegetation is unique to the hot and wet climate, golf courses are built through almost pure jungle. Monkeys swing from the trees and there is little or no roll on the coarse grass fairways. Can they be called parkland? Perhaps, but it would be pushing the boundaries.

In Africa, some courses are built in the dry savanna lands, where the fairways are roamed by wild animals. At Victoria Falls, Zimbabwe, the local golf course is named after the noble beast that trudges over the fairways of Elephant Hills. And at the parkland course at Hans Merensky, on the edge of the Kruger National Park in South Africa, golfers can spot the "Big Five" (lions, rhinos, elephants, buffaloes, and leopards).

RAINFOREST AND LAVA

Golf course developers know no bounds when trying to create a unique golfing experience and turn to ever more bizarre land for building courses. Golf usually goes hand in hand with the tourist dollar, and no more so than in the Hawaiian Islands.

The most northerly island of Kauai is a rainforest paradise, with steep-sided valleys shrouded in exotic flora cutting through the isle. It is almost insulting to label somewhere so dramatic as say, Princeville, as a parkland course, despite it being flanked by trees.

Even more confusing, and less able to be categorized, are the courses on the lava fields of the Big Island.

The shores of the actively volcanic island are encrusted with razor-sharp black lava that has erupted from the massive volcanoes of Mauna Loa and Mauna Kea, or been forced up from the waters of the deep.

The lava is very difficult to walk over and so golf courses seem like a very strange partner. But a lava-munching machine that shreds the rock and spits it out to form smooth surfaces, has made golf a surreal reality. Perfectly manicured strips of fairways using imported soil sweep across the black rock that acts as the rough. These courses are as far away from a links as possible, despite many being right next to the coast.

WHISTLING STRAITS has characteristics of both a links and an ocean course. It lies on a two-mile stretch of the Lake Michigan shoreline north of Sheboygan in Wisconsin.

BEWARE THE 13TH HOLE!

Sun City in South Africa has two magnificent courses and its Lost City Course has a distinctive style. With a background of the Pilansberg Mountains, Lost City runs through high rough and past boulder-strewn lakes. Closest to a desert style, it has an inland linksy feel, too. On the 13th, a vast walled pit between tee and green is home to two dozen Nile crocodiles that laze around in the reeds and water.

■ Crocodile pit on the 13th hole

CARVED FROM BLACK LAVA, the Beach Course at Waikoloa is located along the Kohala coastline on the Big Island of Hawaii. Designed by Robert Trent Jones Jr., the scenic course has many challenging water features and sand bunkers, as well as views of humpback whales in the waters of Anaeho'omalu Bay.

Loch Lomond, SCOTLAND

A DESIGN CLASSIC IN POETIC SURROUNDINGS, Loch Lomond appeals to all the senses. Just north of gritty Glasgow on the "bonnie banks" of a graceful lake, it is an out-and-out feelgood golf course. Considering it only opened for play in 1994, and is an upstart in the "birthplace of golf," it has enjoyed staggering accolades. In 2000, it was voted third best golf course in the British Isles behind Muirfield and Royal County Down, and now ranks in the Top 100 of the world.

UNDENIABLY, LOCH LOMOND is predominantly a parkland course, but its variety and setting make this moniker too simplistic. Yes, the fairways weave through mature woods of oak, pine, Douglas fir, larch, beech, limes, and the odd chestnut, with a few rhododendrons to add color, but there is much more to it than that.

Several holes flirt with marshland edged with untidy areas of broom, heather, reeds, bracken, maram grass, thistles, and bramble. Six holes are directly influenced by the lapping waters of Loch Lomond—the 3rd, 5th, 6th, 7th, 17th, and 18th—while others are crisscrossed with streams and edged by natural ponds. And as you gaze at the panorama, both the loch and the bracken-shrouded highland fells of the Trossachs leave you wide-eyed in appreciation of their natural charms.

EXCEPTIONALLY FAIR AND VARIED

Rating a golf course is mostly a subjective process. Yet to find the real greats, sometimes objective criteria have to be applied, because judgment can be clouded by the surroundings. At Loch Lomond, even if you look away from the sumptuous landscape, you would still be left with a completely awesome course.

In the late 1980s, the expert design team of Tom Weiskopf and Jay Morrish were invited to lay their artistic hands on the land that has been for centuries the ancestral home of the Clan Colquhoun. At its heart was the impressive Rossdhu House overlooking the loch, and the pair of architects would have to fulfil the faith shown in them if they were to match the estate's class and grandeur. While Morrish was most certainly an influence, a heart attack limited his involvement and Weiskopf, the Open Championship winner of 1973 at Troon, became the main player behind its brilliance.

What the course delivers is exceptionally fair and varied holes that have outstanding memorability. All the fairways have "elbow room," but also awkward or nasty hazards to protect them. The forever changing

FEW GOLFERS PLAYING THE COURSE at Loch Lomond can fail to be inspired by the awesome setting of the water and the wonderful panorama of the mountains beyond.

EUROPE'S WOMEN won back the Solheim Cup from the US at Loch Lomond in 2000. Half the team of 12 were Swedish. After the clean sweep of the first morning's foursomes, three and half points of the five Europe won on the final day came from Carin Koch, Helen Alfredsson, Liselotte Neumann and Catrin Nilsmark. Europe won 14 ½ to 11 ½.

FRENCHMAN THOMAS LEVET came from a distant 14th place and 7 behind in the final round to win the Barclays Scottish Open in 2004. His blistering 63 shot him through the field to pip Michael Campbell by one. He came home in just 29 strokes and was 6 under for his last 8 holes, finishing with a birdie 3 for victory and a total of 15 under par.

LOCH LOMOND

ROSSDHU HOUSE, LUSS, DUNBARTONSHIRE G83 8NT, SCOTLAND
www.lochlomond.com

THE COURSE

FOUNDED 1993
LENGTH 7,139 yards (6,528 meters)
PAR 71

DESIGNERS Tom Weiskopf, Jay Morrish
COURSE RECORD 62 Retief Goosen (1997)

SELECTED CHAMPIONS

STANDARD LIFE Lee Westwood (1998); Colin Montgomerie (1999); Ernie Els (2000)
SOLHEIM CUP Europe (2000)
SCOTTISH OPEN Retief Goosen (2001); Eduardo Romero (2002); Ernie Els (2003); Thomas Levet (2004); Tim Clark (2005); Johan Edfors (2006); Gregory Havret (2007)

CARD OF THE COURSE

THE FRONT NINE			THE BACK NINE		
HOLE	YARDS	PAR	HOLE	YARDS	PAR
1	425	4	10	455	4
2	455	4	11	235	3
3	518	5	12	415	4
4	385	4	13	560	5
5	190	3	14	371	4
6	625	5	15	415	4
7	440	4	16	490	4
8	160	3	17	205	3
9	340	4	18	455	4
OUT	3,538	36	IN	3,601	35

■ The picturesque 17th green

■ The brilliant par-3 17th overlooking Loch Lomond

This is probably the best course in Europe, it is a really good layout and the condition is very pure. It is beautiful

ERNIE ELS, WINNER OF THE 2000 AND 2003 SCOTTISH OPENS AT LOCH LOMOND

direction and pace enthral all. The holes change tack no less than 15 times, and the four incredible one-shotters range from 160 to 235 yards (146 to 215 meters), and all play on different bearings.

Two of the short holes are world-beaters. At the 5th, the tees aim you over a pretty, natural waste area toward a green backed by the mirrored lake and framed by huge oaks. Although the loch looks as though it is just over the back there is room for maneuver, but an undulating green and four bunkers keep you on your toes. Of the many ridiculously picturesque holes on the course it is just about the best.

The 5th is rivaled by another par 3. The 17th is a heart-stopping 205 yards (187 meters) over a marsh, with the loch only a few paces to the left. Getting to a back left pin placement takes courage as well as a cultured draw. It was the scene of a great European triumph in the 2000 Solheim Cup, when Sweden's Carin Koch rolled in a 10-foot putt to beat Michelle Redman 2&1 and clinch victory over the US.

HELPFUL BUNKERS

Every hole has its own identity and challenges. Bunkers are used sparingly and not one is wasted. Weiskopf has always believed that sand should present different tests and he was at pains to get it right here. Only one bunker —a small pot on the 8th—is hidden. On every other you get a glimpse of sand, helping with depth perception and visualization of the shot you need to play. On fairways they are reasonably shallow, letting players escape with an exacting shot. They are not only put in troublesome spots, but they help to focus a player's tactics too.

The greenside traps are deeper and settle delightfully into the banks of the trademark slopes and humps. Just

as the sand catches the eye, so too do the wild and ingenious patches of waste and the majestic specimen trees, which in themselves are hazards. On the long and winding par-5 6th that skirts the shore of the loch, magnificent single oaks make their presence felt up both sides of the fairway and definitely fashion your strategy, just as much as the bunkers.

GUILE, GRACE, AND POWER

While this course tends to suit great mid-to-long iron players, being a top putter will always help too. The greens are generous in size but are cambered and swift, providing options for some devious pin positions. This is exemplified by the 18th, an elegant but dangerous par 4 curving left around an inlet of the loch toward the ruins of Rossdhu Castle. A good drive should leave a mid-iron into a steep two-tiered green which has a small shelf at its back-right portion. It may not be so much of a problem to hit the green, but to get your ball in the right spot for the most straightforward putt takes a skilful shot. That is the way of Loch Lomond. It's very fair to all, but to score well, approaches must be pinpoint accurate.

Loch Lomond has become the home of the Scottish Open, and the professionals who come from around the world to play it cannot get enough of it. Nick Faldo once said, "It's just absolutely fabulous. It is by far and away the best golf course in Great Britain by miles." Colin Montgomerie called it "faultless," and Ernie Els, twice winner here, said, "It's in the top five of my world-wide golf venues." High praise, but they are on the mark.

Loch Lomond is an astonishing course enhanced by the splendor of the landscape. It has guile, grace, power, and a soothing quality too, making it one of the most pleasurable rounds of golf you can find anywhere.

BRUSH WITH DEATH

Tom Weiskopf was a hands-on designer who lived in the gardener's cottage on site for 18 months during construction. Early one morning he went for a walk down to the marshy part of the course, near what is the 14th hole, to see if his thoughts could be brought to reality. When Tom tried to jump a burn, he slipped into the marsh, sinking slowly in the mire. He hung on to a grass tuft on the bank, but couldn't pull himself clear. He held on desperately for some hours until he was rescued.

■ Weiskopf at Loch Lomond

■ The breathtaking 5th hole

■ The two-tiered 18th green

THE COURSE

Beguiling in its elegance, Loch Lomond is an architectural masterpiece where holes gracefully saunter through marshlands and mature parkland. Generous off the tee but still a strategic genius, its main dangers lie in the tracts of wild grass, well-placed sand, stands of trees, and large undulating putting surfaces.

The 7th green sits close to the waters of the loch

The 5th green is framed by huge oaks and backed by the loch

Bunkers present danger up the right of the 18th fairway

◀N

THE FRONT NINE ❶ A wide open fairway, with tricky lone oak on the right. **❷** A wall stretching across fairway catches the eye on this strong par 4. **❸** Reachable in two, but a lake short right and the loch long left punish the wayward. **❹** Seems simple, but the double green (shared with the 2nd) is awkward. **❺** A stunning and dangerous par 3 with a carry over a wild marsh. **❻** Massive par 5 with the loch down the right and huge trees to snake through. **❼** Green sits close to the loch. Long iron approaches must be pinpoint accurate. **❽** Missing the green leaves a difficult up and down for par. **❾** Just driveable for the longest, but sand can catch the overbold.

THE BACK NINE ❿ Beautiful swooping par 4. A lake edges across front and left of green. **⓫** Toughest short hole on the course. Slightly uphill and very long, often needing a wood. **⓬** Anything short right of green is drawn back down a steep slope. **⓭** Avoid bunkers on fairway for a good chance of birdie. **⓮** A devious short four. Anything can happen. **⓯** A wicked ridge splits green in two. It can be friend or foe. **⓰** Very difficult par 4 in terms of length and the burn just short of green. **⓱** Awesome par 3 by the loch. Green looks like an oasis across the marsh. **⓲** A dangerous tee shot with the loch down the left and bunkers up the right.

A burn runs across the front of the 16th green

A marsh and towering oak dictate your risk-and-reward strategy

A pond threatens the approach to the 10th green

The green is driveable but the safe route is up the left

HOLE 9 DECEPTIVELY SIMPLE

It may be the shortest par 4 on the course and in range downwind for the biggest hitters, but the 9th can also jump up and grab you. The perfect strategy is to lay up short of the traps up on the right. Traps around the green put pressure on your wedge play. Seems simple, but silly mistakes are common.

A huge nest of traps lies in wait up on the right of the fairway and more still hem in the green

A bunker down the left of the fairway keeps golfers on their toes

Gargantuan oak trees can create visibility problems and may block the view of the green

The green is small and has a few mounds that make putting tricky

HOLE 14 DO OR DIE

This risky hole gives golfers two options. The safer "high road" is an iron or fairway metal down the left, skirting past the marsh and a towering oak. The riskier ploy takes on the carry of 270 yards (247 meters) over the mire and goes directly at the green. Success can bring a simple birdie chance, but failure can lead to a severe penalty.

The fairway turns 90°, leading to a burn and then the awkwardly sloping green

HOLE 6 A LONG AND WINDING HOLE

A huge par 5 unreachable in two for virtually everyone. The secret is not to block yourself out behind any of the oaks dotted along the length of the hole. Nor can you drive it in the rough, or else you will struggle to reach in three–a massive cross bunker means you might have to lay way back from the green after two shots.

Sun City, SOUTH AFRICA

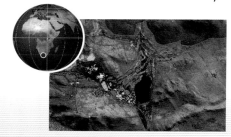

TWO HOURS FROM JOHANNESBURG, this monumental course in the bushveld on the edge of the Pilansberg range, is often ranked as the best course on the continent of Africa. The Gary Player Country Club course at Sun City mixes brawn with brains and is a sapping challenge, both mentally and physically. One of the longest in the world, this course is for big hitters, even with the help of the heat and altitude.

AN AERIAL VIEW of the Gary Player Country Club course, with the 1st hole on the right, the red bunkers around the 14th green in the foreground, and the lake on the left.

THE WATER BESIDE THE 18TH has a habit of capturing a number of wayward balls so they are regularly retrieved.

THE RESORT AT SUN CITY is a purpose-built land of fun, and revelers from all over the world enjoy its decadence and spirit. The Gary Player Country Club course does not reflect this showy style and is more demure than brash. It has been a playground for golfers since 1979, when Gary Player's team cleared tracts of the harsh native bushveld and laid down its softly surging fairways of kikuyu grass.

The course is relatively flat while all around, the hills of the Pilansberg National Park rise and fall, heaved into the air by an ancient volcano. Instead of dramatically swooping holes, it relies on the skill of the route and cleverly placed hazards to keep golfers on their toes. At 7,832 yards (7,162 meters) from the championship tees, it is one of the longest courses in the world. Thankfully, Sun City is 3,675 feet (1,120 meters) above sea level, so the ball flies like an eagle.

Two years after its opening, it staged the first of its now annual Million Dollar events, where an invitation field of 12 top tour professionals fight it out for vast sums of money. Over the years, they have not only lapped up the hospitality, big baying crowds, and the money, but they have loved the golf course, too. It is hard to believe that on a such a long course the best score (but not an official record) is 61 by Padraig Harrington, and back in 1993, when technology was less advanced, Nick Price shot a four-round total of 24 under.

MEAN TRAPS AND TOUGH ROUGH

The course is simply not that easy. Water comes into play on seven holes, most obtrusively on the 9th and 17th, and Player's bunkering is mean and in your face. There is little subtlety to it on the fairways, as most traps appear just at driving distance and pinch already narrow landing zones. By the greens, many are dug into the front corners of the putting surface (or ring the front, like at the 14th). These impinging bunkers force approaches to be towering and precise so they can clear the trouble and hold the greens. Much of the putting surfaces are tucked away behind these traps making flags very difficult to get at.

Most holes do have a channel to roll the ball up through, but they are tight and the greens tend to be slightly raised so a ball can stall on the front. And what adds to the difficulty of missing the fairways and greens is the kikuyu grass rough. While a ball can scamper a

THE COURSE

Ludicrously long and unforgiving, the course takes patience as well as pure striking to play it well, because the clinging rough and sweeps of sand are unrelenting in their full-on challenge. But the heat and altitude help out the power game.

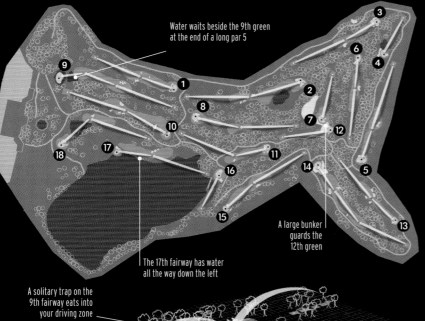

Water waits beside the 9th green at the end of a long par 5

The 17th fairway has water all the way down the left

A solitary trap on the 9th fairway eats into your driving zone

A large bunker guards the 12th green

The 9th green is a wide but shallow island backed by a cascading stream

■ The picturesque 9th

HOLE 9 — A CROWD PLEASER

The challenge from the tee on the truly crowd-pleasing hole is what you would expect, but up by the green it gets interesting. Here, a stream cascades around the green's fringes and empties into the lake at the front. This in turn tumbles down a rocky waterfall into another lake below. It takes a brave man to go for it in two. Ernie Els gives his verdict: "The hole is normally set up so as to encourage the second shot at the green, which can be intimidating. I've gone at the green with 2-irons, but if it's 3-wood distance I back off. Even after laying up short of the lake, if the pin is cut in the back left or right, it is a tough shot; a couple of yards either way and the ball can be in the water."

SUN CITY

P.O. BOX 6, SUN CITY 0316, SOUTH AFRICA
www.sun-international.com

GARY PLAYER COUNTRY CLUB

FOUNDED 1979
LENGTH 7,162 meters
(7,832 yards)
DESIGNER Gary Player
COURSE RECORD 63
Ernie Els (2002)

SELECTED CHAMPIONS

NEDBANK GOLF CHALLENGE (ALSO KNOWN AS THE MILLION DOLLAR CHALLENGE) Nick Price (1997, 1998); Ernie Els (1999, 2000, 2002); Sergio Garcia (2001, 2003); Retief Goosen (2004); Jim Furyk (2005, 2006), Trevor Immelman (2007)
WOMEN'S WORLD CUP OF GOLF Sweden (2006) (Annika Sorenstam and Liselotte Neumann)

CARD OF THE COURSE

THE FRONT NINE			THE BACK NINE		
HOLE	YARDS	PAR	HOLE	YARDS	PAR
1	440	4	10	546	5
2	569	5	11	458	4
3	450	4	12	218	3
4	213	3	13	444	4
5	491	4	14	601	5
6	424	4	15	471	4
7	225	3	16	211	3
8	492	4	17	477	4
9	596	5	18	501	4
OUT	3,900	36	IN	3,931	36

reasonable distance on the fairways, the same grass flanking them is grown up a few inches and is as tough as wire. It is on a par with Bermuda rough, and control from it is virtually non-existent. Outside of the rough, the bushveld creeps in on every hole and is a no-go area. Steamy heat and chirping insects add to the exotic feel.

The last five holes sum up the Country Club's steel. A big par 5 starts the run for home and a massive cross-bunker with islands of rough defends the green. The 15th is two huge smacks to a green with a narrow entrance between traps. Almost half the green sits behind the bunker front right. It is all carry to the 16th, the shortest par 3 on the course, and the 17th is has water all the way down the left. Having to hit a long iron or fairway metal into this green is a scary proposition.

A HERO'S COURSE

If you have survived the kikuyu, water, thorny bush, and superfast greens, all the hard work can be undone on the 18th, a fantastic par 4 that doglegs left over a lake. The closer you can hit your drive to the water, the better, as it leaves a shorter shot in to the gently elevated green. Two gaping bunkers guard the entrance and the back right pin position is a devil to get at. This is the scene of many rowdy moments in the Million Dollar Challenge, as the crowd is often frenzied in support of their heroes.

This is a hero's course. What it lacks in subtlety and ingenuity, it makes up for in precision, power, immaculate conditioning, and a touch of the wild.

UNCOMPROMISING BUNKERS with islands of large, unplayable tufts of kikuyu grass envelop the 14th green.

Mission Hills, CHINA

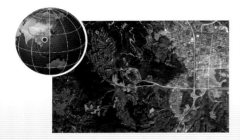

A MIND-BOGGLING RESORT CLOSE TO HONG KONG has become China's golfing success story. The largest golf complex in the world, Mission Hills boasts 12 courses of 18 holes and each has been designed by a renowned figure in golf, mostly touring professionals. The course created by Spanish maestro and double Masters champion José Maria Olazábal is the longest and was chosen to host the Omega Mission Hills World Cup in 2007.

CHINA IS THE FOURTH LARGEST country by area on the planet and has around one quarter of the world's population, yet in golf terms it is a fledgling. Long ago, emperors dabbled, but communism stopped golf from taking any foothold. It wasn't until 1984 that the People's Republic of China unveiled its first 18-hole course, but since then it has caught up and made some serious progress. By 2007, more than 200 courses had been built in China and up to 700 more were either on the drawing board or under construction.

The Mission Hills Resort, near Shenzhen just 35 miles (56 kilometers) from downtown Hong Kong, is leading this remarkable golfing revolution—and on a grand scale. The list of architects who have designed a course reads like a golfing who's who: Jack Nicklaus, Greg Norman, Ernie Els, Annika Sorenstam, Vijay Singh, Nick Faldo, David Duval, Jumbo Ozaki, David Leadbetter, China's own Zhang Lianwei, Pete Dye, as well as José Maria Olazábal.

To add to the head-scratching size of the resort, Mission Hills is proud to have the largest pro shop in Asia and a monumental clubhouse that occupies a whopping 300,000 sq feet—almost 7 acres (2.8 hectares). Despite the resort being quite close to some major industrial cities, it is perched in a secluded valley surrounded by rolling hills. All the courses enjoy the same cracking backdrops, but the design firm Schmidt-Curley, who collaborated with the pros on the courses, made sure that each course should try as much as possible to have its own identity and reflect the player's own thoughts and ideas.

ALTHOUGH IT IS SITUATED very close to Hong Kong, the Mission Hills Resort enjoys the stunning backdrop of tree-covered hillsides.

SANDY FEATURES

Olazábal's course pulls no punches, but is playable by everyone because of its set of five tees. Yet the best players in the world are always tested, thanks to its sheer length and on-the-edge design that uses creeks and lakes. However, there is something else that dominates play. The Spaniard is regarded as one of the finest short-game players that golf has ever seen, and he is particularly adept from bunkers. It is no surprise then that sand is the major feature on this course.

Despite the five par 3s only having 21 bunkers to contend with between them, finding sand at some time in a round is inevitable, given that there are 68 bunkers on the front nine and a phenomenal 86 on the back. Many are not simply small pots of sand but are large amoeba-shaped traps with tongues of hairy grass and steep faces. While the fairway bunkers tend to catch

THE PICK OF THE HOLES

Of Mission Hills' 216 holes of joy, the pick are: Norman's 4th, a downhill one-shotter to a precarious green with drop-offs to a lake on the left and back; Faldo's 16th, slightly downhill to an island green; Els' 4th, which falls 44 yards (40 meters) and has a rocky stream hugging the left side of the arcing left dogleg.

■ The 16th on the Faldo Course

bold drives as they tuck into the corners of the gently shaped holes, others are a saving grace and stop your ball from bounding away into yet more trouble.

ELEVATION CHALLENGES

Olazábal has been kind, too, with the shaping of the fairways—most are set in bowl-like channels, which means there is a little more margin for error from the tee. The 1st starts alongside some of the other courses and gradually the succeeding holes make their way north until the course reaches its furthest point from the clubhouse. Here, the pretty par-3 8th is set on a wooded hillside, with views back down across the resort. The course then intermingles with itself and drops back down the mountain: at two of the par 5s—the 9th and 11th – this descent is particularly spectacular, as they fall some 60 feet (18 meters) to the fairways.

Since there are some big elevation changes, the uphill holes such as the 10th have been treated sensitively. They are shorter but much more fiddly than those that have golfers firing down the valleys. At the signature 15th, which is a long, hook-shaped and downhill par 5 (see right), the course rejoins the mix of other courses.

However, the 18th sits in splendid isolation behind a large hill and is overlooked by the gargantuan clubhouse. At 460 yards (420 meters), this par 4 is a mighty finish—it is located around a bowing lake with no bunkers waterside to catch a tee shot or approach going left. It is a fitting climax to a powerful but fun course in a resort that catches the imagination and is a golfer's dream.

THE COURSE
The Olazábal Course mixes elevation changes with arcing doglegs and fairways with intrusive bunkers. Rippled green surrounds and fast putting surfaces call for a seriously good short game as well as a powerful and exacting long game.

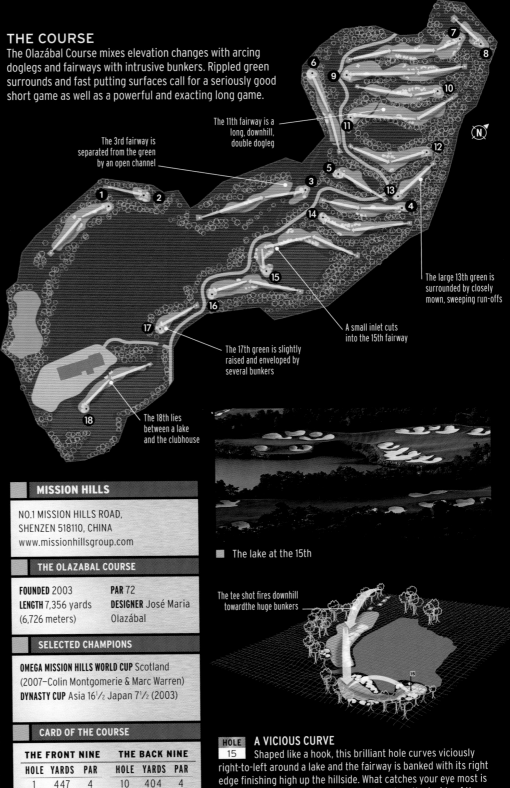

The 3rd fairway is separated from the green by an open channel

The 11th fairway is a long, downhill, double dogleg

The large 13th green is surrounded by closely mown, sweeping run-offs

A small inlet cuts into the 15th fairway

The 17th green is slightly raised and enveloped by several bunkers

The 18th lies between a lake and the clubhouse

The lake at the 15th

The tee shot fires downhill toward the huge bunkers

MISSION HILLS

NO.1 MISSION HILLS ROAD, SHENZEN 518110, CHINA
www.missionhillsgroup.com

THE OLAZABAL COURSE

FOUNDED 2003   **PAR** 72
LENGTH 7,356 yards   **DESIGNER** José Maria
(6,726 meters)   Olazábal

SELECTED CHAMPIONS

OMEGA MISSION HILLS WORLD CUP Scotland
(2007–Colin Montgomerie & Marc Warren)
DYNASTY CUP Asia 16½ Japan 7½ (2003)

CARD OF THE COURSE

THE FRONT NINE			THE BACK NINE		
HOLE	YARDS	PAR	HOLE	YARDS	PAR
1	447	4	10	404	4
2	175	3	11	568	5
3	548	5	12	457	4
4	441	4	13	241	3
5	176	3	14	401	4
6	476	4	15	580	5
7	566	5	16	432	4
8	214	3	17	197	3
9	573	5	18	460	4
OUT	**3,616**	**36**	**IN**	**3,740**	**36**

HOLE 15 A VICIOUS CURVE

Shaped like a hook, this brilliant hole curves viciously right-to-left around a lake and the fairway is banked with its right edge finishing high up the hillside. What catches your eye most is the mass of sand. Nine huge bowl bunkers hug the inside of the dogleg and several more are dotted on the outside line. Depending on how far you have struck your drive, you have three choices. Either lay up short of the small inlet that cuts in, splitting the fairway in two; go for the carry to a heavily bunkered second portion of fairway; or have a crack at the green. The big hitters might be able to reach the green as the hole curves back on itself, but it is all carry over water. From the back tees a drive of around 280 yards (256 meters) will leave a shot of about 240 yards (220 meters) across the lake to the green—a considerable distance saver, but a very risky policy.

TPC Sawgrass, USA

UNCOMPROMISING, AND AN ASSAULT on your game and spirit, The Stadium Course is a purpose-built tournament venue in the steamy swamplands of Florida. All the holes at Sawgrass have their own particular merit but the course is most famous for the daunting island green at the 17th. Sawgrass is one of a number of Tournament Players Clubs (TPCs) where members can experience what it is like to be a touring professional in world golf.

IN THE LATE 1970s the PGA Tour's Commissioner Deane Beman had a brainwave. The headquarters of the PGA Tour were already based in this north Floridian town, so Beman thought it would be a great idea to build a golf course on its doorstep that could permanently host the annual Tournament Players Championship – this was dubbed the "Fifth Major" because of the strength of its field.

Pete Dye was drafted in to turn this swampy area close to the Atlantic Ocean into a world-beating course. But it was a special brief he had to fulfil. Not only was Dye to create a course through the sandy marsh that would test the best, it had to accommodate hordes of spectators and provide superb vantage points for them. No course had ever before been specifically designed with the galleries in mind. Beman also stipulated that he wanted green complexes with at least four different "shelves" so that they could provide four distinct areas for cutting the hole – one for each day of the tournament.

BUILDING THE COURSE

Dye's team reclaimed massive areas of swampland and brought in truckloads of sand to raise the playing areas off the marsh, and as Dye's nickname "Dye-abolical" suggests, he went on to produce a severe test full of tactical nous and bravery.

The Stadium Course opened in 1980 but was not an instant hit with the players. After the first Tournament Players Championship in 1982, won by Jerry Pate, some respected golfers had some harsh words to say. Ben Crenshaw remarked: "It's Star Wars golf, designed by Darth Vader", and Jack Nicklaus left no-one in doubt that it did not suit the way he played: "I've never been good at stopping a 5-iron on the hood of a car." Dye took notice and tweaked his design, making it more friendly, particularly on the greens. While the routeing and the basic course has stayed

THE INFAMOUS AND REMARKABLE 17TH is the one hole that attracts people to Sawgrass, whether to play it for themselves or to watch from the grandstands as the PGA Tour professionals agonize over its devilish charms.

KEY MOMENTS

THE FAN'S FAVOURITE FRED COUPLES came of age at the 1984 TPC at Sawgrass when he set the then course record of 64 in the second round, going on to win the first of his two titles. His course record no longer stands, as it is now 63, shot in 1992 by none other than Couples again! The 17th is one of the holes where Couples entertained the crowd. It's the one hole that people come to Sawgrass for, whether it is to play or simply watch the agony of the Tour pros. Couples made the most incredible comeback on this hole when he found the lake with his first shot, but reloaded and holed out with his next for an amazing par 3.

AT THE AGE OF 48, the diminutive and popular American Fred Funk won the 2005 TPC to become the oldest man to win this prestigious tournament. Funk is known as the straightest hitter on Tour but not the longest, so his feat of holding the world's best at bay in conditions that made scoring very difficult was remarkable. The whole week was beset by heavy rain and swirling winds, and the average score in round four was a heady 76.5, the highest in the tournament's history. Yet Funk clung on gamely to shoot a 71 and finish at 9 under par, winning by one from Luke Donald, Scott Verplank, and Tom Lehman.

TPC SAWGRASS

110 CHAMPIONSHIP WAY, PONTE VEDRA BEACH, FLORIDA 32082, USA
www.tpc.com

THE STADIUM COURSE

FOUNDED 1980 **DESIGNER** Pete Dye
LENGTH 7,215 yards **COURSE RECORD** 63
(6,597 metres) Fred Couples (1992)
PAR 72

SELECTED CHAMPIONS

THE PLAYERS CHAMPIONSHIP Fred Couples (1996); Steve Elkington (1997); Justin Leonard (1998); David Duval (1999); Hal Sutton (2000); Tiger Woods (2001); Craig Perks (2002); Davis Love III (2003); Adam Scott (2004); Fred Funk (2005); Stephen Ames (2006); Phil Mickelson (2007)

CARD OF THE COURSE

THE FRONT NINE			THE BACK NINE		
HOLE	YARDS	PAR	HOLE	YARDS	PAR
1	392	4	10	424	4
2	532	5	11	535	5
3	177	3	12	358	4
4	384	4	13	181	3
5	466	4	14	467	4
6	393	4	15	449	4
7	442	4	16	507	5
8	219	3	17	137	3
9	583	5	18	447	4
OUT	**3,588**	**36**	**IN**	**3,627**	**36**

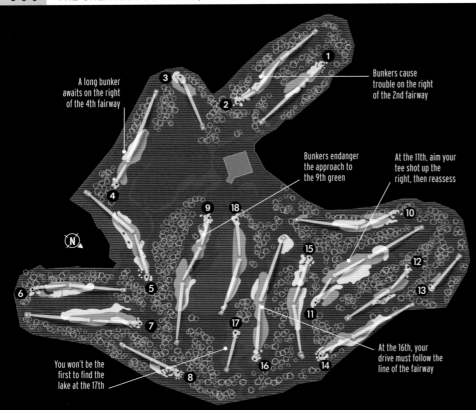

A long bunker awaits on the right of the 4th fairway

Bunkers cause trouble on the right of the 2nd fairway

Bunkers endanger the approach to the 9th green

At the 11th, aim your tee shot up the right, then reassess

At the 16th, your drive must follow the line of the fairway

You won't be the first to find the lake at the 17th

THE COURSE

Designed especially for the world's best to play and for spectators to watch, this modern master trundles over marshland and contains some of the most on-the-edge holes on the planet. The finishing three are worth the entrance fee alone.

THE FRONT NINE ❶ If you dare, drive down the right for the best line into narrow green. ❷ A reachable par 5, but trouble awaits on both sides the entire length. ❸ Short is best as it will leave a chip up the sloping two-tier green. ❹ A snaking bunker protects the right and the small fiendish green is fronted by water. Accuracy is a premium. ❺ Long four with sand everywhere. The sprawl short of the green is unnerving to the eye. ❻ The drive is over a part of a vast trap that wraps around the left side, and grass bunkers and more sand hem in the green. ❼ Slight S-shape hole with three monstrous strips of sand on the flanks.

❽ Ten bunkers protect this long three. Miss the green and par is hard. ❾ A plotter's par 5, with two halves of the hole split by a water channel. Play the third from the right side.

THE BACK NINE ❿ A pull left will end up in the 170-yard (155-meter) bunker, but the line in is best from that side. ⓫ Awesome par 5 with a huge risk-and-reward element thanks to offset green sitting next to lake. ⓬ To get a clear view of green, drive up the right side, flirting with large bunker. ⓭ Going left on this short hole will surely find water. ⓮ Going into the bunker that runs for 250 yards (229 meters) down the right is probably a bogey or worse. ⓯ Slight dogleg right where only the fairway will do. ⓰ Monumental par 5 where eagles and doubles are common. It's all about the second shot, as water awaits right. ⓱ The original island hole that excites and exasperates like no other. A par is one to treasure. ⓲ A sweeping four, edged by water all down the left. But there's little safety out right either.

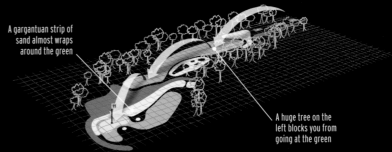

A gargantuan strip of sand almost wraps around the green

A huge tree on the left blocks you from going at the green

HOLE 11 — RISKS GALORE

This tremendous hole is reachable in two with a couple of exacting shots. But many risks await—a massive bunker, a huge tree, a water hazard that splits the fairway, and a strip of sand beside the green that makes even a wedge approach a tricky deal to clinch.

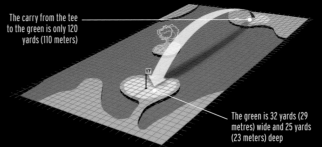

The carry from the tee to the green is only 120 yards (110 meters)

The green is 32 yards (29 metres) wide and 25 yards (23 meters) deep

HOLE 17 — DEVIL ISLAND

The carry to the awesome island green on the 17th is intimidating enough, but the swirling wind makes it worse. Perfectly well struck shots can stall and plunge short of safety, but a knock-down shot risks bounding over the back.

Trees come into play for a water-avoiding drive right

The green is perilously close to the water on the left

HOLE 18 — PLENTY OF PERIL

The 18th is a curving par 4 that arcs around a lake. If you aim to avoid the water on the green's left and bail out right, you find either the grassed humps and hollows or a nasty pot bunker. Chipping and putting from there to a green that slopes toward the water is nerve-racking.

The brilliant 11th hole

The 15th green

The water hazard beside the 13th

the same, a huge overhaul was undertaken in 2006. Bunkers were deepened, more waste areas and the lakes were brought closer into play and 200 palms, oaks, and pines were planted. Most importantly, all the tees, fairways, and greens were rebuilt with a sand base, with the aim of making the course play firmer and faster.

Just when the pros thought they had the course sussed after many years of play, the green slopes were subtly changed and the lines from the tees and into the greens were altered. One thing that hasn't changed a huge amount over the years is the length. In 15 years it has only grown by just over 300 yards (274 meters), but then the trouble is so severe that length hardly matters.

HEART-STOPPING SHOTS

There is no question that great driving is key to playing this course well. Massively long strips of sand flank many of the fairways, and well-placed trees can block out the direct route to the greens. Water comes into play off the tees on 12 holes, although much is defended by the snaking sand. There is always a preferred line from the tee and most definitely a perfect way to approach the greens to get at any given pin position.

All over the course you face heart-stopping shots. Apart from the ultimate challenge at the infamous 17th, two of the finest examinations of mind and body come at the 11th and 16th. Both are in range in two and eagles are on, but the risks are acute. At the 16th, the drive must go right to left to follow the line of the fairway or it will run out into clinging rough, from where the only option is to lay up. A huge overhanging oak on the left just short of the green makes the second shot awkward. It tends to push people right, which spells disaster as the green juts out into a lake and water guards all around the right.

Where the risk-and-reward 16th comes in the round is significant, as it is followed by two of the toughest holes on the course. For the tournament, this trio always shape the outcome. In 2002 New Zealander Craig Perks showed how crucial these three are. Behind by one at 5 under par with three to play, his gambling second with a 4-iron just

■ Devil Island from above

It's like having a **3 o'clock appointment for a root canal.** You're thinking about it all morning and you feel bad all day. You kind of know sooner or later **you've got to get to it**

MARK CALCAVECCHIA, TALKING ABOUT THE 17TH HOLE

cleared the water and stuck in the rough, from where he chipped in for an eagle to go one ahead. He hit the 17th safely and roll in the birdie to go two in front, but it wasn't over. Faced with the 18th, the course's hardest hole, he bailed out right into the trees and had to hack out. This left him a long iron in. He flew the green into the wiry rough. Remarkably, he chipped in again for his winning par.

The Stadium Course is a devil wrapped up in an immaculate and stunning package. A blood, sweat, and tears experience open to all and the ultimate tournament course where the galleries can enjoy the many highs and lows which the best players in the world throw up.

■ Reptilian golf fan

■ The sign for the 17th

■ The clubhouse at Sawgrass

The Ryder Cup

36 Matches
US 24 Wins; **EUROPE** 10 Wins; **Ties** 2

Year	Location	Winner	
1927	Worcester CC, Worcester, MA, USA	**US** 9½	**GB&I** 2½
1929	Moortown GC, Leeds, England	**GB&I** 7	**US** 5
1931	Scioto CC, Columbus, OH, USA	**US** 9	**GB&I** 3
1933	Southport & Ainsdale GC, England	**GB&I** 6½	**US** 5½
1935	Ridgewood CC, Ridgewood, NJ, USA	**US** 9	**GB&I** 3
1937	Southport & Ainsdale GC, England	**US** 8	**GB&I** 4
1939-45	No Matches played due to World War II		
1947	Portland GC, Portland, OR, USA	**US** 11	**GB&I** 1
1949	Ganton GC, Scarborough, England	**US** 7	**GB&I** 5
1951	Pinehurst CC, Pinehurst, NC, USA	**US** 9½	**GB&I** 2½
1953	Wentworth GC, Wentworth, England	**US** 6½	**GB&I** 5½
1955	Thunderbird CC, Palm Springs, CA, USA	**US** 8	**GB&I** 4
1957	Lindrick GC, Yorkshire, England	**GB & I** 7½	**US** 4½
1959	Eldorado CC, Palm Desert, CA, USA	**US** 8½	**GB&I** 3½
1961	Royal Lytham & St. Annes, England	**US** 14½	**GB&I** 9½
1963	East Lake CC, Atlanta, GA, USA	**US** 23	**GB&I** 9
1965	Royal Birkdale GC, Southport, England	**US** 19½	**GB&I** 12½
1967	Champions GC, Houston, TX, USA	**US** 23½	**GB&I** 18½
1969	Royal Birkdale GC, Southport, England	**US** 16	**GB&I** 16
1971	Old Warson CC, St. Louis, MO, USA	**US** 18½	**GB&I** 13½
1973	Muirfield, East Lothian, Scotland	**US** 19	**GB&I** 13
1975	Laurel Valley GC, Ligonier, PA, USA	**US** 21	**GB&I** 11
1977	Royal Lytham & St. Annes, England	**US** 12½	**GB&I** 7½
1979	The Greenbrier, WV, USA	**US** 17	**EUROPE** 11
1981	Walton Health GC, Surrey, England	**US** 18½	**EUROPE** 9½
1983	PGA National GC, Palm Beach Gardens, FL, USA	**US** 14½	**EUROPE** 13½
1985	The Belfry, Sutton Coldfield, England	**EUROPE** 16½	**US** 11½
1987	Muirfield Village GC, Dublin, OH, USA	**EUROPE** 15	**US** 13
1989	The Belfry, Sutton Coldfield, England	**EUROPE** 14	**US** 14
1991	The Ocean Course, Kiawah Island, SC, USA	**US** 14½	**EUROPE** 13½
1993	The Belfry, Sutton Coldfield, England	**US** 15	**EUROPE** 13
1995	Oak Hill CC, Rochester, NY, USA	**EUROPE** 14½	**US** 13½
1997	Valderrama GC, Sotogrande, Spain	**EUROPE** 14½	**US** 13½
1999	The Country Club, Brookline, MA, USA	**US** 14½	**EUROPE** 13½
2002	The Belfry, Sutton Coldfield, England	**EUROPE** 15½	**US** 12½
2004	Oakland Hills CC, Bloomfield Hills, MI, USA	**EUROPE** 18½	**USA** 9½
2006	The K Club, Straffan, County Kildare, Ireland	**EUROPE** 18½	**US** 9½

RYDER CUP - MOST APPEARANCES

US

Billy Casper	8	1961, 1963, 1965, 1967, 1969, 1971, 1973, 1975
Raymond Floyd	8	1969, 1975, 1977, 1981, 1983, 1985, 1991, 1993
Lanny Wadkins	8	1977, 1979, 1983, 1985, 1987, 1989, 1991, 1993
Sam Snead	7	1937, 1947, 1949, 1951, 1953, 1955, 1959
Tom Kite	7	1979, 1981, 1983, 1985, 1987, 1989, 1993
Gene Littler	7	1961, 1963, 1965, 1967, 1969, 1971, 1975
Arnold Palmer	6	1961, 1963, 1965, 1967, 1971, 1973
Gene Sarazen	6	1927, 1929, 1931, 1933, 1935, 1937
Jack Nicklaus	6	1969, 1971, 1973, 1975, 1977, 1981
Lee Trevino	6	1969, 1971, 1973, 1975, 1979, 1981

EUROPE

Nick Faldo	11	1977, 1979, 1981, 1983, 1985, 1987, 1989, 1991, 1993, 1995, 1997
Christy O'Connor Sr	10	1955, 1957, 1959, 1961, 1963, 1965, 1967, 1969, 1971, 1973
Bernhard Langer	10	1981, 1983, 1985, 1987, 1989, 1991, 1993, 1995, 1997, 2002
Dai Rees	9	1937, 1947, 1949, 1951, 1953, 1955, 1957, 1959, 1961
Bernard Gallacher	8	1969, 1971, 1973, 1975, 1977, 1979, 1981, 1983
Bernard Hunt	8	1953, 1957, 1959, 1961, 1963, 1965, 1967, 1969
Ian Woosnam	8	1983, 1985, 1987, 1989, 1991, 1993, 1995, 1997
Neil Coles	8	1961, 1963, 1965, 1967, 1969, 1971, 1973, 1977
Peter Alliss	8	1953, 1957, 1959, 1961, 1963, 1965, 1967, 1969
Sam Torrance	8	1981, 1983, 1985, 1987, 1989, 1991, 1993, 1995
Severiano Ballesteros	8	1979, 1983, 1985, 1987, 1989, 1991, 1993, 1995

RYDER CUP - MOST POINTS WON

US		EUROPE	
Billy Casper	23½	Nick Faldo	25
Arnold Palmer	23	Bernhard Langer	24
Lanny Wadkins	21½	Severiano Ballesteros	22½
Lee Trevino	20	Colin Montgomerie	21½
Jack Nicklaus	18½	José Maria Olazábal	17½
Gene Littler	18	Tony Jacklin	17
Tom Kite	17	Ian Woosnam	16½
Hale Irwin	14	Bernard Gallacher	15½
Raymond Floyd	13½	Peter Oosterhuis	15½
Julius Boros	11	Neil Coles	15½

RYDER CUP - MOST MATCHES PLAYED

USA		EUROPE	
Billy Casper	37	Nick Faldo	46
Lanny Wadkins	34	Bernhard Langer	42
Arnold Palmer	32	Neil Coles	40
Raymond Floyd	31	Severiano Ballesteros	37

The Tours

US TOUR - CAREER EARNINGS (US$)

Tiger Woods	$70,806,251	Fred Funk	$20,573,742
Vijay Singh	$53,209,805	Nick Price	$20,551,208
Phil Mickelson	$43,634,626	Stuart Appleby	$20,375,810
Davis Love III	$35,403,813	Stewart Cink	$20,165,873
Jim Furyk	$33,977,874	Scott Verplank	$20,150,965
Ernie Els	$29,681,047	Tom Lehman	$19,663,876
David Toms	$27,769,092	Mike Weir	$19,562,777
Justin Leonard	$21,735,922	Chris DiMarco	$19,267,352
Mark Calcavecchia	$21,119,798	Fred Couples	$19,172,199
Kenny Perry	$21,048,332	Scott Hoch	$18,487,114

EUROPEAN PGA TOUR - CAREER EARNINGS

Colin Montgomerie	€22,493,466	José Maria Olazábal	€11,444,248
Ernie Els	€19,461,026	Michael Campbell	€10,784,295
Retief Goosen	€17,079,652	Angel Cabrera	€10,626,180
Padraig Harrington	€15,445,592	Sergio Garcia	€9,638,814
Darren Clarke	€15,436,426	Ian Woosnam	€9,584,347
Lee Westwood	€13,124,030	David Howell	€9,235,655
Bernhard Langer	€12,408,558	Paul McGinley	€9,030,886
Thomas Bjorn	€12,017,660	Niclas Fasth	€8,094,693
Miguel Ángel Jiménez	€11,647,100	Ian Poulter	€8,036,562
Vijay Singh	€11,594,502	Nick Faldo	€7,988,684

MOST VICTORIES ON US TOUR

Sam Snead	82	Gene Littler	29
Jack Nicklaus	73	Paul Runyan	29
Ben Hogan	64	Lee Trevino	29
Arnold Palmer	62	Henry Picard	26
*Tiger Woods	57	Tommy Armour	25
Byron Nelson	52	Johnny Miller	25
Billy Casper	51	Gary Player	24
Walter Hagen	44	Macdonald Smith	24
Cary Middlecoff	40	Johnny Farrell	22
Gene Sarazen	39	Raymond Floyd	22
Tom Watson	39	Willie Macfarlane	21
Lloyd Mangrum	36	Lanny Wadkins	21
Horton Smith	32	Craig Wood	21
Harry Cooper	31	Jim Barnes	20
Jimmy Demaret	31	Hale Irwin	20
*Phil Mickelson	31	Bill Mehlhorn	20
*Vijay Singh	31	Greg Norman	20
Leo Diegel	30	Doug Sanders	20

* currently active on the US Tour

MOST VICTORIES IN A SEASON ON PGA TOUR

Byron Nelson	18	1945
Ben Hogan	13	1946
Sam Snead	11	1950
Ben Hogan	10	1948
Paul Runyan	9	1933
Tiger Woods	9	2000
Vijay Singh	9	2004
Horton Smith	8	1929
Gene Sarazen	8	1930
Arnold Palmer	8	1960, 1962
Johnny Miller	8	1974

The Open

(* won after a playoff)

1860 Prestwick (12-hole course)

Willie Park , Sr.	55	59	60	174
Tom Morris , Sr.	58	59	59	176

1861 Prestwick

Tom Morris , Sr.	54	56	53	163
Willie Park , Sr.	54	54	59	167
William Dow	59	58	54	171

1862 Prestwick

Tom Morris , Sr.	54	56	53	163
Willie Park , Sr.	59	59	58	176
Charlie Hunter	60	60	58	176

1863 Prestwick

Willie Park , Sr.	56	54	58	168
Tom Morris , Sr.	56	58	56	170
David Park	55	63	54	172

1864 Prestwick

Tom Morris , Sr.	54	58	55	167
Andrew Strath	56	57	56	169
Robert Andrew	57	58	60	175

1865 Prestwick

Andrew Strath	55	54	53	162
Willie Park , Sr.	56	52	56	164

1866 Prestwick

Willie Park , Sr.	54	56	59	169
David Park	58	57	56	171
Robert Andrew	58	59	59	176

1867 Prestwick

Tom Morris , Sr.	58	54	58	170
Willie Park , Sr.	58	56	58	172
Andrew Strath	61	57	56	174

1868 Prestwick

Tom Morris , Jr.	50	55	52	157
Robert Andrew	53	54	52	159
Willie Park , Sr.	58	50	54	162

1869 Prestwick

Tom Morris , Jr.	51	54	49	154
Tom Morris , Sr.	54	50	53	157
S. Mure Fergusson	57	54	54	165

1870 Prestwick

Tom Morris , Jr.	47	51	51	149
Bob Kirk	52	52	57	161
Davie Strath	54	49	58	161

1871 No Championship

1872 Prestwick

Tom Morris , Jr.	57	56	53	166
Davie Strath	56	52	61	169
William Doleman	63	60	54	177

1873 Royal & Ancient Golf Club, St. Andrews

Tom Kidd	91	88	179
Jamie Anderson	91	89	180
Bob Kirk	91	92	183
Tom Morris , Jr.	94	89	183

1874 Musselburgh

Mungo Park	75	84	159
Tom Morris , Jr.	83	78	161
George Paxton	80	82	162

1875 Prestwick

Willie Park , Sr.	56	59	51	166
Bob Martin	56	58	54	168
Mungo Park	59	57	55	171

1876 Royal & Ancient Golf Club, St. Andrews

Bob Martin won the title after Davie Strath
refused to participate in the playoff

Bob Martin	86	90	176
Davie Strath	86	90	176
Willie Park , Sr.	94	89	183

1877 Musselburgh

Jamie Anderson	40	42	37	41	160
Bob Pringle	44	38	40	40	162
William Cosgrove	41	39	44	40	164

1878 Prestwick

Jamie Anderson	53	53	51	157
Bob Kirk	53	55	51	159
JOF Morris	50	56	55	161

1879 Royal & Ancient Golf Club, St. Andrews

Jamie Anderson	84	85	169
Jamie Allan	88	84	172
Andrew Kirkaldy	86	86	172

1880 Musselburgh

Bob Ferguson	81	81	162
Peter Paxton	81	86	167
Ned Cosgrove	82	86	168

1881 Prestwick

Bob Ferguson	53	60	57	170
Jamie Anderson	57	60	56	173
Ned Cosgrove	61	59	57	177

1882 Royal & Ancient Golf Club, St. Andrews

Bob Ferguson	83	88	171
Willie Fernie	88	86	174
Jamie Anderson	87	88	175

1883 Musselburgh

*Willie Fernie	75	84	159
Bob Ferguson	78	81	159
William Brown	83	77	160

1884 Prestwick

Jack Simpson	78	82	160
Willie Fernie	80	94	164
Douglas Rolland	81	83	164

1885 Royal & Ancient Golf Club, St. Andrews

Bob Martin	84	87	171
Archie Simpson	83	89	172
David Ayton	89	84	173

1886 Musselburgh

David Brown	79	78	157
Willie Campbell	78	81	159
Ben Campbell	79	81	160

1887 Prestwick

Willie Park , Jr.	82	79	161
Bob Martin	81	81	162
Willie Campbell	77	87	164

1888 Royal & Ancient Golf Club, St. Andrews

Jack Burns	86	85	171
David Anderson , Jr.	86	86	172
Ben Sayers	85	87	172

1889 Musselburgh

*Willie Park , Jr.	39	39	39	38	155
Andrew Kirkaldy	39	38	39	39	155
Ben Sayers	39	40	41	39	159

1890 Prestwick

John Ball , Jr.	82	82	164
Willie Fernie	85	82	167
Archie Simpson	85	82	167

1891 Royal & Ancient Golf Club, St. Andrews

Hugh Kirkaldy	83	83	166
Willie Fernie	84	84	168
Andrew Kirkaldy	84	84	168

1892 Musselburgh

First championship to be spread over two
days and 72 holes

Harold Hilton	78	81	72	74	305
John Ball	75	80	74	79	308
Sandy Herd	77	78	77	76	308

1893 Prestwick

W. Auchterlonie	78	81	81	82	322
Johnny Laidlay	80	83	80	81	324
Sandy Herd	82	81	78	84	325

1894 St. George's, Sandwich

J. H. Taylor	84	80	80	81	326
Douglas Rolland	86	79	84	82	331
Andrew Kirkaldy	86	79	83	84	332

1895 Royal & Ancient Golf Club, St. Andrews

J. H. Taylor	86	78	80	78	322
Sandy Herd	82	77	82	85	326
Andrew Kirkaldy	81	83	84	84	332

1896 Muirfield

*Harry Vardon	83	78	78	77	316
J. H. Taylor	77	78	81	80	316
Willie Fernie	78	79	82	89	319

1897 Royal Liverpool, Hoylake

Harold Hilton	80	75	84	75	314
James Braid	80	74	82	79	315
George Pulford	80	79	79	79	317

1898 Prestwick

Harry Vardon	79	75	77	76	307
Willie Park , Jr.	76	75	78	79	308
Harold Hilton	76	81	77	75	309

1899 St. George's, Sandwich

Harry Vardon	76	76	81	77	310
Jack White	79	79	82	75	315
Andrew Kirkaldy	81	79	82	77	319

1900 Royal & Ancient Golf Club, St. Andrews

J. H. Taylor	79	77	78	75	309
Harry Vardon	79	81	80	77	317
James Braid	82	81	80	79	322

1901 Muirfield

James Braid	79	76	74	80	309
Harry Vardon	77	78	79	78	312
J. H. Taylor	79	83	74	77	313

1902 Royal Liverpool, Hoylake

Sandy Herd	77	76	73	81	307
James Braid	78	76	80	74	308
Harry Vardon	72	77	80	79	308

1903 Prestwick

Harry Vardon	73	77	72	78	300
Tom Vardon	76	81	75	74	306
Jack White	77	78	74	79	308

1904 St. George's, Sandwich

Jack White	80	75	72	69	296
James Braid	77	80	69	71	297
J. H. Taylor	77	78	74	68	297

1905 Royal & Ancient Golf Club, St. Andrews

James Braid	81	78	78	81	318
Rowland Jones	81	77	87	78	323
J. H. Taylor	80	85	78	80	323

1906 Muirfield

James Braid	77	76	74	73	300
J. H. Taylor	77	72	75	80	304
Harry Vardon	77	73	77	78	305

1907 Royal Liverpool, Hoylake

Arnaud Massy	76	81	78	77	312
J. H. Taylor	79	79	76	80	314
George Pulford	81	79	80	75	317

1908 Prestwick

James Braid	70	72	77	72	291
Tom Ball	76	73	76	74	299
Ted Ray	79	71	75	76	301

1909 Royal Cinq Ports, Deal

J. H. Taylor	74	73	74	74	295
Tom Ball	74	75	76	76	301
James Braid	79	75	73	74	301

1910 Royal & Ancient Golf Club, St. Andrews

James Braid	76	73	74	76	299
Sandy Herd	78	74	75	76	303
George Duncan	73	77	71	83	304

1911 St. George's, Sandwich

*Harry Vardon	74	74	75	80	303
Arnaud Massy	75	78	74	76	303
Sandy Herd	77	73	76	78	304

1912 Muirfield

Ted Ray	71	73	76	75	295
Harry Vardon	75	72	81	71	299
James Braid	77	71	77	78	303

1913 Royal Liverpool, Hoylake

J. H. Taylor	73	75	77	79	304
Ted Ray	73	74	81	84	312
Michael Moran	76	74	89	74	313

1914 Prestwick

Harry Vardon	73	77	78	78	306
J. H. Taylor	74	78	74	73	309
Harry Simpson	77	80	78	75	310

1915–1919 No Championship – World War I

1920 Royal Cinq Ports, Deal

George Duncan	80	80	71	72	303
Sandy Herd	72	81	77	75	305
Ted Ray	72	83	78	73	306

1921 Royal & Ancient Golf Club, St. Andrews

*Jock Hutchinson	72	75	79	70	296
Roger Wethered	78	75	72	71	296
Tom Kerrigan	74	80	72	72	298

1922 Royal St. George's, Sandwich

Walter Hagen	76	73	79	72	300
Jim Barnes	75	76	77	73	301
George Duncan	76	75	81	69	302

1923 Troon

Arthur Havers	73	73	73	76	295
Walter Hagen	76	71	74	75	296
Macdonald Smith	80	73	69	75	297

1924 Royal Liverpool, Hoylake

Walter Hagen	77	73	74	77	301
Ernest R Whitcombe	77	70	77	78	302
Frank Ball	78	75	74	77	304

1925 Prestwick

Jim Barnes	70	77	79	74	300
Archie Compston	76	75	75	75	301
Ted Ray	77	76	75	73	301

1926 Royal Lytham & St. Annes

Bobby Jones	72	72	73	74	291
Al Waltrous	71	75	69	78	293
Walter Hagen	68	77	74	76	295

1927 Royal & Ancient Golf Club, St. Andrews

Bobby Jones	68	72	73	72	285
Aubrey Boomer	76	70	73	72	291
Fred Robson	76	72	69	74	291

1928 Royal St. George's, Sandwich

Walter Hagen	75	73	72	72	292
Gene Sarazen	72	76	73	73	294
Archie Compston	75	74	73	73	295

1929 Muirfield

Walter Hagen	75	67	75	75	292
Johnny Farrell	72	75	76	75	298
Leo Diegel	71	69	82	77	299

1930 Royal Liverpool, Hoylake

Bobby Jones	70	72	74	75	291
Leo Diegel	74	73	71	75	293
Macdonald Smith	70	77	75	71	293

1931 Carnoustie

Tommy Armour	73	75	77	71	296
Jose Jurado	76	71	73	77	297
Percy Alliss	74	78	73	73	298

1932 Prince's, Sandwich

Gene Sarazen	70	69	70	74	283
Macdonald Smith	71	76	71	70	288
Arthur Havers	74	71	68	76	289

1933 Royal & Ancient Golf Club, St. Andrews

*Denny Shute	73	73	73	73	292
Craig Wood	77	72	68	75	292
Leo Diegel	75	70	71	77	293
Syd Easterbrook	73	72	71	77	293
Gene Sarazen	72	73	73	75	293

1934 Royal St. George's, Sandwich

Henry Cotton	67	65	72	79	283
Sid Brews	76	71	70	71	288
Alf Padgham	71	70	75	74	290

1935 Muirfield

Alf Perry	69	75	67	72	283
Alf Padgham	70	72	74	71	287
Charles Whitcombe	71	68	73	76	288

1936 Royal Liverpool, Hoylake

Alf Padgham	73	72	71	71	287
Jimmy Adams	71	73	71	73	288
Henry Cotton	73	72	70	74	289

1937 Carnoustie

Henry Cotton	74	73	72	71	290
Reg Whitcombe	72	70	74	76	292
Charles Lacey	76	75	70	72	293

1938 Royal St. George's, Sandwich

Reg Whitcombe	71	71	75	78	295
Jimmy Adams	70	71	78	78	297
Henry Cotton	74	73	77	74	298

1939 Royal & Ancient Golf Club, St. Andrews

Dick Burton	70	72	77	71	290
Johnny Bulla	77	71	71	73	292
Johnny Fallon	71	73	71	79	294

1946 Royal & Ancient Golf Club, St. Andrews

Sam Snead	71	70	74	75	290
Johnny Bulla	71	72	72	79	294
Bobby Locke	69	74	75	76	294

1947 Royal Liverpool, Hoylake

Fred Daly	73	70	78	72	293
Reg Horne	77	74	72	71	294
Frank Stranahan	71	74	72	71	294

1948 Muirfield

Henry Cotton	71	66	75	72	284
Fred Daly	72	71	73	73	289
Roberto de Vicenzo	70	73	72	75	290

1949 Royal St. George's, Sandwich

*Bobby Locke	69	76	68	70	283
Harry Bradshaw	68	77	68	70	283
Roberto de Vicenzo	68	75	73	69	285

1950 Troon

Bobby Locke	69	72	70	68	279
Roberto de Vicenzo	72	71	68	70	281
Fred Daly	75	72	69	66	282

1951 Royal Portrush, Co Antrim

Max Faulkner	71	70	70	74	285
Antonio Cerda	74	72	71	70	287
Charlie Ward	75	73	74	68	290

1952 Royal Lytham & St. Annes

Bobby Locke	69	71	74	73	287
Peter Thomson	68	73	77	70	288
Fred Daly	67	69	77	76	289

1953 Carnoustie

Ben Hogan	73	71	70	68	282
Antonio Cerda	75	71	69	71	286
Dai Rees	72	70	73	71	286

1954 Birkdale

Peter Thomson	72	71	69	71	283
Bobby Locke	74	71	69	70	284
Dai Rees	72	71	69	70	284

1955 Royal & Ancient Golf Club, St. Andrews

Peter Thomson	71	68	70	72	281
Johnny Fallon	73	67	73	70	283
Frank Jowle	70	71	69	74	284

1956 Royal Liverpool, Hoylake

Peter Thomson	70	70	72	74	286
Flory van Donck	71	74	70	74	289
Roberto de Vicenzo	71	70	79	70	290

1957 Royal & Ancient Golf Club, St. Andrews

Bobby Locke	69	72	68	70	279
Peter Thomson	73	69	70	70	282
Eric Brown	67	72	73	71	283

1958 Royal Lytham & St. Annes

*Peter Thomson	66	72	67	73	278
Dave Thomas	70	68	69	71	278
Eric Brown	73	70	65	71	279

1959 Muirfield

Gary Player	75	71	70	68	284
Fred Bullock	68	70	74	74	286
Flory van Donck	70	70	73	73	286

1960 Royal & Ancient Golf Club, St. Andrews

Kel Nagle	69	67	71	71	278
Arnold Palmer	70	71	70	68	279
Roberto de Vicenzo	67	67	75	73	282

1961 Birkdale

Arnold Palmer	70	73	69	72	284
Dai Rees	68	74	71	72	285
Neil Coles	70	77	69	72	288

1962 Troon

Arnold Palmer	71	69	67	69	276
Kel Nagle	71	71	70	70	282
Brian Huggett	75	71	74	69	289
Phil Rodgers	75	70	72	72	289

1963 Royal Lytham & St. Annes

Bob Charles	68	72	66	71	277
Phil Rodgers	67	68	73	69	277
Jack Nicklaus	71	67	70	70	278

1964 Royal & Ancient Golf Club, St. Andrews

Tony Lema	73	68	68	70	279
Jack Nicklaus	76	74	66	68	284
Roberto de Vicenzo	76	72	70	67	285

1965 Royal Birkdale

Peter Thomson	74	68	72	71	285
Brian Huggett	73	68	76	70	287
Christy O'Connor, Sr.	69	73	74	71	287

1966 Muirfield

Jack Nicklaus	70	67	75	70	282
Doug Sanders	71	70	72	70	283
Dave Thomas	72	73	69	69	283

1967 Royal Liverpool, Hoylake

Roberto de Vicenzo	70	71	67	70	278
Jack Nicklaus	71	69	71	69	280
Clive Clark	70	73	69	72	284
Gary Player	72	71	67	74	284

1968 Carnoustie

Gary Player	74	71	71	73	289
Bob Charles	72	72	71	76	291
Jack Nicklaus	76	69	73	73	291

1969 Royal Lytham & St. Annes

Tony Jacklin	68	70	70	72	280
Bob Charles	66	69	75	72	282
Roberto de Vicenzo	72	73	66	72	283
Peter Thomson	71	70	70	72	283

1970 St. Andrews

*Jack Nicklaus	68	69	73	73	283
Doug Sanders	68	71	71	73	283
Harold Henning	67	72	73	73	285
Lee Trevino	68	68	72	77	285

1971 Royal Birkdale

Lee Trevino	69	70	69	70	278
Lu Liang-Huan	70	70	69	70	279
Tony Jacklin	69	70	70	71	280

1972 Muirfield

Lee Trevino	71	70	66	71	278
Jack Nicklaus	70	72	71	66	279
Tony Jacklin	69	72	67	72	280

1973 Royal Troon

Tom Weiskopf	68	67	71	70	276
Neil Coles	71	72	70	66	279
Johnny Miller	70	68	69	72	279

1974 Royal Lytham & St. Annes

Gary Player	69	68	75	70	282
Peter Oosterhuis	71	71	73	71	286
Jack Nicklaus	74	72	70	71	287

1975 Carnoustie

*Tom Watson	71	67	69	72	279
Jack Newton	69	71	65	74	279
Bobby Cole	72	66	66	76	280
Johnny Miller	71	69	66	74	280
Jack Nicklaus	69	71	68	72	280

1976 Royal Birkdale

Johnny Miller	72	68	73	66	279
Jack Nicklaus	74	70	72	69	285
Severiano Ballesteros	69	69	73	74	285

1977 Turnberry

Tom Watson	68	70	65	65	268
Jack Nicklaus	68	70	65	66	269
Hubert Green	72	66	74	67	279

1978 St. Andrews

Jack Nicklaus	71	72	69	69	281
Tom Kite	72	69	72	70	283
Simon Owen	70	75	67	71	283
Ben Crenshaw	70	69	73	71	283
Raymond Floyd	69	75	71	68	283

1979 Royal Lytham & St. Annes

Severiano Ballesteros	73	65	75	70	283
Jack Nicklaus	72	69	73	72	286
Ben Crenshaw	72	71	72	71	286

1980 Muirfield

Tom Watson	68	70	64	69	271
Lee Trevino	68	67	71	69	275
Ben Crenshaw	70	70	68	69	277

1981 Royal St. George's

Bill Rogers	72	66	67	71	276
Bernhard Langer	73	67	70	70	280
Mark James	72	70	68	73	283
Raymond Floyd	74	70	69	70	283

1982 Royal Troon

Tom Watson	69	71	74	70	284
Peter Oosterhuis	74	67	74	70	285
Nick Price	69	69	74	73	285

1983 Royal Birkdale

Tom Watson	67	68	70	70	275
Andy Bean	70	69	70	67	276
Hale Irwin	69	68	72	67	276

1984 St. Andrews

Severiano Ballesteros	69	68	70	69	276
Bernhard Langer	71	68	68	71	278
Tom Watson	71	68	66	73	278

1985 Royal St. George's

Sandy Lyle	68	71	73	70	282
Payne Stewart	70	75	70	68	283
Mark O'Meara	70	72	70	72	284

1986 Turnberry

Greg Norman	74	63	74	69	280
Gordon J Brand	71	68	75	71	285
Bernhard Langer	72	70	76	68	286
Ian Woosnam	70	74	70	72	286

1987 Muirfield

Nick Faldo	68	69	71	71	279
Rodger Davis	64	73	74	69	280
Paul Azinger	68	68	71	73	280

1988 Royal Lytham & St. Annes

Severiano Ballesteros	67	71	70	65	273
Nick Price	70	67	69	69	275
Nick Faldo	71	69	68	71	279

1989 Royal Troon

*Mark Calcavecchia	71	68	68	68	275
Wayne Grady	68	67	69	71	275
Greg Norman	69	70	72	64	275

1990 St. Andrews

Nick Faldo	67	65	67	71	270
Mark McNulty	74	68	68	65	275
Payne Stewart	68	68	68	71	275

1991 Royal Birkdale

Ian Baker-Finch	71	71	64	66	272
Mike Harwood	68	70	69	67	274
Mark O'Meara	71	68	67	69	275

1992 Muirfield

Nick Faldo	66	64	69	73	272
John Cook	66	67	70	70	273
José-Maria Olazábal	70	67	69	68	274

1993 Royal St. George's

Greg Norman	66	68	69	64	267
Nick Faldo	69	63	70	67	269
Bernhard Langer	67	66	70	67	270

1994 Turnberry

Nick Price	69	66	67	66	268
Jesper Parnevik	68	66	68	67	269
Fuzzy Zoeller	71	66	64	70	271

1995 St. Andrews

*John Daly	67	71	73	71	282
Costantino Rocca	69	70	70	73	282
Steven Bottomley	70	72	72	69	283

1996 Royal Lytham & St. Annes

Tom Lehman	67	67	64	73	271
Mark McCumber	67	69	71	66	273
Ernie Els	68	67	71	67	273

1997 Royal Troon

Justin Leonard	69	66	72	65	272
Jesper Parnevik	70	66	66	73	275
Darren Clarke	67	66	71	71	275

1998 Royal Birkdale

*Mark O'Meara	72	68	72	68	280
Brian Watts	68	69	73	70	280
Tiger Woods	65	73	77	66	281

1999 Carnoustie

*Paul Lawrie	73	74	76	67	290
Justin Leonard	73	74	71	72	290
Jean Van de Velde	75	68	70	77	290

2000 St. Andrews

Tiger Woods	67	66	67	69	269
Ernie Els	66	72	70	69	277
Thomas Bjorn	69	69	68	71	277

2001 Royal Lytham & St. Annes

David Duval	69	73	65	67	274
Niclas Fasth	69	69	72	67	277
Billy Mayfair	69	72	67	70	278

2002 Muirfield

*Ernie Els	70	66	72	70	278
Steve Elkington	71	73	68	66	278
Stuart Appleby	73	70	70	65	278
Thomas Levet	72	66	74	66	278

2003 Royal St. George's, Sandwich

Ben Curtis	72	72	70	69	283
Vijay Singh	75	70	69	70	284
Thomas Bjorn	73	70	69	72	284

2004 Royal Troon

*Todd Hamilton	71	67	67	69	274
Ernie Els	69	69	68	68	274
Phil Mickelson	73	66	68	68	275

2005 St. Andrews

Tiger Woods	66	67	71	70	274
Colin Montgomerie	71	66	70	72	279
Fred Couples	68	71	73	68	280

2006 Royal Liverpool, Hoylake

Tiger Woods	67	65	71	67	270
Chris DiMarco	70	65	69	68	272
Ernie Els	68	65	71	71	275

2007 Carnoustie

*Padraig Harrington	69	73	68	67	277
Sergio Garcia	65	71	68	73	277
Andres Romero	71	70	70	67	278

The Masters

Augusta National, Augusta, GA, USA
(* won after a playoff)

1934

Horton Smith	70	72	70	72	284
Craig Wood	71	74	69	71	285
Billy Burke	72	71	70	73	286
Paul Runyan	74	71	70	71	286

1935

Gene Sarazen	68	71	73	70	282
Craig Wood	69	72	68	73	282
Olin Dutra	70	70	70	74	284

1936

Horton Smith	74	71	68	72	285
Harry Cooper	70	69	71	76	286
Gene Sarazen	78	67	72	70	287

1937

Byron Nelson	66	72	75	70	283
Ralph Guldahl	69	72	68	76	285
Ed Dudley	70	71	71	74	286

1938

Henry Picard	71	72	72	70	285
Harry Cooper	68	77	71	71	287
Ralph Guldahl	73	70	73	71	287

1939

Ralph Guldahl	72	68	70	69	279
Sam Snead	70	70	72	68	280
Billy Burke	69	72	71	70	282
Lawson Little , Jr.	72	72	68	70	282

1940

Jimmy Demaret	67	72	70	71	280
Lloyd Mangrum	64	75	71	74	284
Byron Nelson	69	72	74	70	285

1941

Craig Wood	66	71	71	72	280
Byron Nelson	71	69	73	70	283
Sam Byrd	73	70	68	74	285

1942

*Byron Nelson	68	67	72	73	280
Ben Hogan	73	70	67	70	280
Paul Runyan	67	73	72	71	283

1946

Herman Keiser	69	68	71	74	282
Ben Hogan	74	70	69	70	283
Bob Hamilton	75	69	71	72	287

1947

Jimmy Demaret	69	71	70	71	281
Byron Nelson	69	72	72	70	283
Frank Stranahan	73	72	70	68	283

1948

Claude Harmon	70	70	69	70	279
Cary Middlecoff	74	71	69	70	284
Chick Harbert	71	70	70	76	287

1949

Sam Snead	73	75	67	67	282
Johnny Bulla	74	73	69	69	285
Lloyd Mangrum	69	74	72	70	285

1950

Jimmy Demaret	70	72	72	69	283
Jim Ferrier	70	67	73	75	285
Sam Snead	71	74	70	72	287

1951

Ben Hogan	70	72	70	68	280
Skee Riegel	73	68	70	71	282
Lloyd Mangrum	69	74	70	73	286
Lew Worsham	71	71	72	72	286

1952

Sam Snead	70	67	77	72	286
Jack Burke , Jr.	76	67	78	69	290
Al Besselink	70	76	71	74	291
Tommy Bolt	71	71	75	74	291
Jim Ferrier	72	70	77	72	291

1953

Ben Hogan	70	69	66	69	274
Ed Oliver	69	73	67	70	279
Lloyd Mangrum	74	68	71	69	282

1954

*Sam Snead	74	73	70	72	289
Ben Hogan	72	73	69	75	289
William Patton	70	74	75	71	290

1955

Cary Middlecoff	72	65	72	70	279
Ben Hogan	73	68	72	73	286
Sam Snead	72	71	74	70	287

1956

Jack Burke , Jr.	72	71	75	71	289
Ken Venturi	66	69	75	80	290
Cary Middlecoff	67	72	75	77	291

1957

Doug Ford	72	73	72	66	283
Sam Snead	72	68	74	72	286
Jimmy Demaret	72	70	75	70	287

1958

Arnold Palmer	70	73	68	73	284
Doug Ford	74	71	70	70	285
Fred Hawkins	71	75	68	71	285

1959

Art Wall , Jr.	73	74	71	66	284
Cary Middlecoff	74	71	68	72	285
Arnold Palmer	71	70	71	74	286

1960

Arnold Palmer	67	73	72	70	282
Ken Venturi	73	69	71	70	283
Dow Finsterwald	71	70	72	71	284

1961

Gary Player	69	68	69	74	280
Charles Coe	72	71	69	69	281
Arnold Palmer	68	69	73	71	281

1962

Arnold Palmer	70	66	69	75	280
Gary Player	67	71	71	71	280
Dow Finsterwald	74	68	65	73	280

1963

Jack Nicklaus	74	66	74	72	286
Tony Lema	74	69	74	70	287
Julius Boros	76	69	71	72	288
Sam Snead	70	73	74	71	288

1964

Arnold Palmer	69	68	69	70	276
Dave Marr	70	73	69	70	282
Jack Nicklaus	71	73	71	67	282

1965

Jack Nicklaus	67	71	64	69	271
Arnold Palmer	70	68	72	70	280
Gary Player	65	73	69	73	280

1966

*Jack Nicklaus	68	76	72	72	288
Tommy Jacobs	75	71	70	72	288
Gay Brewer , Jr.	74	72	72	70	288

1967

Gay Brewer , Jr.	73	68	72	67	280
Bobby Nichols	72	69	70	70	281
Bert Yancey	67	73	71	73	284

1968

Bob Goalby	70	70	71	66	277
Roberto De Vicenzo	69	73	70	66	278
Bert Yancey	71	71	72	65	279

1969

George Archer	67	73	69	72	281
Billy Casper , Jr.	66	71	71	74	282
George Knudson	70	73	69	70	282
Tom Weiskopf	71	71	69	71	282

1970

*Billy Casper , Jr.	72	68	68	71	279
Gene Littler	69	70	70	70	279
Gary Player	74	68	68	70	280

1971

Charles Coody	66	73	70	70	279
Johnny Miller	72	73	68	68	281
Jack Nicklaus	70	71	68	72	281

1972

Jack Nicklaus	68	71	73	74	286
Bruce Crampton	72	75	69	73	289
Bobby Mitchell	73	72	71	73	289
Tom Weiskopf	74	71	70	74	289

1973

Tommy Aaron	68	73	74	68	283
Jesse Snead	70	71	73	70	284
Jim Jamieson	73	71	70	71	285
Jack Nicklaus	69	77	73	66	285
Peter Oosterhuis	73	70	68	74	285

1974

Gary Player	71	71	66	70	278
Dave Stockton	71	66	70	73	280
Tom Weiskopf	71	69	70	70	280

1975

Jack Nicklaus	68	67	73	68	276
Johnny Miller	75	71	65	66	277
Tom Weiskopf	69	72	66	70	277

1976

Raymond Floyd	65	66	70	70	271
Ben Crenshaw	70	70	72	67	279
Jack Nicklaus	67	69	73	73	282
Larry Ziegler	67	71	72	72	282

1977

Tom Watson	70	69	70	67	276
Jack Nicklaus	72	70	70	66	278
Tom Kite	70	73	70	67	280
Rik Massengale	70	73	67	70	280

1978

Gary Player	72	72	69	64	277
Rod Funseth	73	66	70	69	278
Hubert Green	72	69	65	72	278
Tom Watson	73	68	68	69	278

1979

Fuzzy Zoeller	70	71	69	70	280
Ed Sneed	68	67	69	76	280
Tom Watson	68	71	70	71	280

1980

Severiano Ballesteros	66	69	68	72	275
Gibby Gilbert	70	74	68	67	279
Jack Newton	68	74	69	68	279

1981

Tom Watson	71	68	70	71	280
Johnny Miller	69	72	73	68	282
Jack Nicklaus	70	65	75	72	282

1982

*Craig Stadler	75	69	67	73	284
Dan Pohl	75	75	67	67	284
Severiano Ballesteros	73	73	68	71	285
Jerry Pate	74	73	67	71	285

1983

Severiano Ballesteros	68	70	73	69	280
Ben Crenshaw	76	70	70	68	284
Tom Kite	70	72	73	69	284

1984

Ben Crenshaw	67	72	70	68	277
Tom Watson	74	67	69	69	279
David Edwards	71	70	72	67	280
Gil Morgan	73	71	69	67	280

1985

Bernhard Langer	72	74	68	68	282
Severiano Ballesteros	72	71	71	70	284
Raymond Floyd	70	73	69	72	284
Curtis Strange	80	65	68	71	284

1986

Jack Nicklaus	74	71	69	65	279
Tom Kite	70	74	68	68	280
Greg Norman	70	72	68	70	280

1987

*Larry Mize	70	72	72	71	285
Severiano Ballesteros	73	71	70	71	285
Greg Norman	73	74	66	72	285

1988

Sandy Lyle	71	67	72	71	281
Mark Calcavecchia	71	69	72	70	282
Craig Stadler	76	69	70	68	283

1989

*Nick Faldo	68	73	77	65	283
Scott Hoch	69	74	71	69	283
Ben Crenshaw	71	72	70	71	284
Greg Norman	74	75	68	67	284

1990

*Nick Faldo	71	72	66	69	278
Raymond Floyd	70	68	68	72	278
John Huston	66	74	68	75	283
Lanny Wadkins	72	73	70	68	283

1991

Ian Woosnam	72	66	67	72	277
José Maria Olazábal	68	71	69	70	278
Ben Crenshaw	70	73	68	68	279
Steve Pate	72	73	69	65	279
Lanny Wadkins	67	71	70	71	279
Tom Watson	68	68	70	73	279

1992

Fred Couples	69	67	69	70	275
Raymond Floyd	69	68	69	71	277
Cory Pavin	72	71	68	67	278

1993

Bernhard Langer	68	70	69	70	277
Chip Beck	72	67	72	70	281
John Daly	70	71	73	69	283
Steve Elkington	71	70	71	71	283
Tom Lehman	67	75	73	68	283

1994

José-Maria Olazábal	74	67	69	69	279
Tom Lehman	70	70	69	72	281
Larry Mize	68	71	72	71	282

1995

Ben Crenshaw	70	67	69	68	274
Davis Love III	69	69	71	66	275
Jay Haas	71	64	72	70	277
Greg Norman	73	68	68	68	277

1996

Nick Faldo	69	67	73	67	276
Greg Norman	63	69	71	78	281
Phil Mickelson	65	73	72	72	282

1997

Tiger Woods	70	66	65	69	270
Tom Kite	77	69	66	70	282
Tommy Tolles	72	72	72	67	283

1998

Mark O'Meara	74	70	68	67	279
Fred Couples	69	70	71	70	280
David Duval	71	68	74	67	280

1999

José Maria Olazábal	70	66	73	71	280
Davis Love III	69	72	70	71	282
Greg Norman	71	68	71	73	283

2000

Vijay Singh	72	67	70	69	278
Ernie Els	72	67	74	68	281
Loren Roberts	73	69	71	69	282
David Duval	73	65	74	70	282

2001

Tiger Woods	70	66	68	68	272
David Duval	71	66	70	67	274
Phil Mickelson	67	69	69	70	275

2002

Tiger Woods	70	69	66	71	276
Retief Goosen	69	67	69	74	279
Phil Mickelson	69	72	68	71	280

2003

Mike Weir	70	68	75	68	281
Len Mattiace	73	74	69	65	281
Phil Mickelson	73	70	72	68	283

2004

Phil Mickelson	72	69	69	69	279
Ernie Els	70	72	71	67	280
KJ Choi	71	70	72	69	282

2005

Tiger Woods	74	66	65	71	276
Chris DiMarco	67	67	74	68	276
Luke Donald	68	77	69	69	283
Retief Goosen	71	75	70	67	283

2006

Phil Mickelson	70	72	70	69	281
Tim Clark	70	72	72	69	283

2007

Zach Johnson	71	73	76	69	289
Rory Sabbatini	73	76	73	69	290
Retief Goosen	76	76	70	69	290
Tiger Woods	73	74	72	72	290

The US Open

1895 Newport GC, Newport, RI

Horace Rawlins	45	46	41	41	173
Willie Dunn , Jr.	43	46	44	42	175
James Foulis	46	43	44	43	176
A. W. Smith	47	43	44	42	176

1896 Shinnecock Hills, GC Southampton, NY

James Foulis	78	74	152
Horace Rawlins	79	76	155
Joe Lloyd	76	81	157

1897 Chicago GC, Wheaton, IL

Joe Lloyd	83	79	162
Willie Anderson	79	84	163
Willie Dunn , Jr.	87	81	168
James Foulis	80	89	168

1898 Myopia Hunt Club, S. Hamilton, MA

Fred Herd	84	85	75	84	328
Alex Smith	78	86	86	85	335
Willie Anderson	81	82	87	86	336

1899 Baltimore CC, Baltimore, MD

Willie Smith	77	82	79	77	315
Val Fitzjohn	85	80	79	82	326
George Low	82	79	89	76	326
WH Way	80	85	80	81	326

1900 Chicago GC, Wheaton, IL

Harry Vardon	79	78	76	80	313
J. H. Taylor	76	82	79	78	315
David Bell	78	83	83	78	322

1901 Myopia Hunt Club, S. Hamilton, MA

*Willie Anderson	84	83	83	81	331
Alex Smith	82	82	87	80	331
Willie Smith	84	86	82	81	333

1902 Garden City GC, Garden City, NY

Laurence Auchterlonie	78	78	74	77	307
St.ewart Gardner	82	76	77	78	313
Walter Travis	82	82	75	74	313

1903 Baltusrol GC, Springfield, NJ

*Willie Anderson	73	76	76	82	307
David Brown	79	77	75	76	307
St.eward Gardner	77	77	82	79	315

1904 Glen View GC, Club, IL

Willie Anderson	75	78	78	72	303
Gilbert Nicholls	80	76	79	73	308
Fred MacKenzie	76	79	74	80	309

1905 Myopia Hunt Club, S. Hamilton, MA

Willie Anderson	81	80	76	77	314
Alex Smith	76	80	80	80	316
Percy Barrett	81	80	77	79	317
Peter Robertson	97	80	81	77	317

1906 Onwentsia Club, Lake Forest, IL

Alex Smith	73	74	73	75	295
Willie Smith	73	81	74	74	302
Laurie Auchterionie	76	78	75	76	305
James Maiden	80	73	77	75	305

1907 Philadelphia CC, Philadelphia, PA

Alex Ross	76	74	76	76	302
Gilbert Nicholls	80	73	72	79	304
Alex Campbell	78	74	78	75	305

1908 Myopia Hunt Club, S. Hamilton, MA

*Fred McLeod	82	82	81	77	322
Willie Smith	77	82	85	78	322
Alex Smith	80	83	83	81	327

1909 Englewood GC, Englewood, NJ

George Sargent	75	72	72	71	290
Tom McNamara	73	69	75	77	294
Alex Smith	76	73	74	72	295

1910 Philadelphia CC, Philadelphia, PA

*Alex Smith	73	73	79	73	298
John McDermottt	74	74	75	75	298
Macdonald Smith	74	78	75	71	298

1911 Chicago GC, Wheaton, IL

*John J McDermott	81	72	75	79	307
Mike Brady	76	77	79	75	307
George Simpson	76	77	79	75	307

1912 Cricket Club of Buffalo, Buffalo, NY

John J McDermott	74	75	74	71	294
Tom McNamara	74	80	73	69	296
Mike Brady	72	75	73	79	299
Alex Smith	77	70	77	75	299

1913 The Country Club, Brookline, MA

*Francis Ouimet	77	74	74	79	304
Harry Vardon	75	72	78	79	304
Ted Ray	79	70	76	79	304

1914 Midlothian CC, Blue Island, IL

Walter Hagen	68	74	75	73	290
Charles Evans , Jr.	76	74	71	70	291
Fred McLeod	78	73	75	71	297
George Sargent	74	77	74	72	297

1915 Baltusrol GC, Springfield, NJ

Jerome D. Travers	76	72	73	76	297
Tom McNamara	78	71	74	75	298
Bob MacDonald	72	77	73	78	300

1916 Minikahda Club, Minneapolis, MN

Charles Evans , Jr.	70	69	74	73	286
Jock Hutchison	73	75	72	68	288
Jim Barnes	71	74	71	74	290

1917-18 No Championships played due to World War I

1919 Brae Burn CC, West Newton, MA

*Walter Hagen	78	73	75	75	301
Mike Brady	74	74	73	80	301
Jock Hutchison	78	76	76	76	306
Tom McNamara	80	73	79	74	306

1920 Inverness Club, Toledo, OH

Edward Ray	74	73	73	75	295
Jack Burke Sr	75	77	72	72	296
Leo Diegel	71	74	73	77	296
Jock Hutchison	69	76	74	77	296
Harry Vardon	74	73	71	78	296

1921 Columbia CC, Chevy Chase, MD

James M Barnes	69	75	73	72	289
Walter Hagen	79	73	72	74	289
Fred McLeod	74	74	76	74	298

1922 Skokie CC, Glencoe, IL

Gene Sarazen	72	73	75	68	288
John Black	71	71	75	72	289
Bobby Jones	74	72	70	73	289

1923 Inwood CC, Inwood, NY

*Bobby Jones	71	73	76	76	296
Bobby Cruikshank	73	72	78	73	296
Jock Hutchison	70	72	82	78	302

1924 Oakland Hills CC, Bloomfield Hills, MI

Cyril Walker	74	74	74	75	297
Bobby Jones	74	73	75	78	300
Bill Mehlhorn	72	75	76	78	301

1925 Worcester CC, Worcester, MA

*William Macfarlane	74	67	72	78	291
Bobby Jones	77	70	70	74	291
Johnny Farrell	71	74	69	78	292
Francis Quimet	70	73	73	76	292

1926 Scioto CC, Columbus, OH

Bobby Jones	70	79	71	73	293
Joe Turnesa	71	74	72	77	294
Leo Diegel	72	76	75	74	297
Johnny Farrell	76	79	69	73	297
Bill Mehlhorn	68	75	76	78	297
Gene Sarazen	78	77	72	70	297

1927 Oakmont CC, Oakmont, PA

*Tommy Armour	78	71	76	76	301
Harry Cooper	74	76	74	77	301
Gene Sarazen	74	74	80	74	302

1928 Olympia Fields CC, Matteson, IL

*Johnny Farrell	77	74	71	72	294
Bobby Jones	73	71	73	77	294
Roland Hancock	74	77	72	72	295

1929 Winged Foot GC, Mamaroneck, NY

*Robert T. Jones , Jr.	69	75	71	79	294
Al Espinosa	70	72	77	75	294
Gene Sarazen	71	71	76	78	296
Denny Shute	73	71	76	76	296

1930 Interlachen CC, Minneapolis, MN

Robert T. Jones , Jr.	71	73	68	75	287
Macdonald Smith	70	75	74	70	289
Horton Smith	72	70	76	74	292

1931 Inverness Club, Toledo, OH

*Billy Burke	73	72	74	73	292
George von Elm	75	69	73	75	292
Leo Diegel	75	73	74	72	294

1932 Fresh Meadow CC, Flushing, NY

Gene Sarazen	74	76	70	66	286
Bobby Cruikshank	78	74	69	68	289
Phil Perkins	76	69	74	70	289

1933 North Shore GC, Glenview, IL

John Goodman	75	66	70	76	287
Ralph Guldahl	76	71	70	71	288
Craig Wood	73	74	71	72	290

1934 Merion CC, Ardmore, PA

Olin Dutra	76	74	71	72	293
Gene Sarazen	73	72	73	76	294
Harry Cooper	76	74	74	71	295
Wiffy Cox	71	75	74	75	295
Bobby Cruikshank	71	71	77	76	295

1935 Oakmont CC, Oakmont PA

Sam Parks , Jr.	77	73	73	76	299
Jimmy Thomson	73	73	77	78	301
Walter Hagen	77	76	73	76	302

1936 Baltusrol GC, Springfield, NJ

Tony Manero	73	69	73	67	282
Harry Cooper	71	70	70	73	284
Clarence Clark	69	75	71	72	287

1937 Oakland Hills CC, Bloomfield Hills, MI

Ralph Guldahl	71	69	72	69	281
Sam Snead	69	73	70	71	283
Bobby Cruikshank	73	73	67	72	285

1938 Cherry Hills CC, Englewood, CO

Ralph Guldahl	74	70	71	69	284
Dick Metz	73	68	70	79	290
Harry Cooper	76	69	76	71	292
Tony Penna	78	72	74	68	292

1939 Philadelphia CC, West Conshohocken, PA

*Byron Nelson	72	73	71	68	284
Craig Wood	70	71	71	72	284
Denny Shute	70	72	70	72	284

1940 Canterbury GC, Cleveland, OH

*Lawson Little	72	69	73	73	287
Gene Sarazen	71	74	70	72	287
Horton Smith	69	72	78	69	288

1941 Colonial CC, Fort Worth, TX

Craig Wood	73	71	70	70	284
Denny Shute	69	75	72	71	287
Johnny Bulla	75	71	72	71	289
Ben Hogan	74	77	68	70	289

1942–45 No Championships played due to World War II

1946 Canterbury GC, Cleveland, OH

*Lloyd Mangrum	74	70	68	72	284
Vic Ghezzi	71	69	72	72	284
Byron Nelson	71	71	69	73	284

1947 St. Louis CC, Clayton, MO

*Lew Worsham	70	70	71	71	282
Sam Snead	72	70	70	70	282
Bobby Locke	68	74	70	73	285
Ed Oliver	73	70	71	71	285

1948 Riviera CC, Los Angeles, CA

Ben Hogan	67	72	68	69	276
Jimmy Demaret	71	70	68	69	278
Jim Turnesa	71	69	70	70	280

1949 Medinah CC, Medinah, IL

Cary Middlecoff	75	67	69	75	286
Clayton Heafner	72	71	71	73	287
Sam Snead	73	73	71	70	287

1950 Merion GC, Ardmore, PA

*Ben Hogan	72	69	72	74	287
Lloyd Mangrum	72	70	69	76	287
George Fazio	73	72	72	70	287

1951 Oakland Hills CC, Bloomfield Hills, MI

Ben Hogan	76	73	71	67	287
Clayton Heafner	72	75	73	69	289
Bobby Locke	73	71	74	73	291

1952 Northwood Club, Dallas, TX

Julius Boros	71	71	68	71	281
Ed Oliver	71	72	70	72	285
Ben Hogan	69	69	74	74	286

1953 Oakmont CC, Oakmont, PA

Ben Hogan	67	72	73	71	283
Sam Snead	72	69	72	76	289
Lloyd Mangrum	73	70	74	75	292

1954 Baltusrol GC, Springfield, NJ

Ed Furgol	71	70	71	72	284
Gene Littler	70	69	76	70	285
Lloyd Mangrum	72	71	72	71	286
Dick Mayer	72	71	70	73	286

1955 The Olympic Club, San Francisco, CA

*Jack Fleck	76	69	75	67	287
Ben Hogan	72	73	72	70	287
Tommy Bolt	67	77	75	73	292
Sam Snead	79	69	70	74	292

956 Oak Hill CC, Rochester, NY

Cary Middlecoff	71	70	70	70	281
Julius Boros	71	71	71	69	282
Ben Hogan	72	68	72	70	282

1957 Inverness Club, Toledo, OH

*Dick Mayer	70	68	74	70	282
Cary Middlecoff	71	75	68	68	282
Jimmy Demaret	68	73	70	72	293

1958 Southern Hills CC, Tulsa, OK

Tommy Bolt	71	71	69	72	283
Gary Player	75	68	73	71	287
Julius Boros	71	75	72	71	289

1959 Winged Foot GC, Mamaroneck, NY

Bill Casper , Jr.	70	68	69	74	282
Bob Rosburg	75	70	67	71	283
Claude Harmon	72	70	70	71	284
Mike Souchak	71	70	72	71	284

1960 Cherry Hills CC, Englewood, CO

Arnold Palmer	72	71	72	65	280
Jack Nicklaus	71	71	69	71	282
Julius Boros	73	69	68	73	283
Dow Finsterwald	71	69	70	73	283
Jack Fleck	70	70	72	71	283
Dutch Harrison	74	70	70	69	283
Ted Kroll	72	69	75	67	283
Mike Souchak	68	67	73	75	283

1961 Oakland Hills CC, Bloomfield Hills, MI

Gene Littler	73	68	72	68	281
Bob Goalby	70	72	69	71	282
Doug Sanders	72	67	71	72	282

1962 Oakmont CC, Oakmont, PA

*Jack Nicklaus	72	70	72	69	283
Arnold Palmer	71	68	73	71	283
Bobby Nichols	70	72	70	73	285
Phil Rodgers	74	70	69	72	285

1963 The Country Club, Brookline, MA

*Julius Boros	71	74	76	72	293
Jacky Cupit	70	72	76	75	293
Arnold Palmer	73	69	77	74	293

1964 Congressional CC, Washington, DC

Ken Venturi	72	70	66	70	278
Tommy Jacobs	72	64	70	76	282
Bob Charles	72	72	71	68	283

1965 Bellerive CC, St. Louis, MO

*Gary Player	70	70	71	71	282
Kel Nagle	68	73	72	69	282
Frank Beard	74	69	70	71	284

1966 The Olympic Club, San Francisco, CA

*Bill Casper , Jr.	69	68	73	68	278
Arnold Palmer	71	66	70	71	278
Jack Nicklaus	71	71	69	74	285

1967 Baltusrol GC, Springfield, NJ

Jack Nicklaus	71	67	72	65	275
Arnold Palmer	69	68	73	69	279
Don January	69	72	70	70	281

1968 Oak Hill CC, Rochester, NY

Lee Trevino	69	68	69	69	275
Jack Nicklaus	72	70	70	67	279
Bert Yancey	67	68	70	76	281

1969 Champions GC, Houston, TX

Orville Moody	71	70	68	70	281
Deane Beman	68	69	73	72	282
Al Geiberger	68	72	72	70	282
Bob Rosburg	70	69	72	71	282

1970 Hazeltine National GC, Chaska, MN

Tony Jacklin	71	70	70	70	281
Dave Hill	75	68	71	73	288
Bob Charles	76	71	75	67	289
Bob Lunn	77	72	70	70	289

1971 Merion GC, Ardmore, PA

*Lee Trevino	70	72	69	69	280
Jack Nicklaus	69	72	68	71	280
Jim Colbert	69	69	73	71	282
Bob Rosburg	71	72	70	69	282

1972 Pebble Beach GL, Pebble Beach, CA

Jack Nicklaus	71	73	72	74	290
Bruce Crampton	74	70	72	74	293
Arnold Palmer	77	68	73	76	294

1973 Oakmont CC, Oakmont, PA

John Miller	71	69	76	63	279
John Schlee	73	70	67	70	279
Tom Weiskopf	73	69	69	70	281

1974 Winged Foot GC, Mamaroneck, NY

Hale Irwin	73	70	71	73	287
Forrest Fezler	75	70	74	70	287
Lou Graham	71	75	74	70	290
Bert Yancey	76	69	73	72	290

1975 Medinah CC, Medinah, IL

*Lou Graham	74	72	68	73	287
John Mahaffey	73	71	72	71	287
Frank Beard	74	69	67	78	288
Ben Crenshaw	70	68	76	74	288
Hale Irwin	74	71	73	70	288
Bob Murphy	74	73	72	69	288

1976 Atlanta Athletic Club, Duluth, GA

Jerry Pate	71	69	69	68	277
Al Geiberger	70	69	71	69	279
Tom Weiskopf	73	70	68	68	279

1977 Southern Hills CC, Tulsa, OK

Hubert Green	69	67	72	70	278
Lou Graham	72	71	68	68	279
Tom Weiskopf	71	71	68	71	281

1978 Cherry Hills CC, Englewood, CO

Andy North	70	70	71	74	285
J. C. Snead	70	72	72	72	286
Dave Stockton	71	73	70	72	286

1979 Inverness Club, Toledo, OH

Hale Irwin	74	68	67	75	284
Jerry Pate	71	74	69	72	286
Gary Player	73	73	72	68	286

1980 Baltusrol GC, Springfield, NJ

Jack Nicklaus	63	71	70	68	272
Isao Aoki	68	68	68	70	274
Keith Fergus	66	70	70	70	276
Lon Hinkle	66	70	69	71	276
Tom Watson	71	68	67	70	276

1981 Merion GC, Ardmore, PA

David Graham	68	68	70	67	273
George Burns	69	66	68	73	276
Bill Rogers	70	68	69	69	276

1982 Pebble Beach GL, Pebble Beach, CA

Tom Watson	72	72	68	70	282
Jack Nicklaus	74	70	71	69	284
Bobby Clampett	71	73	72	70	286
Dan Pohl	72	74	70	70	286
Bill Rogers	70	73	69	74	286

1983 Oakmont CC, Oakmont, PA

Larry Nelson	75	73	65	67	280
Tom Watson	72	70	70	69	281
Gil Norman	73	72	70	68	283

1984 Winged Foot GC, Mamaroneck, NY

*Fuzzy Zoeller	71	66	69	70	276
Greg Norman	70	68	69	69	276
Curtis Strange	69	70	74	68	281

1985 Oakland Hills CC, Bloomfield Hills, MI

Andy North	70	65	70	74	279
Dave Barr	70	68	70	72	280
Tze-Chung Chen	65	69	69	77	280
Dennis Watson	72	65	73	70	280

1986 Shinnecock Hills GC, Southampton, NY

Raymond Floyd	75	68	70	66	279
Chip Beck	75	73	68	65	281
Lanny Watkins	74	70	72	65	281

1987 The Olympic Club, San Francisco, CA

Scott Simpson	71	68	70	68	277
Tom Watson	72	65	71	70	278
Seve Ballesteros	68	75	68	71	282

1988 The Country Club, Brookline, MA

*Curtis Strange	70	67	69	72	278
Nick Faldo	72	67	68	71	278
Mark O'Meara	71	72	66	71	280
Steve Pate	72	69	72	67	280

1989 Oak Hill CC, Rochester, NY

Curtis Strange	71	64	73	70	278
Chip Beck	71	69	71	68	279
Mark McCumber	70	68	72	69	279
Ian Woosnam	70	68	73	68	279

1990 Medinah CC, Medinah, IL

*Hale Irwin	69	70	74	67	280
Mike Donald	67	70	72	71	280
Billy Ray Brown	69	71	69	72	281
Nick Faldo	72	72	68	68	281

1991 Hazeltine National GC, Chaska, MN

*Payne Stewart	67	70	73	72	282
Scott Simpson	70	68	72	72	282
Fred Couples	70	70	75	70	285
Larry Nelson	73	72	72	68	285

1992 Pebble Beach GL, Pebble Beach, CA

Tom Kite	71	72	70	72	285
Jeff Sluman	73	74	69	71	287
Colin Montgomerie	70	71	77	70	288

1993 Baltusrol GC, Springfield, NJ

Lee Janzen	67	67	69	69	272
Payne Stewart	70	66	68	70	274
Paul Azinger	71	68	69	69	277

1994 Oakmont CC, Oakmont, PA

*Ernie Els	69	71	66	73	279
Loren Roberts	76	69	74	70	279
Colin Montgomerie	71	65	73	70	279

1995 Shinnecock Hills GC, Southampton, NY

Corey Pavin	72	69	71	68	280
Greg Norman	68	67	74	73	282
Tom Lehman	70	72	67	74	283

1996 Oakland Hills CC, Bloomfield Hills, MI

Steve Jones	74	66	69	69	278
Tom Lehman	71	72	65	71	279
Davis Love III	71	69	70	69	279

1997 Congressional CC, Bethesda, MD

Ernie Els	71	67	69	69	276
Colin Montgomerie	65	76	67	69	277
Tom Lehman	67	70	68	73	278

1998 The Olympic Club, San Francisco, CA

Lee Janzen	73	66	73	68	280
Payne Stewart	66	71	70	74	281
Bob Tway	68	70	73	73	284

1999 No. 2 Course at Pinehurst R & CC, Village of Pinehurst, NC

Payne Stewart	68	69	72	70	279
Phil Mickelson	67	70	73	70	280
Vijay Singh	69	70	73	69	281
Tiger Woods	68	71	72	70	281

2000 Pebble Beach GL, Pebble Beach, CA

Tiger Woods	65	69	71	67	272
Miguel Ángel Jiménez	66	74	76	71	287
Ernie Els	74	73	68	72	287
John Huston	67	75	76	70	288

2001 Southern Hills CC, Tulsa, OK

Retief Goosen	66	70	69	71	276
Mark Brooks	72	64	70	70	276
Stewart Cink	69	69	67	72	277

2002 Bethpage State Park (Black Course), Farmingdale, NY

Tiger Woods	67	68	70	72	277
Phil Mickelson	70	73	67	70	280
Jeff Maggert	69	73	68	72	282

2003 Olympia Fields CC, Olympia Fields, IL

Jim Furyk	67	66	67	72	272
Stephen Leaney	67	68	68	72	275
Kenny Perry	72	71	69	67	279
Mike Weir	73	67	68	71	279

2004 Shinnecock Hills GC, Southampton, NY

Retief Goosen	70	66	69	71	276
Phil Mickelson	68	66	73	71	278
Jeff Maggert	68	67	74	72	281

2005 No. 2 Course at Pinehurst Resort, Village of Pinehurst, NC

Michael Campbell	71	69	71	69	280
Tiger Woods	70	71	72	69	282
Sergio Garcia	71	69	75	70	285
Tim Clark	76	69	70	70	285
Mark Hensby	71	68	72	74	285

2006 Winged Foot GC, Mamaroneck, NY

Geoff Ogilvy	71	70	72	72	285
Jim Furyk	70	72	74	70	286
Colin Montgomerie	69	71	75	71	286
Phil Mickelson	70	73	69	74	286

2007 Oakmont CC, Oakmont, PA

Angel Cabrera	69	71	76	69	285
Jim Furyk	71	75	70	70	286
Tiger Woods	71	74	69	72	286

The USPGA

(* won after a playoff)

1916 Siwanoy CC, Bronxville, NY
Jim Barnes bt. Willie MacFarlane 1 up

1919 Engineers CC, Long Island, NY
Jim Barnes bt. Fred McLeod 6&5

1920 Flossmor, Chicago, IL
Jock Hutchinson bt. Douglas Edgar 1 up

1921 Inwood CC, Rockaway, NY
Walter Hagen bt. Jim Barnes 3&2

1922 Oakmont CC, Oakmont, PA
Gene Sarazen bt. Emmett French 1 up

1923 Pelham GC, NY
Gene Sarazen bt. Walter Hagen 1 up (after 38)

1924 French Springs, IN
Walter Hagen bt. Jim Barnes 2 up

1925 Olympia Fields CC, Olympia Fields, IL
Walter Hagen bt Bill Mehlorn 6&5

1926 Salisbury GC, Long Island, NY
Walter Hagen bt. Leo Diegel 5&3

1927 Cedar Crest GC, Dallas, TX
Walter Hagen bt. Joe Turnesa 1 up

1928 Five Farms CC, Baltimore, MD
Leo Diegel bt. Al Espinosa 6&5

1929 Hillcrest GC, Los Angles, CA
Leo Diegel bt. Johnny Farrell 6&4

1930 Fresh Meadows CC, Flushing Meadows, NY
Tommy Armour bt. Gene Sarazen 1 up

1931 Wannamoisett CC, Romford, RI
Tom Creavy bt. Denny Shute 2&1

1932 Keller GC, St. Paul, MN
Olin Dutra bt. Frank Walsh 4&3

1933 Blue Mound CC, Milwaukee, WI
Gene Sarazen bt. Willie Goggin 5&4

1934 Park Club of Buffalo, Williamsville, NY
Paul Runyan bt. Craig Wood 1 up (after 38)

1935 Twin Hills CC, Oklahoma City, OK
Johnny Revolta bt. Tommy Armour 5&4

1936 Pinehurst CC, NC
Denny Shute bt. Jimmy Thomson 3&2

1937 Pittsburgh Field Club, Aspinwall, PA
Denny Shute bt. Harold McSpaden 1 up

1938 Shawnee CC, Shawnee-on-Delaware, PA
Paul Runyon bt. Sam Snead 8&7

1939 Pomonock CC, Flushing, NY
Henry Picard bt. Byron Nelson 1 up (after 37)

1940 Hershey CC, Hershey, PA
Byron Nelson bt. Sam Snead 1 up

1941 Cherry Hill CC, Denver, CO
Vic Ghezzi bt. Byron Nelson 1 up (after 38)

1942 Seaview CC, Atlantic City, NJ
Sam Snead bt. Jim Turnesa 2&1

1943 – No Championship played due to World War II

1944 Manito CC, Spokane, WA
Bob Hamilton bt. Byron Nelson 1 up

1945 Moraine CC, Dayton, OH
Byron Nelson bt. Sam Byrd 4&3

1946 Portland GC, Portland, OR
Ben Hogan bt. Ed Oliver 6&4

1947 Plum Hollow CC, Detroit, MI
Jim Ferrier bt. Chick Harbert 5&4

1948 Northwood Hills CC, St. Louis, MO
Ben Hogan bt. Mike Turnesa 7&6

1949 Hermitage CC, Richmond, VA
Sam Snead bt. Johnny Palmer 3&2

1950 Scioto CC, Columbus, OH
Chandler Harper bt Henry Williams , Jr. 4&3

1951 Oakmont CC, Oakmont, PA
Sam Snead bt. Walter Burkemo 7&6

1952 Big Spring CC, Louisville, KY
Jim Turnesa bt. Chick Harbert 1 up

1953 Birmingham CC, Birmingham, MI
Walter Burkemo bt. Felice Torza 2&1

1954 Keller GC, St. Paul, MN
Chick Harbert bt. Walter Burkemo 4&3

1955 Meadowbrook CC, Northville, MI
Doug Ford bt. Cary Middlecoff 4&3

1956 Blue Hill G&CC, Canton, MA
Jack Burke bt. Ted Kroll 3&2

1957 Miami Valley GC, Dayton, OH
Lionel Heart bt. Dow Finterwald 3&1

1958 Llanerch CC, Havertown, PA

Dow Finsterwald	67	72	70	67	276
Billy Casper	73	67	68	70	278
Sam Snead	73	67	67	73	280

1959 Minneapolis GC, St. Louis Park, MN

Bob Rosburg	71	72	68	66	277
Jerry Barber	69	65	71	73	278
Doug Sanders	72	66	68	72	278

1960 Firestone CC, Akron, OH

Jay Herbert	72	67	72	70	281
Jim Ferrier	71	74	66	71	282
Doug Sanders	70	71	69	73	283
Sam Snead	68	73	70	72	283

1961 Olympia Fields CC, Olympia Fields, IL

Jerry Barber	69	67	71	70	277
Don January	72	66	67	72	277
Doug Sanders	70	68	74	68	280

1962 Aronimink GC, Newton Square, PA

Gary Player	72	67	69	70	278
Bob Goalby	69	72	71	67	279
George Bayer	69	70	71	71	281
Jack Nicklaus	71	75	69	67	281

1963 Dallas Athletic Club, TX

Jack Nicklaus	69	73	69	68	279
Dave Ragan	75	70	67	69	281
Bruce Crampton	70	73	65	74	282

1964 Columbus CC, Columbus, OH

Bobby Nichols	64	71	69	67	271
Jack Nicklaus	67	73	70	64	274
Arnold Palmer	68	68	69	69	274

1965 Laurel Valley GC, Ligonier, PA

Dave Marr	70	69	70	71	280
Billy Casper	70	70	71	71	282
Jack Nicklaus	69	70	72	71	282

1966 Firestone CC, Akron, OH

Al Geiberger	68	72	68	72	280
Dudley Wysong	74	72	66	72	284
Billy Casper	73	73	70	70	286

1967 Columbine CC, Denver, CO

*Don January	71	71	70	68	281
Don Massingale	70	75	70	66	281
Jack Nicklaus	67	75	69	71	282

1968 Pecan Valley CC, San Antonio, TX

Julius Boros	71	71	70	69	281
Bob Charles	72	70	70	70	282
Arnold Palmer	71	69	72	70	282

1969 NCR CC, Dayton, OH

Ray Floyd	69	66	67	74	276
Gary Player	71	65	71	70	277
Bert Greene	71	68	68	71	279

1970 Southern Hills CC, Tulsa, OK

Dave Stockton	70	70	66	73	279
Bob Murphy	71	73	71	66	281
Arnold Palmer	70	72	69	70	281

1971 PGA National, Palm Beach, FL

Jack Nicklaus	69	69	70	73	281
Billy Casper	71	73	71	68	283
Tommy Bolt	72	74	69	69	284

1972 Oakland Hills CC, Bloomfield Hills, MI

Gary Player	71	71	67	72	281
Tommy Aaron	71	71	70	71	283
Jim Jamieson	69	72	72	70	283

1973 Canterbury GC, Cleveland, OH

Jack Nicklaus	72	68	68	69	277
Bruce Crampton	71	73	67	70	281
Manson Rudolph	69	70	70	73	282
J. C. Snead	71	74	68	69	282
Lanny Wadkins	73	69	71	69	282

1974 Tanglewood GC, Clemmons, NC

Lee Trevino	73	66	68	69	276
Jack Nicklaus	69	69	70	69	277
Bobby Cole	69	68	71	71	279

1975 Firestone CC, Akron, OH

Jack Nicklaus	70	68	67	71	276
Bruce Crampton	71	63	75	69	278
Tom Weiskopf	70	71	70	68	279

1976 Congressional CC, Bethseda, MD

Dave Stockton	70	72	69	70	281
Ray Floyd	72	68	71	71	282
Don January	70	69	71	72	282

1977 Pebble Beach GL, Pebble Beach, CA

*Lanny Wadkins	69	71	72	70	282
Gene Littler	67	69	70	76	282
Jack Nicklaus	69	71	70	73	283

1978 Oakmont CC, Oakmont, PA

*John Mahaffey	75	67	68	66	276
Jerry Pate	72	70	66	68	276
Tom Watson	67	69	67	73	276

1979 Oakland Hills CC, Bloomfield Hills, MI

*David Graham	69	68	70	65	272
Ben Crenshaw	69	67	69	67	272
Red Caldwell	67	70	66	71	274

1980 Oak Hill CC, Rochester, NY

Jack Nicklaus	70	69	66	69	274
Andy Bean	72	71	68	70	281
Lon Hickle	70	69	69	75	283

1981 Atlanta Athletic Club, Duluth, GA

Larry Nelson	70	66	66	71	273
Fuzzy Zoeller	70	68	68	71	277
Dan Pohl	69	67	73	69	278

1982 Southern Hills CC, Tulsa, OK

Ray Floyd	63	69	68	72	272
Lanny Wadkins	71	68	69	67	275
Fred Couples	67	71	72	66	276
Calvin Peete	69	70	68	69	276

1983 Riviera CC, Pacific Palisades, CA

Hal Sutton	65	66	72	71	274
Jack Nicklaus	73	65	71	66	275
Peter Jacobsen	73	70	68	65	276

1984 Shoal Creek CC, Birmingham, AL

Lee Trevino	69	68	67	69	273
Gary Player	74	63	69	71	277
Lanny Wadkins	68	69	68	72	277

1985 Cherry Hills CC, Eglewood, CO

Hubert Green	67	69	70	72	278
Lee Trevino	66	68	75	71	280
Andy Bean	71	70	72	68	281

1986 Inverness Club, Toledo, OH

Bob Tway	72	70	64	70	276
Greg Norman	65	68	69	76	278
Peter Jacobson	68	70	70	71	279

1987 PGA National, Palm Beach, FL

*Larry Nelson	70	72	73	72	287
Lanny Wadkins	70	70	74	73	287
Scott Hoch	74	74	71	69	288

1988 Oak Tree GC, Edmond, OK

Jeff Sluman	69	70	68	65	272
Paul Azinger	67	66	71	71	275
Tommy Nakajima	69	68	74	67	278

1989 Kemper Lakes GC, Hawthorn Woods, IL

Payne Stewart	74	66	69	67	276
Andy Bean	70	67	74	66	277
Mike Reid	66	67	70	74	277
Curtis Strange	70	68	70	69	277

1990 Shoal Creek CC, Birmingham, AL

Wayne Grady	72	67	72	71	282
Fred Couples	69	71	73	72	285
Gil Morgan	77	72	65	72	286

1991 Crooked Stick GC, Carmel, IN

John Daly	69	67	69	71	276
Bruce Lietzke	68	69	72	70	279
Jim Gallagher , Jr.	70	72	72	67	281

1992 Bellerive CC, St. Louis, MO

Nick Price	70	70	68	70	278
John Cook	71	72	67	71	281
Nick Faldo	68	70	76	67	281
Jim Gallagher , Jr.	72	66	76	67	281
Gene Sauers	67	69	70	75	281

1993 Inverness Club, Toledo, OH

*Paul Azinger	69	66	69	68	272
Greg Norman	68	68	67	69	272
Nick Faldo	68	68	69	68	274

1994 Southern Hills CC, Tulsa, OK

Nick Price	67	65	70	67	269
Corey Pavin	70	67	69	69	275
Phil Mickelson	68	71	67	70	276

1995 Riviera CC, Pacific Palisades, CA

*Steve Elkington	68	67	68	64	267
Colin Montgomerie	68	67	67	65	267
Ernie Els	66	65	66	72	269
Jeff Maggert	66	69	65	69	269

1996 Valhalla GC, Louisville, KY

*Mark Brooks	68	70	69	70	277
Kenny Perry	66	72	71	68	277
Steve Elkington	67	74	67	70	278
Tommy Tolles	69	71	71	67	278

1997 Winged Foot GC, Mamaroneck, NY

Davis Love	66	71	66	66	269
Justin Leonard	68	70	65	71	274
Jeff Maggert	69	69	73	65	276

1998 Sahalee CC, Redmond, WA

Vijay Singh	70	66	67	68	271
Steve Stricker	69	68	66	70	273
Steve Elkington	69	69	69	67	274

1999 Medinah CC, Medinah, IL

Tiger Woods	70	67	68	72	277
Sergio Garcia	66	73	68	71	278
Stewart Cink	69	70	68	73	280

2000 Valhalla GC, Louisville, KY

*Tiger Woods	66	67	70	67	270
Bob May	72	66	66	66	270
Thomas Bjorn	72	68	67	68	275

2001 Atlanta Athletic Club, Duluth, GA

David Toms	66	65	65	69	265
Phil Mickelson	66	66	66	68	266
Steve Lowery	67	67	66	68	268

2002 Hazeltine National GC, Chaska, MN

Rich Beem	72	66	72	68	278
Tiger Woods	71	69	72	67	279
Chris Riley	71	70	72	70	283

2003 Oak Hill CC, Rochester, NY

Shaun Micheel	69	68	69	70	276
Chad Campbell	69	72	65	72	278
Timothy Clark	72	70	68	69	279

2004 Whistling Straits, Kohler, WI

*Vijay Singh	67	68	69	76	280
Chris DiMarco	68	70	71	71	280
Justin Leonard	66	69	70	75	280

2005 Baltusrol GC, Springfield, NJ

Phil Mickelson	67	65	72	72	276
Thomas Björn	71	71	63	72	277
Steve Elkington	68	70	68	71	277

2006 Medinah CC, Medinah, IL

Tiger Woods	69	68	65	68	270
Shaun Micheel	69	70	67	69	275
Luke Donald	68	68	66	74	276
Sergio Garcia	69	70	67	70	276
Adam Scott	71	69	69	67	276

Kraft Nabisco Championship

Formerly Colgate Dinah Shore, 1972–81; Nabisco Dinah Shore, 1982–99; The Nabisco Championship, 2000–01. Mission Hills Country Club, Rancho Mirage, CA

1972
Jane Blalock 213 (-3)
Carol Mann 216
Judy Rankin 216

1973
Mickey Wright 284 (-4)
Joyce Kazmierski 286

1974
*JoAnn Prentice 289 (+1)
Jane Blalock 289
Sandra Haynie 289

1975
Sandra Palmer 283 (-5)
Kathy McMullen 284

1976
Judy Rankin 285 (-3)
Betty Burfeindt 288

1977
Kathy Whitworth 289 (+1)
JoAnne Carner 290
Sally Little 290

1978
*Sandra Post 283 (-5)
Penny Pulz 283

1979
*Sandra Post 276 (-12)
Nancy Lopez 277

1980
Donna Caponi 275 (-13)
Amy Alcott 277

1981
Nancy Lopez 277 (-11)
Carolyn Hill 279

1982
Sally Little 278 (-10)
Hollis St.acy 281
Sandra Haynie 281

1983
Amy Alcott 282 (-6)
Beth Daniel 284
Kathy Whitworth 284

1984
*Juli Inkster 280 (-8)
Pat Bradley 280

1985
Alice Miller 275 (-13)
Jan St.ephenson 278

1986
Pat Bradley 280 (-8)
Val Skinner 282

1987
*Betsy King 283 (-5)
Patty Sheehan 283

1988
Amy Alcott 274 (-14)
Colleen Walker 276

1989
Juli Inkster 279 (-9)
Tammie Green 284
JoAnne Carner 284

1990
Betsy King 283 (-5)
Kathy Postlewait 285
Shirley Furlong 285

1991
Amy Alcott 273 (-15)
Dottie (Pepper) Mochrie 281

1992
*Dottie (Pepper) Mochrie 279 (-9)
Juli Inkster 279

1993
Helen Alfredsson 284 (-4)
Amy Benz 286
Tina Barrett 286

1994
Donna Andrews 276 (-12)
Laura Davies 277

1995
Nanci Bowen 285 (-3)
Susie Redman 286

1996
Patty Sheehan 281 (-7)
Kelly Robbins 282
Meg Mallon 282
Annika Sorenstam 282

1997
Betsy King 276 (-12)
Kris Tschetter 278

1998
Pat Hurst 281 (-7)
Helen Dobson 282

1999
Dottie Pepper 269 (-19)
Meg Mallon 275

2000
Karrie Webb 274 (-14)
Dottie Pepper 284

2001
Annika Sorenstam 281 (-7)
Karrie Webb 284
Janice Moodie 284
Dottie Pepper 284
Akiko Fukushima 284
Rachel (Hetherington) Teske 284

2002
Annika Sorenstam 280 (-8)
Liselotte Neumann 281

2003
Patricia Meunier-Lebouc 281 (-7)
Annika Sorenstam 282

2004
Grace Park 277 (-11)
Aree Song 278

2005
Annika Sorenstam 273 (-15)
Rosie Jones 281

2006
*Karrie Webb 279 (-9)
Lorena Ochoa 279

2007
Morgan Pressel 285 (-3)
Catriona Matthew 286
Brittany Linicome 286

McDonald's LPGA Championship

Formerly LPGAChampionship, 1955–86; Mazda LPGA Championship, 1987–93; McDonalds LPGA Championship, 1994–2000; McDonald's LPGA Championship presented by AIG, 2001–03.

1955
Orchard Ridge, CC, Ft Wayne, IN
††Beverly Hanson   220   4&3
Louise Suggs   223

1956
Forest Lake CC, Detroit, MI
*Marlene Hagge   291
Patty Berg   291

1957
Churchill Valley CC, Pittsburgh, PA
Louise Suggs   285
Wiffi Smith   288

1958
Churchill CC, Pittsburgh, PA
Mickey Wright   288
Fay Crocker   294

1959
Sheraton Hotel CC, French Lick, IN
Betsy Rawls   288
Patty Berg   289

1960
Sheraton Hotel CC, French Lick, IN
Mickey Wright   292
Louise Suggs   295

1961
St.ardust CC, Las Vegas, NE
Mickey Wright   287
Louise Suggs   296

1962
St.ardust CC, Las Vegas, NE
Judy Kimball   282
Shirley Spork   286

1963
St.ardust CC, Las Vegas, NE
Mickey Wright   294   (+10)
Mary Lena Faulk   296
Mary Mills   296
Louise Suggs   296

1964
St.ardust CC, Las Vegas, NE
Mary Mills   278   (-6)
Mickey Wright   280

1965
St.ardust CC, Las Vegas, NE
Sandra Haynie   279   (-5)
Clifford A. Creed   280

1966
St.ardust CC, Las Vegas, NE
Gloria Ehret   282   (-2)
Mickey Wright   285

1967
Pleasant Valley CC, Sutton, MA
Kathy Whitworth   284   (-8)
Shirley Englehorn   285

1968
Pleasant Valley CC, Sutton, MA
†Sandra Post   294   (+2)   68
Kathy Whitworth   294   75

1969
Concord GC, Kiameshia Lake, NY
Betsy Rawls   293   (+1)
Susie Berning   297
Carol Mann   297

1970
Pleasant Valley CC, Sutton, MA
*Shirley Englehorn   285   (-7)
Kathy Whitworth   285

1971
Pleasant Valley CC, Sutton, MA
Kathy Whitworth   288   (-4)
Kathy Ahern   292

1972
Pleasant Valley CC, MA
Kathy Ahern   293   (+1)
Jane Blalock   299

1973
Pleasant Valley CC, Sutton, MA
Mary Mills   288   (-4)
Betty Burfeindt   289

1974
Pleasant Valley CC, Sutton, MA
Sandra Haynie   288   (-4)
JoAnne Carner   290

1975
Pine Ridge GC, Baltimore, MD
Kathy Whitworth   288   (-4)
Sandra Haynie   289

1976
Pine Ridge GC, Baltimore, MD
Betty Burfeindt   287   (-5)
Judy Rankin   288

1977
Bay Tree Golf Plantation, N. Myrtle Beach, SC
Chako Higuchi   279   (-9)
Pat Bradley   282
Sandra Post   282
Judy Rankin   282

1978
Jack Nicklaus Golf Center, Kings Island, OH
Nancy Lopez   275   (-13)
Amy Alcott   281

1979
Jack Nicklau Golf Center, Kings Island, OH
Donna Caponi   279   (-9)
Jerilyn Britz   282

1980
Jack Nicklaus Golf Center, Kings Island, OH
Sally Little   285   (-3)
Jane Blalock   288

1981
Jack Nicklaus Golf Center, King's Island, OH
Donna Caponi   280   (-8)
Jerilyn Britz   281
Pat Meyers   281

1982
Jack Nicklaus Sports Center, Kings Island, OH
Jan St.ephenson   279   (-9)
JoAnne Carner   281

1983
Jack Nicklaus Sports Center, Kings Island, OH
Patty Sheehan   279   (-9)
Sandra Haynie   281

1984
Jack Nicklaus Sports Center, Kings Island, OH
Patty Sheehan   272   (-16)
Beth Daniel   282
Pat Bradley   282

1985
Jack Nicklaus Sports Center, Kings Island, OH
Nancy Lopez   273   (-15)
Alice Miller   281

1986
Jack Nicklaus Sports Center, Kings Island, OH
Pat Bradley   277   (-11)
Patty Sheehan   278

1987
Jack Nicklaus Sports Center, Kings Island, OH
Jane Geddes   275   (-13)
Betsy King   276

1988
Jack Nicklaus Sports Center, Kings Island, OH
Sherri Turner   281   (-7)
Amy Alcott   282

1989
Jack Nicklaus Sports Center, Kings Island, OH
Nancy Lopez   274   (-14)
Ayako Okamoto   277

Women's US Open

1990
Bethesda CC, Bethesda, MD
Beth Daniel   280   (-4)
Rosie Jones   281

1991
Bethesda CC, Bethesda, MD
Meg Mallon   274   (-10)
Pat Bradley   275
Ayako Okamoto   275

1992
Bethesda CC, Bethesda, MD
Betsy King   267   (-17)
JoAnne Carner   278
Karen Noble   278
Liselotte Neumann   278

1993
Bethesda CC, Bethesda, MD
Patty Sheehan   275   (-9)
Lauri Merten   276

1994
DuPont CC, Wilmington, DE
Laura Davies   279   (-5)
Alice Ritzman   280

1995
DuPont CC, Wilmington, DE
Kelly Robbins   274   (-10)
Laura Davies   275

1996
DuPont CC, Wilmington, DE
Laura Davies   213   (E)
Julie Piers   214

1997
DuPont CC, Wilmington, DE
*Chris Johnson   281   (-3)
Leta Lindley   281

1998
DuPont CC, Wilmington, DE
Se Ri Pak   273   (-11)
Donna Andrews   276
Lisa Hackney   276

1999
DuPont CC, Wilmington, DE
Juli Inkster   268   (-16)
Liselotte Neumann   272

2000
DuPont CC, Wilmington, DE
*Juli Inkster   281   (-3)
St.efania Croce   281

2001
DuPont CC, Wilmington, DE
Karrie Webb   270   (-14)
Laura Diaz   272

2002
DuPont CC, Wilmington, DE
Se Ri Pak   279   (-5)
Beth Daniel   282

2003
DuPont CC, Wilmington, DE
*Annika Sorenstam   278   (-6)
Grace Park   278

2004
DuPont CC, Wilmington, DE
Annika Sorenstam   271   (-13)
Shi Hyun Ahn   274

2005
Bulle Rock GC, Havre de Grace, MD
Annika Sorenstam   277   (-11)
(a) Michelle Wie   280

2006
Bulle Rock GC, Havre de Grace, MD
*Se Ri Pak   280   (-8)
Karrie Webb   280

2007
Bulle Rock GC, Havre de Grace, MD
Suzann Pettersen   274   (-14)
Karrie Webb   275

1946
Spokane CC, Spokane, WA
††Patty Berg   5&4
Betty Jameson

1947
St.armount Forest CC, Greensboro, NC
Betty Jameson   295
(a) Sally Sessions   301
(a) Polly Riley   301

1948
Atlantic City CC, Northfield, NJ
Babe Zaharias   300
Betty Hicks   308

1949
Prince Georges CC, Landover, MD
Louise Suggs   291
Babe Zaharias   305

1950
Rolling Hills CC, Wichita, KA
Babe Zaharias   291
(a) Betsy Rawls   300

1951
Druid Hills Golf Club/Course,
Atlanta, GA
Betsy Rawls   293
Louise Suggs   298

1952
Bala Golf Club/Course, Philadelphia, PA
Louise Suggs   284
Marlene Hagge   291
Betty Jameson   291

1953
Country Club of Rochester,
Rochester, NY
†Betsy Rawls   302   70
Jackie Pung   302   77

1954
Salem CC, Peabody, MA
Babe Zaharias   291
Betty Hicks   303

1955
Wichita CC, Wichita, KA
Fay Crocker   299
Mary Lena Faulk   303
Louise Suggs   303

1956
Northland CC, Duluth, MN
†Kathy Cornelius   302   75
Barbara McIntire   302   82

1957
Winged Foot CC, Mamaroneck, NY
Betsy Rawls   299
Patty Berg   305

1958
Forest Lake CC, Detroit, MI
Mickey Wright   290
Louise Suggs   295

1959
Churchill Valley CC, Pittsburgh, PA
Mickey Wright   287
Louise Suggs   289

1960
Worcester CC, Worcester, MA
Betsy Rawls   292
Joyce Ziske   293

1961
Baltusrol GC, Springfield, NJ
Mickey Wright   293
Betsy Rawls   299

1962
Dunes Golf Club, Myrtle Beach, SC
Murle Breer   301
Jo Anne Prentice   303
Ruth Jessen   303

1963
Kenwood CC, Cincinnati, OH
Mary Mills   289   (-3)
Sandra Haynie   292
Louise Suggs   292

1964
San Diego CC, Chula Vista, CA
†Mickey Wright   290   (-2) 70
Ruth Jessen   290   72

1965
Atlantic City CC, Northfield, NJ
Carol Mann   290   (+2)
Kathy Cornelius   292

1966
Hazeltine GC, Minneapolis, MI
Sandra Spuzich   297   (+9)
Carol Mann   298

1967
Hot Springs Golf & Tennis Club,
Hot Springs, VA
(a) Catherine LaCoste 294 (+10)
Susie Berning   296
Beth St.one   296

1968
Moselem Springs GC, Fleetwood, PA
Susie Berning   289   (+5)
Mickey Wright   292

1969
Scenic Hills CC, Pensacola, FL
Donna Caponi   294   (+2)
Peggy Wilson   295

1970
Muskogee CC, Muskogee, OK
Donna Caponi   287   (+3)
Sandra Haynie   288
Sandra Spuzich   288

1971
Kahkwa CC, Erie, PA
JoAnne Carner   288   (even)
Kathy Whitworth   295

1972
Winged Foot CC, Mamaroneck, NY
Susie Berning   299   (+11)
Kathy Ahern   300
Pam Barnett   300
Judy Rankin   300

1973
Country Club of Rochester,
Rochester, NY
Susie Berning   290   (+2)
Gloria Ehret   295

1974
La Grange CC, La Grange, IL
Sandra Haynie   295   (+7)
Carol Mann   296
Beth St.one   296

1975
Atlantic City CC, Northfield, NJ
Sandra Palmer   295   (+7)
Jo Anne Carner   299
Sandra Post   299
(a) Nancy Lopez   299

1976
Rolling Green CC, Springfield, PA
†Jo Anne Carner   292   (+8)   76
Sandra Palmer   292   78

1977
Hazeltine GC, Chaska, MI
Hollis St.acy   292   (+4)
Nancy Lopez   294

1978
Country Club of Indianapolis,
Indianapolis, IN
Hollis St.acy   289   (+5)
Jo Anne Carner   290
Sally Little   290

1979
Brooklawn CC, Fairfield, CT
Jerilyn Britz   284   (even)
Debbie Massey   286
Sandra Palmer   286

1980
Richland CC Nashville, TN
Amy Alcott   280   (-4)
Hollis St.acy   289

1981
La Grange CC, La Grange, IL
Pat Bradley   279   (-9)
Beth Daniel   280

1982
Del Paso CC, Sacramento, CA
Janet Anderson   283   (-5)
Beth Daniel   289
Sandra Haynie   289
Donna White   289
Jo Anne Carner   289

1983
Cedar Ridge CC, Tulsa, OK
Jan St.ephenson   290   (+6)
JoAnne Carner   291
Patty Sheehan   291

1984
Salem CC, Peabody, MA
Hollis St.acy   290   (+2)
Rosie Jones   291

1985
Baltusrol GC, Springfield, NJ
Kathy Baker (Guadagnino) 280 (-8)
Judy Dickinson   283

1986
NCR Golf Club, Dayton, OH
†Jane Geddes   287   (-1) 71
Sally   Little   287   73

1987
Plainfield CC, Plainfield, NJ
†Laura Davies   285   (-3) 71
Ayako Okamoto   285   73
Jo Anne Carner   285   74

1988
Baltimore CC, Baltimore, MD
Liselotte Neumann   277   (-7)
Patty Sheehan   280

1989
Indianwood Golf & Country Club,
Lake Orion, MI
Betsy King   278   (-4)
Nancy Lopez   282

1990
Atlanta Athletic Club, Duluth, GA
Betsy King   284   (-4)
Patty Sheehan   285

1991
Colonial CC, Ft Worth, TX
Meg Mallon   283   (-1)
Pat Bradley   285

1992
Oakmont CC, Oakmont, PA
†Patty Sheehan   280   (-4) 72
Juli Inkster   280   74

1993
Crooked St.ick GC, Carmel, IN
Lauri Merten   280   (-8)
Donna Andrews   281
Helen Alfredsson   281

1994
Indianwood CC, Lake Orion, MI
Patty Sheehan   277   (-7)
Tammie Green   278

1995
The Broadmoor Colorado Springs, CO
Annika Sorenstam   278   (-2)
Meg Mallon   279

1996
Pine Needles Lodge & Golf Club,
Southern Pines, NC
Annika Sorenstam   272   (-8)
Kris   Tschetter   278

1997
Pumpkin Ridge GC, Cornelius, OR
Alison Nicholas   274   (-10)
Nancy Lopez   275

1998
Blackwolf Run Golf Resort, Kohler, WI
†*Se Ri Pak   290   (+6) 73
(a) Jenny Chuasiriporn   290 73

1999
Old Waverly GC, West Point, MS
Juli Inkster   272   (-16)
Sherri Turner   277

2000
Merit Club, Libertyville, IL
Karrie Webb   282   (-6)
Meg Mallon   287
Cristie Kerr   287

2001
Pine Needles Lodge & GC, Southern
Pines, NC
Karrie Webb   273   (-7)
Se Ri Pak   281

2002
Prairie Dunes CC, Hutchinson, KA
Juli Inkster   276   (-4)
Annika Sorenstam   278

2003

Pumpkin Ridge GC, North Plains, OR

†Hilary Lunke	283	(-1)	70
Angela St.anford	283		71
Kelly Robbins	283		73

2004

Orchards GC, South Hadley, MA

Meg Mallon	274	(-10)
Annika Sorenstam	276	

2005

Cherry Hills GC,
Cherry Hills Village, CO

Birdie Kim	287	(+3)
(a) Brittany Lang	289	
(a) Morgan Pressel	289	

2006

Newport CC, Newport, RI

†Annika Sorenstam	284	(E)	70
Pat Hurst	284		74

2007

Pine Needles Lodge & Golf Club,
Southern Pines, NC

Cristie Kerr	279	(-5)
Angela Park	281	
Lorena Ochoa	281	

Women's British Open

1994

Woburn G&CC, Milton Keynes,
England

Liselotte Neumann	280	(-12)

1995

Woburn G&CC, Milton Keynes,
England

Karrie Webb	278	(-14)

1996

Woburn G&CC, Milton Keynes,
England

Emilee Klein	277	(-15)

1997

Sunningdale GC, Berkshire, England

Karrie Webb	269	(-19)

1998

Royal Lytham & St. Annes, Lancashire,
England

Sherri St.einhauer	292	(+4)

1999

Woburn G&CC, Milton Keynes,
England

Sherri St.einhauer	283	(-9)

2000

Royal Birkdale Golf Club, Southport,
England

Sophie Gustafson	282	(-10)

2001

Sunningdale Golf Club, Berkshire,
England

Se Ri Pak	277	(-11)
Mi Hyun Kim	279	

2002

Turnberry GC, Ailsa Course,
Ayrshire, Scotland

Karrie Webb	273	(-15)
Michelle Ellis	275	
Paula Marti	275	

2003

Royal Lytham & St. Annes
Lancashire, England

Annika Sorenstam	278	(-10)
Se Ri Pak	279	(-9)

2004

Sunningdale GC, Berkshire, England

Karen St.upples	269	(-19)
Rachel (Hetherington) Teske	274	(-14)

2005

Royal Birkdale GC, Merseyside, England

Jeong Jang	272	(-16)
Sophie Gustafson	276	

2006

Royal Lytham & St. Annes
Lancashire, England

Sherri St.einhauer	281	(-7)
Sophie Gustafson	284	
Cristie Kerr	284	

2007

St. Andrews, Scotland

Lorena Ochoa	287	(-5)
Maria Hjorth	291	
Jee Young Lee	291	

The Solheim Cup

Year	Location	Europe	US
1990	Lake Nona, FL, USA	4.5	11.5
1992	Dalmahoy, Edinburgh, Scotland	11.5	6.5
1994	Greenbrier, WV, USA	7.0	13.0
1996	Marriott St. Pierre Hotel, Wales	11.0	17.0
1998	Muirfield Village GC, OH, USA	12.0	16.0
2000	Loch Lomond Golf Club, Scotland	14.5	11.5
2002	Interlachen Country Club, MN, USA	12.5	15.5
2003	Bärseback Golf & CC, Sweden	17.5	10.5
2005	Crooked St.ick Golf Club, IN, USA	12.5	15.5
2007	Halmstad Golfklubb, Sweden	12	16
Total		3	7

Key

*	Won sudden-death playoff
†	Won 18-hole playoff
††	Won match-play final

Index

Page numbers in **bold** refer to main articles on players and courses. Page numbers in *italics* refer to illustrations and information in captions.

Chamonix, France 338
Charles, Bob **141**, *141*
Chart Hills, Kent, England 164
Cherry Hills, USA 54, 129
chip and run: with hybrid club 61, *61*
chip shot 84-5, *84-5*
    of top players 86-7, *86-7*
Choi, KJ 200
    chip shots 87, *87*
Churchill, Winston 16
Clark, Tim 357
Clarke, Darren **186**, *186*
Clarke, Heather 186
Clinton, Bill *255*
Clooney, George 349
clothing *26-7*, 27
clubs (equipment):
    Big Bertha *242-3*, 243
    drivers 46-9, *46-9*
    fairway metals 56-7, *56-7*
    hybrids 56-7, *56-7*
    irons 64-7, *64-7*
    number allowed in bag 167
    putters 92-3, *92-3*
    wedges 78-9, *78-9*
clubs (places) 19
    earliest 16
coaches 38, 40, *40-1*
Collett, Glenna 114
Colonial 179
Colt, Harry S. 245, 307, 308, 310, 311, 319
Combe, George: course design 256
Congressional 175
Cook, John 163
Corcoran, Fred 118
Cotton, Henry **115**, *115*, 252
Couples, Fred **170**, *170*, 348, 365, *365*
course management 100-1
course marshalls 38
courses:
    design 27
        player-designers **245**
    number of holes 268
Crans sur Sierre, Switzerland 338
Creamer, Paula 31, 204, *206*
Crenshaw, Ben 154, **156**, *156*, *177*, 234, 237, 298, 313, 364
    course design 245
crocodiles *355*
Crooked Stick, Indiana, USA 169
Crosby, Bing *117*, 332

"Crosby Clambake" (The Crosby) 332
Crump, George 318, 319, 321, *321*
Cupit, Jackie 127
Curtis, Ben 272
Curtis Cup: champions 272
Cypress Point, California, USA 324-5, **328-9**, *328-9*

D

Dallas Open 116
Dalmahoy 171
Daly, Fred 190
Daly, John **169**, *169*, 269
Darcy, Eamonn 234, *295*
Darwin, Bernard 105
Davies, Laura **171**, *171*, 204
Del Monte 330
Derksen, Robert Jan 347
desert courses 342-51
    water on 344
Desert Forest, Carefree, Arizona, USA *343*
Desert Mountain, Arizona, USA 344
Desert Ridge Resort, Arizona, USA: Faldo Course *344-5*
design 27
    player-designers **245**
Diegel, Leo 219
DiMarco, Chris 181
    on Woods 195
Doak, Tom 326, 327
Donald, Luke 198, *198*, 365
    business interests 27
    pitch shots 82, *82*
Donald, Mike 147
Doonbeg, Ireland *250*
Dougherty, Nick 164
    title 261
draw: hitting 70, *70*
Dredge, Bradley 269
drive 52-3, *52-3*
    big hitters 54-5, *54-5*
    distances 48
    swing 52-3, *52-3*
drivers:
    Big Bertha *242-3*, 243
    clubhead design 46
    custom fitting 49
    evolution 46, 49, *49*

flex 48, *48*
loft 48, *48*
    moment of inertia 46, 47
    multi-material construction 47
    shafts: materials 48, *48*
    size 47
    square-headed 46, 47, *47*
    sweet spot 46, *47*
    weights 46, *46*
Drum, Bob 130
Dubai Desert Classic 346, 347
Dudley, Ed *216-17*
Dundrum Bay *249*, 257
Dunn, Tom 307
Dunn, Willie 279
Duval, David 167, 168, **185**, *185*, 197
    course design 362
    course record 331
    title 365
Dye, Alice 276, 367
Dye, Pete: course design 276, 277, 334, *334*, 335, 362, 364, 365
Dynasty Cup 363

E

Eastwood, Clint *332*
Edfors, Johan 357
Edwards, Bruce *151*
Eichenheim, Austria 338
Eisenhower Trophy 335
Elephant Hills, Zimbabwe *353*, 354
Elkington, Steve 175, 365
Els, Ernie *40-1*, **174-5**, *174-5*, 177, 181, 198, 200, 238, *313*, *346*, 358, *358*
    bunker shots 90, *90*
    business interests 27
    course design 27, 245, 362
    course records 313, 361
    iron shots 72, *72*
    titles 301, 346, 347, 357, 361
Emirates, Dubai **346-7**, *346-7*
    clubhouse *346*
English Amateur Championship 311
English Ladies Championship 114
equipment manufacturers: Tour reps 38
Ernie Els & Fancourt Foundation 175
Espirito Santo Trophy 335
European Masters 155

ACKNOWLEDGMENTS

Dorling Kindersley would like to thank: Gill Sheldon at the Phil Sheldon Golf Picture Library, Jenny Baskaya, and Liz Moore for picture research; Angus Murray for photography; Julian Small, Annie Nicholson and all the greens staff at Wentworth Golf Club; Stuart Collier, Jason Brant, Kelly Ford, and Ajay Patel for modeling the instruction photographs; Julian Sandys at Mizuno, Gary McQuaid at TaylorMade, and Jon Parsons at Srixon for the loan of golf equipment.

PICTURE CREDITS

The publisher would like to thank the following for their kind permission to reproduce their photographs:

Key:
a-above; b-below/bottom; c-center; f-far; l-left; r-right; t-top

Alamy Images: Helene Rogers: 346b

Angus Murray Photography: 2l (scoreboard), 34-35, 35br, 36-37, 39br, 39crb, 39tr, 55b, 67bl, 102-103

Tony Arruza: 335b

Bob Atkins: 248-249, 250tr, 251t, 260-261, 276-277, 280-281, 282-283t, 286cl, 286-287, 287cr, 323tl, 324-325, 343tl, 358tr, 359tl

Tom Breazeale: 363cr

Callaway Golf: 49tr, 67br, 92br, 93bl

Steve Carr: 281tl, 296-297

Corbis: 182t, 196bl; Lewis Alan/Corbis Sygma 255br; Yann Arthus-Bertrand 345b; Denis Balibouse/Reuters 171t; David Bergman 30; Bettmann 2r (lee trevino), 3cr (jess sweetser), 8-9, 20-21, 23b, 23c, 24, 24-25, 64bl, 109r, 111bl, 111cr, 112bl, 112br, 112fbr, 112tl, 113bc, 113bl, 113br, 113fbl, 113fbl (trophy), 113fbr, 116t, 117b, 117tc, 117tr, 118t, 119br, 120-121, 121l, 122bl, 122r, 122t, 126c, 126t, 127bl, 127br, 127t, 128r, 130bc (1961), 130bl, 130br, 130fbl, 130fbr, 130-131t, 131bl, 132l, 132tr, 135cr, 137l, 137r, 138bc, 138br, 138-139tc, 140t, 142bl, 144br, 146t, 148r, 149t, 150tl, 160tr, 212-213, 219tr, 220tl, 220-221, 222-223, 262bl, 293b, 301tl, 319tl, 329b, 332cla; Mike Blake/Reuters 131crb, 186b; Will Burgess/Reuters 171c; Matt Campbell/epa 297tl; Sebastian Derungs/Reuters 182br; Richard Dole 196bl (1994); Duomo 189r, 196fbl; Don Feria 332tr; Robert Galbraith/Reuters 197tr, 317br; Raymond Gehman 341tl; Sam Greenwood/NewSport 73b; John Gress/Reuters 202l; Gunter Marx Photography 339b; Hulton-Deutsch Collection 30-31 (background), 112bc, 114crb, 123t, 159cra; Dimitri Iundt 161t; Dimitri Iundt/TempSport 131br; Mark A. Johnson 338; Eddie Keogh/Reuters 205; Keystone 19br; Justin Lane/epa 301tc; Christian Liewig 207tl; Peter Macdiarmid/Reuters 308cr; Paul McErlane/Reuters 29r; Yuriko Nakao/Reuters 188t; Juda Ngwenya/Reuters 275br; Reuters 3fcl, 32-33, 90r, 168bl, 169t, 176l, 180br, 331tr; Jim Richardson 325cra; Tony Roberts 109bl, 147bl, 156t, 166t, 170l, 257, 259crb, 294b, 320tc, 321tl, 332bc, 343tr, 344l, 344-345, 349b, 351tl; Galen Rowell 355tr; Christina Salvador/Sygma 196tl; Larry W. Smith/epa 187b; Scott T. Smith 307bl; John Sommers II/Reuters 148l; Jim Sugar 323tr, 324br; Swim Ink 2, LLC 340cr; Tim Thompson 336-337; Underwood & Underwood 31br, 108tl; Nik Wheeler 355cla; Rick Wilking/

Reuters 178bl; Julia Xanthos/EPA 189b; Michael S. Yamashita 14-15

Ernie Els Wines: 27br

Flickr.com: Carl Doose 353br; Farrel Lifson 353bc; ludwig428 351cb

Getty Images: Time & Life Pictures 20bl, 23t, 45bl, 118-119, 121r, 128l, 130bc, 134bl, 138bl, 142cl, 216tl, 232tl, 285tl; 4b, 4t, 5b, 5t, 29bl, 29br, 32bl, 40bc, 54l, 55t, 62r, 63b, 63t, 72l, 73t, 82l, 82r, 83b, 86, 87bl, 87t, 91b, 93, 98b, 98r, 99b, 99t, 104ftr, 105ftr, 105l, 105tr, 106ftr, 106tc, 108bl, 112-113t, 113tc, 115b, 124l, 125b, 125cra, 129, 131fbl, 134fbr, 136cr, 138bc (1969), 138fbr, 139bc, 139bl, 139fbl, 142t, 147br, 147t, 148t, 153b, 153t, 155fbr (trophy), 160l, 162cr, 162tr, 167b, 167t, 168t, 170b, 170t, 172t, 173t, 175b, 175t, 177t, 178t, 181t, 183t, 184t, 186cr, 186t, 187t, 189t, 190tl, 191t, 193t, 195t, 196br, 198br, 198l, 199, 200br, 200-201, 201bl, 203bl, 203br, 204l, 206bl, 206t, 207r, 208-209, 225tr, 228-229, 232-233, 238-239, 240-241, 241tr, 243tr, 245tr, 250bl, 252r, 256br, 258bl, 259bl, 264-265, 265tc, 267tr, 269tl, 269tr, 270br, 271br, 274c, 275c, 276cla, 277crb, 277tl, 278b, 284b, 284r, 289tl, 297tr, 301tr, 302bc, 303bl, 303br, 309b, 310b, 311bc, 311tl, 312-313, 314bl, 314cla, 315br, 316c, 318-319, 319tr, 325b, 326c, 327cb, 327tl, 334cl, 341cb, 349c, 349cra, 356-357, 357tl, 358tl, 360c, 362-363, 365tc, 365tl, 367bc, 367c, 368-369; AFP 28-29t, 72r, 131fbr, 139br, 197fbl, 202br, 215tr, 313tl; Aurora 165br, 207cl; Focus On Sport 128tr; Stuart Franklin 357tr; Gerald French 328b; Hulton Archive 16-17, 46ca, 111tl, 114t, 120tl, 210-211, 218-219; Jonathan Kantor 1; Brian Morgan 131bc; Don Morley 130-131b; National Geographic 321crb; Panoramic Images 353bl; PGA 2r, 203tc, 334br, 364-365, 366bl, 366br, 367bl, 367br, 367t; WireImage 135fbr, 300-301

Google Earth: 2007 Digital Earth Technology 292tl; 2007 DigitalGlobe 252tl, 264tl, 274tl, 312tl, 316tl, 328tl, 346tl, 350tl, 356tl; 2007 DigitalGlobe/Europa Technologies 362tl; 2007 DigitalGlobe/Image AMBAG 330tl; 2007 DigitalGlobe/NASA 276tl; 2007 DigitalGlobe/TerraMetrics 254tl, 326tl; 2007 DigitalGlobe/TerraMetrics/ Tele Atlas 256tl; 2007 New York GIS 278tl; 2007 State of New Jersey 318tl; 2007 TerraMetrics 258tl, 268tl, 340tl; 260tl, 262tl, 284tl, 294tl, 296tl, 300tl, 306tl, 308tl, 334tl, 348tl; Cnes/Spot Image 286tl, 288tl; Infoterra Ltd & Bluesky 272tl, 310tl; NASA 364tl

Eric Hepworth: 250c, 305bl, 305br, 307crb, 310cr

Historic Golf Photos: 112fbl, 119tr, 138fbl, 140crb, 150b, 157bl

iStockphoto.com: Dan Cooper 337bl; Chris Neale 337br; Jess Wiberg 339t

Bryan Izatt: 335ca

Barry Jennings (ViewCalgary.com): 340b

Craig Jones: 330-331

Kingsbarns Golf Links: Iain Lowe 260cr

Russell Kirk / golflinksphotography.com: 246-247, 251br, 279b, 281tc, 281tr, 282b, 283b, 288-289, 304-305, 306-307, 307tr, 322-323, 342-343, 343tc, 350c, 352-353, 354-355, 366bc

Lambrecht Photography : 249br

Mirrorpix: 125t

Picture by Brian D Morgan: 358crb

Old Golf Images: 16l, 44bl, 104cra, 104tr, 106bl, 106br, 107l, 107r, 108r, 110b, 110t, 113cr, 115cr, 116br, 120bl, 123b, 298crb, 313tr

PA Photos: PA Archive 134fbl, 138cl, 142cr, 145tl, 158-159; Elise Amendola/ AP 192l; AP 112crb, 114bl, 116bl, 134bc (trophy), 161bl; AP Photo 162l, 212tl, 214-215, 216-217, 224-225, 238tl; Matthew Ashton/Empics Sport 347br; Chris Bacon/PA Archive 252cl; Barry Batchelor/PA Archive 172l; Michael Boyd/ PA Wire 165fbr; Michael Conroy/AP 91t; Olivier Douliery/ABACA 139fbr;

Damien Eagers/PA Wire 155tr; Phelan M. Ebenhack/AP 160cr; EMPICS
Sport 105br; HC/AP 140bl; Charles Krupa/AP 202-203; Rebecca Naden/PA
Archive 176cr, 201br; Chris O'Meara/AP 26-27; PA Photos 211tr; David J.
Phillip/AP 180t; S&G 87bc, 106tr, 124br, 141bl, 141br, 150tc; Scanpix 179l

Pine Valley Golf Club, NJ: 321br

popperfoto.com: 115t, 124t, 136tr, 141t, 144t, 151t, 157t, 158t

PunchStock: Comstock 42-43

Reuters: 185t; John Sommers II 151r

Phil Sheldon: 2l (annika sorenstam), 22, 38-39, 39cra, 40tr, 40-41, 41t, 62bl,
90l, 104bl, 118b, 131cra, 131tc, 133l, 133r, 134br, 134tl, 134-135, 135bc, 135bl,
135br, 135fbl, 136crb, 136l, 139tr, 143l, 143r, 144l, 145r, 146bl, 146br, 149l, 149r,
151b, 152br, 152cr, 152l, 154bc, 154bl, 154br, 154fbl, 154fbr, 154tc, 154-155c,
155bl, 155br, 155fbl, 155fbr, 156l, 156r, 157r, 158b, 159br, 161br, 163l, 163r,
164bc, 164bl, 164br, 164fbl, 164fbl (1978), 164fbr, 164l, 164r, 164-165b, 165bc,
165bl, 165br (MBE), 165fbl (trophy), 165t, 166l, 166r, 167cl, 167cla, 167r, 168br,
168r, 169l, 169r, 171b, 172r, 173bl, 173br, 174l, 174r, 175r, 176tr, 177b, 179r, 180l,
181r, 182bl, 183b, 183c, 184b, 184l, 185b, 185c, 188b, 190b, 190c, 191bl, 191r,
192br, 192tr, 193b, 193r, 194, 195b, 196fbr, 196-197, 197bc, 197bl, 197br, 197fbr,
200bl, 201tr, 204r, 206br, 222tl, 226tl, 226-227, 228tl, 230-231, 231tr, 234tl, 234-
235, 236-237, 237tr, 239r, 242-243, 244-245, 254c, 255c, 256bc, 261tc, 262c,
263bl, 263br, 263tl, 265tl, 266tc, 266tl, 266tr, 267b, 267tl, 268-269, 270bc, 270bl,
270crb, 270t, 271bl, 272b, 273b, 273t, 274br, 276clb, 278c, 279cla, 285c, 289tr,
290bc, 290bl, 290br, 291bl, 291br, 291cra, 291tl, 295br, 295cr, 298br, 298cl,
298tc, 298tl, 298tr, 299tc, 299tl, 299tr, 302bl, 302br, 303bc, 303t, 308bl, 309cl,
314br, 314tr, 315bl, 317cla, 320tl, 320tr, 321tc, 321tr, 329cla, 329crb, 331tl, 332bl,
332br, 332cb, 333bc, 333bl, 333br, 346cl, 358cra, 359tr, 360bl, 361b, 361tc, 362cr

TopFoto.co.uk: 109tl

Tufts Archives: 317clb

Visions in Golf: 293t; Hobbs Golf Collection 54br; Michael Hobbs/Mark
Newcombe 104br, 134bc; Christer Hoglund 178br; Mark Newcombe 18-19, 83t

Waterville Golf Links: 3cr (waterville), 249bl, 253b, 253ca

All other images © Dorling Kindersley. For further information see:
www.dkimages.com